State Crime:
Current Perspectives

CRITICAL ISSUES IN CRIME AND SOCIETY
Raymond J. Michalowski, Series Editor

Critical Issues in Crime and Society is oriented toward critical analysis of contemporary problems in crime and justice. The series is open to a broad range of topics, including specific types of crime, wrongful behavior by economically or politically powerful actors, controversies over justice system practices, and issues related to the intersection of identity, crime, and justice. It is committed to offering thoughtful works that will be accessible to scholars and professional criminologists, general readers, and students.

For a list of titles in the series, see the last page of the book.

State Crime:
Current Perspectives

EDITED BY
DAWN L. ROTHE AND
CHRISTOPHER W. MULLINS

FOREWORD BY
WILLIAM J. CHAMBLISS

INTRODUCTION BY
M. CHERIF BASSIOUNI

RUTGERS UNIVERSITY PRESS
New Brunswick, New Jersey, and London

LIBRARY OF CONGRESS CATALOGING-IN-PUBLICATION DATA

State crime : current perspectives / edited by Dawn L. Rothe
and Christopher W. Mullins.
    p. cm. — (Critical issues in crime and society)
    Includes bibliographical references and index.
    ISBN 978-0-8135-4900-2 (alk. paper) — ISBN 978-0-8135-4901-9 (pbk. : alk.
paper)
    1. Political crimes and offenses. I. Rothe, Dawn, 1961– II. Mullins, Christopher W.,
1971–
    HV6273.S73 2010
    364.1'31—dc22

                                                          2010008404

A British Cataloging-in-Publication record for this book is available
from the British Library.

This collection copyright © 2011 by Rutgers, The State University
Individual chapters copyright © 2011 in the names of their authors

Visit our Web site: http://rutgerspress.rutgers.edu

Manufactured in the United States of America

Contents

FOREWORD

WHEN I ASK MY STUDENTS "What makes an act a crime?" the most common answer, even among seniors majoring in criminology, is "Acts that violate cultural norms." The answer raises more questions than it answers. I usually follow the question of what makes an act a crime with another: What is the difference between civil and criminal law? That question is usually greeted with silence.

While it is true in a tautological sense that criminal acts violate societal norms, this answer misses much more than it hits. First and foremost, fortunately, not all acts that violate societal norms are criminal. When a congressman screams "You lie!" at the president of the United States during the president's address to Congress, the congressman is certainly violating a widely held societal norm, but it is not a crime. More mundane acts like loudly burping in a restaurant, eating loudly with your mouth open, or not shaking hands when someone's hand is offered as a greeting all violate widely held U.S. societal norms, but none are crimes.

Perhaps more important is the fact that there is rarely consensus even on widely held societal norms. In contemporary America the norms that generate the most widespread disagreement over whether or not they should be crimes include the use of marijuana and other so-called illicit substances; a woman's right to have an abortion and, if so, at what stage of pregnancy or under what circumstances; and, most recently, the use of cell phones while driving. Even the most widely held norms are riddled with exceptions. The norm "Thou shalt not kill" does not apply to police officers acting in the line of duty, executioners in penitentiaries, soldiers in battle, people acting in self-defense, or individuals coerced into killing someone.

The point is that the answer that criminal law is a simple, straightforward codification of widely held norms is misleading. For an act to be a crime, it must meet at least six criteria:

1. There must be a written law prohibiting an act or requiring the person to act.
2. There must be a punishment prescribed for acting or failing to act in a certain way.

3. There must be an *act*. That is, the person has not committed a crime simply because he or she has thought about it. The individual must actually take some positive action toward carrying out the crime.
4. There must be a *harm*.
5. The actor must *intend* to commit the act. In Latin this requirement is called *mens rea*.
6. The individual's *act* must have *caused* the *harm*.

For centuries criminologists have debated whether or not the foregoing legal definition of crime is sufficient for the social scientific study of crime. The problem with the legal definition is that it restricts scientific inquiry to those acts defined by legislators as criminal. Given the political nature of legislation, it is clear that a legal definition does not lead to a sociologically homogeneous set of behaviors. Rather it leads essentially to the end result of a political process that does not include some of the most harmful acts committed by individuals, especially those committed by the people who are making and enforcing the laws.

Recognizing that a strictly legal definition limits the scope of criminological inquiry has led in recent years to the broadening of the conception of crime to include social harms. One need only reflect for a moment to realize that historically some of the most heinous social harms were not criminal but in fact were legally sanctioned: the murder of eleven million Jews, Gypsies, and homosexuals in Nazi Germany, the slaughter and forced removal to reservations of Native Americans, and the forced incarceration of Japanese Americans in concentration camps during World War II, to name a few.

In this magnificent collection of research on state crime, the advantage of a social harm approach to the study of crime is demonstrated. While some of the state crimes explored in this volume are legally prohibited acts, others, although clearly extremely important social harms, have escaped the legislative process that transforms social harms into crimes. In most cases serious social harms escape legislative action, because it is not in the interest of the ruling class or the legislators to define them as crimes. The fact that some of the most serious social harms occurring in the twentieth century are *not* defined as crime makes the study of state crime in the global age even more urgent. It is with great satisfaction, then, to have a collection of outstanding researches addressing the issue of state crime in the global age. This volume will not only be widely read, it will also stimulate further research that will continue to expose and explain the social, political, and economic forces that lead to state crimes, and which in turn should lead to social policies curtailing this all too prevalent characteristic of the modern state.

William J. Chambliss

PREFACE

WHEN WE FIRST began discussing editing a collection of classical and current research on crimes of the state for a book, we envisioned including some reprints and a couple of new pieces to serve as a one-stop reference for scholars and students of state crime. As such, we wanted to emphasize not only crimes by states but also responses and/or controls. However, as time progressed, it seemed to make more sense to ask the authors of the classical works (Barak 1991a; Chambliss 1989; Friedrichs 2000; Kauzlarich and Kramer 1998; Ross 1995, 2000b) to revisit their original works, expanding and/or revising upon their previous research, to give a bit of the old with the new. Additionally, we wanted to include previously unpublished pieces, as well as include scholars beyond the walls of U.S. academics. We are most pleased that we accomplished all of the above.

As William Chambliss's presidential address to the American Society of Criminology (1989) is often cited as the impetus behind the criminological interest in crimes of the state, we opened this book with his foreword. We were also honored to have Cherif M. Bassiouni contribute an introduction. As one of the leading forces behind the development of international criminal law, the International Criminal Tribunal for the former Yugoslavia, and the Rome Statute, his insightful introduction hones in on the key issues surrounding impunity, accountability, and realpolitik: thus providing a perfect opening to the field of state crime and subsequent examples of case studies presented here.

From that, the book begins with an introductory chapter briefly highlighting not only the development of the field but also the definitional debate (e.g., a legalistic or social harm approach) that continues to be an issue for some scholars of state crime. The first several chapters revisit original works with excellent expansions and/or revisions of thoughts and research, highlighting the advancements of the field. Indeed, the area of state crime continues to expand its boundaries and its impact.

This book represents such developments by offering case studies not only of capitalistic state crimes motivated by a desire for empire or economic and military supremacy, but also of current events and various types of governmental

regimes. Here issues of motivation and opportunity include not just the ideological, economic, or military interests, but also issues of ethnocism, political
power and representation, scarce resources, disparities, religion, postcolonial histories, and governments that are weakened, illegitimate, or overtly authoritarian.
Beyond these themes, issues of impunity, lack of accountability, and social justice
emerged in many of these contributions, which should come as no surprise since
the history of head-of-state impunity illustrates the level of accountability for
those most responsible for crimes by the state.

Given this, the second section pays particular attention to issues of
accountability, impunity, and social justice that are available and/or have been
initiated in an effort to address these horrific forms of state criminality,
taking into account not only the progress made in the field of state crime
control but also in the world over the past two decades. Chapters offer case-
specific examples of social justice mechanisms and accountability, including
domestic law, localized responses, moral and ethical dilemmas, restorative justice, and the international institution of control. Here the issue of "ought"
versus "does" becomes visible as the extant body of international criminal law
and the cry for the end of impunity do little to address the dissonance
between what is and what should be. As noted in the introduction, much of
this dissonance is the result of realpolitik.

As scholars of state crime, our hope is that someday we will see justice
for those victimized by crimes of the state; an equal application of the rule of
law, even for heads of state; social justice that moves beyond accountability to
incorporate measures of inclusion and victims' needs; and, ideally, no more
cases to analyze as crimes by states cease to occur.

Acknowledgments

We are thankful to the contributors for their willingness to be a part of this volume and for laying the foundation for our own scholarship on crimes of the state. Thank you to our colleagues for the support, guidance, and knowledge you so willingly share. We also want to thank William Chambliss and M. Cherif Bassiouni for their willingness to provide the foreword and introduction to this volume. We are truly honored by your contributions. We also would like to acknowledge Barb Perry for reviewing the manuscript and providing insightful comments and suggestions. Thank you, Barb. Thank you also goes out to our editors at Rutgers for their support and guidance during this process, and to Hope for all of her hard work. We also would like to acknowledge the International State Crime Research Consortium, housed at Old Dominion University, College of Arts and Letters. Of course, no acknowledgment would be complete without mentioning how grateful we both are to our families for their love and support.

State Crime:
Current Perspectives

Introduction

CRIMES OF STATE AND OTHER FORMS
OF COLLECTIVE GROUP VIOLENCE BY
NONSTATE ACTORS

M. Cherif Bassiouni

THROUGHOUT HISTORY, abuses of power by tyrannical rulers and ruling-regime elites, which are carried out under their direction by state actors, have occasioned significant human, social, and economic harm to their respective national societies and those of others. Under the guise of war, large-scale human depredations have taken place, as well as in the colonization context and in other contexts manifesting oppression or repression by states that victimize groups in other states or territories.

Since the end of World War II forms of collective violent social interactions have increased significantly, but no reliable data have been gathered to document this phenomenon.[1] Political, social, and behavioral sciences have developed different techniques and methodologies for determining the causes of these violent manifestations, as well as some measurements to assess their outcomes. But they were not sufficiently developed to influence policy making in connection with preventing or limiting violent interaction, whether at the interstate or domestic levels. Whether or not this is the reason for international law's failure to take into account the findings and insights of other disciplines is speculative. More likely, international law, which is the product of state decision making, has simply ignored social and behavioral sciences in order to be less encumbered by scientific findings in reflecting state interests.

Notwithstanding its solid growth in the last few decades, International Criminal Law (ICL)[2] continues to lag behind the needs of the international community to enhance its goals of peace, justice, and the protection of human rights (Bassiouni 1999b, 1999c, 2000a, 2000b). This is due to ICL's almost inevitable linkage to states' strategic, economic, and political interests, which has historically hampered its development.

While international law has primarily focused on state actors, experience evidences that violent social interactions do not only derive from state actors' conduct, but also from nonstate actors. "Other forms of collective group violence by nonstate actors," as that formulation appears in the title, refers to aberrant conduct having some of the characteristics of "crimes of state" when committed by nonstate actors acting outside the state structure. Both share similar phenomenological characteristics, produce significant human and material harm, and are not adequately controlled by social and legal mechanisms. Thus, a parallel concept for "crimes of state" needs to be developed to apply to nonstate actors. This is a complex task in view of the fact that nonstate actors' roles and participation in violent interactive processes varies and is characterized by extraordinary flexibility. This is true with respect to nonstate actors who are noncombatants but whose participatory or support roles in conflicts of a noninternational character and in purely internal conflicts are not covered under international humanitarian law norms. These groups drift in and out of the combatant role and engage in criminal conduct that falls within the legal meaning of organized crime.

In the context of conflicts of noninternational and purely internal conflicts, nonstate actors have conducted themselves similarly to state actors in connection with abuse of power against civilian populations. This includes the commission of, or participation in, the commission of genocide, crimes against humanity, war crimes, torture, piracy, and slavery and slave-related practices. Thus, nonstate actors who have some of the characteristics of states, such as control of a defined territory and its population, exercise dominion and control over some territory and population, and are capable of developing an organizational policy should be held accountable to the same level as states.

Etiology

The etiology of crimes of state and similar crimes committed by nonstate actors needs to be addressed from a perspective other than physical human harm. This is necessary in order not to exclude a range of abuses of power that impact internationally protected social, economic, and cultural rights—for example, the following forms of domestic abuse of power: plundering of a state's public treasury by a dictator or members of a ruling-regime and large-scale corruption by public officials. Abusive state actors, particularly heads of state, who rule regimes and oligarchies that fall outside international law's control regime also engage in a whole range of domestic and international activities. Presumably these types of unlawful conduct fall under domestic law, which makes these activities subject to the control of those who have the power to engage in them. It also places those who perform them above or beyond the reach of the law. Thus, they can self-define their conduct as legitimate. When the determination of what is and is not legitimate is left in the hands of those who wield unbridled power, the result is invariably manipulated to the benefit of those who are in power.

There is also an array of issues that affect the interests of the international community but are either internationally unprotected or are so lightly regulated that it amounts to no regulation, thus leaving the determination of power actions in the hands of those who wield power. This applies to international protection of the environment and to the manufacturing of and trafficking in weapons, particularly weapons of mass destruction. Conduct by states in connection with these activities notwithstanding, their harmful human consequences remain subject to the discretion of states, even though a variety of treaties prohibiting the use of certain weapons exists. The doctrinal basis for such a prohibition is that these weapons produce indiscriminate harm to civilian population and cause combatants unnecessary pain and suffering. The record of states in the use of such weapons throughout the history of armed conflicts reveals how little effect these international norms have had on the usage of such weapons. Exceptionalism rests in the power of state unilateralism.

Another contemporary activity controlled by states that is outside international regulation is the use of private contractors who engage in violent activities. But, neither the law in general nor armed conflict law regulates such groups and their violent activities. The members of private organizations are subject to the law of the place where their conduct takes place or under their respective national laws, provided that they have extraterritorial jurisdictional application. There are no existing international controls, and where there is some regulation, it is weak and ineffective. In addition, there is virtually no enforcement.

All of the above points to the need for a traditional etiology for crimes of state (see Drost 1959; Power 2003) and atrocity crimes (see Drumbl 2007; Scheffer 2006).

Some Phenomenological Observations

Crimes of state have existed, in some form or another, throughout human history and have essentially manifested themselves when a state's organizational structure was under the control of a tyrannical ruler or a ruling elite engaging in abuse of power. Robespierre, Stalin, Hitler, and Pol Pot are among the most salient historic examples of rulers who exercised complete control over the apparatus of state and consequently over all of society, thereby generating an extraordinarily large number of victims with no viable internal opposition capable of preventing or mitigating the harmful outcomes. Victimization at the hands of ruling-elite regimes have also produced significant, though quantitatively less harmful, outcomes.

Violence initiated by a tyrannical ruler rather than a ruling elite generates more violence because of the ruler's ability to marshal the resources of a state's apparatus. Most tyrannical rulers are charismatic leaders who have a significant impact on their respective populations, which ruling elites are not likely to have. Their ability to use propaganda and to control the means of mass communications enhance their ability to affect collective behavior. Tyrannical rulers have the ability to create facts, impressions, and perceptions that they can convert into violent action.

Violent group dynamics that erupt in conflict are different. In fact, they are often beyond the state's ability to control. Violent group dynamics are almost always occasioned by interethnic, intertribal, and interreligious groups. They can be initiated by tyrannical rulers and ruling elites, but they are essentially the product of group dynamics. In postmodern manifestations, this formal collective violence has evidenced increased harmful consequences while revealing that in absence of forceful internal or external controls very little else is useful in preventing, curtailing, or stopping these collective violent dynamics.

The differences that exist between the two typologies, that which is initiated by tyrannical rulers and ruling elites and that which is the product of violent group dynamics, are relevant to the choice of policies needed to address these phenomena. Following are their differences:

1. Tyrannical-ruler and ruling-elite initiated violence originates from the top and involves a state's organizational structure, while violent group dynamics originates from the bottom and does not involve a state's structure.
2. State organizational structure violent practices tend to be systematic, and their tactics direct violence in a discriminate manner, whereas violent group dynamics tend to be indiscriminate.
3. Both are widespread, though in the case of violent group dynamics there may be a more limited geographic focus.
4. External or internal state intervention to halt violence is more likely to produce effective results in violent group dynamics.
5. State organizational structure violence can essentially be halted only by external intervention.
6. State-sponsored violence usually produces more human harm than violent group dynamics.
7. State-sponsored violence constitutes a betrayal of trust by the state actors violating the rights of those who have entrusted them with their protection. The abuse of power by state actors renders even more helpless a civilian group because its attackers are those entrusted with their protection.
8. Both forms of violence have the potential for collateral consequences such as generating new cycles of domestic and regional violence, disrupting world peace and security, and compelling high economic costs of peace-keeping and reconstruction.

9. Both engender criminogenic factors that characterize them in ways that should be relevant to understanding their phenomenology.
10. Both have predictability factors that are consistently ignored or underestimated at the domestic and international levels.

These observations are both elementary and self-evident. Scientific research is needed to make available more data and options to policy makers. More important, government elites should become more aware of the phenomenology of these forms of collective violent interactions to prevent and control them and deter and punish their perpetrators.

Human experience indicates that control mechanisms, including external use of force, reduce the number of victims and the levels of harm. Why this has only sporadically taken place is due to realpolitik.

The Protagonists

Accounts of mass atrocities since 1915, to pick a starting date for the modern and postmodern periods, reveal that atrocity crimes committed with the involvement of state organizations or as a result of violent group dynamics invariably involve the participation of a large number of protagonists. Some are directly or indirectly active, while others are passive participants or mere observers of these violent processes. Carrying out mass atrocities is more like an industrial mass production model, except that in the situation of atrocities, it is mass infliction of human harm ranging from physical extermination and injury to violations of social, economic, political, and cultural rights. Thus, the larger the scale of harm the more it requires a large number of persons to be actively or passively involved in carrying out the harmful conduct.

The numbers of active protagonists vary from one situation to another: Stalin's and Hitler's bureaucracies included millions in the army, police, security services, civil service, and party personnel. At a minimum, the respective numbers of protagonists in the atrocities committed had to exceed a million active participants. In addition, there had to be at least a similar number of those in the state apparatus who facilitated the process of committing mass atrocities by running prisons, transportation systems, disposing of the dead, and so on. Moreover, since these mass atrocities did not occur in a social vacuum, there had to be millions whose conduct ranged from the supportive to the indifferent, thereby contributing in some way to the overall outcomes.

In addition to this large number of domestic participants, supporters, and passive bystanders, there are also external participants who contribute to these outcomes. They include other states and their respective societies whose roles range from the supportive to the indifferent, and other nonstate actors operating outside the territorial arena of the conflict but who have a bearing on the conflict. In the supportive category are those states who provide weapons and needed commodities, make credits available, and provide political support. Indeed, what better way for a tyrannical ruler or regime to have international support in the Security Council? This was evidenced during the cold war when the USSR and the United States used surrogate states to fight their geopolitical war. When the surrogates committed genocide, crimes against humanity, and war crimes, they were protected by their principals from being held accountable.

Neutralization

Since the states' decision makers cannot direct their abuses of power against all of society, they have to find ways to neutralize some of its elements capable of opposing it. Neutralization of existing and potential opponents is by providing incentives and disincentives, offering advantage and profit from the victims' plight, and threatening inclusion in the victim category. Time and again, these simple techniques have been successfully used. (Recall the practices of the USSR's Communist regime under Lenin and Stalin [1917–1950s] and the Nazi regime under Hitler [1932–1945].) Other approaches are used with the rest of society in order to allow the intended outcomes to be obtained without resistance, mainly through techniques likely to produce reactions of apathy, indifference, and passivity. Combining or alternating misinformation about factual situations and using propaganda to create climates of fear based on perception of internal or external dangers and threats have been consistently employed.

Experience in these types of situations indicates that a variety of mechanisms operate, sometimes simultaneously, to engender the highest level of public compliance through propaganda and fear; and by means of compartmentalization of the perpetrators' actions. Paradoxically, the larger the scale of social involvement, the easier it is to manipulate the larger numbers that can be stimulated in what social psychologists call crowd-conditioning psychology. This is paradoxical because the same group of persons, if taken individually, would for the most part not act in the same way as they would if swept into collective frenzy. These observations, though basic to behavioral scientists, have hardly had an effect on law, which harkens to the simplistic conception of individual criminal responsibility and thus fashions legal norms to suit only this model of individual conduct.

The obvious conclusion is that the more persons involved in the mass production of human harm, the greater the resulting harm. Even though the harmful outcomes are determined by the number of protagonists, it does, however, matter whether human social organizations inherently produce these outcomes or they are more susceptible to producing a higher level of victimization than group dynamics or violent collective action by nonstate actors. Understanding phenomenological differences is necessary in order to devise appropriate social and legal control mechanisms.

Apathy, Indifference, and Passivity

Atrocity crimes are characterized by the apathy, indifference, and passivity of the societies in which they occur. This reaction also applies to other states and their respective societies. At the domestic and international levels, apathy, indifference, and failure to act, intervene, or create obstacles to the unfolding of the various manifestations of state abuse of power and other forms of violent social interaction have in some way contributed to the commission of atrocity crimes. This phenomenon was best described by Pastor Martin Niemöller during World War II when he stated about the Nazi regime:

> In Germany, [the Nazis] first came for the Communists, and I did not speak up, because I was not a communist. Then they came for the Jews, and I did not speak up, because I was not a Jew. Then they came for the trade unionists, and I did not speak up, because I was not a trade unionist. Then they came for the Catholics, and I did not speak up, because I was a Protestant. Then they came for me—and by that time no one was left to speak up. (Marcuse 2008)

Modern and postmodern manifestations of the phenomenon of atrocity crimes also reveal that the organizational structure of such endeavors keeps its various components separate from one another or without knowledge of the ultimate goal. The Nazi regime's organizational structure, in a perverse sense, is the perfect example of how so many persons could have been marshaled, with so much effectiveness, to produce such a high level of human harm with little or no resistance from the rest of society. Through the compartmentalization of the execution of mass atrocities, by means of apportioning and preassigning tasks, the state apparatus as a whole and society can be kept relatively unknowing of the overall plan and how it is executed. If nothing else, it facilitates the task of those who prefer to ignore the facts by allowing them not to connect the dots—the disassociative effect. This approach also contributes to the neutralization of possible opposition or obstacles by certain segments of the state's apparatus or by society. Concealing the overall scheme also gives other states the opportunity to claim political plausible deniability in connection with their failure to act. The same observations apply to violent group dynamics, which may or may not be directly attributable to a state's organizational structure and may be totally independent of it, or even contrary to state policy and beyond its control.

This is evident in situations involving certain forms of interethnic and inter-religious conflict.

The question thus arises as to why these and other forms of collective violence that involve large numbers can take place. Answering this question requires a diagnosis of various forms and types of mass social violence. No matter how tentative this diagnosis may be, it is necessary in order to devise the social and legal techniques to address this form of collective aberrant behavior. The need for countervailing social and legal controls, both domestic and international, are necessary to prevent and contain atrocity crimes and, when all else fails, to punish those who commit such crimes.

The well-known Milgram experiment proved what commonsense observation recognizes. Humans respond to authority, and the more authoritarian a society becomes, the more compliance it elicits from its members. In the age of globalization, Western societies have so well isolated the individual from traditional family, tribal, village, and other group contact that it makes response to authority more likely than when there are inhibiting factors deriving from social values and practices.

Dehumanization, Subhumanization, and Objectification

Almost every violent social interaction, whether at the domestic or inter-state level, has the characteristic of dehumanizing, subhumanizing, or objec-tivizing the other upon whom violence is to be unleashed. This technique is necessary, since a variety of human inhibitory mechanisms would prevent a person from engaging in indiscriminate and mass killing, torturing, and raping of those who are the same. The victim has to be perceived as at least different or undeserving of humane treatment. If all else fails, the rationaliza-tion can always be the necessity of survival due to the dangerous threat posed by the group about to be victimized. This characteristic exists irrespec-tive of whether the violence is initiated by a tyrannical ruler or a ruling elite, or whether it is the outcome of ethnic, religious tribal, or national rivalries. This is why the best predictor of such impending violence is hate propaganda. In this respect, as in others, the psychological mechanism is cognitive dissidence.

The Banality of Evil

In her observations on the Eichmann trial in Jerusalem in 1961, Hannah Arendt (1963) described certain aspects of the Holocaust as representing the banality of evil. Another way of putting it is that evil is frequently done under the appearance of banality. Thus banality is the outer appearance of evil. In all cases, banality is intended to make evil not appear as such. Consequently, evil acts can be performed by many with greater ease.

The commission of human wrongs is for many, particularly those who are followers of the Abrahamic faiths, the product of human evil. How that evil is theologically defined varies in faith-belief systems. In most faiths evil is the breach of a divinely revealed obligation. The same transgressions of human laws are deemed social or secular, in that they remove the connection between wrongdoing and evil. The former is deemed subject to free will and is devoid of a moral content other than what the social content of the prohibition incorporates of an unarticulated moral significance.

Evil per se is both a theological and teleological concept that presupposes for certain faith-belief systems that every human being is created by God with inherent characteristics of good and evil. These faith-belief systems vary as to their interpretations of the connection between freewill/free choice and predetermination/predestination. But this is not the place to argue the merits of these propositions. It is, however, relevant to examine the processes by which atrocity crimes produce the appearance of banality and thus remove from its commission the perception of the evil or wrongdoing being accomplished. Another perspective is how evil can be transformed into an appearance of banality, whereas the moral significance of a person's conduct is lost to that person.

Compartmentalization neutralizes actors' negative reactions by letting them see only a small part of the whole. This technique conveys the impression that the singular acts, unrelated to the whole, are not wrongful, and it neutralizes actors' inhibitions against carrying out such acts by means of banalizing the specific conduct taken outside the overall scheme. Banalization induces people to engage in the commission of these horrible and inhuman acts without facing the evil, moral/social wrongdoing of their actions or inactions. The study of this human phenomenon is particularly relevant in identifying social and legal controls designed to prevent it.

What transforms a banal act into a wrongful act resides in its outcome. Two examples illustrate this proposition. The first is a form letter produced by a manufacturer to a client indicating that the merchandise ordered has been produced and is ready to be picked up. On its face, it is a banal form of everyday commercial communication. If the merchandise, however, is a crematorium for human beings intended for shipment to Auschwitz in 1943, the evil resulting from the use of the crematorium is obvious. The second is one of the many similar situations I encountered in the former Yugoslavia between 1992 and 1994 when I chaired the United Nations Security Council Commission to Investigate War Crimes in the former Yugoslavia. This case involved a Serb militiaman assigned to the front desk of a motel near Pale, in the mountains above Sarajevo. He gave out keys to the rooms in the motel to other Serb militiamen who kept coming in and out. On its face this is a banal function, but the rooms were occupied by Bosnian women who had been seized by force and imprisoned there. The keys allowed the militiamen access to these women, whom they raped. The rapes transformed the banal act of passing out door keys into an evil act. This, too, may fall under the category of cognitive dissidence.

Legal Controls

Considerations on Legal Philosophy

Does the banality of an isolated act that in itself is ordinary and devoid of moral significance make it easier for the human mind, some would say the human conscience, to detach itself from the resulting proximate cause of the person's action? Should the law accept such distinctions concerning acts that are part of an enterprise whose end is to commit mass atrocities? To all but strict legal positivists, the answer is clearly no. Yet, the influence of positivism on domestic criminal law and international criminal law is still strong enough to make it difficult to effectively prosecute such persons.

Moral philosophers have long addressed these questions, but their findings have not sufficiently permeated legal thinking. Jurists are still divided among positivists, relativists, naturalists, and other philosophical bents. But criminal law, both at the domestic and international levels, remains largely positivistic and substantially devoid of the understanding of what motivates human behavior and how to impact it using social and legal controls. Natural law philosophy, like other philosophical doctrines, has different premises leading to different perspectives. The naturalists are in part opposed by legal positivists because natural law has been associated with Christianity. But Judaism and Islam also have their counterpart to Christian natural law, with the significant difference that for the latter, divine law is codified in their respective holy books. In turn, however, theologians have interpreted these legal canons, either literally or in accordance with their intended purposes and scope. Because these religions are in force in states which declare themselves to be binding as a state religion, religious norms constitute the higher-law background of positive law. Irrespective of what higher law exists in a given legal system, whether it is the constitution or treaties or both, every legal system has a hierarchy of sources of law. Resorting to higher sources of law beyond positive law inevitably leads to another sphere of inquiry for substantive content. This was the dilemma for the drafters of International Military Tribunal (IMT). Do they go by the positive law of the Third Reich, do they consider these laws null and void because they violated some higher-law principle, or do they fashion norms that largely partake of ex post facto, but with some plausible legal connection to extant international law in order not to violate the principles of legality? The latter formula was chosen, though a declaration of nullity of Nazi laws and the recognition of validity of the pre-1932 German laws would have boosted the legitimacy of prosecuting the Nazis before the IMT and before the Allied Tribunals established pursuant to Control Council Order No. 10. The comparison between the pre-1932 laws of Germany, particularly its Criminal Code of 1871, would have shown how unjust the Nazi laws were by comparison to these preexisting legal norms. This led German philosopher Gustof Radbruch to articulate a post–World War II rationale for retroactive application based on the relativity of the positive law's violation in comparison with the harm committed. Since the Nazi atrocities were not only a case of *lex iniusta*, but of *lex iniustissima*, retroactive application of the law under the Radbruch formula was deemed acceptable. But where does this qualitative judgment come from, if not from a higher source of law, whether that be morality or ethics as reflected in the social values of a given society? Why then is the identification and formulation of these values such a daunting task for jurists? The answers, varied as they may be, inevitably include political considerations. This is not only the case for the *grande politique* but also for the *petite politique* that animates the public life of every state. As for the undemocratic states, the question is never reached, let alone addressed.

Crimes of state are a form of aberrant social/collective criminality, which generates so much harm that it should compel jurists at both the domestic and international levels to address the phenomenon with clear and precise legal norms and effective enforcement measures. Why this has not occurred is a political or policy choice by states represented by state actors who have demonstrated their reluctance to do so, if for no other reason than to avoid personal responsibility under the theory of command responsibility. To many jurists and other social scientists, the answer is democracy and the rule of law. Both are intended to produce checks and balances likely to prevent, or bring to an early halt, the excesses of rulers and ruling elites: the assumption being that democracies eliminate tyrannical rulers and provide checks and balances on the exercise of the majority's power. Based on experience, however, this assumption has many limitations. In fact, experience proves that political and legal controls have their limits and limitations. They either cannot go far enough or they cannot encompass the range of their intended goals. In the end, even if there were one controller for every citizen in a given country, who would control the controllers?

Moralists counter with the need to strengthen internalized individual controls. But virtue also has its limits. If nothing else, as history demonstrates, the virtuous are not likely to stop the violence of others only with their virtue. And so long as they do not respond to force with force, the courage of speaking truth to power seldom prevents power from pursuing its goals. The exception is mass social disobedience, as Gandhi demonstrated in India during its struggle for independence. Peaceful resistance alone in Apartheid South Africa was not enough to bring the regime to its end. It took a combination of domestic violence and external political and economic pressures to bring about the end of that regime.

International and Domestic Criminal Law Considerations

Consensus must be reached as to the social interests sought to be protected in order to proceed on a policy-oriented basis to devise the different social, political, economic, and legal mechanisms that need to be brought to bear on the phenomenon of mass atrocities in order to achieve prevention and control, and when needed to punish the individual perpetrators and the class (collectively) of perpetrators. This means the making of normative and enforcement choices at the domestic and international levels.

The normative choices include whether there is to be state criminal responsibility under international criminal law; collective or group criminal responsibility under international and domestic criminal law; new forms of vicarious criminal responsibility; new types of penalties to be applied; the extension of legal mechanisms to both international and domestic to civil and administrative sanctions. Adding to these normative policy-based choices are the enforcement mechanisms of interstate and international cooperation for the apprehension, investigation, prosecution, and punishment of persons accused, charged, or convicted of crimes arising out of the established norms. All of this translates into the need for an international and domestic policy of accountability to guard against impunity.

An examination of the national criminal laws of all states reveals that none contain a crime labeled as crimes of state. It also reveals that the state is never collectively responsible. No domestic laws exist anywhere that hold criminally responsible those who have collectively participated in mass atrocity crimes, including that which is otherwise defined as a common crime under domestic criminal laws. State officials are criminally responsible on an individual basis in every state, but the forms of criminal responsibility, the evidentiary requirements, and the political influences on the investigation, prosecution, and adjudication processes afford wide latitude of impunity to state actors. As for legal forms of group or vicarious criminal responsibility, which exist in some states, they are scarcely enforced. A low percentage of prosecutions occur under these legal forms in comparison to the estimated black figures (unknown estimates) of those who could, and maybe should, be prosecuted for mass atrocities.

Understandably, elites in any state are not likely to criminalize their conduct or to allow the law to easily reach them. Thus, there are many ways by which rulers and ruling elites can place themselves above the law or beyond the reach of the law and also protect those who carried out their misdeeds. The same is true under international criminal law, where there is no established criminal responsibility of states, where international crimes apply only to individuals, and where heads of state have *de jure* temporal immunity, though not substantive immunity, for certain *jus cogens* crimes.

The responsibility of heads of state for certain international crimes exists but is still a work in progress. The political reasons for such a state of affairs are too obvious for comment. That fact is generally well accepted among the world's ruling elite, notwithstanding the western state's professions to the contrary. Nondemocratic leaders and regimes such as those in Africa, Asia, and the Arab World have no need to hide behind a fig leaf of support for the principle. They blatantly stand against it. They are comforted by the fact that western states are largely passive. In any event, states know that double-standards and exceptionalism still prevail, and that it is essentially how well a state plays its political cards at a given moment that allows it to avoid being placed in the category of perpetrators of crimes of states, no matter how episodic and elusive accountability may be.

The historical record shows some recent successes, but they are scant. Kambanda of Rwanda was prosecuted by the International Criminal Tribunal for Rwanda (ICTR) after his regime was toppled and is now in prison. Milosevic of Serbia was prosecuted by the International Criminal Tribunal for Former Yugoslavia (ICTY) after he left office on the heels of his renewed aggressive plan in Kosovo, which led to the United States lifting its protection of him. He died during the proceedings. Taylor of Liberia is on trial before the Special Court of Sierra. He was surrendered by Nigeria, which initially gave him asylum under the Lomé Peace Accords and allowed him to resign as president of Liberia, after making millions from the sale of blood diamonds. He is believed to have moved that money from Liberia to Switzerland and the UK. Then there is Pinochet of Chile, who after leaving power was about to be prosecuted but managed to avoid extradition to Spain compliments of the UK. He returned to Chile, where he is presently living at home and not subjected to prosecution on grounds of illness and old age. Habré of Tchad avoided prosecution by obtaining asylum in Senegal, who did not surrender him to Belgium when they asked to prosecute him. Al-Bashir of the Sudan was indicted by the ICC and so far sits uneasily as head of state, with the support and comfort of African and Arab states and also China, due to its oil interests in that country. The United States is also a passive contributor to the situation for a variety of strategic and political considerations. Although the lessons are self-evident, they have yet to be learned or acted upon. These and other examples are intended to show that no matter what is obvious, the cynicism of realpolitik prevails all too often, the cost and consequences to humankind notwithstanding.

When the conduct of state actors has the characteristics described here and is committed wholly within the confines of a given state, domestic criminal law applies, unless the conduct in question falls within the definition of a given international crime. If the conduct is across state boundaries and takes place in another state, then international criminal law applies, as well as the domestic criminal law of the state wherein the conduct occurred, or the state whose nationals have been victimized, or the state whose nationals have committed the crime. Universal jurisdiction also applies to certain international crimes, but few states presently have legislation that allows a state to exercise this form of jurisdiction. No state, however, has legislation that can be described as pure universal jurisdiction, meaning that no link to the prosecuting state is required.

The absence of adequate legal norms and their effective and consistent enforcement gives rise to two basic questions. The first is how domestic and international law legislatively addresses crimes of state, and the second is how effective is the enforcement of these applicable norms. These two questions raise others, such as the following:

1. How do we fill the gaps that exist in domestic criminal laws and in international law?
2. How do we address the overlaps that exist between domestic and international laws?
3. How do we reconcile the multiplicity of international legal regimes and their subregimes, which apply to the same protected interest?
4. How do we assess the effectiveness of coercive enforcement capabilities of the domestic and international law regimes?
5. How do we develop noncoercive compliance-inducing legal and social mechanisms?

The aggregate effect of these questions raises the ultimate question of the limits of social and legal controls in the prevention of mass atrocity crimes, particularly in the face of realpolitik's manipulation of these processes because of their inherent limitations. Those who are inclined to moralist solutions tend toward reinforcing internalized individual controls and inhibiting factors likely to prevent individual involvement in crimes of violence. But, as stated earlier, virtue has its limits, which are lost in the frenzy of collective violence. The more effective approach is a comprehensive strategic one that combines these personal internalized controls with a wide array of external social and legal controls deriving both from international and domestic measures, including what is presently advocated as the international responsibility to protect, which includes external intervention by force when needed.

International Criminal Law

International Criminal law comes closest to addressing crimes of state, though not by that name. The crimes in question are aggression, genocide, crimes against humanity, and torture. Other international crimes may also fall within that meaning if committed by state actors and others in furtherance of a state plan or policy. These crimes include war crimes, slavery and slave-related practices, and a variety of terrorism of distinct prohibitions (airplane hijacking, kidnapping of diplomats, taking of hostages, piracy and certain types of violent crimes aboard ships, use of explosives, and theft and attack upon nuclear materials and facilities). But careful consideration of these international crimes reveals how realpolitik manipulates them for the benefit of the state and state actors.

Aggression is not defined in any international treaty that criminalizes its commission, and it does not extend to neo-imperial forms of foreign domination and exploitation. Genocide is only limited to national ethnic or religious groups, thus excluding social and political groups, and there has to be a specific intent to destroy the group in whole or in part, which is a very high legal standard to prove. Crimes against humanity require proof of a state policy and do not extend to nonstate actors. War crimes will depend on which legal subregime applies, since there is one regime concerning conflicts of an international character and another one concerning conflicts of a non-international character, the latter being weaker and offering no inducement for compliance to belligerents not granted POW status (instead, they are to be treated as common criminals under domestic criminal laws for performing the very same acts that state actors engage in). Moreover, neither conventional nor customary international humanitarian law applies to purely domestic conflicts; thus the commission of crimes of state in these contexts is beyond the reach of the law. Torture is limited to its use by state actors seeking to extract a confession or statement from the victim and does not therefore extend to the sole infliction of harm. Terrorism is not comprehensively defined in any given treaty and does not include acts of state. It is compartmentalized by a series of twelve conventions essentially applicable to nonstate actors.

More important, the piecemeal approach of international criminal law allows for significant normative and enforcement gaps. For example, there are very few manifestations of environmental harm that are criminalized. While there are crimes to protect endangered species that apply to individuals, more harmful state conduct such as global warming and hazardous waste dumping remain outside the sphere of international criminalization.

International criminal law criminalizes certain international human right violations, but not every violation of human rights is criminalized, even when that violation constitutes a crime under the domestic laws of every country in the world. This is the case for murder, which is criminalized in every country of the world but does not, in and of itself, constitute an international crime. It is only when the mass killing of persons is committed on a widespread or systematic basis that it constitutes crimes against humanity.

Even so, there is a legal requirement that a link be established between the conduct in question and a state policy directing that conduct against a given civilian population.

International criminal law has, since the end of World War I, sought to criminalize individual conduct for certain crimes committed by state actors that are the product of state action or state policy. This includes crimes against peace (now aggression) that are not necessarily the product of state action or state policy, crimes against humanity, and war crimes. All three crimes were included in the Charter of the International Military Tribunal (IMT), as well as under the Statute of the International Tribunal for the Far East (IMTFE). Even though aggression and crimes against humanity are among the quintessential crimes of state, they have not, for political reasons, been included in an international convention. Aggression has also not been the subject of any prosecution since both the IMT and IMTFE.

Since the end of World War II, international criminal law has added genocide, apartheid, and torture to the category of crimes of state. The elements of all three crimes require that the conduct be performed by state actors, as part of state action, or reflecting state policy. All international crimes, however, address only individual and not state criminal responsibility. Individual criminal responsibility also exists for the perpetuators of some international crimes under the concept of *jus cogens*.

Genocide and crimes against humanity, which require the element of state policy or state action, are contained in the statutes of several international tribunals established between 1993–1998, namely International Criminal Tribunal for the Former Yugoslavia (ICTY), the International Criminal Tribunal for Rwanda (ICTR), the International Criminal Court (ICC), and, the mixed-model tribunals: the Special Court for Sierra Leone (SCSL), the Extraordinary Chambers in the Courts of Cambodia (ECCC), the Special Panels of the Dili District Court (also called the East Timor Tribunal) for Timor-Leste, and the Serbian War Crimes Tribunal (for Kosovo). War crimes are also included in these statutes, but they do not require state policy or state action because they can be committed by individuals acting on their own. They can also be the product of state policy or state action. Aggression is not criminalized under these statutes. The ICC is in the process of debating the definition of "aggression" to be included in the statute.

There is no norm under ICL that embodies the principle of state criminal responsibility, even though it was applied to Germany and Turkey after World War I. It derived from the historic concept of reparations, which arose from the historic practices of exactions imposed upon the defeated. This concept was rejected after World War II in favor of individual criminal responsibility. The new approach was premised on the belief that any form of collective criminal responsibility is inherently unjust, because it does not distinguish between those deemed responsible and those who are not. Aside from this basic assumption, no studies were developed on the possible deterring and preventive impact of collective criminal responsibility on the future conduct of collectivities that are part of the international community.

International Human Rights Law

The International Human Rights Law regime provides only certain administrative and civil remedies. Whenever the state conduct is deemed "wrongful conduct," this is actionable by one state against another. But it does not give rise to functions other than damages. It does not provide for state criminal sanctions against the state or the collectivity that engages in such conduct. The European human rights system provides direct access to justice by individuals against states, but the remedy is only monetary. The Inter-American Regional human rights is a close follow-up, which has made much progress but is yet to have reached its European counterpart. This is due in part to U.S. nonparticipation. The African human rights system is barely nascent. But none of these regimes have effective enforcement mechanisms. Compliance with these regimes remains at the discretion of states.

THE ENFORCEMENT GAP

The greatest manifestations of crimes of state remain, as they have been throughout history, the despotism of domestic power holders over the vast majority of the populations they control and the exercise of power and hegemony, be it military or economic, by stronger states over weaker ones. Killings, slavery, torture, deprivation of civil, economic, political, and cultural rights, and other forms of oppression and exploitation, whether at the domestic or international level, are all on the same continuum when they are the product of state policy or action. For all practical purposes, these and other similar state actions benefit from a combined normative and enforcement gap at the domestic and international levels that create an open window of opportunity for the commission of atrocity crimes and other crimes. Combined with the few and far between international and national prosecutions for atrocity crimes, the result is impunity for the perpetrators. Moreover, the cynicism of the international community's prevailing realpolitik approach is exemplified by the false dichotomy of peace versus justice. This translates into offering immunity and amnesty in exchange for the cessation of violence. The result is the triumph of impunity over accountability. This approach escalates conflicts until they reach a level where it can be argued that offering immunity to the leader and amnesty to the followers is wiser than insisting on accountability. The cynicism of this argument derives from the fact that had it not been for the failure of major states to intervene these situations would not have occurred in the first place.

It should be noted, however, that in states which have achieved a certain level of democratization secured by the rule of law, the manifestations of state abuses of power are circumscribed; thus they are either reduced or eliminated. But in the majority of the world's 198 states, this is not the case, as is evidenced by the level of atrocity crimes in failed states. The number of these states has for the past few decades been almost permanently at 40. They are known, as are the conditions likely to drive them toward mass atrocities. Yet even in relatively easy cases to address by collective external intervention, as in Somalia, the world stands immobile. One has only to consider the self-imposed powerlessness of the world's major navies in the face of a few pirates on power boats armed with a few rocket launchers and Kalashnikovs.

In 1939, when Hitler visited the front lines of his troops about to invade Czechoslovakia, he gathered his generals, many of whom were reluctant to invade a peaceful neighboring country. Hitler reportedly said the following to quiet their concerns: "And who now remembers the Armenians?" Even if the story is untrue, it is a valuable reminder that norms on crimes of state and their enforcement have some general prevention. But whenever norms are not comprehensive or have escape hatches, and whenever their enforcement is periodic, symbolic, or selective, the preventive effect is sharply attenuated.

Effective and selective prosecutions have proven how in a perverse way they accomplish the opposite result of what is intended by the form of justice allowing states to put their past behind them and hand their collective responsibility on the few token guilty ones who were prosecuted. After World War II, Austria conducted a few prosecutions, but having declared itself the first victim of Nazism, it was able to put its past behind it as of the mid-1950s. The United States conducted the prosecution for the infamous Mauthausen Prison camps, which were in Austria, as were others. Italy did not address the crimes of its fascist leaders and their military action overseas. Only a year ago Italy signed a compensation agreement with Libya, but the funds will go to the Italian companies heading development projects there. Over the past thirty years, Italy has pursued a few token prosecutions for crimes committed in occupied Italy between 1943 and 1945, such as the *Priebke* case. Thousand of Italian military and civilians were killed by Germany, and yet the Italian authorities did not pursue any action except for opening a number of investigatory files by military prosecutors, which still remained closed or not acted upon. The crimes against humanity committed by France's Vichy collaborationist government, such as the deportation of French Jews for slave labor in Germany, and the delivery of escaped Jews from German-controlled territory back to Germany to be killed or sent to slave-labor camps, resulted in only three major prosecutions between the 1960s and 1980s. They are the cases of *Barbie, Touvier,* and *Pappon,* and with that the record was closed.

The serious effort to address crimes of state must also close the loophole that allows states to engage in the deceptive game of holding some token aspects of postconflict justice modalities, such as domestic prosecutions and truth commissions, only to justify issuing general and indiscriminate amnesties and then conveniently absolving itself from all past responsibility. The Vichy government's slate was wiped clean with three prosecutions some twenty to thirty years after the fact (there were, however, many prosecutions between 1945 and1955) for collaboration with the Nazi occupiers, but they had nothing to do with international crimes and crimes of state. Italy wiped its slate clean after signing the 1945 Armistice Agreement and the prosecution, on false grounds, of the scapegoat General Bellomo. Spain for years did not address its Franco regime past on the grounds that Franco himself made the transition to democracy possible. A truth commission has recently been established, and with the issuance of its report and a few measures to be implemented that slate too will be cleaned.

To revisit Hitler's quip: How many today remember the 1 million Ibo killed in Nigeria in the sixties, the 1 million Bangladeshi killed in the seventies, and the 1 million Khmer killed in Cambodia between the seventies and eighties? And who even knows of the estimated 3 million killed in the DRC in the last five years? Who will remember in a few years the 800,000 killed in Rwanda, and the 500,000 killed in Liberia and Sierra Leone? The list is tragically long, and the memory of what happened in a given generation may survive for one or two succeeding ones, but then it is lost to the future. To paraphrase George Santayana, the forgotten lessons of the past are what makes possible repeating the same mistakes.

CONCLUSION

There has been a reduction in violent power takeovers in states and fewer tyrannical rulers who abuse power and victimize their societies. However, whether the overall consequences of regime victimization will be reduced in the coming decades is speculative at best. Political realism is reasserting itself in this era of globalization. States and multinational corporations, whose goals and policies are characterized by the pursuits of power and wealth over the values of human, social, and economic justice, are reacquiring a predominant position in international affairs. The present tendency is marked by an abandonment of the ideals of universal justice that emerged during the age of enlightenment. These ideals compel the search for redressing imbalances of power and wealth instead of accepting them as the natural order of things. As a consequence, the focus of states has shifted from trying to strengthen commonly shared values as a factor that unites peoples of the world to accepting that which divides peoples of the world as part of the natural order of things. Accepting disparities in power and wealth between states eliminates the value

of universal social solidarity that requires sharing wealth, reducing power disparities, and eliminating exceptionalism for the mighty. The consequences of
this new paradigm shift includes accepting power outcomes instead of legitimacy outcomes, placing order above justice, and confirming the primacy of
power and wealth over the values of universal justice.

In a perverse sense, the law, which has yet to catch up with crimes of state
when committed by state actors, is already lagging behind the needs of
addressing the same manifestations of aberrant social behavior when committed by nonstate actors. There are few indicators that international criminal
law's future development may address the issues of state and collective
responsibility, both criminal and civil, and the inclusion of nonstate actors in
a parallel category to state actors for purposes of individual and group criminal responsibility. But that may well be wishful thinking.

Atrocity crimes are not inevitable; they are preventable, though not
entirely or at all times, and their harmful consequences can be limited.
The international community's adoption of *inter alia* and the responsibility to
protect includes the following measures:

1. Establishing early warning systems at the level of the United Nations
   and other international governmental organizations (IGOs) and
   maintaining a database on the causes and consequences of postconflict justice
2. Institutionalizing preventive diplomacy
3. Developing assistance programs to enhance national capacity-building
   to observe and enforce the rule of law
4. Addressing human rights grievances at the IGO level before they
   erupt into conflicts
5. Providing and enforcing credible sanctions as a means of prevention
   and control of violent social interactions by the Security Council,
   IGOs, and responsible states
6. Developing at the IGO level effective crisis-management techniques,
   including monitoring systems of impending and actual conflicts
7. Providing economic and other forms of assistance to failed states and
   those on the verge of becoming failed states

Recent developments in the area of international criminal justice, such as
the establishment of the International Criminal Tribunal for the former
Yugoslavia, the International Criminal Tribunal for Rwanda, the International
Criminal Court, and mixed-model tribunals for Cambodia, Sierra Leone,
Timor-Leste, and Kosovo are definite signs of progress, but they have yet to pro-
duce a deterring effect on widespread transgressions against basic human rights
and atrocity crimes. International criminal justice is still a work in progress.
Between 1992 and 2009, the international community has witnessed many

tragedies with large-scale human victimization, as in Darfur (Sudan) and the Democratic Republic of Congo. Crimes of state in these and other areas of the world are alive and well. The promise of accountability, however, is yet to be redeemed by the international community. Clearly, the post–World War II promise of "never again" is far from having been redeemed. Will it ever be redeemed? A question that has periodically been posited during the ages after major cataclysmic warring events. The end of the Napoleonic wars brought about such a question as did WWI. Each one of these and other devastating wars brought about the same questions. In her celebrated song, "Where Have All the Flowers Gone?" Joan Baez's words echo vividly: "when will they ever learn?"

NOTES

1. The exception to this is a project undertaken by the author, Fighting Impunity and Promoting International Justice, through the International Institute of Higher Studies in Criminal Sciences, as a European Commission funded initiative whose results are soon to be published. The data reveal that between 1948 and 2008, 310 conflicts have taken place, killing 92 million to 101 million people. Prosecutions occurred for no more than 1 percent of the perpetrators.
2. For a more detailed discussion of international criminal law, see Bassiouni (2003, 2008a). For more detailed discussion of issues to particular crimes, see above and Bassiouni (1998, 1999a, 2000c, 2002a, 2002b).

PART ONE

◆ Crimes of the State

SCHOLARLY ATTENTION to crimes committed by states or governments has steadily increased over the past few decades. Coming from many disciplinary perspectives—criminology, history, law, political science, socio-legal studies, and sociology—this field of scholarship has been united by two central concerns: identifying the etiological dimensions of crimes committed by states and forms of control that have been or can be devised and implemented. A simple perusal of headlines in major newspapers highlights the importance of such a field of inquiry: the continued fallout from the United States' and Britain's illegal invasion of Iraq, an ongoing genocide in the Darfur region of Sudan, mass atrocities and crimes against humanity committed in the Democratic Republic of the Congo, political violence and oppression in Zimbabwe, Russia's invasion of Georgia, and the list goes on. Yet, despite the seeming ubiquity of these crimes, mainstream criminology still turns away from an attempt to understand and explain them as *crimes*.

A major point of resistance from more traditional criminological schools has been the very definition of state crime. Within the boundaries of criminological literature, the vast majority of scholars focus on street crime with clear legally based definitions. Even the study of white-collar crimes (see Sutherland 1949) has proved controversial and tends to be limited to what is termed "occupational crime"—employee theft, fraud, and embezzlement (see Friedrichs 2004). It is not surprising, given a field's seeming discomfort of examining more routine crimes of the powerful, that studies of the crimes of state themselves have gone relatively underexamined.

DEFINITIONAL DEBATES

The origin of the study of state crime is traced to William Chambliss's 1988 presidential address to the American Society of Criminology.[1] Chambliss (1989, 184) defined the concept of state-organized crime as "acts defined by law as criminal and committed by state officials in pursuit of their jobs as representatives of the state." While controversial within the field at large,

Chambliss's initial definition was quite conservative—limiting the concept to acts deemed illegal by a state itself (i.e., aiding and abetting pirates) and carried out by agents acting in the name of the government. Growing out of his earlier work on organized crime and influenced by Sutherland's (1949) explorations of corporate crimes, this work logically extended the criminological lens to the actions of a different set of complex organizations: states.

Chambliss's initial call for the study of crimes by states did inspire several criminologists to take up his challenge. As we explore later, this work began to extend the boundaries of his initial definition, creating the debate this introductory chapter centers upon. Chambliss returned to his concept of state-organized half a decade later. In 1995 he called for resolving the key question at the foundation of the discipline, the definition of crime, so that the discipline could remain viable and vital. He stated, "State organized crimes, environmental crimes, crimes against humanity, human rights crimes, and the violations of international treaties increasingly must take center stage in criminology. . . . Criminologists must define crime as behavior that violates international agreements and principles established in the courts and treaties of international bodies" (Chambliss 1995, 9). This is a call that some criminologists would heed, producing a definition of state crime grounded in international law.

Yet, more immediate responses and work drew upon other definitions of crime in general and state crime specifically. The first major issue to arise in the literature was the very question of states being labeled as criminal actors. Barak points out that "the study of state criminality is problematic because the concept itself is controversial, in part because of a debate over whether one should define crime in terms other than law codes of individual nations. Some argue that if a state obeys its own laws, it should be judged by no higher criterion" (1991b, 8). Sharkansky (1995) presented such a critique, arguing that while states may commit many undesirable behaviors, one cannot call them criminal unless they expressly violate their own state's laws. Doing so, he suggests, violates key precepts of national sovereignty and a country's right to regulate itself. This critique sees even well-recognized instances of state criminality, like the Holocaust, as "nasty" but not criminal behaviors. Allowing states to be the sole arbitrator of the legality of their own behavior is highly problematic, as nearly no state will voluntarily define its own actions as criminal. Even from a narrowly legalistic perspective, Sharkansky ignored the fact since their inception modern states have voluntarily surrendered portions of their sovereignty via the making of international compacts and treaties.

The tensions and debates over defining state crime reflect a broader debate within criminology itself. Utilization of state-produced legal codes has long been the stated and unstated norm. Such a reliance on state-produced definitions has caused tensions within street crime and white-collar crime studies, with critically orientated criminologists rejecting state-produced definitions (see Michalowski 1985). The political nature of law production has long been the main rationale for this rejection. One cannot separate the nature of the political process that guides legislatures (and legislators) from the legislation produced. This is highly relevant when studying crimes of the state. If law is produced by states, and states, at least in Enlightenment-inspired liberal democracy, are constituted by political representatives, law becomes a *sui generis* political tool and activity. States have an inherent drive to fulfill their own self-interest and not define harmful and problematic behavior as criminal (especially their own).

Even in instances where state crimes have come under legal prosecution, the selection of what is and is not prosecuted (or prosecutable) is highly political and contingent upon realpolitik. For example, many have noted that the ubiquity of sexual violence during war and lamented the fact that only recently has it been prosecuted as a war crime (Card 1996; Gottschall 2004; Graybill 2001; Salzman 1998). Pointing specifically to Nuremberg and Tokyo, these calls descry the lack of attention to these crimes as a function of patriarchal worldviews held by leaders and war makers. These critiques miss one of the main factors of the absence of rape prosecutions in the postconflict justice mechanism imposed after the Second World War: the Allied powers were just as guilty of the crimes as were the Axis. Similarly, mass bombings and other civilian-focused attacks were not prosecuted, as they were widely used by the Allied powers (e.g., the fire bombings of Dresden and Tokyo, as well as the use of nuclear devices on Hiroshima and Nagasaki). Such examples highlight the intensely politicized and contextualized definitional processes that come into play within the field. Of course, in the past decades the processes and dynamics of the creation of international law have become even richer and more complex as a multitude of state holders bring their own interests and perceptions to the table.

Additionally, there have been points of contention regarding the larger question of ownership and expertise. In its reliance on legal codes, criminology became a rarity among academic disciplines: one that relies on outsiders for the definition of subject matter. This is not a new debate, with criminologists as early as Sellin (1938) raising this objection. At core is the question of legitimacy and expert authority. If those who study a phenomenon do not take an independent initiative to define, but rather cede, this essential aspect of definitional conceptualization to outsiders, then that group of scholars is merely the adjunct of those whom they allow to define their subject matter for them. From this standpoint, criminology as a discipline "must either declare its independence of the state or serve as an arm of the state" (Reiman 2006, 362). While Reiman is referring to the general tendency of criminologists to rely upon state definitions of crime as well as their use of state monies to study topics of state interest, thus creating policy information relevant to the positional interests of those in power, his statement is highly relevant to the overall foundational issue of defining crime itself.

The substance of a debate about definitions goes beyond merely critiquing the source or the substance of a given definition. One must also provide an alternative conceptualization. The Schwendingers (1970) suggested using human rights as the core definition of crime (see also Galliher 1989). Others have advocated that crimes are any socially injurious actions, regardless of the actor in question. Michalowski (1985, 357) defines these acts as "legally permissible acts or sets of conditions whose consequences are similar to those of illegal acts." Here the potential vagaries and political nature of law are circumvented while maintaining a general focus on the sorts of actions criminologists have long investigated. More recently, some criminologists have called for the abandonment of the concept of crime entirely in favor of zemiology, the study of harm (Hillyard, Pantazis, Tombs, and Gordon 2004). Establishing the generation of harm to individuals or communities as the common fact all crimes hold as a class of phenomena, a zemiology would expand the foundation of the field favoring a broad consistency of categorization over a narrow specificity. While this might add a conceptual and ideological purity to definitional processes, it takes an already broad subject matter and casts the net ever wider to nearly the entirety of individual and institutional behavior within contemporary societies. Additionally, as with any other standard, the question becomes who then defines what is or is not a harm?

While this is a debate that ranges across some segments of the criminological community, here we want to focus specifically on those approaches relative to the definition of state crime. In general, three positions have emerged within this debate: crime as a socially injurious action (social harm definition); social response approach (deviance as socially defined); and a legalistic approach. Legalists' use of extant statute identifies an external reference point, while the social harm standard uses a more amorphous and relativistic definitional rubric. The social response approach rejects the ability to define something absolutely, and looks backward to positions advanced by the sociology of deviance in the 1960s, specifically the social response tradition.

Responding to Chambliss's call for the study of state criminality, in 1991 Kramer and Michalowski began their long-standing inquiry into crimes that occur at the intersection of state and corporate apparatuses. Typically called state-corporate crimes, these crimes have been defined as "illegal or socially injurious actions that result from a mutually reinforcing interaction between (1) policies and/or practices in pursuit of the goals of one or more institutions of political governance and (2) policies and/or practices in pursuit of the goals of one or more institutions of economic production and distribution" (Michalowski and Kramer 2006, 20).[2] They followed their classic conceptualization piece with two solid case studies: the destruction of the space shuttle *Challenger* (Kramer 1992) and the fire at the Imperial Chicken plant in Hamlet, North Carolina (Aulette and Michalowski 1993). Each explored the ramifications of the interaction of corporate and government interests and negligence and presented compelling studies of actions that were harmful, yet did not meet any extant legal definition of crime. These papers produced a chain of state-corporate crime studies, establishing it as a line of inquiry in its own right, separate but related to state crime studies (see Michalowski and Kramer 2006).

The use of socially injurious action as the key criteria for labeling something criminal opened up a wide variety of activities for study (e.g., Tunnell 1993b). Aulette and Michalowski's (1993) piece also supplemented the original conceptualization through labeling state agency omissions as criminal in addition to commissions. To clarify and order much of this work, Kauzlarich, Mullins, and Matthews (2003) presented a continuum harm-based definition of state and state-corporate crime. First, the authors defined state crime as a phenomenon that

- Generates harm to individuals, groups, and property
- Is a product of action or inaction on behalf of the state or state agencies
- Relates the action or inaction directly to an assigned or implied trust/duty
- Is committed, or omitted, by a governmental agency, organization, or representative
- Is committed in the self-interest of the state itself or the elite groups controlling it

In the tradition of socially injurious actions, this definitional approach united the conceptual elements of harm, omission, and actor identification. The approach further refines omission from any failure of a body to an express failure on an extant trust. The authors continued by establishing a continuum of complicity separating commissions from omission, then adding another dimension that classifies state crimes based upon how the crimes tie to explicit state goals and actions (e.g., the Holocaust and U.S. mining of Nicaraguan harbors) or implicit state ideologies and conditions (e.g., perpetration of inequity). Some recent papers on state crime have used this continuum as a core aspect of their conceptualization of state responsibility, especially in the area of omissions (e.g., Hogan et al. 2006; Faust and Kauzlarich 2008).

While the socially analogous harms approach offers one way around the problem of defining what constitutes state crime, it has some key weaknesses.

First, none of the above pieces clearly define and conceptualize harm. In the loosest sense of the term, anything can be a state crime if there is any amount of deprivation or pain and the introduction of negative or the removal of positively desired stimuli. If the state can be remotely tied either in action or inaction, then one has a state crime.

An alternative to the socially analogous or harm-based approach definition is the attempt to generate a social response definition. Green and Ward (2000) argue that the true definition of state crime rests within the eyes of a social audience. Borrowing heavily from the work of Howard Becker (1963) and the social response school of the sociology of deviance, their position is that what constitutes (or does not constitute) a state crime should be determined from the perspective of social audiences witnessing (directly or indirectly) the behavior. When a given audience perceives an action committed by a state that it sees as criminal in nature and responds to it as if it were criminal, then that action is a state crime. In many ways, this is much vaguer than a harm-based definition. A key problem is that this perspective never establishes what can constitute a social audience, leaving that open to a given social context. As with Sharhansky's (1995) definition discussed earlier, much of what could be objectively defined as criminal would fail to reach that bar. For example, Kauzlarich (2007) recently published a qualitative study of anti-Iraq war protestors examining their views on the nature and legality of the war. While this population saw the war as harmful, wrong-headed, and illegitimate, the majority of his interviewees balked at labeling the war (or its progenitors) as criminal. If we were to apply Green and Ward's reasoning here, assuming this to be the social audience from which we define its potential criminality, the war itself should not be seen as criminal in nature—something that those drawing on either the social harm perspective or the use of international law would strongly disagree with. At its core, this definition fails as it places the primary burden of definition on an unknown social audience or a mass public that is easily molded by propaganda and other forms of claims making to produce anything solid or concrete. As with zemiology, this is far too vague to be useful in either theoretical or empirical research. While it has value as a potential epistemological description of how such events become defined as state crimes, it gives scholars little in the way of explaining such events.

In response to the critiques of these approaches, some state crime scholars have drawn upon the framework of international law to define state crimes. In the most general sense, the scholarship done by legal scholars on these phenomena implicitly take this approach. Recently labeled "supranational criminology," this focus tends to limit itself to war crimes, genocide, and crimes against humanity (see Smeulers and Haveman 2008)—critical state crimes but not inclusive of all such entities. Some within the critical criminological tradition have upheld international law and domestic law as a general baseline for defining state crime for several reasons, many of which are founded on the critiques of the other approaches. Works in this tradition have often devoted large segments of papers or entire chapters to the explication of relevant international laws to a given case (e.g., Kauzlarich and Kramer 1998; Rothe and Mullins 2008b). A definition of state crime grounded in international law would be "any action that violates international public law, and/or a states' own domestic law when these actions are committed by individual actors acting on behalf of, or in the name of the state even when such acts are motivated by their personal economical, political, and ideological interests" (Rothe and Mullins 2008b, xxx). Further, it is our contention that using extant international law as a foundation adds legitimacy to the field's definition. If a critique of state crime studies is that they are not truly scientific but rather politically inspired diatribes, establishing the illegality of such actions under a legal code is a fitting response to such critiques. The gravitas associated with international law is transferred to the subject matter under study. This response has then been a meeting of a more traditional criminology on its own terms and turning the critique of mainstream studies away from labeling the work as a tool of the state, as zemiology does, to something very similar to Sutherland's critique of criminology when he initiated the study of white-collar crime (Sutherland 1939, 1949). Indeed, such an approach insists this topic qualifies as an appropriate area of criminological study.

The use of international law provides clarity and precision in the definitional processes. One need not negotiate the problematic aspects of defining "harm" and seeking connections to states and state actors that may be direct or indirect. As with any legal code—due to the very nature of law itself—actions are clearly defined. Responsibilities are firmly established. However, no legal code is universally applied, and on occasion criminologists studying such crimes might come to different interpretations about whether or not a given event meets the definitional criteria under international law. For example, there has been quite a bit of public/political discourse as to whether or not Sudan's continuing destruction of the Fur, Massalit, and Zaghawa constitutes genocide (see Rothe and Mullins 2007), even though the actions in Darfur have been subjected to criminological attention and have been academically labeled as and studied as genocide (see Hagan, Rymond-Richmond, and Parker 2006; Mullins and Rothe 2007, 2008a).

As with other positions, there are critiques of drawing on international law as well. The foremost is that, as with state-produced law, international law is the result of a political process and thus as suspect as any other body of law. Further, the political nature of these laws is even more transparent due to the multiparty negotiations that occur in its creation. In fact, international law often fails to be created or is created in a nonjusticable way due to express politicization of its construction. The most obvious case in point is the attempt to define the crime of aggression. While there is general agreement amongst state and nonstate bodies as to what constitutes an aggressive action between states, and there has been a longstanding definition produced by the United Nations, it has never been codified into law, as states refuse to subject themselves to the definition they all agree upon. However, unlike state-based laws, international law is *designed* to address states and their behaviors, making it a more obvious definitional source.

Our purpose here is not to solve this argument. In some senses it is an intractable debate that will continue (see Rothe and Friedrichs 2006). This volume rightfully contains pieces that draw upon a variety of definitional approaches. These definitional differences not only matter in a conceptual sense but also have led state crime scholars to address a number of different subject matters.

STUDIES OF STATE CRIME

Chambliss's "State-Organized Crime" (1989) is hailed as the first attempt to bring crimes by states under a criminological lens. In this groundbreaking article he explores piracy, drug smuggling, and aspects of the U.S. Iran Contra scandal as type cases, which if not directly committed by polities are tacitly approved of and encouraged. Piracy was illegal under the domestic laws of all major world powers in the eighteenth and nineteenth centuries. However, due to interstate power struggles and a cold war on the seas, the advantages of allowing pirates safe harbor so long as they only attacked one's enemies overrode any commitment to law or its legitimacy. The issuance of letters of marque simply formalized informal relationships. Similarly, the gains offered to U.S. intelligence agencies in participating in a south Asian drug trade during the Vietnam era overrode the fact that such behaviors were banned by U.S. law. His last example, the Regan administration's violation of the Boland amendments to provide aid to the Nicaraguan Contras, highlights the same pattern—when law is found in opposition to political expediency, realpolitik holds sway and laws are violated (for a more thorough analysis of state crime in this case, see Rothe 2009b).

Needless to say, Chambliss's piece catalyzed critical criminologists especially. Three edited volumes were published in its wake: Barak's *Crimes by the Capitalist State* (1991a); Tunnell's *Political Crime in Contemporary America* (1993b); and Ross's *Controlling State Crime* (1995a). All three of these books contained chapters addressing issues of conceptualization or theory and cases. They begin with Sutherland's (1939) call for an extension of criminological thought to white-collar crime studies and then extend to the next logic step—a criminology of political institutions. Taken as a whole, these books represent thirty-four analyses of various types and controls of state crime by twenty-eight scholars. Specific case discussions range from corruption to police misconduct to state omissions (i.e., bad policies). Most of the works here focus on contemporary western states (i.e., Canada, the United States, and the United Kingdom)—a trend that continued for some time in the field. Varied in approach and presentation, these contributions served as a catalyst for future works.

State crime studies began to appear in peer-reviewed journals as well. Kauzlarich, Kramer, and Smith (1992) published the first of many pieces on crimes regarding nuclear weapons (see also Kauzlarich 1995, 1997; Kauzlarich and Kramer 1998), explicitly framing the issue in terms of state crime. Since then a number of venues have frequently highlighted state crime studies: *Contemporary Justice Review; Crime, Law, and Social Change; Critical Criminology: An International Journal; Humanity and Society*; and *Social Justice*. Studies have appeared in other areas, with the *British Journal of Criminology* devoting a special issue to state crime in 2005 and *Critical Criminology: An International Journal* in 2009.

Kauzlarich and Kramer's *Crimes of the American Nuclear State: At Home and Abroad* (1998) holds a central place in the history of state crime studies, as it is the first research monograph focused upon state crime. Drawing upon international law to frame their discussions, the authors provide well-contextualized explorations of the criminal nature of the United States' use of nuclear weapons as a threat to do so in both the Korean and Vietnam conflicts, criminal aspects of weapons development vis-à-vis environmental pollution, and the Department of Energy's illegal utilization of prisoners in Oregon and Washington State as test subjects. Drawing on an integrated theory of state offending, the volume provides rich and in-depth analysis of how numerous motivational and opportunity catalysts at three levels of analysis, as well the ability of the U.S. nuclear state to invalidate controls, allowed the political and organizational drives behind these crimes. Over a decade later, this volume stands as one of the exemplarily case studies in state crime scholarship.

In 1998 David Friedrichs also published a landmark two-volume anthology titled, simply, *State Crime*. Collecting some of the articles mentioned, as well as pieces from legal scholars and historical and political scientists, it is a definitive anthology on crimes committed by nation-states, whether or not the studies were framed specifically within criminological terms or not. Volume 1 focuses on definitional and theoretical issues concerning war, genocide, state terror, and nuclearism, thus casting a wide net and presaging the direction of state crime studies in the twenty-first century. Volume 2 features a series of foundational essays on law and social controls central to work discussed later in this book. In 2000 Ross published *Varieties of State Crime and*

Its Control, a follow-up volume to *Controlling State Crime* (1995). It explores state violations of international and domestic law among developed democracies (e.g., Canada, France, Japan, Israel, Britain, and the United States), bringing together scholars from many different fields of inquiry.

Since 2000, the number of papers published on state crime has grown markedly. In addition, state crime studies have expanded their purview, taking on a number of types of crimes and including ongoing cases of state crime, and definitional and conceptual discussions have continued to develop. A number of pieces have examined the criminality of specific wars. Kramer (1995) explicitly framed the U.S. invasion of Panama as a violation of international laws. Two pieces also examine the range of illegalities surrounding the U.S. invasion and occupation of Iraq in 2003 (Kramer and Michalowski 2005; Kramer, Michalowski, and Rothe 2005). Rothe (2009a, 2009b) has recently published an exploration of the illegal activities of the Regan administration's conduct of its Nicaragua policy, as well as a book solely dedicated to state crime.

Along these lines, a number of works have examined genocide, war crimes, and crimes against humanity. Friedrichs (1996, 2000) has published two pieces on the Holocaust as state crime. Mullins and Kauzlarich (2000) examined the Wounded Knee massacre in the context of broader U.S. governmental Plains Indian policy during the Sioux Wars. Ward (2005) has explored the behavior of the Belgian government in the Congo Free State as a state crime. Additionally, Rothe and Mullins, in various authorial combinations, have pushed the study of state crime into violations of international criminal law, especially international humanitarian law. Their works have explored the situation in the Democratic Republic of the Congo, the Rwandan genocide, Sudan's ongoing genocide in Darfur, and Uganda's civil war. They have also extensively developed the integrated model of state offending, which proved productive earlier in the field's history.

Recent papers also explore state culpability in the Katrina disaster in the United States (Faust and Kauzlarich 2008) and in the damage from Turkish earthquakes (Green 2005). Other works have explored the suppression of terrorism funding (McCulloch and Pickering 2005), campaign contributions (Hogan et al 2006), the use of depleted uranium in weapons (White 2008) and sexual violence in Nigeria (Lenning and Brightman 2009). Victimology-focused studies are still rare in the field. Kauzlarich, Matthews, and Miller (2001) first broached this topic, calling for more criminological attention to victims, their experiences, and victimization typologies. Most recently, Kauzlarich (2008) extended this call for an examination of victimization issues relevant to supranational crimes, especially calling for work that examines types of victims as well as state and international institutions designed to bring victim redress to the fore.

Concluding Thoughts

No longer in its infancy, the past two decades have seen the promulgation of a wide variety of conceptual and theoretical approaches to studying the most serious of crimes. Yet even at the most fundamental level of definition there is much work to be done. The vast number of labels used to describe these sorts of crime is increasing rather than coalescing. State crime, state-corporate crime, political crime, transnational crime, supranational crime, violations of international criminal law or international humanitarian law (as well as the subcategories of genocide, war crimes and crimes against humanity) are all extant descriptors for the types of crimes examined here. While diversity of topics and conceptual approaches is healthy in any field, the overall umbrella term must be codified to maintain coherence of thought and purpose. That is why throughout this book we use the term "state crime" to refer to all of these types of offenses and harms.

Notes

1. Chambliss was not the first to study crimes committed by the state. See Rothe and Friedrichs (2006) for a discussion of some early scholars in this area.
2. This citation refers to the original statement that was first presented at a conference in 1990, which has been often cited and has inspired much work, even if it took sixteen years to find itself in print (see Michalowski and Kramer 2006).

CHAPTER 1

Revisiting Crimes by
the Capitalist State

Gregg Barak

CRIMES BY THE CAPITALIST STATE: An Introduction to State Criminality (CBCS) was the first book devoted entirely to the study of state crime, to call for the development of a criminology of the state, and to present several case studies of state crimes from North America, Latin America, Europe, and Down Under. Some of the state crimes covered in this early volume included but were not limited to aboriginal deaths in custody, multitiered terrorism, air piracy, contract policing, and sexual assault. Since that time, I would argue that while the criminological study of state crimes has matured significantly, its influence as a subfield or specialty has thus far remained marginal to the discipline of criminology as measured globally by its lack of success to become a core component of university curriculums and to engage a sizable number or percentage of criminologists devoted to researching this subject matter as an area of expertise. Given the enormity of state criminality around the globe today, these contradictory relations are reflective of the dialectics of law, power, and the social construction of crime and justice.

CBCS was not made available as part of an edited series within criminology; rather, it was published by the State University of New York Press as a volume in the Radical Social and Political Theory series, edited by Roger S. Gottlieb, professor of philosophy at the Worchester Polytechnic Institute. Tony Platt's blurb on the back cover called attention to the "comparative/ international perspective" of *CBCS,* as evidenced by the work's mix of contributors, which included three Canadians, political scientist Stuart Farson and sociologists Ronald Hinch and R. S. Ratner; two criminological transplants to the United States, Stuart Henry from Britain and Daniel E. Georges-Abeyie from the West Indies; one Australian criminologist, Kayleen Hazlehurst; one practicing criminal attorney from Cali, Colombia, Jose Maria Borrero; three

American-born and trained criminologists, Susan Caulfield, Mark Hamm, and me; one U.S.-born and Scottish trained criminologist, Christina Johns; and one American sociologist, John Wildeman.

Back in the eighties and early nineties, I did not assume that capitalist states had a monopoly over state crimes. The title of the book was primarily descriptive and politically and economically correct since there were no socialist states examined. It reflected the reality that whether the state crimes we examined were committed by the United States, Canada, Peru, Israel, or Australia, each of these nation-states expressively and instrumentally represented capitalist state formations as differentiated, for example, from criminal or police state formations steeped in the interstices of the larger global political economy of corruption, like some of those failed states found in contemporary postcolonial Africa (Mullins and Rothe 2008a). As underscored in the book's preface: "The nature, patterns, or seriousness of state crime will not necessarily be the same for all types of state formation. In fact, a structural and dialectical analysis of state criminality, such as the one presented here, would predict that crimes by the state would vary according to the changing interaction between a particular state formation and the developing political economy. It is assumed that a fully developed criminology of state criminality would have to incorporate the full array of state crimes committed by the varying kinds of state formations" (Barak 1991a, x).

TOWARD A CRIMINOLOGY OF STATE CRIMINOLOGY

The prologue to *CBCS* differentiated between conventional offenses typically defined as crimes against the state, including acts committed in the street or in the suite, from traditionally overlooked or downplayed offenses, such as acts/actions or inactions/omissions "committed by government agencies or caused by public policies," whose victims suffer harm as a result of "social, political, and economic injustice . . . racial, sexual, and cultural discrimination . . . [and] abuse of political and/or economic power" (Barak 1991a, 3–4). The prologue also established the need for a criminology of states and linked the study of "state criminality (both domestic and international) . . . [to] the fundamental and irreconcilable conflict between empire and social justice" and to the then historical reality that "although students of comparative crime and criminal justice [had] paid some attention to political crimes committed against the state" in the past and present, "they [had] seriously neglected the political crimes committed by the state" (6). In addition, the section identified the roles that state criminality play in creating "inherent contradictions which simultaneously threaten the legitimacy of the prevailing political order yet accommodate the very same behavior in the name of common interests or national security" (7).

Some twenty years later, I do believe that the subfield or specialty area of state crime has achieved a small place at the criminological table. And, while it may be that criminologists of state criminality no longer have to make a case for the study of state crimes, it is still accurate to say that the majority of criminology textbooks, as well as the core curriculum in our criminology and criminal justice programs, have not appreciated the need to adopt, incorporate, and spread the study of state criminality. State criminality still remains marginal to the study of criminology as a whole, even though these acts or omissions have become pivotal to some strands of critical criminology. For example, just as *CBCS* at the time of its publication was "compatible with the philosophies and practices of the emerging schools of 'new left realism' and 'peacemaking criminology'" (11), the study of state crimes today represents a reciprocally integrated approach of the realist and peacemaking criminologies gone global.

Similarly, beyond the narrow boundaries of the conventional disciplinary and state criminologies are the frontiers of the broader studies of globalism and world justice, which bring together activists and theorists from a vast multidisciplinary community. In this regard, it makes sense for criminologists of state criminality to network with myriad worldwide ecological movements in general and with various international human rights and/or antigenocidal campaigns, conflict resolution and positive peacemaking interventions, and the up-and-coming criminology of international crimes or "supranational criminology" (Smeulers and Haveman 2008), as well as with the emerging paradigm of "global criminology" in particular (Morrison 2006). Herein lays the newest criminology to date where the study and reduction of state crimes is central to the transnational project of building an integrated global order of peace, security, and sustainable growth (Barak 2009).

Since the end of the cold war and the breakup of the former USSR, the number of state crimes has picked up momentum worldwide to where there is now a plethora committed annually (Barak 2000). These trends in the expanding cases of state crimes globally, domestically, and internationally no longer require that criminologists, critical or mainstream, make the argument for the study of state criminality. Paralleling these developments, I would argue that the criminological journey establishing a criminality of states has also come a long way in a relatively short time. For example, the study of state crimes in general and of terrorism or of genocide in particular has not only overcome criminology's historical "tendency to treat political violence and state criminality one-dimensionally" (Barak 1991a, 8), but also, during the same time period, become far more empirical and theoretically grounded compared to studies that dominated the field twenty to forty years earlier (Ross 1988).

Finally, consistent with the thrust and trajectory of *CBCS*, today's study of state crimes typically examines the intersections of state sovereignty, domestic and international legalisms, and the need to transcend those studies of individual offenders and their punishments divorced from the "structural and organizational nature of governmental abuse." Careful attention has also been "given to the relationship between the changing global political economy and the reproduction of class and social injustice worldwide" (Barak 1991a, 12). These developments in the study of state criminality reflect favorably on the maturation of this subfield of criminology.

CLASSICAL FORMS OF STATE CRIME

The two case studies presented in *CBCS* to illustrate expressions of what could be labeled classical forms of state crimes resonates throughout history and are every bit as relevant today. In "Passion and Policy: Aboriginal Deaths in Custody in Australia (1980–1989)," Hazlehurst (1991) examined the relationship between the crimes against and by the Aboriginal peoples. She specifically examined the role of the state and the governmental agencies of law enforcement, adjudication, and incarceration in the oppression of that nation's indigenous people. Situated historically and in a neocolonial context, Hazlehurst described the events, activities, and protests that led to establishing the Royal Commission into Aboriginal Deaths in Custody.

She also critiqued the commission's findings and how the inquiry actually obscured the fact that far too many Aboriginals were imprisoned unnecessarily. Moreover, since Australia was a cosignatory nation to the International Covenant on Civil and Political Rights, Hazlehurst defined the treatment of the aboriginal peoples within the larger context of international human rights as well as in relation to racism, genocide, and psychological state terrorism. She utilized evidence from national and international inquiries supporting the claims that aboriginal people were "dying prematurely from ill health, imprisonment, despair and defeat." Finally, Hazlehurst raised the pertinent question of whether or not the domestic situation (e.g., acts of repression and neglect by state authorities) in Australia warranted international intervention. Explicitly, she underscored the daily "intervention by police, abuse and neglect of community needs, cruel and degrading treatment of aboriginal prisoners, intimidation of witnesses to national inquiries, and unashamed attempts by state agencies to terminate the Royal Commission into Aboriginal Deaths in Custody" (Hazlehurst 1991, 19).

In "Subcultures as Crime: The Theft of Legitimacy of Dissent in the United States," Caulfield tapped into the classical role of the state generating politically subversive or criminal subcultures. At the same time, she captured "the dialectical processes involved in state activities which create criminals by violating rather than protecting citizens' fundamental rights as guaranteed in the Constitution and other laws" (Caulfield 1991, 20). Caulfield focused her attention on the state's interaction with two political groups, the Co Madres of El Salvador and the Committee in Solidarity with the People of El Salvador.

In a theoretically informed discussion of subcultural formation, Caulfield examined the relationship between First Amendment dissent and being sub-jected to government harassment, break-ins, illegal monitoring, and so forth. She also explained the classic ways in which the "state-created illusion of legit-imate intervention (stopping crime)" provided "a cover for the political crimi-nality of state agents." Finally, she argued that the state's use of this "subcultural methodology" resulted in vast and serious harms. These ranged from "the theft of basic constitutional rights to the infliction of monetary hardship on U.S. citizens, and monetary and physical hardship, including death, on citizens in Central America and elsewhere" (Caulfield 1991, 20).

Each of these classical case studies in state criminality certainly resonates with many state crimes found throughout history. Today, the relevance of the treatment of indigenous persons in Australia still reverberates with the treat-ment of indigenous and/or ethnic others in both developing and developed nation-states. In the case of Caulfield's trenchant analysis of dissent and its relation to the dialectics of law enforcement, nothing rings more true post 9/11 than the myriad violations perpetrated by the executive and legislative branches of the U.S. government.

For purposes of brevity, I refer specifically to the torturing of noncitizens by state agents or, in the case of extraordinary renditions, by U.S. proxies, and to spying on our own citizenry courtesy of the surveillance-industrial com-plex, all in the name of homeland security. The problem with prosecuting these state crimes, of course, is made all the more difficult because of the Bush administration's repetitive and systemic twisting of "the law to immunize its criminal conduct" aided by the authorization of "executive branch lawyers, particularly in the Justice Department's Office of Legal Counsel," who have provided a strong defense for governmental perpetrators vis-à-vis legal mem-orandums, not to mention the congressional granting of legal immunity to potential defendants through the passage of the Military Commissions Act of 2006 and other statutes (Balkin 2009).

ON THE DIALECTICAL NATURE OF STATE CRIMES

The four case studies in this section of *CBCS* covered the selective repres-sion of illegalities and various legal and human rights abuses committed dur-ing the 1980s. Primarily, these state crimes were enacted by the nation-states of Colombia, Israel, Peru, and the United States in association with their over-lapping ideological wars against communism, drugs, terrorism, and revolu-tionary liberation movements. Situated within both the historical, dialectical, and ongoing struggles between neoliberal capitalist crime control and global policies of social justice, on the one hand, and the interdependent developing relations between democratic and authoritarian regimes, on the other hand, each of these contributions—"The War on Drugs: Nothing Succeeds Like Failure" (Johns and Borrero 1991); "Multi-Tiered Terrorism in Peru" (Ratner 1991); "Piracy, Air Piracy, and Recurrent U.S. and Israeli Civilian Aircraft Interceptions" (Georges-Abeyie 1991), and "The Abandoned Ones: A History of the Oakdale and Atlanta Prison Riots" (Hamm 1991)—sought to describe and examine the contradictory nature of these state crimes from the perspectives of evolving national and/or international law.

Furthermore, each of these case studies, among other things, depicted the ways in which the manufacturing of fear and state intervention into these areas of crime control and security often caused disproportionate harm and victimization against both real and alleged violators. For example, in the case of "The Abandoned Ones: A History of the Oakdale and Atlanta Prison Riots," Hamm not only exposed the creation by the mainstream U.S. media of an untrue picture of alleged human rights abuses in the "Cuban Gulag," but also demystified the extent of the dangerousness of the Cuban detainees, as it turned out that less than one-half of 1 percent of the entire Freedom Flotilla was found to have serious criminal backgrounds. The same could be said of the ongoing counterproductive war on drugs at home and in Central America. As Johns and Borrero (1991, 65) concluded in "The War on Drugs: Nothing Succeeds Like Failure," although decriminalization is a much more rational and less costly approach to the abuse of illegal drugs than a criminal approach is, the "battles are likely to go on and on, escalating the attendant crime and violence and increasing the exploitation and control of the periphery by the center. The war on drugs is, simply put, too useful a legitimation of state crime to abandon."

These violations of domestic and international law also included state crimes specifically involving counterterrorist or counternarcotics scenarios of law and order. Whether exploring the vagaries of the war on drugs in the United States and Colombia, the multitiered terrorism in Peru and the programs in counterinsurgency and counternarcotics control, the recurrent civilian aircraft piracy interceptions by U.S. and Israeli uniformed personnel, or the lack of access to due process for the Mariel Cubans who had committed no crimes but were being held captives in two U.S. prisons, the subcultural and semantic methodologies used to define these "dangerous classes" afforded the state opportunities to violate its own sovereign laws as well as other international laws. These actions also resulted in the passage of new domestic laws that were often in violation of their own constitutions as well as other universal covenants and treaties.

For example, the Constitutional Court of Peru in 2004 declared some parts of the counterterrorism law passed in June of 2002 by the Peruvian congress and enacted by President Fujimori unconstitutional and therefore void, as these antiterrorist sections were viewed as contrary to international human rights (Privacy International 2004). The contradictions in state crime control and the multitiered terrorism that Ratner described in *CBCS* have continued to be political and warring forces in contemporary Peru. Specifically, the developing wars on the antigovernment guerillas and the wars on the narcotic trafficking in cocaine and more recently heroin, as well as the resistance to the various practices of state terrorism in Peru, were also given a shot in the arm in 2002, thanks in part to the George W. Bush administration's escalation of both the war on terrorism (e.g., the resurgence of the Shining Path [Sendero Luminoso] guerrilla terrorists whose goals under the earlier leadership of Abimael Guzman were to achieve a "peasants-workers republic") and the war on drugs (e.g., tripling U.S. antidrug aid in Peru to US$150 million annually).

During the 1980s and beyond, as Ratner described in his chapter, Peru fought a bloody and brutal war against the Shining Path guerrillas, with some thirty thousand Peruvians killed by one side or the other. In "the midst of a government-corruption scandal uncovering decades of misdeeds by some of the U.S. government's closest drug-war partners—including bribery, drug running, arms dealing, and death squads," this "war culminated in the 1990s during the early days of the Presidency of Alberto Fujimori, when thousands of suspected Shining Path were captured" with the assistance of the CIA (Kopel and Krause 2002, 1). Subsequently, a review commission released more than 600 of some 3,900 persons convicted of terrorism in secret courts. At the same time, the victory over the Shining Path was accompanied by the destruction of Peru's constitutional democracy, when Fujimori in 1992 "launched a coup, dissolved the courts and Congress, erased constitutional protections, and instituted military tribunals" (Kopel and Krause 2002, 1).

In the mid-nineties, the U.S. State Department's report on Peruvian human rights violations explained: "The military and the police continue to be responsible for numerous extra-judicial killings, arbitrary detentions, torture, rape and disappearances . . . Besides beatings, common methods of torture include electric shock, water torture and asphyxiation . . . credible reports indicate the total number of female detainees raped in the past few years (by police and military forces) to be in the hundreds . . . Violence against women and children . . . [a]re continuing problems" (Kopel and Krause 2002, 2). Keeping in mind that half the population of Peru lives in abject poverty, many farmers who had turned to cultivating coca for international consumption in the 1970s and 1980s were also early in this century starting to grow poppies as part of an expanded networking between the Peruvian and Colombian drug trade.

Historically, it is interesting that both Bush presidencies simultaneously emphasized the war on drugs and the war on terrorism. These dual war strategies have consistently undermined each other or both of these wars in Peru. During each of the Bush administrations Peru tried to prioritize counterinsurgency over counternarcotics, leaving coca farmers unhindered, even promoting a coca-growers cooperative, to the dismay of the United States. In the case of Bush I, the Peruvian military had conducted more than three hundred offenses against the Shining Path and had killed more than seven hundred guerillas. However, U.S. officials at the time were "concerned that General Alberto Arciniega had not done enough to fight coca cultivation," and they "pressed the Peruvian government for his transfer," in the process weakening the war against terrorism there (Kopel and Krause 2002, 2).

Beginning with President George H. W. Bush, continuing with Bill Clinton, and more recently with George W. Bush, the combined wars against terrorists and against drug farmer-producers and narco-distributors not only helped to drive up the price and make coca production a thriving and highly profitable business, but also brought together narco-traffickers, guerilla terrorists, and coca and poppy farmers whose combined interests have done much to resist and compromise the programs of eradication and interdiction. In a nutshell, the dual wars on terrorism and drugs had virtually guaranteed income for narco-traffickers and the terrorists who taxed the drug cultivation and protected the farmers from income fumigation. According to unclassified documents, Washington was also aware that some of their go-to guys on these wars might be working both sides of the street as narco-traffickers and supporters of the death squads (Kopel and Krause 2002).

For example, throughout the 1990s the CIA was working with a retired chief of the Armed Forces Joint Command, General Nicolas Hermoza, who plead guilty to profiting from illegal arms deals and who had been charged with running a drug-flight protection racket. During the same period, the CIA had given US$10 million to Vladimiro Montesinos, the de facto head of the Peruvian National Intelligence Service and Director of the Narcotics Intelligence Division. By 2002, Montesinos was residing in a Lima jail cell "charged with over eighty crimes ranging from money laundering, organizing death squads, protecting drug traffickers, and illegal-arms trafficking (selling 10,000 AK-47s to the Colombian FARC terrorists)" (Kopel and Krause 2002, 4). At the time, in excess of US$200 million of Montesinos's illicit fortune had been tracked down and seized, including over US$50 million in U.S. banks.

CRIMES OF STATE OMISSION

State crimes of omission have been and still are more diverse and less developed comparatively than are the state crimes of commission. Conceptually, crimes of state omission encompass the failure to protect the rights and to serve the needs of all persons subject primarily (but not exclusively) to the territory of a particular nation-state. The four contributions to this section of

CBCS presented analyses of various kinds of state omissions that threatened the well-being of vulnerable populations and that harmed both innocent and not innocent persons. Two of these case studies were focused on policing, the first on the roles, abuses, and reforms of law enforcement intelligence agencies; the second on the roles, abuses, and circumventions of law enforcement norms by way of privatization and contract policing. The third contribution examined the development and changing nature of sexual assault laws. The final contribution examined the free market economy and its relationship to particular forms of street criminality. In "Old Wine, New Bottles, and Fancy Labels: The Rediscovery of Organizational Culture in the Control of Intelligence," Farson (1991) examined the overlapping worlds of organizational culture, deviance, and reform. Specifically, he analyzed the McDonald Commission of Inquiry into the wrongdoing of the Royal Canadian Mounted Police. He also reexamined past and present legislative reform efforts to alter the criminal behavior of the RCMP and its security service in the context of new laws, organizational structures, and control mechanisms. Although Farson believed that lessons had been learned and that, for example, strategic as opposed to case-by-case approaches to intelligence gathering could "not only increase organizational efficacy in dealing with security, but may also reduce the abuse of civil liberties of particular individuals and groups by eliminating them from the targeting decision agenda," he still concluded that despite the establishment of new mechanisms for ensuring political knowledge and accountability which were put in place, "the control of wrongdoing has remained ever elusive" (Farson 1991, 183).

The contribution from the late John Wildeman, "When the State Fails: A Critical Assessment of Contract Policing in the United States," provided an overview of the historical and contemporary developments in the growth and practice of contract policing—with an eye toward examining both the legal abuses and legal circumstances associated with the privatization of many of the law enforcement functions of the state. Specifically questioned by Wildeman (1991, 219) was whether or not these developments represented "a decline in the state's responsibility and effort to protect civil rights and liberties of its citizens." He concluded, "the exponential growth in contract policing has been accompanied by a diminution of civil liberties and rights such as privacy, confidentiality, and due process as well as by a vast and largely unrecognized increase of power of the capitalist state" (183).

In "Contradictions, Conflicts, and Dilemmas in Canada's Sexual Assault Law," Hinch (1991, 184) argued that although the state created the impression with Bill C-127 that it had found a compromise between feminist and patriarchal interests in the prosecution of Canadian rape cases, the fact remained that the compromise did "little to alter the patriarchal or class nature of either the law itself or of the law enforcement." Specifically, with respect to the actual changes in the sexual assault laws, he pointed out that contradictory clauses or sections in effect canceled each other out in the four areas examined. These included the abolition of the exemption from prosecution granted married men, the abolition of the penetration requirement, the definitions of sexual assault, and the admissibility of evidence on reputation. In his analysis, Hinch also provided an examination of the "feminist criticism of the old law and the state's response to that criticism," as well as an assessment of "the ways in which the state's response can be shown to be protective of patriarchal and class interests."

In the final contribution to CBCS, "The Informal Economy: A Crime of Omission by the State," Henry examined the relationship between a "free market" economy and various forms of street criminality. He argued specifically that "some people's participation in informal economic activity can be traced to governmental policies, and therefore, such state-organized activities can be held co-responsible for their crimes" (Henry 1991, 184). Henry reasoned, "By excluding some people from a legitimate share of the wealth they create, governments force marginalized sections of the population to participate in informal economies wherein some people are introduced to opportunities for criminal activity which harms both themselves and others." He ultimately concluded that because government policy could be developed so as not to force some economic activity underground, failure to do so could be construed as a crime of omission by the state.

Consistent with all of the contributions to CBCS, Henry's analysis implied that confronting and reducing state criminality in general, but especially crimes of state omission, would have the spin-off effect of reducing other forms of crime because of the inherently criminogenic nature of state crime.

RESISTING STATE CRIMINALITY AND THE STRUGGLE FOR JUSTICE

The epilogue to CBCS was primarily concerned with resisting state criminality and struggling for social justice. At least part of that struggle, both then and now, seems to be the need for the fields of criminology as a whole to stop marginalizing, at best, and ignoring, at worst, state criminality. Moreover, the same question I asked in 1991 remains today: How and why have criminologists let such oftentimes horrendous behavior on the part of states escape their attention and inquiry? Of course the answer to this question has partially to do with the political nature of state criminality and the lack of concern of states about their own or other states' criminality.

More fundamentally, as Pat O'Malley (1987, 79) explained in "Marxist Theory and Marxist Criminology," crimes by and against the modern state are merely the expressions of specific historic conditions, "variably present and having variable effects" subject to the "historical continuities and discontinuities in capitalist production and accumulation." In this sense, acts committed and omitted by, on behalf of, or of the state have usually become repressive means directed at the real and imagined enemies of a given state and its associated relations to the prevailing political and economic arrangements. As some of the following excerpts from the epilogue exemplify, these passages are just as relevant today when it comes to explaining the crimes of the capitalist U.S. state in its post–September 11, 2001, war on terrorism as they were when used to explain, justify, or deny the state crimes committed in the name of anticommunism or socialist revolution when *CBCS* was published:

> With respect to the United States' capitalist state power, former case officer and agent for the CIA Phillip Agee (1988, 8) has concluded that the covert and overt activities, for example, of his former organization's role in the political oppression and denial of fundamental human rights in developing nations (especially in Latin America) have always had the primary objective of maintaining "long-range control of the natural resources, the labor, and the markets of other countries." Allegedly, however, this type of intervention was engaged in for the purposes of making the world freely democratic and anticommunist. In the anticommunist political culture of the West, "any popular revolutionary movement that seeks revolutionary change or fundamental radical change in favor of the worker" is equally threatening to the capitalist state (Agee 1988, 9). . . . Hence, the actions taken by the CIA and the local oligarchies (e.g., banking and commercial interests) in Latin America against Juan Bosch in the Dominican Republic or Salvador Allende in Chile—and against the vast majority of rural peasants or of marginalized urban workers—were rationalized through the emotional and political rhetoric of anticommunism used to justify subversive operations abroad. "They are subversive in the sense that from the very beginning, the CIA has used money and control of the people to seek control over the so-called free, pluralistic, democratic institutions of other countries" (Agee 1988, 6) . . . state-supported terrorism of the kind waged by the U.S. trained Contras in Nicaragua has also resulted in fifty thousand wounded and twenty thousand dead Nicaraguans in less than ten years. But these expressions of state criminality are not limited to the torturing and murder of political enemies; they also include the crimes against self-determination committed by trade policies, for example, that assert adverse economic pressures on political parties, the church, and the press, or by waging disinformation campaigns inside and outside these Third World countries. As former Contra pubic relations person Edgar Chamorro has noted about the

actions and consequences of various disinformation campaigns aimed at
the people of Nicaragua:"Our psychological wars [were] very cleverly oriented to use people or to lie and they [were] very cruel to the recipient.
Because there is cruelty not only in rapes, or in assassinations, but also in
destruction of the economy, in making people suffer for lack of full electricity and water (Chamorro 1988, 24). . . .With respect to the more general economic, political, and social development of countries and peoples
of Asia, Africa, and Latin America, the role of the U.S. intervention
through its foreign policy has certainly been a deterrent to the material-
ization of the rights of Third World people, at least since 1945. And . . .
"it is unfortunately the United States of all governments in the West that has
most consistently opposed the realization of the right of self-determination
by the peoples of the Third World and is, therefore, portrayed as an
implacable foe of the rights of people" (Falk 1989, 60).The record of the
United States, for example,"when it comes to the ratification of the major
multilateral human rights instruments has one of the very worst . . .
among all of the so-called Western liberal democracies" (Boyle 1989b, 71)
[including the contemporary failure of the United States to have recognized and endorsed the International Criminal Court]. The arguments
implicitly and explicitly developed throughout this book suggest that the
reduction of wholesale as opposed to retail forms of state criminality
would have a far greater impact on the levels of violence and suffering
worldwide—especially since the former are often criminogenic of the
latter. Our nontraditional arguments about the legal and non-legal relationships of the crimes by state omission are particularly salient here. Take, for
example, the "crime of homelessness" which results in both crimes by and
against homeless people (Barak and Bohm 1989).This crime of omission
by an advanced, post-industrialized, capitalist state consists of laws that do
not guarantee and policies that do not provide permanently affordable
housing for all residents.The fact that the current social relations of bour-
geois legality do not directly, or even remotely, recognize permanent
housing as a fundamental human right does not preclude either the
struggle for or the eventual development of such a de jure or de facto
right. In other words, human rights exist in both theory and practice, and
as such they may be viewed as part and parcel of the historical development in the ever-evolving status of the collective rights of all human
beings (Felice 1989). (Barak 1991a, 275–277)

Seems like we are in pretty much the same boat today as we were twenty
years ago, when the systematic study of state crime first emerged. Just as the
contributions to *CBCS* are as spot on today as they were two decades ago,
so is the same fundamental question that I posed in 1991: How do citizens of

a given state and peoples from multiple states intervene into the various state apparatuses of the world for the purposes of controlling both the crimes and the criminogenic nature of state power? Since those days, two positive incremental changes have occurred. First, thanks to globalization there are measurably more pathways to the examination and resistance of state criminality and there are more globally oriented movements on behalf of human rights and social justice than there were some twenty years ago. Second, the fields of state criminality, thanks to some of the contributors to this anthology, such as Dave Kauzlarich, Ron Kramer, Ray Michalowski, Christopher Mullins, and Dawn Rothe, have developed an overlapping body of integrated theories of state-organized and state-corporate crimes (Kauzlarich and Kramer 1998; Kramer and Michalowski 2006b; Mullins and Rothe 2008a; Rothe 2009a; Rothe and Mullins 2006a, 2008b, 2009). These theoretically informed and reciprocally formulated models are, indeed, capable of providing improved explanatory models for many of the case studies found in *CBCS* and for state crimes more generally.

Some twenty years ago when *CBCS* was in a state of becoming, the U.S. government was busy sweeping the state crimes (e.g., Iran-Contragate and the illegal bombings of Nicaragua) of the Reagan administration under the proverbial rug of the threats of the cold war. Today, the U.S. Congress and the new Barack Obama administration (three days away from its inauguration at the writing of this chapter) is about to sweep the state crimes, including the torture, murder, illegal surveillance, denial of habeas corpus, and other war crimes committed by the Bush II administration, under the rug of denial associated with the threats of the War on Terrorism. Once again, the subcultural methodology, the semantic slew of sound bite rationales, and the lack of lawful accountability for these state crimes will allow the executive and legislative branches of the U.S. government responsible for these crimes to escape both culpability and justice under law.

In light of the lessons learned over the past two decades about the prosecution of state crimes and the various efforts by nation-states, the United Nations and other supranational bodies, and the courts—domestic and international—to address these violations and to attempt to provide some kind of closure—justice, punishment, and/or recovery—what course of action do I think makes the most sense to pursue in light of what I believe the Obama administration is likely to do? In point of fact, I do not believe that the attorney general, an independent prosecutor, or the federal Congress will pursue criminal prosecutions, not because of a supposed lack of political will or because of the allegedly protracted divisiveness that this would cause when the economic crisis calls for us to pull together; but because of the legal defenses that exist for those charged with these state crimes due to the executive and legislative actions mentioned earlier in this chapter. Even if criminal prosecutions materialized, I am not confident that legal justice would be accomplished regardless of the criminal verdicts and punishments reached. Moreover, I do not believe that the victims of these state crimes, such as those innocent persons held and abused in Guantánamo, would receive their appropriate reparations or amends.

Nevertheless, I do believe that for symbolic reasons such trials for state crimes perpetrated by the U.S. government would acknowledge to the world that whatever the outcome of such tribunals, the United States is fully repudiating these practices of state criminality carried out in the name of counterterrorism, homeland security, and global democracy. These state crimes, in other words, should be acknowledged and not abandoned to the judgment of history, at least not U.S. history. As for world opinion on the state crimes committed by the principal players in the Bush administration, such as the vice president, the secretary of defense, and the attorney general, the guilty verdicts are already in. Even though Americans may want to turn the page on the state crimes of the second Bush administration, in terms of a global consensus, if Americans desire acceptance back into the international community, some acknowledgment, if not apology, is called for, some demonstration of condemnation of past illegalities is called for, as is remorse. A formal disposition or recognition of these state crimes committed on behalf of the war on terrorism and in violation of international law, however, need not call for exhibits of humiliation, exile, or death.

In terms of realpolitik, I believe that the best course to pursue should be to discover the truth and to repudiate the crimes rather than to punish the wrongdoing or to bring about reconciliation between the perpetrators and the victims. Truth and repudiation in the form of presidential commissions and congressional oversight hearings on various subjects, including detention and interrogation practices, extraordinary renditions, reform of military commissions, and reform of surveillance practices, should be commenced. Doing so would restore America's commitment to human rights by exposing and condemning U.S. abuses. It would counteract the tendency toward secret laws that facilitate these types of violations. And it would create a public record of government misconduct as a lesson to future generations and a caution to future administrations (Balkin 2009). Even with the new political administration, however, it will likely be state business and state crime control as usual. As for the myriad state crimes committed by the Bush II administration, they will probably dissipate the way of the state crimes of the Reagan administration, evaporating into the narrative abyss of a long and ignoble history of state criminality by the United States.

CHAPTER 2

The Crime of the Last Century—And of This Century?

David O. Friedrichs

THE CRIME OF THIS CENTURY: TOWARD A PROSPECTIVE CRIMINOLOGY

The turn of a century inevitably gives rise to much retrospective interpretation and prospective speculation: What have been the central events and trends of the century now ending, and what are the most likely key events and trends of the century now beginning? An article entitled "The Crime of the Century: The Case for the Holocaust," published in 2000, was my contribution to the former project. With the first decade of the new century drawing to a close, an opportunity has arisen to use this retrospective interpretation as a foundation for a provisional contribution to the project of prospective speculation as it relates to the realm of crime. Of course one should acknowledge that the concept of a "century" is ultimately an artificial construct (Badiou 2007). Many historians accept the proposition that the twentieth century was a "short" century, extending from approximately 1914 and the outbreak of World War I to 1991 and the collapse of the Soviet Union. But with that caveat in mind, it remains the case that "century" continues to be a widely invoked device for framing the whole range of historical and societal developments.

The forecasting of future events and trends has been an inexact science, to say the least, and history has been full of surprises and unexpected twists and turns. Many of the most momentous events and trends of the twentieth century were not anticipated by those—relatively few and far between—who engaged in the exercise in the nineteenth century and at the outset of the twentieth in attempting to put forth projections of the future. I have not been able to identify published work that anticipated clearly and accurately the forms and patterns of crime that characterized the twentieth century, and certainly not the scale of crimes of states that were such a central feature of twentieth-century history. While it may be true that there is a long European history of calls for the destruction of the Jewish people by a long line of anti-Semites, it is less clear that the Holocaust itself, in the specific form that it took, was anticipated in a meaningful sense. Although salient dimensions of the Holocaust as crime are addressed more fully further on in this article, this large-scale crime as industrial killing is a theme that links it with some of the noteworthy crimes of states in the twentieth century: that increasingly sophisticated forms of technology during the course of the century amplified immensely the scale and scope of killing in ways quite unimaginable in earlier times. Of course the development and deployment of atomic weapons at Hiroshima and Nagasaki, in the period approximating the middle of the twentieth century, ramped up exponentially the potential scope of state crime killing. These weapons of mass destruction could hardly be even imagined prior to certain key developments in physics within the first couple of decades of the twentieth century. But what does all this mean for the future as we consider the century now in its earliest stages? Unfortunately, any reflection of the past century, especially in relation to crimes of states, offers up a truly frightening vision of the possible crime—or crimes—of the twenty-first century in this realm. The premise set forth here, then, is that it can hardly be overstated what is at stake in a collective anticipation of such crime, and the identification and implementation of policies and practices that might at least minimize the chances of its occurrence. The study of crimes of states, then, has been largely a retrospective criminology. What is needed now—arguably desperately needed—is a prospective criminology of crimes of states.

A prospective criminology of crimes of states that focuses upon possible crimes of the future rather than historical crimes of the past could be regarded as an exercise in idle speculation and, in practical terms, as futile and unrealizable. As was suggested earlier, the historical record of anticipating large-scale catastrophes—at least those caused by human actions—has hardly been successful in any meaningful sense. And on balance the impact of scholarly work, including criminological work, on policies and practices that prevent or limit such catastrophes has been either exceptionally modest or simply nil. But the core thesis adopted here is that if we contemplate what is at stake—which, without hyperbole, is potentially the very survival of the human species and life on Earth—then we are saddled with the moral imperative of engaging in the endeavor just suggested. Criminologists working alone cannot expect to have any meaningful impact on human history or on the adoption of policies and practices that prevent or contain large-scale crimes of states. However, if criminologists can contribute to a collective, cooperative endeavor of participants in a broad range of disciplines and scholarly interests directed toward this ambitious goal, then it does not seem entirely far-fetched that some real impact on human history can be realized. And this has to be one of the ultimate goals of responsible, engaged scholarly activity in the twenty-first century.

If we adopt the hopeful assumption that human life will still exist at the end of the twenty-first century and, more narrowly, that a recognizable criminological discipline will exist as well, what might a criminologist writing at that point identify as "the crime of the twenty-first century"? Again, in the worst-case scenario, a crime of such momentous proportions will have occurred during the course of the century that there will be no criminologists, or anyone else, left to write about the crime. Famously, in *The Fate of the Earth*, Jonathan Schell, writing in 1982, set forth the possibility of the extinction of the human species itself—the "death of death"—unless we humans collectively succeeded in addressing the looming threat of a global nuclear war (Schell 1982). Early in the twenty-first century this threat can hardly be said to have disappeared (Reed and Stillman 2009). Countries such as North Korea and Iran—with unstable and fanatical dimensions to their leadership—continue to have the potential to develop nuclear weapons. Tensions between states that already have such weapons—for example, India and Pakistan—are ongoing. The threat of nuclear weapons in countries such as Pakistan falling into the hands of fundamentalists with a terrorist agenda remains pronounced. And the broader problem of nuclear proliferation and effective control over or elimination of existing nuclear stockpiles is unresolved. Historically, criminologists have, with few exceptions, almost wholly ignored nuclear war and nuclear issues as criminological phenomena. In the new century, going forward, it should be self-evident that engagement with these issues by the whole range of scholarly disciplines, including criminology, is imperative. Imagine, if you will, this nightmare fantasy: A meeting of the American Society of Criminology has taken place in some major city at some future time. A devastating nuclear attack destroys that city and much of the country itself. A survivor of this nuclear holocaust picks through the rubble of the hotel where criminologists were meeting at the time of the attack and finds a charred conference program. Rifling through the program, the survivor encounters countless sessions devoted to such matters as evaluation research, drugs and crime, childhood victimization, police stress, juvenile justice policy formation, professional crime, bullying, and the like. But not one session on nuclear weapons in relation to crime is listed? This comment is not intended to be dismissive of the wide range of conventional criminological concerns and their significance. But it does go to a long-standing perception of a lack of proportionality in criminological concerns, and that it sometimes seems to be the case that there is an inverse relationship between the amount of measurable harm caused by some form of human activity and the level of criminological attention to it.

The 9/11 attack on America, with some three thousand deaths, at the very outset of the twenty-first century, was experienced by Americans in particular as a "crime of the century"—so far. It incorporated traditional and modern elements of crime—box cutters and airplanes as weapons—and had an element of the postmodern as well, in light of the central role of simulations in the representation of the event. The immense attention to this event, however, was perceived in some quarters to reflect a U.S.-centric orientation—that is, crimes involving American fatalities are greatly privileged in terms of media attention to those involving non-Americans, and especially victims of color in developing countries (e.g., the 800,000 dead in the Rwandan genocide). The meaning of the event itself was widely contested, and it was celebrated in some parts of the world as a justifiable attack on a country widely regard as a criminal state (Aronowitz and Gautney 2003; Denzin and Lincoln 2003; Calhoun, Price, and Timmer 2002). And the American response—with a preemptive invasion of Iraq as part of it—was taken by many critics, including many Americans, as a further manifestation of a long history of crimes of states committed by the United States. Of course the George W. Bush administration characterized all its actions in response to 9/11 as justifiable policing responses to international terrorism and protective measures in relation to the prevention of further terrorism. It remains to be seen exactly how 9/11 will fare as a historical event in the long term, but it is certainly unlikely in the extreme to be viewed as the crime of the twenty-first century at the end of this century. Some elements of the 9/11 drama—both the original attack and the range of responses to it—may well foreshadow much larger scale historical crimes yet to occur.

The first decade of the twenty-first century has not been especially encouraging, if the relegation to the history books of crimes of the state as a phenomenon is an aspiration. During the course of the first decade of the twenty-first century we have the depressing spectacle of an ongoing genocide, in Darfur, with a remarkably feeble response by the rest of the world, including the United States. The true meaning of Darfur—characterized by one commentator as "the ambiguous genocide"—is contested (see Just 2008; Mamdani 2008). And its long-term historical status and significance is presently unsettled. Will it be largely forgotten in the future, which has been the fate of the genocidal attack on the Hereros in what was then Southwest Africa, at the outset of the twentieth century (in 1904), with some sixty-five thousand victims? Or will it assume the status of a historically momentous event that transformed historical responses to genocide in some measurable way? Only a few criminologists have addressed Darfur as a criminological issue. Europe, Russia, and China were the locus of monumental crimes of states in the twentieth century. By some interpretations, Africa, the Middle East, and the subcontinent are today more likely to be the locus of major crimes of states. But certainly the major powers—including the United States, Russia, and China—have the resources to be initiators of or complicit in large-scale crimes of states.

Whether or not one agrees with the characterization of the Holocaust as the crime of the twentieth century, as put forth in what follows, there can be no denying that it has been the source of immense amount of ongoing attention, at least since the 1960s. One need hardly document the vast scope of this attention in terms of books, journal articles, films, conferences, and so forth. As someone who has been engaged with this topic in some form through much of his life, I certainly support attention to it as serving a number of useful purposes. But on the other side, we have the pejorative claims of a Holocaust industry. Even those who recognize the enduring importance of the Holocaust can experience some discomfort in the face of the fact that, by some measures, far more attention continues to be directed at an event more than sixty-five years in the past than to ongoing genocidal activity in the world today, such as that in Darfur. In certain respects, it is easier and arguably more comfortable to address events of the past than those of the present—to say nothing of the future. But, again, an issue of appropriate proportionality arises. The tensions between doing justice to events past and to events present and future is reflected in the 2007 debate over whether the U.S. Congress should pass a resolution condemning the Armenian genocide—by the Ottoman Empire in 1915 (Krauthammer 2007; Power 2007). That this genocide occurred is amply documented, and Armenian activists have campaigned for decades for formal acknowledgment of this fact, in the face of ongoing, historical denial by the Turkish state that genocide occurred (Akcam 2006). But a legitimate question was raised: Should the U.S. Congress privilege official acknowledgment of a historical fact over the possibility of compromising relations with an important ally in combating present and future terrorist threats in the Middle East? In a somewhat parallel vein, should continued attention to the Holocaust be privileged over more sustained attention to the prospective obliteration of Israel—and its Jewish people—by its many enemies in the Middle East? Israeli attacks on Gaza early in 2009, as this is written, have led to ramping up of already widespread hostility toward the Jewish state and calls for action against it. That the survival of Israel as a Jewish state faces formidable challenges is quite evident (see Morris 2008). It is a terrible thought that a criminologist writing at the end of the twenty-first century on the crime of this century would identify the systematic obliteration of Israel and the extermination of its Jewish people as that crime. During the 1920s and the 1930s surely scholarly attention focused more on crimes of the past—including those connected with World War I—than on the possibility of an evolving, ultimately emerging crime of the future: the Holocaust. On the one hand, we have much of value to learn from studying crimes of states of the past in some depth, with knowledge ideally applicable to address crimes of states of the present and potentially the future. On the other hand, one could argue that there is some lack of proportionality here as well, with too much attention to past crimes in their unique dimensions and too little to present and prospective crimes.

Criminology throughout its history has been principally focused upon conventional forms of crime and their control. And this remains true early in the twenty-first century. But it has also been true that the parameters of criminological concerns were considerably broadened during the course of the past century. White-collar crime—introduced to the discipline in 1939 by Edwin H. Sutherland—had by the last couple of decades of the twentieth century received significant attention from at least some criminologists (Sutherland 1939). The emergence of radical criminology—and subsequently the various strains of critical criminology—from the early 1970s on, directed more criminological attention to the crimes of the powerful. William J. Chambliss's 1988 American Society of Criminology presidential address on "State-Organized Crime" was influential in fundamental ways in calling criminological attention to crimes of states. Early in the twentieth-first century attention to such crime has grown measurably (Chambliss 1989). Altogether, many criminological initiatives have been undertaken to transcend traditional criminological parochialism. In addition to white-collar crime and crimes of states, we have more attention to transnational and global crime. European criminologists have been at the forefront of promoting attention to supranational crime, incorporating crimes of states. In my own participation in some of these initiatives I have attempted to lay out an agenda for an emerging criminology of transnational, international, and global criminology (Friedrichs 2007a, 2008). Concepts and phenomena that are identified as central to any such criminology include sovereignty, nationalism, legitimacy, human rights, humanitarian intervention, international law, international tribunals, the global justice movement, and global governance. In my view these are among the phenomena with which criminologists prepared to undertake a prospective criminology of crimes of the state must address. But in the present context I limit myself to reproducing, selectively, a consideration of the crime of the last century as one important foundation for any such criminological initiatives.

The reproduced sections of my 2000 article "The Crime of the Century" that follows should be read in this context: Our attempts to understand the crime of the twentieth century should be applied to our imperative moral obligation to anticipate as best as we can the crime of the twenty-first century and contribute in any way possible to a collective effort to minimize the chances of this crime occurring. If it is naive to hope that no monstrous crimes of the twenty-first century will occur—indeed, some quite monstrous crimes have already occurred early in the century and are occurring as this is written—it does not follow that one must abandon hope of preventing at least some potentially monstrous crimes and much—perhaps everything—is at stake in preventing the worst of the worst possible crimes of states.

THE CRIME OF THE LAST CENTURY: THE CASE FOR THE HOLOCAUST

With the twentieth century now ended, we have many attempts at retrospective assessments and evaluations and any number of lists of the greatest achievements, books, leaders, minds, and so on of this century. What of the crime of the century? This term has been applied most readily to sensational murder cases, such as the killing of Bobby Franks by Nathan Leopold and Richard Loeb, the kidnapping/death of the young son of Charles Lindbergh (with Bruno Richard Hauptmann convicted and executed in this case), and the murder of Nicole Simpson and Ronald Goldman, with her ex-husband O. J. Simpson tried (and acquitted) for the crime (Geis and Bienen 1998). What should the criteria be for designating the crime—or one of the crimes—of the century? Any such designation has an inevitable dimension of arbitrariness and artificiality to it.

The crime of the century for Americans is not likely to be the crime of the century for people in other countries. Ultimately any such claims have a subjective aspect as well. For victims of heinous crimes—or their survivors—the crime against them is likely to be experienced as the crime of the century. Nevertheless, a relatively small number of crimes, and trials, acquire a status—at least within a particular culture—that clearly separates them from other crimes, and such crimes, and trials, become eligible for "of the century" designation. The degree of harm, of evil intent, and of unusualness (in some aspect) are possible criteria, but any such designation also importantly incorporates the level of public and media interest, impact on popular imagination, and endurance as an iconic or mythic event. Obviously we have countless cases where children were not merely killed—as in the Leopold and Loeb and Lindbergh cases—but were tortured, where the purity of evil intent, to the extent that such a thing can be measured, was as great or greater, and where especially bizarre aspects were present. The cases identified earlier are distinctive, then, more for the immense public and media interest in them, the massive coverage of the subsequent trials, and their assumption of iconic or mythic status in our culture than for the nature of the crime itself.

If any event merits the designation of "crime of the century" in broader terms the case is made here for the Holocaust perpetrated by the Nazis in the early 1940s.[1] Or at least the claim is made on behalf of the Holocaust for Western developed nations, and between such nations the salience of the Holocaust varies (i.e., highest for Israel and in a different way for Germany;

perhaps much lower for some South American countries).The claim that the Holocaust has a special or universal significance has not gone unchallenged. For example, a lawyer defending one of the last Nazis to be brought to trial (Klaus Barbie, the "Butcher of Lyon") denigrated the Holocaust as a "Eurocentric preoccupation," or simply one of the unfortunate but hardly unique consequences of a wartime situation (Finkielkraut 1992). Indeed, the Holocaust had both unique and nonunique aspects as a genocidal event. Is the claim for the Holocaust as "crime of the century" made on the basis of the number of victims, the scope of suffering, the purity of evil intentions, the degree of cruelty inflicted, or the uniqueness of this event? No. On each of these criteria one could identify other criminal events during the course of the twentieth century that equaled, or possibly exceeded, the Holocaust.

No claim is made here, then, that the Holocaust was necessarily the worst case of genocide in history. Indeed, some have argued that other cases of genocide—for example, the genocide directed at Native Americans—were more enduring and resulted in much greater loss of life (see Stannard 1996). By some estimations, more people died as a result of policies and practices pursued in Stalin's Soviet Union and in Mao's People's Republic of China than died in the Holocaust. Specific acts of gratuitous cruelty carried out in many genocidal campaigns (for example, in the rape of Nanking by Japanese soldiers and in the "dirty war" in Argentina carried out by the military leadership) are no less extreme than those carried out in conjunction with the Holocaust. Is it really possible (or desirable) to have a comparative sociology of cruelty or relative evil? Rather, the combination of the events of the Holocaust, the response to them, the massive literature and analysis, the Holocaust's role as metaphor, the impact and influence of the event—that is, the totality of the event itself and its aftermath—renders the Holocaust a criminal event apart from all others. Without systematically documenting the claim that the literature pertaining to the Holocaust and the number of references to the Holocaust far exceeds that for any other genocide (or specific crime) occurring in the twentieth century, one hopes that the claim can be stipulated (to use the legal term meaning a claim is accepted in court without having to be proven).

Why has the Holocaust inspired such an immense response? First, one should note that relatively little attention was directed toward it until the 1960s, and the application of the term "the Holocaust" to this event only occurred during this decade. But several reasons can then be identified for this singular level of attention.The Holocaust occurred in the heart of Europe in conjunction with a widely covered war; the Nazis lost the war; an unprecedented international tribunal was formed to try the surviving Nazi leadership, and evidence of their crimes was systematically collected; the Nazis had documented their crimes to an extent, surely unusual for genocides; Hitler and the Nazis were always uncommonly colorful media copy, whatever else one says about them; their primary target group, Jewish people, has a long and enduring tradition of commitment to literacy, higher education, and scholarship, contributing greatly to the Holocaust-related literature, and at least from the 1960s many Jewish (as well as non-Jewish) scholars focused on the Holocaust as a cataclysmic event in Jewish (and world) history; the Jewish state of Israel in various ways promoted attention to the Holocaust; and so on. No other criminal event, then, has so fully captured the attention of so many people. No other criminal event has produced such a large (and ever-expanding) literature. The Holocaust perpetrated by the Nazis is often invoked as the paradigmatic case of genocide in the modern world.

It has been commonly noted that genocide itself is hardly new to the twentieth century, although the concept of genocide is and the mass technology of genocide is as well. The term "genocide" was introduced in 1944 by Raphael Lemkin, who applied it to the destruction of a nation or ethnic group (Lemkin 1944). In subsequent decades the term has been invoked in quite different ways: broadly—for example, the nonlethal destruction of indigenous cultures—and narrowly—for example, intentional mass killing with the purpose of exterminating an identifiable group of human beings. The destruction of the Hittites and of Carthage in the ancient world, the Albigensian Crusades, and the witch hunts in medieval Europe have all been identified as historical cases of genocide. In the twentieth century genocides have occurred in many different parts of the world and have involved many different nationalities and ethnic groups. Fairly or not, the German involvement in genocide has been highlighted in most accounts on the subject. As was noted earlier, the massacre of some sixty-five thousand Southwest African Herero tribesmen by German colonial forces, beginning in 1904, may be the first significant case of genocide in the twentieth century. And, as was suggested earlier, the Holocaust engineered by German Nazis near the midpoint of the century is surely the most famous twentieth-century case of genocide. At century's end, Germany undertook its first military action since World War II, participating in the NATO effort to stop the ethnic cleansing (or genocidal enterprise) in Kosovo. The overall German repudiation of its genocidal past in the final decades of the century was heartening; the outbreak of genocidal campaigns in the former Yugoslavia and in other parts of the world during the final years of the twentieth century was disheartening. Learning from history was both possible and far from assured.

CRIMINOLOGY AND THE HOLOCAUST

A massive and ever-growing literature on the Holocaust has developed, especially since the 1960s. Many different disciplines have contributed to this literature, including history, philosophy, theology, political science, literature, and art. The social sciences—for example, psychology and sociology—have also made some noteworthy contributions to the literature. Many other disciplinary or transdisciplinary perspectives—for example, a feminist perspective—have been applied to an understanding of the Holocaust, although at least some such applications are controversial. But a specifically criminological approach to the Holocaust has been largely, although not wholly, absent.

If a case can be made for the Holocaust as the crime of the century, why has it been largely neglected by criminologists, what are its specifically criminological dimensions, and what can criminologists contribute to its understanding? Few if any contemporary criminologists would deny that the Holocaust was a terrible "crime," in some sense of the term, yet very few criminologists have focused on the Holocaust as a criminological phenomenon. We may speculate that this neglect can be attributed to viewing the Holocaust as a topic lying outside the boundaries of appropriate criminological concerns (that is, a topic more appropriately addressed by historians and other specialists); that criminologists would in any case have nothing very useful to contribute to the understanding of the Holocaust; that criminologists who might even contemplate addressing the Holocaust are overwhelmed by the prospect, on different levels, and have a sense of impotence on effectively responding to the problem of genocides generally; and that criminological attention to the Holocaust would deflect attention from other legitimate criminological concerns. Criminologists in the course of their graduate training and professional socialization are not typically taught to regard the Holocaust as a criminological phenomenon.

Through much of its early history criminology was principally concerned with conventional crime and delinquency. Edwin Sutherland's call for criminological attention to white-collar crime—issued in 1939—did not elicit much of a response from criminologists until the 1970s; since that time we have witnessed significant criminological attention to white-collar crime. Although Sutherland was undertaking his principal work on white-collar crime during the period of the Holocaust (the 1940s), he did not address genocide as a form of white-collar crime (Sutherland 1949). Some contemporary students of white-collar (or occupational) crime have explored the generic relationship between such crime and genocide. We can identify parallels as well as significant differences between white-collar crime offenders and state criminals, or between corporate executives with complicity in illegal pollution, production of unsafe products or unsafe working conditions, and Hitler and the Nazi leadership and a genocidal campaign (Friedrichs 1996). Political crime has also been a marginal concern of criminologists. Earlier treatments of political crime focused principally on antistate activities such as political assassination or terrorism, and on corruption, although a more recent text identifies genocide as a form of political crime (Friedrichs 1996). In the final decades of the twentieth century some prominent criminologists called for attention to the threat of nuclear war as crime (Harding 1983), state-organized crime (Chambliss 1989), and violations of human rights (Cohen 1993). Inspired at least in part by such initiatives, we have begun to witness the emergence of a criminology of state crime (e.g., Barak 1991a; Ross 1995a; Friedrichs 1998; Kauzlarich and Kramer 1998; Ross 2000b). Jeffrey Ian Ross has documented some of the grounds of resistance to criminological attention to state crime and has formulated an agenda for such attention (Ross 1998; see also Ross et al. 1999). Alexander Alvarez (1998) has initiated an ambitious call for criminological attention to genocide specifically. It seems likely that such calls will eventually be widely heeded, but, as in the case of white-collar crime, this may take time.

Some commentators on the great expansion of studies of the Holocaust from many different disciplinary viewpoints have expressed reservations that could hypothetically be applied to a criminological approach to the Holo-caust. Gabriel Schoenfeld (1998) contends that the Holocaust has become "academized," so that the application of various "explanatory variables" diminishes the natural horrors of the Holocaust itself. On this view the Holo-caust has now been invoked on behalf of many special agendas—for example, feminism—and has been misappropriated for careerist reasons. In a somewhat related vein, Alvin Rosenfeld has criticized "the Americanization of the Holo-caust," or its invocation to call attention to a wide range of social problems (Rosenfeld 1995). The concern here is with an excessive relativism and abstraction as applied to the Holocaust, feeding into a broad cult of victim-hood. This commentator, along with others, expresses reservations about a search for redemptive meaning in the Holocaust (see Langer 1995). Elie Wiesel (1970), arguably the best-known contemporary commentator on the Holocaust, has questioned whether we can understand it at all; rather, we should commemorate it. For some, explanation inevitably leads us to a posture of excusing, in some sense, the actions of the perpetrators. Such concerns have to be taken seriously, but it seems to me we can separate the commemoration of the Holocaust (and its victims) from the endeavor of attempting to learn whatever we can both about and from the Holocaust, and in the latter case should not be constrained by anyone's claims of "correctness" in this enter-prise. Serious attempts to explain and understand the Holocaust, from what-ever disciplinary or ideological vantage point, should not be equated with the pernicious phenomenon of Holocaust denial.

Accordingly, some specific counterarguments can be offered on behalf of criminological attention to the Holocaust and genocide. The threat and scope of harm from intentional (typically illegal) genocidal actions vastly exceeds that from crime more conventionally defined. And genocide may well be more of a threat in the twenty-first century than conventional crime and violence. Criminologists should be able to apply some of what they have learned about conventional crime and violence to the study of genocide and should in turn be able to enrich their understanding of conventional crime and violence from the study of the Holocaust. By failing to define the Holocaust and genocide as specifically criminological events, criminologists may well contribute—however unwittingly—to a public resistance to viewing criminality and crime more inclusively.

Discussion of criminological theory—explaining crime—does not always clearly differentiate between explaining criminality or the propensity of individuals and entities to commit crime; explaining crime, or the occurrence of an event involving the violation of law; and explaining criminalization, or the process of certain activities being defined as criminal. Crime generally—including a state crime such as the Holocaust—can only be properly understood by addressing these several levels of explanation.

Understanding the Holocaust in Terms of Criminality

Any discussion of criminality and the Holocaust must begin with recognition of the Nazi endeavor of ascribing criminality to those whom they wished to defeat or obliterate. One must discriminate between an ascription of criminality based upon beliefs and behavior and one based upon "race" or condition. The Nazi ascription of criminality to communists, then, belongs in a somewhat different category than the Nazi ascription of inherent criminality to Jews. The first case is quite consistent with a widely diffused tendency to ascribe criminality to those who are viewed as a direct threat to the state; the second is a somewhat extreme version of a biogenetic view of criminality. For example, one difference between the Holocaust and the Stalinist genocides is that the latter did not target children but was focused on adults perceived to be enemies of the state.

In addition, what of the sources of the criminality of the Nazi elite? The Nazi leadership did not regard itself as criminal and was not so regarded by most of the German people during their reign of power. The leadership gave criminal orders without, for the most part, being directly involved in the implementation of these orders. Genocide differs from conventional interpersonal violent crime by virtue of this distancing effect, or the separation of those who administer criminal orders from those who carry them out. Although Hitler is widely believed to have given the order setting the Holocaust into motion, he was not involved directly in its implementation, and he seems to have spent the war years primarily focused on the military campaigns and never visited the death camps (Lukacs 1997). Although the second primary architect of the Holocaust, Heinrich Himmler, did visit the camps, he was reportedly made ill by what he observed (Breitman 1992).[2] Adolf Eichmann, who oversaw the process of transporting millions of Jews to the death camps, also claimed to have been sickened by a rare, direct encounter

with the actual process of extermination (Arendt 1963). We need to understand more fully differences in the psychodynamics of instigators as opposed
to hands-on perpetrators. Those who formulate the instigating orders in cases
of genocide might not be capable of implementing these orders; and those
who implement the orders might not be capable of instigating them. In one
approach (which I find generally persuasive), the actions of the Nazi elite
(including Hitler) of the middle-level German bureaucrats (not all of whom
were Nazis) and of the police battalion or death camp personnel who actually
carried out the killing process are explainable by different processes or combinations of factors (Browning 1992). An ideological commitment to exterminate the Jews, a careerist concern on the part of bureaucrats, an adaptation
to extraordinary circumstances and peer conformity on the part of
perpetrators, contributed to the lethal dynamic of the Holocaust.

Finally, on the matter of criminality, one must note the role of "ordinary"
criminals in the extermination process. Some of the higher level personnel
of the extermination process—notably Rudolf Hoess, commandant of
Auschwitz—had records as conventional offenders (Fest 1970, 411). And some
ordinary criminals were enlisted within the concentration camps in connection with the extermination process (Sofsky 1996). We have a case here of
conventional criminality being harnessed, so to speak, in service of state
crime, with a conflation of individual and state motives for criminal conduct.

That humans are capable of murder has always been disturbing, but that
murders on a monumental scale have been carried out on behalf of states is
still more disturbing. Yet murder per se has been identified primarily with
individual offenders. Murders carried out on behalf of states, or with the
approval, knowledge, and support of state authorities, have often been viewed
as a fundamentally different phenomenon than interpersonal murders. We can
recognize that such murders are both driven by different dynamics than conventional murders but also have some features in common with conventional
murders. Humans killing other humans takes many different forms along a
continuum ranging from the intensely personal to the utterly impersonal. One
of the intellectual challenges here is to delineate both the differences and the
similarities between impulses for committing genocidal murder and for committing interpersonal murder.

In this section, then, the relevance of the concept of criminality for the
Nazi case has been explored. The specific criminological challenge is to
explore the parallels and differences between criminality in the Nazi case and
in relation to more conventional forms of criminal conduct.

Understanding the Holocaust in Terms of Crime

In terms of explaining the Holocaust as a crime, one must address the
configuration of circumstances making this "event" possible. On one end of

the spectrum we have the view that the Holocaust cannot be explained and understood, it can only be commemorated; on the other hand we have a massive literature that attempts to identify the circumstances and factors explaining the Holocaust (see also Hartman 1996; Hayes 1991; Langer 1995; Rosenfeld 1997; Rosenberg and Myers 1988). In my view we can identify factors that contributed to the occurrence of the Holocaust, although it does not follow from this that we can achieve a total understanding of how such a crime could have occurred. In efforts to explain the Holocaust we have a division between those who essentially adopt mono-causal explanations and those who adopt multi-causal explanations. Daniel Goldhagen's highlighting of "eliminationist anti-Semitism" is a conspicuous example of the former approach; most large-scale studies of the Holocaust adopt some form of a multi-causal approach. In the recent era we also have a division between those who adopt an intentionalist approach and those who adopt a functionalist approach to an understanding of the Holocaust (see Browning 1992). The intentionalist approach holds that the genocidal program was a specific objective of Hitler and the Nazis from the outset; the functionalist approach holds that the Holocaust came about primarily due to the circumstances that arose in the context of World War II.

First, I strongly adhere to the multi-causal explanation approach. Second, I adopt the view that intentionalist aspirations (or fantasies) could be realized due to a complex of circumstances favorable to genocide. Altogether, we can only approach an understanding of the crime of the Holocaust in terms of the interaction of structural, organizational, social psychological, and individualistic factors.

The crime of genocide is different from conventional forms of mass murder because it is carried out by a regime that is widely regarded by a large proportion of its citizens as undertaking many positive or progressive initiatives. Considerable evidence documents the claim that support for Hitler and the Nazi Party—by the German people as well as admirers in many other countries—was primarily a function of the perception that Hitler and the Nazis would provide strong leadership to effectively address economic and political turmoil, would restore law and order, would revive national pride, and would initiate many constructive programs. The anti-Semitic aspect of the Nazi program was certainly of primary importance to some supporters of Hitler and the Nazis, but apparently not to the majority of its supporters. William Brustein (1996), in The Logic of Evil, makes the somewhat contentious case that support for the Nazis and Nazi Party membership was driven primarily by rational, instrumental considerations (see also Fischer 1995; Hamilton 1982; Muhlberger 1990). And through much of the 1930s Hitler and the Nazis were viewed by many Germans (and foreign admirers) as successful in addressing many of the problems confronting Germany. Some commentators believe that had Hitler died in 1938 history would have regarded him as a great German leader (although surely the relentless anti-Semitic campaign, totalitarian rule, and ruthlessness of the Nazis would continue to be assessed negatively) (Lukacs 1997). In a book with the surprising title *The Nazi War on Cancer*, Robert N. Proctor (1999) explores the Nazi campaign on behalf of good health and reveals that German scientists during this period were the first to establish a link between smoking and cancer, and the German health authorities were the first to promote breast self-examination for women. The Nazi campaign to obliterate the "cancer" of a Jewish presence—as they defined it—as well as other "societal cancers" such as homosexuals and Gypsies is well known, but these campaigns on behalf of the supposed social health of society were intertwined with a campaign on behalf of good health in more conventional terms. The complex intermixture of the good with the bad, and the complex of motivations involved on the part of both Nazis and their supporters, has to be fully appreciated, because the crime of genocide occurs in this context and not as a wholly independent endeavor. Good things have been promoted by evil, criminal states, and, conversely, terrible crimes have been carried out on behalf of generally beneficent, democratic states. State crime has in common with corporate crime that it is intertwined in complex ways with productive and beneficial activities.

This section has considered some of the circumstances making the crime of the Holocaust possible. Criminologists can address the parallels and differences between such organizational homicide and homicides involving conventional criminal entities, such as juvenile gangs.

Understanding the Holocaust in Terms of Criminalization

Criminalization is the third fundamental criminological issue pertaining to the Holocaust. This issue has two basic dimensions for criminologists. First, how did the Nazis effectively criminalize those whom they sought to destroy; second, what was the process involved in criminalizing the genocidal activities of the Nazis?

On the first question, in one view, the predominance of legal positivism as a jurisprudential philosophy in Germany in the early decades of the twentieth century facilitated the Nazi crimes; a challenge to this view holds that an emerging national socialist jurisprudence—with the "Fuhrer principle" privileging Hitler's commands over legislative acts and the claimed needs of the state taking precedence over formal law—really operated at odds with the fundamental tenets of legal positivism (Ott and Buob 1993). Despite Hitler's written authorization for the pre–World War II euthanasia program directed at various "defective" human beings, the strictly "legal" status of these (and later) mass killing activities was questionable, at best, and challenged by at least some members of the judiciary and the larger German public (Friedlander

1995). That law-making overall became increasingly dominated by the Nazis, and that the judiciary for the most part cooperated willingly or even initiated some Nazi law, has been quite thoroughly documented (Fraser 1996; Lippman 1993; Miller 1995; Muller 1991; Stolleis 1998). A criminological approach to the Holocaust, then, requires some attention to the criminalization of Jews and other perceived enemies of the Nazi state.

By what criteria and process does the Holocaust come to be defined as a crime? That the Holocaust was not only a crime but also a crime on a monumental scale is certainly a widely accepted proposition, and the term "crime" is commonly applied to the Holocaust. The term "crime" is invoked in somewhat different ways, however. In moralistic and humanistic terms, the Holocaust was a crime by virtue of violating widely embraced views of morality and by causing objectively identifiable harm as a consequence of intentional policies and actions. In political terms, the Holocaust was a crime because it was so defined by opposing political entities (in the form of other nations and oppositional political forces within Germany). In legalistic terms, the status of the Holocaust as crime is somewhat more complicated. But the postwar indictment of leading surviving Nazis and the Nuremberg Trials determined that various policies and actions of Nazi Germany (including the Holocaust) were violations of widely recognized international law, and many Nazis were then found guilty of crimes by a formal, adjudicatory process (see Bassiouni 1979; Conot 1983; Hackett 1998; Taylor 1992; Wolfe 1998). In a criminological context, the status of international law as comparable to state law, and the validity of the international tribunals, arises.

The process of criminalization in relation to the Holocaust has been considered here. How does the process of criminalization of a genocide such as the Holocaust compare with, and how does it differ from, the process of criminalization for conventional forms of crime?

AN INTEGRATIVE CRIMINOLOGICAL FRAMEWORK FOR UNDERSTANDING THE HOLOCAUST

We can explain and understand the Holocaust. We cannot explain and understand the Holocaust. Both of these statements are correct. We can explain and understand many of the contributing factors; we cannot fully and wholly explain how the Holocaust could have occurred. Theories can be invoked in trying to explain and understand the Holocaust; no rigorous theory of the Holocaust is possible.

The need for an integrative criminological framework would seem to be exemplified by the case of the Holocaust specifically and by genocide more generally. Such a framework draws upon the widest possible range of disciplines; it adopts a fairly inclusive concept of crime, transcending narrow legalistic boundaries; and it draws upon a humanistic tradition as opposed to being limited to a narrowly positivistic (or "scientific" tradition) (Barak 1998). Diane Vaughan has argued that the study of organizational crime calls for a theoretical framework linking the macro and the micro level, or the integration of structural, social psychological, and individualistic levels of explanation (Vaughan 1999). An integrative criminological approach to the Holocaust must draw upon as many disciplines as possible and must address it on historical, societal, organizational, communal, peer group, situational, and psychological levels. More specifically, the Holocaust can only be understood in the context of an understanding of European and German history; the character and composition of post–World War I society; the nature and dynamic operation of the government bureaucracies (from departments of the state to death camp administrations) and nongovernmental organizations (e.g., the IG Farben corporation); intergroup relations within German communities and within concentration camps; peer group pressures (for example, within the Einsatzgruppen killing squads); situational factors arising in the specific circumstances of the killing process, which can take on a life of its own; and psychological dimensions involving the perpetrators on all levels. Although biogenetic factors may be relevant for understanding some manifestations of crime, their contribution to explaining the Holocaust is questionable. I share with Gregg Barak the view that both the complexity of crime (especially genocidal crime) and immense methodological challenges preclude the development of a truly testable integrated theory. At best, we can hope to achieve a rough approximation of the relative weight of a broad range of factors in contributing to the genesis of the Holocaust and to specific actions within the Holocaust. At the end of our analysis we have a residual dimension, or something left over that we cannot fully explain.

CONCLUSION

One can now turn, full circle, to questions raised in the opening section of this article. In the year 2099, or 2100, a criminologist will surely address the "crime of the century" issue as assessments of the twenty-first century are made. What will it be? From our present vantage point, as was suggested in the opening section, a nuclear holocaust on a monumental—and species-exterminating level—appears to be the single most disturbing candidate for a "crime of the century" designation for the present century. Could there be even worst forms of large-scale crimes, involving, for example, an exponential, global spread of a devastating, fatal disease or crime carried out with cruel, massive means that we cannot even envision? If the world escapes a major nuclear holocaust or some crime parallel in scope in the twenty-first century, it seems improbable in the extreme that it will avoid some major genocidal campaigns, possibly of a magnitude hitherto not experienced due to the use of advanced technology.

What, then, will a review of crime in the twenty-first century look like at its end? Conventional crime will hardly have disappeared during the course of this century, but the contours, demographics, and distribution of crime are likely to be quite different from what they are today. Surely some forms of crime will have largely disappeared (perhaps syndicated crime), just as some forms of crime (e.g., safecracking and train robberies) largely disappeared by the end of the twentieth century. Altogether, it seems more likely that we will have had greater success in addressing the least sophisticated forms of crime (e.g., conventional crime) than the most sophisticated (e.g., finance crime), and the crimes of the powerless over the crimes of the powerful. In particular, the crimes of states (and nonstate political entities) are likely to be far harder to control and far more consequential.

The characterization of the Holocaust as the crime of the century is inspired at least in part by the conviction that we must promote a general transformation of public (and professional) consciousness that tends to separate conventional crime from state crime and homicide from genocide. Genocides such as the Holocaust are widely characterized as crimes, but they are typically thought of as quite unrelated to conventional forms of crime. A criminological approach to the Holocaust should clarify as specifically as possible ways in which genocidal homicide both differs from and has elements in common with conventional homicide. A criminological approach to the Holocaust should introduce concepts and insights that have been largely absent from the analysis of this event, as interpretation and analysis of the Holocaust has been dominated by other disciplines. A criminological approach to the Holocaust should contribute to the legitimation of state crime as a proper and fruitful realm of inquiry for criminologists. Above all, a retrospective criminology of the Holocaust ideally contributes in a fundamental way to the development of a prospective criminology of crimes of states, one that contributes measurably to the anticipation of such crimes— and ideally their containment or prevention.

The case for recognition of the Holocaust as the crime of the century is rooted in the conviction that criminology must attend more fully to genocide, that if we can order crimes at all by seriousness, then genocide should be recognized as the worst of all crimes, and that the societal response to crimes is one vital dimension of their overall significance. In accord with these criteria, then, a case can be made for the Holocaust as the crime of the century.

NOTES

The core section of this article was originally presented at the Annual Meeting of the American Society of Criminology, Toronto, November 1999, and was published in *Crime, Law and Social Change* in 2000. I want to thank Jeffrey Scott McIllwain, the guest editor of the special issue of this journal, on "Criminology and Genocide," for comments and encouragement. The assistance of a University of Scranton Faculty Research Grant facilitated research on my original paper, and a Judaic Studies Committee travel grant made it possible to present the paper in Toronto; both grants are gratefully acknowledged. My collaboration since 1994 with several colleagues on an interdisciplinary course on the Holocaust has been an important stimulus to my thinking on this topic, as was our shared journey to Auschwitz, Majdanek, and Theresienstadt; they are Jody Dunn, Frank Homer, Darlene Miller-Lanning, Bill Rowe, Carl Schaffer, and Marc Shapiro. Finally, I wish to thank Dawn L. Rothe, the editor of this volume, for encouraging me to undertake an adaptation and update of my original article.

1. The term "the Holocaust" here refers to the systematic extermination of millions of people by the Nazis during the early 1930s, with Jews as the principal victims. The term "holocaust" has been applied to other genocides and events—somewhat controversially—and some Jews prefer the term "the Shoah" for the Nazi war against the Jews.

2. Clendinnen (1999, 91) points out the bizarre incongruities in Himmler's apparent outlook, when he commends the SS killers for their "decency" but condemns the immorality of stealing a watch.

CHAPTER 3

Nuclear Weapons, International Law, and the Normalization of State Crime

Ronald C. Kramer and David Kauzlarich

IN THIS CHAPTER WE ARGUE THAT THE USE, threat to use, and continued possession of nuclear weapons by the United States constitute international state crimes and can be subjected to a sociological/ criminological analysis. We have previously addressed some of these issues in our book, *Crimes of the American Nuclear State: At Home and Abroad*, but here we cover substantial new ground. One new theoretical argument that we advance, following the work of Diane Vaughan (1996), is that the crimes of the American nuclear state have become, over time, normalized within the broader political culture and specific national security agencies of the United States. We conclude that such a sociological analysis of the normalization of nuclear crimes is a necessary, but not sufficient, component of any effort to prevent the greatest criminal threat that the world faces today: the threat of nuclear catastrophe.

The use, threat to use, and continued possession of nuclear weapons by any government are state crimes because they involve decisions and actions by state officials, "in the pursuit of their jobs as representatives of the state" (Chambliss 1989, 184), that violates specific public international laws, such as International Humanitarian Law (IHL) and the Nuclear Non-Proliferation Treaty (NPT) of 1968. Following the Nuremberg Charter, these illegal state actions can be designated as crimes against humanity and/or war crimes (Boyle 2002). Richard Falk (2008a, 43) argues "that we need to recognize the *intrinsic* criminality of any threat or use of nuclear weapons, its nonderogability [which means that in times of emergency these laws may not be suspended or limited], whether we look backward in time to World War II or forward to possible situations where it serves political or military goals to threaten or actually use such weaponry." Furthermore, since nuclear weapons indiscriminately target and do violence to civilian populations for political goals, their use or threatened use can also be defined as a form of state terrorism (Falk 2004a; Kauzlarich and Kramer 1995; Selden and So 2004).

A number of criminologists have argued (Friedrichs 1985, 2007a; Harding 1983; Kauzlarich and Kramer 1998) that criminality related to nuclear weapons can and should be brought within the purview of the discipline of criminology. There are two major reasons for a criminological inquiry concerning these state crimes. One reason is for the scholarly purposes of describing, analyzing, and explaining these illegal acts as a special form of crime, a form of crime that has been almost completely neglected by criminologists. Another, more important, reason is because the prevention of nuclear war and nuclear terrorism, and the abolition of nuclear weapons, are the most critical crime prevention policy issues of all time.

As we enter the seventh decade of the nuclear age there are both old and new dangers that we must confront. Jonathan Schell (2007, 3) has noted: "The birth of nuclear weapons in 1945 opened a wide, unobstructed pathway to the end of the world." An all-out exchange of nuclear weapons between the United States and Russia, for example, would likely constitute the crime of omnicide (the annihilation of all human life on earth) or what Michael Bess (2006) calls ecocide (the extermination of almost all forms of life on the planet). Even a more limited use of these deadly weapons, say between India and Pakistan, or by the United States against Iran, would still be a historic genocidal act. The worldwide environmental consequences of even a delimited use of nuclear weapons would still be catastrophic.

While it has less disastrous physical consequences, the alarming act of threatening to use nuclear weapons can still be used by nuclear powers to force imperial domination on other countries that do not possess these weapons (Gerson 2007). Attempts to impose an unjust economic or political order may also lead to global instability as dominated nations seek nuclear weapons to deter the nuclear powers, as North Korea and Iran have recently done. The greatest imperial power in the world today, the United States, falsely claimed that it was forced to respond to the potential destabilizing proliferation of weapons of mass destruction when it engaged in an illegal preventive war against Iraq in 2003 (which, as Kramer and Michalowski show in this volume, did not have any weapons of mass destruction or even a nuclear weapons program at the time), and then threatened to resort to the use of force to halt an alleged nuclear weapons program in Iran. These so-called counterproliferation efforts of the United States and other nuclear powers ironically assign nuclear weapons a key strategic role in this policy (Schell 2007). Finally, the most ominous new nuclear danger is the possibility of the use of a nuclear device by a non-state terrorist group. As Schell (2007, 6) observes, "the world is awash in nuclear-weapon technology, adding a new dimension to the dangers of proliferation, and raising the terrifying specter of a terrorist group that acquires and uses a nuclear weapon . . . to lash out against a great city somewhere in the world."

INTERNATIONAL LAW AND NUCLEAR WEAPONS

Governmental decisions to use, threaten to use, or continue to possess nuclear weapons can be classified as state crimes and brought within the boundaries of criminology because they are illegal—that is, they violate public international law. While some criminologists have made this argument in the past (Friedrichs 1985; Kauzlarich, Kramer, and Smith 1992; Kauzlarich and Kramer 1995, 1998), drawing on the legal analysis provided by a number of international law scholars (Boyle 1989a; Falk 1983a, 1983b; Lawyers' Committee on Nuclear Policy 1990; Meyrowitz 1990; Weston 1983), their position received a tremendous boost on July 8, 1996, with the delivery of an important decision by the International Court of Justice (ICJ), also known as the World Court. In an advisory opinion, *The Legality of the Threat or Use of Nuclear Weapons*, the ICJ ruled that the threat or use of nuclear weapons would generally be illegal under international law. This decision, which has been called by some "the most important opinion by a court in the history of the world" (Ginger 1998, 1), came in response to requests from the World Health Organization (WHO) and the United Nations General Assembly (UNGA) for advisory opinions on the legality of nuclear weapons. In a complicated and controversial ruling, the ICJ stated "the threat or use of nuclear weapons would generally be contrary to the rules of international law applicable in armed conflict, and in particular, the principles and rules of humanitarian law" (ICJ 1996, para. 105 [2] E).

Background to the ICJ Case

Public international law binds states to a set of rules of policy and practice and is normally created by treaties, customs, judicial decisions, international and regional conventions, and arguably UNGA resolutions (Bledsoe and Boczek 1987). Its history is rich, especially in the area of international humanitarian law, the laws of war. International agreements limiting the military practices of states date as far back as 1868, when the Declaration of St. Petersburg prohibited the express attack of civilians in times of war. The laws of war evolved over the following century and a half and include the spirit and substance of such international agreements as the Hague Conventions (1899 and 1907), the Nuremberg Principles (1946), the Genocide Convention (1948), and the 1949 Geneva Conventions (Byers 2005; Gutman, Rieff and Dworkin 2007; McCormack and Durham 2009). International law is forcefully endorsed by the United Nations, although its application and definition are certainly subject to the whims of the powerful states that sit on the Security Council and possess the veto.

The International Court of Justice is the judicial organ of the United Nations. The ICJ has the power to both decide contentious cases, which are usually disputes between two member states, and to provide advisory opinions on important legal matters. The court gives these advisory opinions when it is asked a legal question by the UNGA or one of the specialized agencies affiliated with the United Nations. An advisory opinion is intended to clarify some aspect of international law related to the work of the agency requesting the opinion.

The two requests for advisory opinions on the legality of the threat or use of nuclear weapons were stimulated by the efforts of a number of nongovernmental organizations dedicated to the goals of peace and nuclear disarmament (Kramer and Kauzlarich 1999). After written submissions were received and several hearings held, the ICJ delivered two opinions. In one it concluded that the WHO lacked competence to request an advisory opinion on the legality of nuclear weapons, and thus the court did not rule on the substance of the WHO request. In the other opinion however, the court did rule on the request it had received from the UNGA and declared that generally the threat or use of nuclear weapons was illegal.

The Advisory Opinion

The ICJ began its substantive analysis of the UNGA question by dealing with a series of human rights, health, and environmental arguments that had been made by some of the states. The court rejected these arguments based on human rights and environmental law and instead turned to the law relating to the use of armed force as the basis on which the legality of the threat or use of nuclear weapons should be judged. The ICJ concluded the following:

> The most directly relevant applicable law governing the question, of which it was seized, is that relating to the use of force enshrined the United Nations Charter and the law applicable in armed conflict which regulates the conduct of hostilities, together with any specific treaties on nuclear weapons that the Court might determine to be relevant. (ICJ 1996, para. 34)

The court then added:

> In consequence, in order correctly to apply to the present case the Charter law on the use of force and the law applicable in armed conflict, in particular humanitarian law, it is imperative for the Court to take account of the unique characteristics of nuclear weapons, and in particular their

destructive capacity, their capacity to cause untold human suffering, and their ability to cause damage to generations to come. (ICJ 1996, para. 36)

The ICJ then first considered the provisions of the UN charter relating to the threat or use of force. The judges came to a unanimous conclusion that any use of nuclear weapons contrary to Article 2(4) of the United Nations Charter (generally prohibiting the threat or use of force), and not vindicated by Article 51 (recognizing every state's inherent right of self-defense if an armed attack occurs) is unlawful. The court then turned to the law applicable in situations of armed conflict. Here it faced two questions:

1. Are there specific rules in international law regulating the legality or illegality of recourse to nuclear weapons per se?
2. What are the implications of the principles and rules of humanitarian law applicable in armed conflict and the law of neutrality?

By way of introduction, the ICJ notes that international customary and treaty law does not contain any specific prescription authorizing the threat or use of nuclear weapons. Likewise, the court also concluded (by a vote of 11–3) that "there is in neither customary nor conventional international law any comprehensive and universal prohibition of the threat or use of nuclear weapons" (ICJ 1996, para. 105). Not having found any specific rules in international law prohibiting nuclear weapons per se, the court considered whether recourse to nuclear weapons could be declared illegal in light of the general principles and rules of international humanitarian law applicable in armed conflict and of the law of neutrality. The cardinal principles of humanitarian law according to the court are the protection of the civilian population and civilian objects, the prohibition of weapons incapable of distinguishing between combatants and noncombatants, and the prohibition of causing unnecessary suffering to combatants. All the judges agreed that there could be no doubt as to the applicability of these principles to a possible threat or use of nuclear weapons, despite the fact that these principles and rules had evolved prior to the invention of nuclear weapons. This is a key point we will come back to.

While all fourteen judges agreed that these principles apply to nuclear weapons in general, there was a sharp divergence of opinion concerning their specific application. There were two points of view (Bekker 1997). According to one view, the fact that recourse to nuclear weapons is subject to and regulated by the law of armed conflict does not necessarily mean that such recourse is prohibited. The other view holds that recourse to nuclear weapons could never be compatible with the principles and rules of humanitarian law and is therefore always prohibited. Although, the court admitted that, "in view of the unique characteristics of nuclear weapons . . . the use of such weapons in fact seems scarcely reconcilable with respect for such requirements.

Nevertheless, the Court considers that it does not have sufficient elements to enable it to conclude with certainty that the use of nuclear weapons would necessarily be at variance with the principles and rules of law applicable in armed conflict in any circumstance" (ICJ 1996, para. 95).

Accordingly, the ICJ's overall finding on this point (by a vote of 8–7, decided by the second vote of President Bedjaouri) was a qualified one: "it follows from the above-mentioned requirements that the threat or use of nuclear weapons would generally be contrary to the rules of international law applicable in armed conflict, and in particular the principles and rules of humanitarian law" (para. 105 [2] E). The court goes on to say: "However, in view of the current state of international law, and of the elements of fact at its disposal, the court cannot conclude definitely whether the threat or use of nuclear weapons would be lawful or unlawful in an extreme circumstance of self-defense, in which the very survival of a State would be at stake" (para. 105 [2] E). Several points need to be made about this qualified finding. First of all, of the seven dissenting judges, three voted against the finding because it does not go far enough and prohibit the threat or use of nuclear weapons in all circumstances. Second, the qualification in the finding applies only to the most extreme cases where the survival of a state is at stake. Finally, as Falk points out, "The court is clearly not validating a threat or use of nuclear weapons in an extreme circumstance of self-defense but asserting that it cannot conclude definitely one way or the other with respect to the legality of such a claim even in that situation" (1997, 68).

It is important to stress that the ICJ advisory opinion did not create new law. Rather, the decision clarified that existing public international law, particularly the general principles and rules of international humanitarian law applicable in armed conflict (the laws of war), did apply to the use or threat to use nuclear weapons. The court's ruling could be characterized, in the words of Justice Robert H. Jackson, U.S. chief of counsel at the Nuremberg Tribunal, as "declaratory of existent law" (1946, xii). This legal position supports the ruling of the Japanese court in the *Shimoda* case that the United States did violate international law by dropping atomic bombs on Japan (Falk 1965).

As the Nuremberg Tribunal made clear, the violation of the laws or customs of war are war crimes, and inhumane acts committed against civilian populations are crimes against humanity. Thus, the use, threat to use, and possession of nuclear weapons are not only illegal but also criminal. As Boyle points out concerning the ICJ ruling:

> Whenever the court discusses violations of the laws and customs of war; or violations of the Hague Conventions and Protocols; or violations of international humanitarian law, etc. with respect to the threat and use of

nuclear weapons, the reader must understand that such violations are not just "illegal" and "unlawful" but are also "war crimes" and thus "criminal" under basic principles of international law that have been fully subscribed to by the United States government itself. Hence my basic conclusions (1) that both the threat and use of nuclear weapons are criminal; and (2) that nuclear deterrence itself is criminal. (2002, 71–72)

STATE CRIMES RELATED TO NUCLEAR WEAPONS

Since the ICJ ruling states that the use or threat to use nuclear weapons would be a violation of the long-standing laws of war, a war crime, then any actual use or threat to use nuclear weapons by the United States would be a criminal event, a state crime, subject to criminological analysis.

The Use of Atomic Bombs against Hiroshima and Nagasaki

The basic facts concerning the atomic bombings of Hiroshima and Nagasaki are clear. On August 6, 1945, at 8:15 A.M., the *Enola Gay*, a Superfortress B-29 bomber plane piloted by Paul Tibbets, dropped a five-ton uranium-235 atomic weapon above the Shima Hospital in Hiroshima, a Japanese city of some 350,000 people. The explosion of "Little Boy," as the bomb was called by the U.S. military, completely destroyed the city. Between 70,000 and 100,000 people died in the blast. Others would continue to die from radiation sickness and other bomb-related causes for years. The final death toll is estimated to be around 200,000. Three days after the bombing of Hiroshima, another B-29, *Bock's Car*, piloted by Charles W. Sweeny, dropped a plutonium bomb called "Fat Man" over Nagasaki, Japan, a city of about 270,000, killing between 40,000 and 70,000 people. The final death toll of the Nagasaki bombing is estimated to be around 140,000. The vast majority of those who died in the two atomic bombings were civilian noncombatants.

While these facts seem clear, the social meanings given to them vary tremendously. The political, military, moral, and legal interpretations of the atomic bombings of Hiroshima and Nagasaki are, to this day, bitterly contested. One historian, Michael Bess, has concisely summarized most of the core issues involved in these controversies with a series of basic questions concerning the decision to drop the atomic bomb:

Was it necessary to drop the bomb in order to get the Japanese to surrender?

Was this weapon qualitatively different from all the other weapons used during the war?

Did the use of the bomb speed up the Japanese surrender?

Were there plausible alternatives for achieving surrender without invading Japan or dropping the bomb?

Did the atomic bombing of Japan, by shortening the war, result in a net saving of lives?

Was the Nagasaki bomb necessary?

Was there a plausible alternative for achieving surrender with a lower loss of life, by using the bomb differently than the United States actually did?

Did the United States drop the bomb to intimidate the Soviet Union?

Did U.S. leaders rush to drop the bomb, in the hope of bringing about Japanese surrender before the Soviets could enter the Pacific War?

Was the bomb used out of racism?

Did the use of this weapon violate the basic principles of a just war?

Was the dropping of the atomic bomb justified? How to judge the morality of this act? (2006, 198)

While all of these questions are important, and the answers to some of them will later play an important role in the theoretical interpretation we offer concerning the normalization of the crimes of the nuclear state, this section asks several different and prior questions: Was the use of atomic weapons against Japan illegal? Was the use of the bomb a war crime and a crime against humanity?

It is difficult to address these and other criminological questions about the atomic bomb without first taking into account the more general phenomenon that developed among all the major airpowers during World War II of the movement from sporadic, selective, and tactical attacks on military and military-industrial targets "to the use of airpower to destroy cities and terrorize and kill civilians" (Selden 2004, 30). The aerial bombardment of civilian populations in urban areas, variously referred to as "area bombing," "strategic bombing," or "total war," has been examined by numerous scholars (Bess 2006; Conway-Lanz 2006; Falk 2004a; Grayling 2006; Schaffer 1985, 2009; Selden 2004, 2009; Sherry 1987, 1995, 2009; Tanaka and Young 2009). Most of them concur with the assertion that "deliberately mounting military attacks on civilian populations, in order to cause terror and indiscriminate death among them, is a moral crime" (Grayling 2006, 4). Bess characterizes these bombings, often carried out with incendiary substances such as thermite or napalm, as atrocities. Selden and Falk each define them as state terrorism. While we are focused in this section on the use of atomic weapons against Hiroshima and Nagasaki, we will point out in our theoretical narrative that those acts cannot be analyzed separately from the aerial bombing of civilians in cities that preceded them. According to Selden (2004, 30), the atomic attacks simply "marked an additional cruel step in erasing the combatant/noncombatant distinction." And as Cirincione points out, there is "compelling evidence that most senior officials did not see a big difference between killing civilians with fire bombs and killing them with atomic bombs. The war had brutalized everyone. The strategy of intentionally attacking civilian targets, considered beyond the pale at the beginning of the war, had become commonplace in both the European and Asian theaters. Hiroshima and Nagasaki, in this context, were the continuation of decisions reached years earlier" (2007, 13).

We return to the question at hand: Was the use of atomic weapons against Hiroshima and Nagasaki unlawful? The answer is yes. The atomic bombings were objectively illegal, a war crime, because they violated the rules and principles of international humanitarian law that existed in 1945, the same laws the ICJ would rely on in its momentous decision in 1996. The leading authority on this point according to most legal scholars is the *Shimoda* case, decided by the District Court of Tokyo, on December 7, 1963. In May of 1955, five Japanese nationals instituted a legal action against their government to recover damages for the injuries they had suffered as a result of the atomic bombings of Hiroshima and Nagasaki. Part of their claim for compensation was based on the assertion that the dropping of the atomic bombs as an act of hostilities was illegal under the rules of positive international law. In its important ruling on the case, the Japanese court held that the atomic bomb attacks on Hiroshima and Nagasaki did indeed violate international law, although it rejected the plaintiffs' claims for compensation. In his classic appraisal of the Shimoda case, Falk clearly summarizes the principle reasons the court gave for its decision that the attacks were illegal:

> International law forbids an indiscriminate or blind attack upon an undefended city; Hiroshima and Nagasaki were undefended;

> International law only permits, if at all, indiscriminate bombing of a defended city if it is justified by military necessity; no military necessity of sufficient magnitude could be demonstrated here;

> International law as it has specifically developed to govern aerial bombardment might be stretched to permit zone or area bombing of an enemy city in which military objectives were concentrated; there was no concentration of military objectives in either Hiroshima or Nagasaki;

> International law prohibits the use of weapons and belligerent means that produce unnecessary and cruel forms of suffering as illustrated by the prohibition of lethal poisons and bacteria; the atomic bomb causes suffering far more severe and extensive than the prohibited weapons. (Falk 1965, 776)

According to Falk (1965, 770), the Japanese court based its ruling of the illegality of the atomic attacks on the following legal documents: The St. Petersburg Declaration (1868), the Hague Conventions on the Law and Customs of Land Warfare (1899 and 1907), the Declaration Prohibiting Aerial Bombardment (1907), the Treaty of Five Countries Concerning Submarines and Poisonous Gases (1922), the Draft Rules of Air Warfare (1923), and the Protocol Prohibiting the Use of Asphyxiating, Poisonous, or Other Gases (1925). These international legal rules for the conduct of warfare were codified and promulgated by the United States government itself in the War Department's Field Manual 27-10, entitled *Rules of Land Warfare*, which was issued on October 4, 1940 (and amended on November 15, 1944). As Boyle has conclusively demonstrated, the principles of international law specified in Field Manual 27-10 were binding on U.S. officials throughout World War II and thus prohibited the use of atomic weapons against Japan. Therefore, "all U.S. civilian government officials and military officers who ordered or knowingly participated in the atomic bombings of Hiroshima and Nagasaki could have been (and still can be) lawfully punished as war criminals" (Boyle 2002, 73).

The *Shimoda* decision, the U.S. government's own Army Field Manual, the ICJ ruling "declaratory of existent law," and the considered opinion of many international law scholars make it clear that from an objective legal perspective at least, the atomic attacks on Japan did constitute a state crime. As Falk notes, "the unavoidable legal conclusion [is] that these attacks remain unacknowledged crimes against humanity of the greatest magnitude. The use of the atomic bomb in World War II was not merely a violation of the laws of war . . . but was also a criminal act of the greatest severity for which the perpetrators were given impunity" (2008a, 42).

Threats to Use Nuclear Weapons: Korea, Vietnam, and Beyond

A second form of state crime related to nuclear weapons that the United States has repeatedly engaged in is the threat to use these weapons in a variety of conflict situations to gain geopolitical and/or military advantage. As Gerson (2007, 2) has documented: "On at least 30 occasions since the atomic bombings of Hiroshima and Nagasaki, every US president has prepared and/or threatened to initiate nuclear war during international crises, confrontations, and war—primarily in the Third World." These threats, he argues, have been used to illegally "expand, consolidate, and maintain" the American empire (Gerson 2007, 1).

On some occasions the threats to use nuclear weapons were made in an attempt to coerce a Third World government into negotiating an end to a military conflict on terms more favorable to the United States than the current conventional warfare strategy could produce. President Eisenhower's threat to use a nuclear device during the "police action" in Korea in 1953 and President Nixon's "November ultimatum" to North Vietnam in 1969 during the Vietnam War are the two primary examples of this practice (Kauzlarich and Kramer 1998). Implicit nuclear threats, which some have called nuclear terrorism, have also been used since World War II in an attempt to impose a global American imperial order and to provide a "nuclear shield" or "umbrella of U.S. power" (Chomsky 1994, 1999) to cover the use of conventional forces and make them, in the words of former Secretary of Defense Harold Brown, more "meaningful instruments of military and political power" (Gerson 2007, 2). Numerous presidents have used the specter of nuclear weapons in an attempt to secure "vital interests" in the Middle East, particularly with regard to Iraq and Iran, and also in East Asia (Chomsky 2006; Gerson 2007). Nuclear weapons in space and missile defense systems, viewed as offensive weapons, have also increasingly been brandished as part of the nuclear shield designed to advance U.S. hegemony in a post–cold war world (Chomsky 2003, 2006). Finally, the threat to use nuclear weapons to reciprocate for a first strike by the former Soviet Union (a guarantee of "mutual assured destruction") was the basis for "nuclear deterrence" policies during most of the years of the cold war (Kurtz 1988).

All of these threats by the American nuclear state to use nuclear weapons, regardless of the circumstances, are unlawful. First of all, as we noted above, the ICJ explicitly ruled that in all but the most extreme circumstances, the threat to use nuclear weapons would be illegal under international law. The legal logic here, as the Lawyers' Committee on Nuclear Policy has pointed out, is that "if a given use of nuclear weapons is judged to be contrary to the humanitarian rules of armed conflict, then logically any threat of such use should be considered contrary to the humanitarian rules of armed conflict as well" (1990, 19). In the view of several legal scholars, these threats, as violations of international law, constitute state crimes. Boyle has concluded that "the threat to use nuclear weapons (i.e., nuclear deterrence/terrorism) constitutes ongoing international criminal activity: Namely, planning, preparation, conspiracy and solicitation to commit crimes against peace, crimes against humanity, war crimes, as well as grave breaches of the Four Geneva Conventions of 1949, their Additional Protocol One of 1977, the Hague Regulations of 1907, the Geneva Gas Protocol of 1925, and the International Convention on the Prevention and Punishment of the Crime of Genocide of 1948, inter ali" (2002, 74).

In *Crimes of the American Nuclear State* we extensively analyzed the threats to use nuclear weapons by the U.S. during the wars in Korea and Vietnam (Kauzlarich and Kramer 1998). In addition, Kurtz (1988), Gerson (2007) and Chomsky (1994, 2003, 2006) have documented and analyzed numerous other situations in which the U.S. government has engaged in criminal acts of nuclear terrorism. In these studies, the important role of imperial motives for state crimes related to nuclear threats is stressed. We would simply add here that, just as the bombing of civilians, with either conventional weapons or atomic bombs, became a form of normalized criminal behavior over the course of World War II (Kramer 2008, 2010), so too did the threat of using nuclear weapons become a normal and acceptable criminal act in the pursuit of empire during the cold war and on down through the George W. Bush administration.

The Possession of Nuclear Weapons and the Failure to Disarm

The third form of state crime related to nuclear weapons that the United States (and, we would hasten to add, all of the other nuclear weapons states) is engaged in is the continued possession of these "indefensible weapons" (Lifton and Falk 1982). Since the end of the Second World War the U.S. government has maintained varying stockpiles of atomic and nuclear weapons. Today, despite the end of the cold war and substantial negotiated reductions, there are still over 10,000 nuclear weapons in the American arsenal, out of the total of 27,000 such weapons existing among the worldwide nuclear club, which now numbers nine members (Cirincione 2007).

Shortly after World War II the UNGA was determined to eliminate the production and possession of atomic weapons through arms control treaties. Given the Cold War and the technical problems of monitoring, inspection, and enforcement, this proved impossible to accomplish at the time. As the former UN weapons inspector Hans Blix has admitted, "we have not been able to achieve rules specifically banning the production, stockpiling and use of nuclear weapons" (2008, 42). Does the lack of a specific rule banning the possession of nuclear weapons mean that the stockpiling of these weapons is lawful?

Since both the use and the threat to use nuclear weapons are illegal under international law and, as Falk argues, intrinsically criminal, would not the mere possession of weapons that cannot be legally used in any practical way also be illegal and criminal? One could certainly attempt to make that legal argument. However, there is another legal agreement that can be used to evaluate the lawfulness of the continued possession of nuclear weapons under international law. That agreement is the Nuclear Non-Proliferation Treaty (NPT) of 1968. The NPT was a "double bargain" (Blix 2008, 44). The non-nuclear weapons states agreed not to develop the weapons and accepted international inspection. On the other side, the five nuclear weapons states at the time committed themselves to negotiations that would lead to general and complete nuclear disarmament. According to Falk (2008b), the United States and the other nuclear weapons powers are in material and flagrant breach of this treaty today.

To appreciate the significance of the NPT to the question of the legality of the possession of nuclear weapons, we return once again to the 1996 ICJ decision. One of the most important aspects of the ICJ's ruling on the illegality of nuclear weapons is the call, by all fourteen judges, for the abolition of such weapons. The ICJ concluded its advisory opinion with an examination of the duty of states to negotiate in good faith a complete nuclear disarmament. The relevant treaty obligation the court relied on is that found in Article 6 of the NPT that states: "Each of the Parties to the Treaty undertakes to pursue negotiations in good faith on effective measures relating to cessation of the nuclear arms race at an early date and to nuclear disarmament, and on a treaty on general and complete disarmament under strict and effective international control."

On the basis of this provision, a unanimous court found that "there exists an obligation to pursue in good faith and bring to a conclusion negotiations leading to nuclear disarmament in all its aspects under strict and effective international control" (ICJ 1996, para. 105 [2] F). The ICJ interpreted the NPT provision as imposing an obligation to achieve a precise result—nuclear disarmament in all its aspects. This part of the opinion can be interpreted as a strong rebuke of the nuclear weapons states. As Falk observed at the time:

> The unanimity of the Court as to the disarmament obligation thus goes against the prevailing outlook of the declared nuclear weapons states, especially that of the United States and the United Kingdom, and could become substantively important at some subsequent time. Indeed, it gives indirect encouragement to peace groups around the world that have been calling for nuclear disarmament ever since the first atomic explosions in 1945. This legal endorsement of disarmament also amounts, even if unwittingly, to a sharp criticism of the nuclear weapons states of their abandonment of any serious pursuit of disarmament goals in recent decades. (1997, 66–67)

And as Boyle also notes:

> Since 1968 it cannot be said that the world's nuclear weapons states have ever pursued negotiations on nuclear disarmament in good faith. Indeed, since 1968, except perhaps for the 1986 Gorbachev proposals, not one of the nuclear weapons states has ever given any serious consideration to their solemn legal obligation of nuclear disarmament, let alone general and complete disarmament, as required and called for by NPT Article VI. Hence, all of the nuclear weapons states currently stand in material breach of these twin obligations under NPT Article VI and/or customary international law as authoritatively determined by the world court itself. (2002, 192)

By failing to engage in good faith efforts to achieve complete disarmament and continuing to possess nuclear weapons, the U.S. and the other nuclear states are in violation of the NPT and engaged in a form of international lawlessness. This lawlessness presents a host of nuclear problems and dangers that bear on the question of the criminality of continued possession. First of all, the fact that the U.S. maintains a stockpile of nuclear weapons provides American state officials with the opportunity to illegally threaten to use them, as they have on numerous occasions that we documented above, or actually use them in a future conflict situation. Second, as we also noted above, keeping the world "awash in nuclear-weapons technology" raises "the terrifying specter of a terrorist group that acquires and uses a nuclear weapon" (Schell 2007, 6). Perhaps most important, by failing to disarm and thus violating the NPT, the United States encourages the proliferation of nuclear weapons among other states, making the world a much more dangerous place. India and Pakistan never signed the NPT and both joined the nuclear club in the 1990s. More recently, North Korea withdrew from the treaty and has since acquired several nuclear devices. Other states are sure to follow and seek nuclear weapons for reasons of security and international prestige (Schell 2007). The final danger, then, is that the United States has pledged in its National Security Strategy (2002 and 2006) to stop the proliferation of weapons of mass destruction through preventive warfare, and has even assigned its own nuclear weapons a counterproliferation role in the 2002 Nuclear Posture Review (Blix 2008; Schell 2007). These imperial policies led to the George W. Bush administration's illegal invasion of Iraq in 2003 (Kramer and Michalowski 2005 and this volume), and the threat to destroy the alleged nuclear weapons program in Iran and bring about regime change there through the use of military force, that could escalate to the use of nuclear weapons (Ritter 2006).

The continued possession of nuclear weapons in violation of the NPT, therefore, not only abandons international law but also creates a criminogenic international environment that poses a variety of clear nuclear dangers. As Schell has pointed out, the nuclear dilemma is an "indivisible whole," meaning "proliferation and possession cannot be considered in isolation from each other." As the world drifts toward "nuclear anarchy," he warns that "not since the world's second nuclear bomb was dropped on Nagasaki has history's third use of a nuclear weapon seemed more likely" (Schell 2007, 12–13, 14).

THE NORMALIZATION OF THE CRIMES OF THE AMERICAN NUCLEAR STATE

In *Crimes of the American Nuclear State* we developed a theoretical narrative to explain state crimes related to nuclear weapons that drew on a revised integrated framework for the study of organizational crime that we originally created with Ray Michalowski (Kramer and Michalowski 1990, 2006b). This theoretical schema, an effort at theory elaboration (Vaughan 2007), links three levels of analysis, macro-, meso- and micro-, with three catalysts for action: motivation (goals), opportunity (means), and formal social control (sanctions). Our objective was to inventory and highlight the key factors that contribute to or restrain organizational deviance at each intersection of a catalyst for action and a level of analysis. We viewed the organization as the key unit of analysis, nested within an institutional and cultural environment, and engaged in social action through the decisions of individual actors who occupied key positions within the structure of the organization. According to this schema, organizational deviance is most likely to occur when pressures for organizational goal attainment intersect with attractive and available illegitimate organizational means in the absence or neutralization of effective formal social controls.

In our theoretical narrative in the book we suggested that as organizational goals shaped by the geopolitical and economic environment (U.S. national security and imperialistic interests) were pursued with available illegitimate means (the threat to use nuclear weapons), certain ideological or cultural beliefs could develop to support these pursuits. We did not, however, draw explicitly on Diane Vaughan's (1996) concept of the normalization of deviance, which she developed in her landmark study of the Space Shuttle *Challenger* launch decision. We have come to see this concept as particularly relevant to our analysis of state crimes related to nuclear weapons. According to Vaughan, the normalization of deviance occurs when actors in an organizational setting, such as a corporation or a government agency, come to define their deviant acts as normal and acceptable because they fit with and conform to the cultural norms of the organization within which they work. Even though their actions may violate some outside legal or social standard and be labeled as criminal or deviant by people outside the organization, organizational offenders do not see these actions as wrong because they are conforming to the cultural mandates that exist within the workgroup culture and environment where they carry out their occupational roles.

Vaughan's concept of the normalization of deviance makes a number of important contributions to our understanding of organizational deviance. First, it offers a useful corrective to the tendency to see all crimes, including organizational crimes, as the result of individual rational choices; that is, calculated decisions where the costs and benefits of wrongdoing are weighed by the actors before acting. Second, it advances our sociological understanding of how organizational cultures narrow choices and shape social definitions of what is rational and acceptable at any given moment, and how these choices and definitions can lead to unlawful or deviant behavior on behalf of the organization. Finally, it shows how organizational culture can be the mediating factor between macro- and micro-social forces. As Vaughan points out, "Organizational settings make visible the ways that macro-institutional forces outside of organizations and occupations are joined with micro-processes, thus affecting individual decisions and actions. Organizations provide a window into culture, showing how culture mediates between institutional forces, organizational goals and processes, and individual illegality so that deviance becomes normalized in organizational settings" (2007, 4).

We believe that in order to understand the crimes of the American nuclear state, we must first examine how the war crime of bombing civilian populations in violation of the legal and moral principle of noncombatant immunity became normalized during World War II. In 1937, prior to the official start of the war, there was international outrage and horror over the terror bombing of civilians at Guernica (Gernika) by the Nazis during the Spanish Civil War and within several coastal cities in China by the Japanese. At the onset of the war in Europe in 1939, President Franklin D. Roosevelt appealed to the warring nations not to permit the bombardment of civilian populations from the air (Grayling 2006). Schaffer (1985, 2009) has documented that at the start of the American involvement in the war there was considerable opposition within the U.S. Army Air Force (USAAF) to directing air attacks at primarily civilian targets. In addition to their own misgivings about this strategy, U.S. air generals thought that this would cause problems with the Congress and the American people, "who did not appear to have the stomach for annihilating ordinary Germans" (Schaffer 2009, 36). Disapproving of the British approach, the Americans initially agreed to a division of labor where the USAAF would carry out daytime "precision bombing" against military and industrial targets while the Royal Air Force would engage in nighttime "strategic or area" bombing, which caused far more civilian deaths.

The evidence, therefore, suggests that at the outset of World War II there was little normative support within American political culture or military institutions for the illegal practice of bombing civilians. By the end of the war, however, the normative constraints on the terror bombing of cities had almost completely collapsed. The area bombing of civilians in Germany and Japan by the allied nations during World War II wrought "a revolution in the morality of warfare" (Schaffer 1985, 3). Bombing civilians became normalized, culturally approved by state officials and the American public alike. Once normalized, accepted, and supported within the larger political culture and specific war planning bureaucracies, this form of state crime, the "most barbaric style of warfare imaginable" (Englehardt 2008, 161), would lead to the use of the atomic bomb against Japan and then continue to characterize American war fighting, including the numerous threats to use nuclear weapons, right up to the present. As Selden observes, "The strategy of killing of noncombatants through air power runs like a red line from the bombings of 1944–1945 through the Korean and Indochinese wars to the Gulf, Afghanistan, and Iraq wars" (2009, 93).

The theoretical question, then, is how did the illegal and criminal bombing of civilian populations, including the threat and use of nuclear weapons, become normalized, culturally accepted, and approved? Space does not permit an extended examination of this question, but we will present a summary of Kramer's (2008, 2010) recent analysis of this normalization of deviance process. His account argues that over the course of World War II, the socially constructed morality of nationalistic and imperialistic war goals, the "technological fanaticism" of the bureaucracies charged with military planning, and the legitimation of state violence through the weaknesses of international law, all contributed to the overall erosion of social and moral constraints on the state crime of terror bombing and the development of normative supports for this practice.

The Social Construction of the Morality of War Goals

The primary goal of the United States and its allies during World War II, of course, was to win the war. The "precision bombing" of military and war-related industrial targets, with its attendant collateral damage, and then the "area bombing" of enemy civilian populations to destroy their morale, were two of the means to that ultimate end. But by 1944 military victory was all but assured in both the European and Pacific theaters. At this point, secondary war goals emerged to the forefront: ending the war as quickly and decisively as possible and, by accomplishing those objectives, saving the lives of Allied military personnel. The majority of American political and military leaders came to believe that the accomplishment of these national goals necessitated a change from a sole reliance on precision bombing to an increasing use of terror bombing of enemy civilian populations, including the utilization of newly developed atomic weapons (Schaffer 1985; Walker 2004).

Many historians argue that the atomic bombings did help to shorten the war somewhat and thus they did save some American lives (Bess 2006; Walker 2004). After the war, however, Henry Stimson, former secretary of war, President Truman, and others who had participated in the decision to drop the atomic bombs created an elaborate mythology that the bombings of Hiroshima and Nagasaki had been the only way to end the war short of a costly invasion of Japan, and that the lives of up to a million soldiers had been saved by shortening the war and avoiding the invasion. Neither of these assertions was true. Walker (2004, 109) argues that the bomb "was not necessary to prevent an invasion of Japan" and that it "saved the lives of a relatively small but far from inconsequential number of Americans." But, according to the principle of noncombatant immunity found in both the just war moral tradition and the international laws of war, it is never permissible to target innocent civilians or noncombatants to accomplish war aims or save the lives of military combatants.

The mythology created by Stimson and Truman, however, served to legitimate the atomic bombings and, by extension, all forms of terror bombing during the war, in the eyes of the American people. The goals of shortening the war and saving the lives of American boys were presented as self-evidently "good" and "just." Even before this, of course, the entire conflict, in a nationalistic fervor, was defined as the "Good War" (Terkel 1984; Wood 2006). Defeating what was, to most Americans, the obvious "evil" of Hitler and the fascists, whose own state crimes during the war were massive, exacting "just retribution" for the "sneak" attack on Pearl Harbor and other Japanese atrocities during the war, and defending the American ideals of freedom and democracy at home against the criminal aggression of the Axis powers were such clear moral goals that any means necessary to accomplish them came to be viewed as acceptable and legitimate to most American leaders and the public. The social construction of the goodness and morality of the war in general, and the specific objectives of shortening the bloody conflict and saving the lives of "our boys in uniform," overwhelmed and short-circuited any attempt to critically evaluate the morality and legality of the terror bombing of the civilian populations of the "evil" enemy as a means to those legitimate ends.

In addition, as a number of historians have documented, the United States also shared with its adversaries certain other nationalistic and expansionist motives. The war "propelled the U.S. to a hegemonic position" that provided a unique opportunity for American leaders to pursue these imperial designs (Selden 2009, 91). Enhancing the economic power and geopolitical position of the American empire became central goals of U.S. wartime policies, including the policy of terror bombing (Gerson 2007; Zinn 1980).

The United States has been an imperial project from its earliest years (Anderson and Cayton 2005; Ferguson 2004; Nugent 2008; Wright 2008). Throughout its early history, American growth relied on expansion through force, including enslavement of Africans, expropriation of Native lands in the name of "manifest destiny," claiming North and South America as an exclusive American sphere of influence (the Monroe Doctrine), expansionist war with Mexico, and using American warships to ensure Asian trading partners (Beard and Beard 1930; Kolko 1984; Williams 1969, 1988). As the nineteenth century drew to a close, structural contradictions in American capitalism provoked an intensification of America's imperial reach through formal colonization in Cuba, Puerto Rico, and the Philippines. The United States would soon abandon its brief experiment with colonization as too economically and politically costly. The United States became an "informal" empire as opposed to a formal or colonial empire. As Selden (2009, 91) points out: "In contrast to earlier territorial empires, this took the form of new regional and global structures facilitating the exercise of American power."

World War II provided an opportunity for the United States to greatly expand this informal empire by confronting and defeating rival imperial powers and by creating some of these new regional and global structures. A clash of imperial ambitions precipitated the "Day of Infamy" at Pearl Harbor. This clash necessitated the decisive defeat of Japan and the complete destruction of Japanese militarism and imperialism. According to some historians, the firebombing of Japanese cities and the use of the atomic bombs were viewed as important means to accomplish these goals and exact just retribution for wartime atrocities (Gerson 2007; Zinn 1980).

As the war progressed and it became clear that the United States would be able to exercise hegemonic power in the postwar era, American leaders began to plan for the construction of new global institutions that would greatly advance their imperial designs. As Zinn (1980, 414) notes: "Before the war was over, the administration was planning the outlines of the new international economic order, based on partnership between government and business." This new international economic order would enhance and expand the informal "Open Door" imperialism the United States had been practicing since the early years of the twentieth century (Williams 1988).

Even as World War II was putting the United States into a position from which it could dominate the world, American political and military leaders recognized that the Soviet Union, their wartime ally, would be their chief rival in the postwar period. The contest for power and domination between the Soviet Union and the United States that would later be dubbed the cold war was already under way before the "hot" war against fascism was over. American officials increasingly came to view Stalin and the Soviets as a threat to their postwar imperial designs both in Europe and East Asia. And the perception of this threat would be an important factor in the most momentous decision of the war: the decision to drop the atomic bomb.

A number of historians have argued that the decision to use the atomic bomb was motivated more by political factors related to the perceived Soviet threat than by purely military factors. Alperovitz (1965, 1995) presents persuasive evidence that American leaders dropped atomic weapons on Hiroshima and Nagasaki in an effort to impress Stalin with the power of the bomb and to intimidate the Soviet Union in the coming postwar contest for domination. He argues that Japan was on the verge of surrender in the summer of 1945 and that Truman and his advisors were well aware that alternatives to using the bomb existed. Nevertheless, Alperovitz contends, for diplomatic considerations U.S. leaders decided to use this powerful new weapon on Japan. To gain political leverage over the Soviets in the postwar period, the

United States carried out the terror bombing of two cities using atomic weapons.

Another political factor that played a role in the decision to drop the atomic bomb was the threat of Soviet expansionism in the Far East. Once the war in Europe was over, Stalin had pledged to enter the Pacific war by attacking Manchuria, eventually driving the Japanese out of China and perhaps becoming involved in a prospective invasion of the Japanese home-lands. As Hasegawa (2005) points out, alarmed by the prospect of Soviet terri-torial gains in East Asia and a shared occupation of Japan, American leaders hoped to use the atomic bomb to end the war quickly before the Soviet Union could enter the fight and become a major player in the end game in the Pacific. Again, imperial rivalry rather than military necessity seemed to drive the decision to bomb civilian populations with a new weapon of mass destruction.

While numerous scholars have concluded that the use of atomic weapons against Japan was both a moral and legal crime (Boyle 2002; Falk 2004a, 2004b; Gerson 2007; Grayling 2006; Lifton and Mitchell 1995; Zinn 1980), the majority of Americans did not see it that way at the time, and still to this day do not see it that way. Considerations of the morality and legality of the decision to use the atomic bomb, or of area bombing during World War II in general, were overwhelmed by the social construction of the morality of the "Good War." To most political and military leaders and the majority of the American people, the goals of winning the war as quickly as possible, saving the lives of American boys in uniform, and exacting a just retribution on the evil German and Japanese empires were paramount, and they justified the use of any means, including the terror bombing of enemy civilians. Other nation-alistic and imperialistic goals were either not recognized or were interpreted within the mythic idealism that has from the very beginning characterized American culture.

The mythic ideals of political leaders in the United States are usually drawn from a broad, historical, cultural narrative often referred to as American exceptionalism (Fiala 2008; Hodgson 2009). American exceptionalism gener-ally portrays the United States as a nation of exceptional virtue, a moral leader in the world with a unique historical mission to spread "universal" values such as freedom, democracy, equality, popular sovereignty, and increasingly global capitalism. This mythic cultural construction of exceptionalism "thoroughly informs US constructs of its identity" (Ryan 2007, 119). According to Hodgson, the "myth of American exceptionalism" often takes a "missionary" form, with the U.S. viewed as "a city upon a hill" with a "God-given destiny" to "spread the benefits of its democratic system and of its specific version of capitalism to as many other countries as possible" (2009, 159). Americans have always viewed their country as a "city set upon a hill" with a special duty and destiny to spread their values and wisdom, their freedom and democracy, to the rest of the world. This myth of American exceptionalism (Hodgson 2009) has often shielded the American people from a critical examination of their history and the imperial motives that so often drive U.S. foreign policy.

The Good War only reinforced the mythic idealism at the heart of American exceptionalism. In *Worshipping the Myths of World War II*, Edward W. Wood Jr. points out that one of the myths of that war is the idea that "when evil lies in others, war is the means to justice" (2006, 143). In the end, the fight against evil and the advancement of America's exceptional ideals justifies any of the means, including violent means; we select to accomplish our national goals. In the wartime environment, conformity to these cultural mandates helped to make the bombing of civilians, even with the most horribly destructive weapon that humans had ever devised, a normal and acceptable act.

Weapons Technology, Military Planning, and Technological Fanaticism

A second factor in the normalization of terror bombing was the way in which the destructive technologies of air power increasingly came to be the means that were relied upon to accomplish wartime aims within U.S. political and military institutions and organizations such as the White House, the War Department, the Joint Chiefs, the Army Air Force, the Manhattan Project, and the Interim Committee. As Selden (2009, 87) notes, in a variety of wartime organizational settings, "Technology was harnessed to the driving force of American nationalism." In order to realize its military goals, the United States would increasingly rely on advancements in the technologies of mass destruction. The rise of American air power in particular would serve as the technical means by which these wartime aims would be secured. The B-29 Superfortress bomber, the Norden bomb-sight, the napalm bomb and other incendiary devices, improved radar, and, of course, the development of the atomic bomb all made possible the greater use of aerial bombardment as a primary tool of war.

Throughout the war, an instrumental rationality that fixates on the most effective and efficient means to accomplish pre-given and unquestioned ends developed within the institutions and organizations associated with military planning that led inexorably to the terror bombing of civilian populations. Organizational and bureaucratic imperatives concerning the development of technologies of mass destruction increasingly came to drive the war planning process, and moral and legal concerns about these technologies were pushed aside. As Jackall points out: "The rational/technical ethos of bureaucracy transforms even those issues with grave moral import into practical concerns" (1980, 355). Thus, the instrumental rationality of the organizational form itself appears to be partially responsible for the state terrorism of bombing civilians. Again, Jackall observes that "the very rationality which makes bureaucratic structures effective administrative tools seems to erode moral consciousness" (1980, 356).

Historian Michael Sherry (1987, 1995, 2009) has developed a compelling analysis of this rational bureaucratic process in its association with the development of American air power. He terms it "technological fanaticism." Sherry argues "that among policymakers, if not in the public at large, a technological fanaticism often governed actions, an approach to making war in which satisfaction of organizational and professional drives loomed larger than the overt passions of war" (1987, xi).

The very concept of "precision bombing," which American political and military leaders clung to for much of the war, implies a faith that advances in technology allowed attacks to be carried out on military and war-related industrial targets with only minimal and unintentional "collateral damage" to civilians and noncombatants. As Conway-Lanz points out, both during and after the war, "many Americans tenaciously clung to the optimistic assumption that violence in war could still be used in a discriminating manner despite the increased destructiveness of weapons" (2006, 19). Buttressing this assumption was the fact that the advancing technology of air power provided both a physical and psychic distance from the people being harmed for scientists and military personnel. As Sherry observes: "By virtue of their economic and technological superiority, Americans could act out war's destructive impulses while seeing themselves as different from their enemies. Rarely witnessing the human costs to the enemy, scientists could press new technologies on the armed forces, air force crews could incinerate enemy cities, and battleships could pummel Japanese-held islands from miles offshore. The intricate technology of war provided physical and psychic distance from the enemy" (1995, 81).

Within the organizational settings in which World War II military planning took place, an instrumental rationality concerning the application of the new technological means of mass destruction through the use of air power to the unquestionable moral goals of the war took hold. As Selden points out, "What was new was both the scale of killing made possible by the new technologies and the routinization of mass killing or state terrorism" (2009, 87). This technological fanaticism served to override and displace moral and legal concerns over the use of terror bombing within the various political and military bureaucracies charged with wartime decision making. It also provided both the optimistic assumption that air attacks could be carried out in a discriminating way, as well as physical and psychological distance from the actual consequences of bombing civilian populations. Technological fanaticism, therefore, was one more factor in the dynamic social process that spawned terror bombing during war and allowed it to become normal and acceptable.

The Laws of War: The Absence of Enforcement
and the Legitimation of Violence

Despite the long-standing principle of noncombatant immunity, or any of the formal legal standards found in the laws of war as they existed at the time, the terror bombing of civilian populations became widespread during World War II, including the atomic bombings of Japan. The final factor that influenced the normalization of these bombing attacks on civilians was the weakness of international law itself. The primary problem with international law in general is the lack of any effective enforcement mechanism. While a plethora of laws and legal standards have been promulgated over the years (particularly with regard to conduct during war), states have been unwilling to give up too much sovereignty to allow for any formal controls or coercive enforcement tools to be created that may be able to effectively punish or deter violations of these standards. Absent any effective formal legal controls, the compelling drive to achieve nationalistic and imperialistic goals during the course of the war through the effective and available means of terror bombing was not deterred by the mere existence of the legal principle of noncombatant immunity.

While no effective coercive enforcement mechanisms existed under international law at the time of actual hostilities, following the war there was an important effort to hold states and political and military leaders to account for their actions during the conflict that constituted "war crimes" broadly conceived. The International Military Tribunals at Nuremberg and Tokyo prosecuted, convicted, and then sanctioned a number of German and Japanese government officials for illegal acts they had allegedly engaged in during the war. Space does not permit an extended discussion of these international tribunals, but it is important to note that the aerial bombardment of civilian populations, whether to destroy their morale or for any other purpose was not one of the crimes that was prosecuted. As Jochnick and Normand point out, "In order to avoid condemning Allied as well Axis conduct, the war crimes tribunal left the most devastating forms of warfare unpunished" (1994, 89). They go on to argue that the decision not to include terror bombing among the war crimes to be prosecuted at Nuremberg or Tokyo helped to legitimate this behavior: "By leaving morale bombing and other attacks on civilians unchallenged, the Tribunal conferred legal legitimacy on such practices" (Jochnick and Normand 1994, 91). So even the most significant effort in history to actually enforce the laws of war, along with its undeniably important humanitarian accomplishments in advancing the legal categories of "crimes against peace" and "crimes against humanity," failed to even define the bombing of civilians as a crime, let alone punish the behavior or attempt to deter it in the future with formal sanctions. Thus, the legal legitimacy conferred upon terror bombing by the International Military Tribunals helped to normalize the practice and ensure that it would be a normal and acceptable method of warfare in the future.

But alongside the failure to control terror bombing due to a lack of formal enforcement mechanisms, there is an even more fundamental way that that international law legitimizes state violence and contributes to its normalization. As Jochnick and Normand have convincingly argued, the laws of war provide "unwarranted legitimacy" and "humanitarian cover" for violence during wartime due to the way in which states have created and codified an elastic definition of "military necessity" within the codes and conventions that constitute this body of law (1994, 56). Through overly broad and unchallenged conceptions of military necessity and military objectives, international law has legitimized and facilitated state practices during war such as terror bombing. During World War II the Allies did not openly violate the laws of war as much as they simply interpreted them in such a way as to justify and legalize their resort to the aerial bombardment of civilian populations in Germany and Japan. Jochnick and Normand conclude that:

> In both World Wars the laws of war played analogous roles. In each conflict the law served as a powerful rhetorical device to reassure anxious publics that the conflict would be confined within just limitations. The First and Second World Wars both saw the law subverted to the dictates of battle, reduced to a propaganda battlefield where belligerents traded attacks and counterattacks. And in the end, the law ultimately failed to protect civilians from horrifying new weapons and tactics. The scope of permissible violence expanded under a flexible definition of military objective and military necessity that eventually, and predictably, justified relentless terror bombing campaigns. (1994, 89)

In several ways, then, international law played a significant role in the development and normalization of terror bombing. By the failure to create effective mechanisms to enforce the legal standards that purport to provide immunity for noncombatants, and by the refusal of the Allies to include area bombing as a war crime to be prosecuted by the military tribunals formed after World War II, the international legal community helped to institutionally facilitate and culturally legitimate the targeting of civilians by air during wartime. Furthermore, the elastic definition of military necessity that was deliberately written into the laws of war over the years has allowed states to interpret their bombing behavior as legal and has provided them with a rhetorical device to assure their publics that the deaths of innocent civilians in such attacks are regrettable but necessary to accomplish military aims. Thus, terror bombing becomes normalized and culturally approved.

CONCLUSION

Despite the fact that the bombing of civilian populations, including the use of atomic weapons, was objectively illegal and criminal under existing international humanitarian law in 1944–1945, it is important to stress, from a sociological perspective, that the state officials who ordered these attacks and the military personnel who carried them out, did not see themselves as criminal. Nor did the American public. Those who thought otherwise, such as Vera Brittain (1944) were a small minority. The state officials and military leaders who engaged in these criminal acts did not make a calculated decision to violate any laws. Instead they were conforming to cultural mandates concerning ending the war, saving American lives, and advancing national interests that were derived from the mythic idealism of American exceptionalism. They utilized the technological means at their disposal within bureaucratic settings that were dominated by a form of instrumental rationality that erodes moral consciousness. They interpreted international law through the lens of an elastic concept of military necessity and were never forced to contemplate the threat of formal legal sanctions. In a few short years during the war, bombing civilians, even with a new weapon of mass destruction, had become normalized.

Winning this war, the Good War against evil, and purportedly winning it through the use of the atomic bomb, helped to cement the normalization of the state crime of bombing civilians. As Falk observes, "The winners in a war such as World War II, which was, in the deepest sense, widely regarded a just war, exerted a strong influence in determining which practices in war are to be tolerated" (2008b, 228). The bombing of civilians and the use of atomic weapons would now be tolerated. They had become normal and acceptable. In the immediate postwar period, the Stimson-Truman mythology concerning the necessity of the use of the atomic bomb to end the war without an invasion, thus saving over a million American lives, would further cement the normalization of the use and threat to use nuclear weapons. The cultural belief in this myth is so strong that the slightest deviation from the conventional wisdom concerning the morality and necessity of the atomic attacks can cause enormous outrage and controversy, as we witnessed in 1994–1995 when the Smithsonian's Air and Space Museum attempted to use a more historically balanced script for an exhibit of the *Enola Gay* (Bird and Lifschultz 1998).

The normalization of the practice of bombing civilians that emerged during the Second World War has continued to exert an enormous influence on the conduct of U.S. foreign policy ever since. In the early 1950s, three years of bombing and shelling reduced Korea, North and South, to a "shambles" (Zinn 1980, 481). The total tonnage of all airborne ordnance during the Korean War was 698,000, with a death toll of between two to three million (Young 2009,157). And when this level of conventional bombing did not end the conflict, President Eisenhower resorted to the threat to use nuclear weapons.

In Vietnam, from Lyndon Johnson's Operation Rolling Thunder in 1965 to Richard Nixon's Christmas bombing of the North in 1972, called by James Carroll (2004,150) "terror bombing pure and simple," the use of air power was incredible. Some eight million tons of bombs were dropped on Indochina during the Vietnam War (compared to two million tons in all of World War II), and the death toll was from two to four million (Young 2009, 157). Once again, when the conventional bombing of civilians did not resolve the conflict, the president of the United States, Richard Nixon, illegally threatened to go nuclear.

The "shock and awe" bombing of Baghdad in March 2003 and the increasing use of air strikes to battle insurgents and suspected terrorists in Iraq, Afghanistan, and other parts of the Middle East, South Asia, and Africa are only the most recent examples of how normal and acceptable this way of war, this "religion of air power," has become for both American political and military leaders and the U.S. public (Englehardt 2008). And when U.S. presidents publicly state that "all options are on the table," as they often do in conflict situations, it is clear that one of the options on that table is the still sizable stockpile of American nuclear weapons. Given this stockpile, the considerable Russian stockpile, and the recent proliferation of nuclear arms in the Middle East and South Asia, it is clear that nuclear catastrophe still hangs over the world like the Sword of Damocles.

One of the first steps toward ending the nuclear threat, the greatest crime prevention policy issue of all, and moving toward the complete abolition of nuclear weapons, is to challenge the normalization of the state crime of bombing civilians. And criminologists and sociologists have much to contribute to this effort. We need to expose and dismantle the cultural mandates that make such criminal acts normal and acceptable. We need to change the political culture that defines nuclear weapons as necessary for national security, indiscriminate air strikes as an appropriate military tactic, and civilians slaughtered by bombing attacks as "collateral damage." We need to restore a culture of compliance with international law to all the organizational settings that deal with foreign policy, national security, and military planning. We need to engage the American people and their political leaders in a critical examination of the mythic idealism that is at the core of the concept of American exceptionalism. Good intentions are not an excuse for destructive criminal acts that kill innocent people. High ideals and good ends cannot be reached through evil means. Only by stripping away normative support for the crimes of bombing civilians and clinging to nuclear weapons can we clear a space, sociologically and politically, to take the other hard steps that will be necessary in a conflict-ridden world to abolish nuclear weapons and end the nuclear threat once and for all.

CHAPTER 4

Empire and Exceptionalism

THE BUSH ADMINISTRATION'S CRIMINAL WAR AGAINST IRAQ

Ronald C. Kramer and Raymond J. Michalowski

ON MARCH 19, 2003, the United States and Great Britain, in conjunction with several inconsequential members of the "coalition of the willing," launched an unprovoked invasion of Iraq and subsequently inaugurated a formal military occupation of that once sovereign nation. The Bush administration's legal and political justifications for this attack migrated from the eradication of weapons of mass destruction, to the advancement of democracy, to fighting terrorism, and back to the advancement of democracy. Economic and geopolitical motives, such as controlling Iraqi oil, reconstructing Iraq's economy into a radical free market system, or establishing permanent military bases in the heart of the Middle East, were publicly disavowed as goals of the invasion by the administration.

The initial war of aggression, followed by years of a belligerent and still ongoing military occupation, has subjected the Iraqi people to a "tidal wave" of death, destruction and misery (Schwartz 2008). The chain of events set into motion by the invasion and occupation of Iraq has—so far—resulted in the deaths of over one million Iraqis, based on extrapolations from studies carried out by researchers from Johns Hopkins University and published in the highly respected British medical journal *Lancet* (Burnham et al. 2006; Roberts et al. 2004; Schwartz 2008). In addition, over four million people have been displaced from their homes and the social and economic infrastructure of Iraq has been devastated (Schwartz 2008). By the time George W. Bush left office in January 2009, over four thousand American military personnel had been killed in the war, and, according to Stiglitz and Bilmes (2008), the total cost of the invasion and occupation to American taxpayers would eventually exceed $3 trillion.

In several earlier publications we have argued that the U.S. war on Iraq must be understood as a state crime (Chambliss 1989), a claim we have supported through a criminological analysis of the Bush administration's actions in launching a war aggression against Iraq and overseeing the subsequent military occupation of that country (Kramer and Michalowski 2005, 2006a; Kramer, Michalowski, and Rothe 2005). Our analysis centered on two key questions: Was the invasion of Iraq illegal and criminal? If so, what were the historical and contemporary forces that shaped the decision of these state officials to undertake such a war?

Is War Criminal? International Law and the Invasion of Iraq

In the original legal analysis (Kramer, Michalowski, and Rothe 2005) we established the validity of the following claims:

1. The 2003 invasion and subsequent occupation of Iraq by the United States and its allies was a criminal violation of public international law.
2. Insofar as the invasion and occupation of Iraq took place under the auspices of state authority, they are state crimes.
3. The state officials responsible for the violations of law pursuant to the invasion and occupation of Iraq are guilty of war crimes.
4. The illegal and criminal war on Iraq poses a grave threat to the UN Charter System and a law-governed approach to world order.

The body of public international law governing a state's recourse to war and legitimate conduct during war provided the legal framework for our analysis in this case. While we offered some historical background on public international law in general and the United Nations Charter in particular at the beginning of that analysis, we only mentioned the importance of the Nuremberg Charter in passing. We also neglected to discuss the significant role that the mid-twentieth century criminologist Sheldon Glueck played in organizing the Nuremberg trials and in defining aggressive war as criminal. A review of the contributions of Glueck's work and the Nuremberg prosecutions helps confirm the validity of our original legal analysis and places it in a broader historical context.

Sheldon Glueck, the Nuremberg Trial, and the Crime of Aggressive War

Sheldon Glueck was a criminologist and professor of law at Harvard University before and after World War II. He is best known for the work he did with his wife, Eleanor, on the causes of juvenile delinquency, in which they argued that multiple biological and psychological traits play an important role in the explanation of delinquent behavior. Given the pioneering work that the Gluecks did in the field of what is now called developmental criminology, it is somewhat surprising that in the 1940s Sheldon Glueck taught a graduate seminar and published a number of books and articles on war criminals, aggressive war, and the Nuremberg trial (see Glueck 1943a, 1943b, 1944, 1946). John Hagan and Scott Greer (2002, 234–235) have recently restored to criminological memory Glueck's contributions to the literature on international law and international crimes, noting that he "also played a major public and private role in establishing the legal foundations for the Nuremberg trials."

Sheldon Glueck was elected a "corresponding member" of the London International Assembly on the Trial of War Criminals in September 1942, gave a statement to Congress concerning a resolution on governmental policy concerning war criminals in 1945, and was in regular communication with the Office of Strategic Services (OSS) during the planning for the Nuremberg prosecutions, and eventually joined the OSS team and served as a consultant during the preparations for the trials (Hagan and Greer 2002). He developed a strong relationship with the head of the OSS, General James B. "Wild Bill" Donovan, and with Justice Robert H. Jackson, the U.S. chief of counsel during the Nuremberg trials. Glueck also devised a control system for summarizing and indexing the mass of documents utilized throughout the trials (Hagan and Greer 2002; Jackson 1946). It is important for criminologists, such as ourselves, who study state crime in the hope of reducing its occurrence, to remember that our concern reaches back to one of the founders of modern criminology who played a central role in developing the legal strategy for the prosecution of Nazi war criminals and implementing that strategy during the Nuremberg trials.

Sheldon Glueck closely identified with the philosophy of legal realism developed by Roscoe Pound (which argues that law can be used as an instrument of social engineering), and according to Hagan and Greer, "exhibited a sweeping vision of the scope of the [Nuremberg] trial" (2002, 251). They note that he believed that "the full range of crimes against humanity . . . should be tried, and that out of this experience a permanent international criminal court could emerge" (237). Given this "sweeping vision," it is interesting to assess Glueck's position on one of the most controversial questions that faced the International Military Tribunal (IMT) at Nuremberg and remains a pressing issue for us today as we examine the invasion of Iraq: Is a war of aggression criminal?

A heated and politicized debate occurred within the tribunal as a whole, as well as within the American prosecution team, over the priority that was to be given to the charge that Germany engaged in an illegal and criminal war of aggression (a crime against peace) compared to charges of crimes against humanity and war crimes related to the atrocities of the Holocaust and the conduct of the war (Hagan and Greer 2002). Justice Jackson (1946) was a strong advocate for focusing on the aggressive war charges. He wanted to firmly establish that such a war was illegal and criminal. On the other hand, the OSS and General Donovan, among many others, wanted to emphasize the Nazi crimes committed as a part of the Holocaust. In his earlier congressional statement, Sheldon Glueck had recommended against giving higher priority to the charge of conspiring to commit aggressive war. And as he began to write on the subject of war crimes he admitted, "I was not at all certain that the acts of launching and conducting an aggressive war could be regarded as international crimes" (Glueck 1946, 4). After the war, he shared the frustration of many other Jews "with the failure to confront the criminal scale and horror of the Holocaust" (Hagan and Greer 2002, 249). In the end, the control system devised by Glueck for gathering and presenting evidence, along with "the overwhelming nature of the nondocumentary evidence," shifted the focus of the Nuremberg trial "from the aggressive war charges that Jackson favored to the crimes against humanity in the form of the Holocaust" (250).

But in 1946, upon further reflection on the problem, Glueck did come to the conclusion that aggressive war could be conceived as an international crime. In *The Nuremberg Trial and Aggressive War* he argued the case that launching a war of aggression can be considered a criminal violation of international law. He started his analysis by citing Article 6(a) of the Nuremberg Charter, which defines "crimes against peace" as, "namely, planning, preparation, initiation or waging of a war of aggression, or a war in violation of international treaties, agreements or assurances, or participation in a common plan or conspiracy for the accomplishment of any of the foregoing." Glueck defended this article against its critics by arguing that an international custom had developed that held aggressive war to be an international crime. Under customary international law, he noted, "All that is necessary is to show that during the present century a widespread custom has developed among civilized States to enter agreements expressive of their solemn conviction that unjustified war is so dangerous a threat to the survival of mankind and mankind's law that it must be branded and treated as criminal" (Glueck 1946, 26).

Glueck was referring to a number of specific developments that had taken place in public international law in the twentieth century. Public international law consists of both customary state practices and specific treaties that govern the relations among states. The legal rules that Glueck cited are those that focus on the use of force and recourse to war in international affairs (*jus ad bellum*) and those that regulate the conduct of combatants in armed conflicts (*jus in bello*). Both of these international legal frameworks were of relatively recent origin. In the state system that emerged from the peace settlement at Westphalia that ended the Thirty Years War in 1648, war appeared to be a necessary evil. However, according to Richard Falk (2004a, 14), by the end of the nineteenth century, "there was a constituency for the thesis that war was at once integral to the Westphalian world of interacting sovereign states and increasingly intolerable as a recurrent international practice associated with conflict resolution." The Geneva Convention for the Amelioration of the Condition of the Wounded in Armies in the Field in 1864, the creation of the International Red Cross, and the two Hague peace conferences in 1899 and 1907 started the international community down the path toward the development of International Humanitarian Law (IHL), also known as the law of armed conflict or laws of war. The original objective of the two Hague Conventions was to limit the use of force in international affairs, but as William Slomanson (2003, 485) points out, "Once the conference participants realized that there would be no international agreement to eliminate war, the central theme became how to conduct it."

The catastrophic Great War of 1914–1918 (World War I) shattered Europe, the Middle East, and other parts of the world and brought renewed efforts to outlaw war. The most significant result of the Paris Peace Conference following the "war to end all wars" was a new organization of states called the League of Nations. The covenant of the league did not prohibit war or the use of military force, but it did attempt to reduce their likelihood through "structures of consultation and arbitration." Following the creation of the League of Nations and the 1925 Treaties of Locarno (an international agreement that was supposed to have "buried" the Great War), there was some optimism throughout Europe that future wars could be averted. But as Paul Kennedy (2006, 12) observed: "Yet for all the hopes placed in the League, and the various advances made in the growth of international civic society after 1919, the system failed within less than two decades of its founding."

While the covenant of the League of Nations did not contain an outright ban on the use of force in international relations, the 1928 Treaty for the Renunciation of War, commonly called the Kellogg-Briand Pact or the Paris Pact, did explicitly prohibit "recourse to war for the solution of international controversies." Initially signed by fifteen countries and eventually ratified by sixty-two, the Kellogg-Briand Pact was an outright condemnation of war that specified that states "shall" only use peaceful means to settle their disputes. Unfortunately, Kellogg-Briand also had little practical effect in a world slouching toward another catastrophic conflict. As Slomanson noted, "The Pact contained unassailable principles but it lacked any effective enforcement provisions to stop the outbreak of another world war" (2003, 487). Despite the fact that the League of Nations and the Kellogg-Briand Pact did not prevent World War II, they represented, along with the earlier Hague Conventions, serious legal efforts on the part of the international political community to restrict and even outlaw war.

These efforts were part of the body of "solemn international pronouncements" that Glueck (1946, 26–27) drew on as evidence of the custom and the conviction that aggressive war had been "branded and treated as criminal." Glueck's argument here, in the words of Jackson (1946, xi), is simply "declaratory of existent law." Glueck rejected as "specious" the claim that "in the absence of a specific, detailed, pre-existing code of international penal law to which all States have previously subscribed, prosecution for the international crime of aggressive war is necessarily ex post facto" (38). He concluded by pointing out that: "Every custom and every recognition of custom as evidence of law must have a beginning some time; and there has never been a more justifiable stage in the history of international law than the present, to recognize that by the common consent of nations as expressed in numerous solemn agreements and public pronouncements the instituting or waging of an aggressive war is an international crime" (1946, 45).

The creation of the International Military Tribunal at Nuremberg to hold personally liable senior Nazi officials accused of crimes against peace, crimes against humanity, and war crimes was a transformative moment for international law. Whatever one thought of Glueck's argument that aggressive war was a crime under customary international law prior to World War II, after Nuremberg there could be no doubt. As Jackson pithily noted, "Whatever the state of the law has been, such conduct is a crime now" (1946, x). The constituting treaty for the trials, the charter for the Nuremberg Military Tribunal was agreed to on August 8, 1945, by the victorious Allied powers. The principles contained in the charter were later approved by the UN General Assembly (Resolution 95–1), which explicitly incorporated them into international law. One of these principles is that a state that wages a war of aggression commits the "supreme international crime." As Louis Henkin concluded, "At Nuremberg, sitting in judgment on the recent past, the Allied victors declared waging aggressive war to be a state crime (under both treaty and customary law) as well as an individual crime by those who represented and acted for the aggressor state" (1995, 111).

The Charter of the United Nations and the Use of Military Force

In addition to the Nuremberg Charter, we also drew on another significant development in international law in our effort to analyze whether the invasion and occupation of Iraq was illegal and criminal: The Charter of the United Nations. The UN Charter, the current legal framework governing the use of military force in international affairs, grew out of the ambitious and sustained effort by the Allied victors and other members of the world community after World War II to minimize the likelihood of future armed conflict. The starting point was the Atlantic Charter signed in August 1941 by American President Franklin Delano Roosevelt and British Prime Minister

Winston Churchill. Philippe Sands (2005, 9) points out that the key principles of the Atlantic Charter, an end to territorial aggrandizement or territorial changes, respect for self-government, social security, peace, freedom from fear or want, high seas freedoms, and restraints on the use of force would serve "as the guidelines for a new world order and were later enshrined in the United Nations Charter."

The principles of the Atlantic Charter captured the public imagination and eventually led to the creation of the United Nations and the signing of the UN Charter in 1945 as the war drew to a close. The Charter of the United Nations is the fundamental document, the bedrock, of the contemporary international legal system. It is the highest treaty in the world, the embodiment of international law that codifies and supersedes all existing international laws and customs. The charter's legal authority rests with its status as a treaty to which most nations of the world have agreed to abide. Violations of a treaty are violations of law no less than are violations of domestic law. In the United States, most legal scholars take a monist position and argue that no legal bright line separates international law from domestic law, despite assertions to the contrary by the dualist position adopted by some members of the Bush administration, as well as Supreme Court Justice Anton Scalia. Once the U.S. Senate has ratified a treaty, it becomes the "supreme law of the land" under Article 6, Clause 2, of the U.S. Constitution. Whether or not treaties are "self-executing"—that is, whether a "treaty may be enforced in the courts without prior legislation"—has been a source of jurisprudential controversy in the United States since the passage of the constitution (Vasquez 1995). However, the fact that the U.S. government agreed when it entered into the UN Charter that its core principles are nonderogable (i.e., they cannot be rescinded) argues forcefully that a violation of the charter is also a violation of domestic law in the United States.

At the heart of the UN Charter is the prohibition against war. The preamble sets out the context for and the spirit of the charter. It begins: "We, the Peoples of the United Nations determined to save succeeding generations from the scourge of war which twice in our lifetime has brought untold sorrow to mankind." The purposes and principles of the charter are spelled out in the first paragraph of Article 1. The fundamental purpose of the United Nations is "to maintain international peace and security. And to that end to take effective, collective measures for the prevention and removal of threats to the peace, and for the suppression of acts of aggression, and other breaches of the peace and to bring about by peaceful means and in conformity with the principles of justice and international law the adjustment and settlement of international disputes."

The specific prohibition against aggressive war is found in Article 2, Section 4, of the charter, which requires that "all members shall refrain in their international relations from the threat or use of force against the territorial integrity or political independence of any state, or [behave] in any other inconsistent with the purposes of the United Nations." We will come back to this critical provision shortly, but here it is important to stress that the ban on war is the crucial thread that runs throughout the purpose and structure of the United Nations. As C. G. Weeramantry, a former judge of the International Court of Justice, points out, "by its very structure, by its express provisions and by its underlying intent the UN Charter completely outlaws unilateral resort to armed force" (2003, 22). As with Nuremberg, Michael Byers argues that "the introduction of legal limits on the use of force through the UN Charter was a transformative moment in international affairs, and it was entirely consensual" (2005, 2).

While the UN and Nuremberg Charters outlawed the recourse to war, the four Geneva Conventions of 1949 advanced international law concerning how wars are to be fought. The Geneva Conventions are an important part of International Humanitarian Law (IHL). This body of international law requires parties to an armed conflict to protect civilians and noncombatants, limits the means or methods that are permissible during warfare, and sets out the rules that govern the behavior of occupying forces. Violations of IHL are war crimes.

Thus, in a relatively short period of time, under the leadership of the United States, a new world order was fashioned by the establishment of the United Nations, the passage of the UN Charter, the adoption of the Nuremburg Charter, and the creation of the Geneva Conventions. After 1945 a new international legal framework for judging aggression and war crimes was born. It was this legal framework that we applied to the 2003 invasion and occupation of Iraq to classify it as illegal and criminal. The major points of that analysis still hold. The following section provides a brief overview of the case we made.

The Invasion of Iraq as Illegal and Criminal

As noted earlier, the UN Charter is the fundamental law of international relations, superseding all existing laws and customs. The heart of the charter is the prohibition of aggressive war found in Article 2(4). Article 2(4) is a peremptory norm having the character of supreme law that cannot be modified by treaty or by ordinary customary law. Insofar as the United States and its allies invaded a sovereign nation without provocation or legal authorization from the international community, the invasion of Iraq was a prima facie violation of Article 2(4). It was illegal and criminal. A large number of legal scholars concur in this opinion (Boyle 2004; Brecher, Cutler, and Smith 2005; Dyer 2004; Falk, Gendzier, and Lifton 2006; Farebrother and Kollerstrom 2004; Mandel 2004; McGoldrick 2004; Sands 2005; Weeramantry 2003).

However, U.S. and British officials argued that this judgment was rendered null by the charter's exceptions to Article 2(4), and by the emerging concept of humanitarian intervention. In our original analysis we carefully considered these exceptions and demonstrated why they should be rejected.

Article 51 of the UN Charter recognizes that states have an "inherent right" to use force in self-defense in the face of an armed attack. Iraq, however, had not attacked the United States, nor was there ever any claim that such an attack was imminent. Thus, Article 51 would appear to not apply. The Bush administration, however, sought to retain Article 51 justification by linking Iraq to the Al Qaeda attacks of September 11, 2001.

However, as we will detail below, not only were the claims of Iraq's links to Al Qaeda questionable, the evidence indicates that the Bush administration knew there were no data to support them (Clark 2004). In late 2003, both President Bush and former Secretary of State Colin Powell publicly conceded that there was no evidence linking Saddam Hussein to 9/11 or other terrorist attacks against the United States.

Even as the 9/11 and Al Qaeda links were being debunked, the Bush administration also claimed that the United States had a legal right to attack any nation it perceived as a *potential* threat to U.S. interests (the Bush Doctrine). Based on this claim, administration officials repeatedly argued that the United States could legally attack Iraq because Hussein's government possessed weapons of mass destruction (WMD) that might eventually be used against the United States, either directly or through terrorist networks. But the claim of the Bush Doctrine, that the United States possessed the legal right to initiate preventive war, was an attempt to unilaterally rewrite international law. International law does provide some latitude for preemptive strikes in the face of an imminent threat. It does not, however, authorize the kind of preventive warfare the Bush administration claimed for the invasion of Iraq. The reason for this is clear. History is dense with wars initiated by governments that claimed an absolute need to invade enemy territory to prevent some claimed future threat. As international law, the Bush Doctrine would provide easy legal cover for any nation with aggressive intentions.

Although it had no status in international law, the administration's claim to a right of preventive war focused much of the prewar debate around the question of whether or not Iraq possessed WMD—which we know it did not. What was lost in this debate, however, was the fact that in the absence of a clearly defined, imminent threat from Iraq, invading that country did not meet the test of legality under international law. That is, even if Hussein had possessed some WMD, absent explicit authorization from the UN Security Council, the invasion would still have been a violation of international law. This brings us to the second exception.

The second exception to the Article 2(4) prohibition against war is found in Chapter 7 of the UN Charter. Article 41 authorizes the UN Security Council to implement various measures short of war to respond to a threat to or breach of international peace and security as determined by Article 39. If the nonmilitary measures allowed under Article 41 are judged to have failed, then, and only then, can the Security Council authorize the use of force to restore or maintain international peace and security under the auspices of Article 42. There was no such authorization for the use of force against Iraq in March of 2003. In early 2003 the United States, along with the United Kingdom and Spain, sought Security Council support for a draft resolution that would have declared Iraq to be in violation of an earlier disarmament resolution (Resolution 1441), and that this noncompliance posed a threat to international peace and security. Although the draft resolution did not explicitly authorize war, it was clear to Security Council members that the drafters intended to use it as a warrant to invade Iraq. Faced with strong resistance from Security Council members France, Russia, and Germany, the pro-invasion forces withdrew their resolution. As UN weapons inspector Hans Blix concluded, "By withholding an authorization desired if not formally requested, the Council dissociated the U.N. from an armed action that most member states thought was not justified" (2004, 218).

Lacking Security Council authorization, American and British officials argued that previous Security Council resolutions, dating back to the Gulf War of 1991, already provided sufficient legal justification for the invasion of Iraq. Indeed, this is the only argument that Lord Goldsmith, the UK attorney general, utilized in his March 17, 2003, presentation to Parliament seeking support for the invasion of Iraq (Sands 2005). At the start of the invasion, the U.S. ambassador to the United Nations, John Negroponte, made similar claims to the Security Council, as did legal advisors for the State Department (Taft and Buchwald 2003). These claims, however, in the words of international legal experts, have proven to be little more than selective, misleading, creative, problematic, and ultimately unsustainable interpretations of the resolutions in question. Simply put, if the members of the UN Security Council had believed that an invasion of Iraq was legally justified, they would have endorsed the draft resolution authorizing military action instead of forcing its withdrawal in early 2003.

The third possible exception to Article 2(4) can be found in what Roger Normand calls "the legally dubious doctrine of humanitarian intervention" (2003, 8). The United States and the United Kingdom argued that they had a right and a duty to use military force for the humanitarian purpose of saving Iraqis from human rights violations by the Hussein government. In pre-war arguments for invading Iraq, however, Bush and Blair rarely discussed liberation of the Iraqi people, and when they did it was most often a distant third to the threat of WMD and Iraq's ties to terrorism. It was only in the aftermath of the invasion, once the WMD argument proved to be hollow, that humanitarian concerns were reframed as the primary justification for the invasion of Iraq.

Even if the Bush and Blair administrations were motivated primarily by humanitarian concerns, which, as we show below, they were not, the legality of humanitarian invasions remains in question. Many international lawyers question their legality because unilateral humanitarian invasions circumvent established procedures and principles within the UN Charter and international law for addressing humanitarian crises (Byers 2005). Beyond the question of legality, there is also little evidence that Hussein's government was engaged in large-scale political atrocities at the time of the invasion. The worst offenses of Hussein's Baathist regime occurred in the 1980s and early 1990s, when he was supported by the Reagan and first Bush administrations (Chomsky 2003). Human Rights Watch concluded that at the time of the U.S./British invasion, political killings in Iraq were "not of the exceptional nature that would justify such intervention," nor was invasion "the last reasonable option to stop Iraqi atrocities" (Roth 2004, 9).

In conclusion, none of the exceptions apply, and we must judge that the invasion of Iraq violated Article 2(4) and was therefore illegal. According to the Nuremberg Charter, an illegal war of aggression is an international crime, the supreme international crime. Thus, the invasion of Iraq was illegal and criminal, a state crime. The state officials responsible for the decision to prosecute a criminal war are, under international law, war criminals. The following sections will revisit the criminological analysis we offered of the historical and contemporary origins of this decision.

Explaining a Criminal War: Empire and Exceptionalism

In our original analysis we examined the ways in which the U.S. invasion of Iraq was not a single, isolated act of international criminality, but rather a logical expression of a nexus of forces involving the long- and short-term interests of corporate capital on the one hand, and the imperial designs of the U.S. government under the administration of George W. Bush on the other (Kramer and Michalowski 2005, 2006a). Our primary goal was to provide a critical narrative of the historical and contemporary forces that came together in the days after the Al Qaeda attacks against the United States on September 11, 2001. In developing this critical analysis of the Iraq war, we drew on the integrated model for the study of organizational deviance we had created with David Kauzlarich (Kauzlarich and Kramer 1998; Michalowski and Kramer 2006), and that is utilized in the Kramer and Kauzlarich chapter in this volume.

In our criminological analysis of the invasion and occupation of Iraq we proceeded in two steps. First, we examined the historical context within which U.S. open-door imperialism has served as a breeding ground for repeated wars of aggression since the end of the nineteenth century. Second, we analyzed the relationship between this history and the specific Bush-era neoconservative reliance on unilateralist and militarist strategies to promote longstanding U.S. interests in making the world safe for international capitalism under the aegis of an American hegemon. In retrospect, we believe that the analysis holds up well and that much of it has been confirmed by the emergence of additional data concerning the decision to invade Iraq. However, we also think that the analysis can be sharpened by the introduction of some different conceptual language concerning American exceptionalism and the addition of some new factual details.

Upon further reflection we believe that it is helpful to sort the Bush administration's goals concerning the invasion and occupation of Iraq into three major categories. First, as we noted earlier, there were the publicly proclaimed war goals of eliminating Iraq's alleged weapons of mass destruction, fighting terrorist groups such as Al Qaeda, and avenging the September 11 attacks of 2001. These presumed threats were creatively linked to the negative emotions of anger, fear, and vengeful nationalism that arose in the wake of the 9/11 attacks. Recent analyses have demonstrated that Bush administration officials and allied political pundits then used this concocted stew of events, emotions, and trumped-up threats to frame Saddam Hussein and his Baathist Party as new "folk devils" in the hopes of stirring a moral panic that would ensure support for the invasion of Iraq (Rothe and Muzzatti 2004).

When no weapons of mass destruction were found in Iraq, and Saddam Hussein's alleged connections to Al Qaeda and the 9/11 attacks were eventually discounted, the Bush administration turned to a second category of motives that we, following Fiala (2008), call mythic ideals. The mythic ideals of political leaders in the United States are usually drawn from a broad, historical, cultural narrative often referred to as American exceptionalism (Fiala 2008; Hodgson 2009; Koh 2003). American exceptionalism generally portrays the United States as a nation of exceptional virtue, a moral leader in the world with a unique historical mission to spread universal values such as freedom, democracy, equality, popular sovereignty, and increasingly global capitalism. This mythic cultural construction of exceptionalism "thoroughly informs US constructs of its identity" (Ryan 2007, 119). The myth of American exceptionalism often takes the form of missionary zeal that reaches back to John Winthrop's 1630 sermon to the Puritans before they disembarked to found the new Massachusetts Bay Colony: "[The colony] shall be as a city upon a hill. The eyes of all people are upon us so that if we shall deal falsely with our God in this work we have undertaken . . . we shall shame the faces of many of God's worthy servants, and cause their prayers to be turned into curses upon us" (Collins 1999, 64). Winthrop's image of this new society as a city on a hill bearing a special burden to outshine other nations has been quoted repeatedly by U.S. presidents to promote claims that the United States has a "God-given destiny" to "spread the benefits of its democratic system and of its specific version of capitalism to as many other countries as possible" (Hodgson 2009, 159).

The historical narrative of American exceptionalism, particularly after World War II, has lead to the normalization of military force and warfare as legitimate and acceptable means to advance the mythic ideals and geopolitical interests of the United States (see Kramer and Kauzlarich, this volume). Thus, starting before the Iraq war, but increasingly after no WMDs were found, Bush administration officials fell back on the cultural mandates embedded in the narrative of American exceptionalism to explain and justify the invasion and occupation. The goals of the war, we were told repeatedly, were to bring freedom and democracy, not only to Iraq but also to the Middle East as a whole and thus "change the political culture of the region" (Dorrien 2004, 182).

While conflict goals and mythic ideals were publicly proclaimed by the Bush administration as justifications for war, many critics pointed to a third category of goals as the "real" motives behind the invasion of Iraq: Imperial designs. According to many analysts, including us, this was a war for empire (Bacevich 2008; Bello 2005; Callinicos 2003; Chomsky 2003; Dorrien 2004; Englehardt 2006; Everrest 2004; Hartnett and Stengrim 2006; Harvey 2003; Juhasz 2006; Klein 2007; Ryan 2007; Schwartz 2008). These analysts argue that economic interests, geopolitical concerns, military power projection, and imperial domination were the primary motives for invading Iraq. Although Bush administration officials have repeatedly denied imperial ambitions, the extensive data and documentation offered by the works cited here offer a convincing case that the Bush administration sought a position from which it could control Iraqi oil, reconstruct Iraq's economy to create a model free-market economic system, establish permanent military bases in the heart of the Middle East, consolidate American power in the region, and communicate a message about the futility of opposing the world's "lone superpower" in the post–cold war, "unipolar" world. Whatever their denials, whatever their understanding of imperialism, these expressed goals of imposing a U.S. version of order and politics on the Middle East are clearly imperial in nature.

As we noted above, the available evidence strongly suggests that the first category of goals were not the operative goals of the Bush administration in going to war with Iraq. Saddam Hussein did not have WMDs, and there was solid evidence of that prior to the invasion (Pitt 2002; Ritter 2003). A UN weapons inspection team (UNMOVIC) and the International Atomic Energy Agency were in Iraq actively searching for WMDs in early 2003 and making regular reports that they were finding none (Blix 2004). There was never any evidence whatsoever that Iraq was involved in the 9/11 attacks or that Saddam Hussein had a working relationship with Al Qaeda, and President Bush was told that directly by his National Coordinator for Security, Infrastructure Protection and Counterterrorism (Clark 2004). As the British government pointed out in the famous "Downing Street Memo" in the summer of 2002, the Bush administration had made the decision to invade Iraq, and the facts were now being "fixed around the policy" (Danner 2006). There is a considerable amount of evidence that the intelligence concerning WMDs in Iraq was being manipulated, distorted, and in some cases fabricated to support the case for war (Bamford 2005; Corn 2003; Dickinson and Stein 2006; Isikoff and Corn 2006; Pillar 2006; Prados 2004; Ricks 2006; Risen 2006; Scheer, Scheer, and Chaudry 2003; Suskind 2006). The cynical manipulation of intelligence and the alarmist public statements from administration officials about "mushroom clouds" were part of a "marketing" campaign, a public relations effort to "sell" the war to Congress and the American people (Rich 2006). As Suskind notes, "evidence, loosely defined, was summoned at the convenience of action" (2006, 177). Some legal scholars have even argued that this deceptive marketing campaign to take the country to war could provide the basis for criminal charges of "Conspiracy to Defraud the United States" (de la Vega 2006) or for "the prosecution of George W. Bush for murder" (Bugliosi 2008).

If eradicating WMDs, fighting terrorists, and avenging 9/11 were not the operative goals of the invasion of Iraq, what were the Bush administration's motives in this case? In our revised analysis, presented below, we argue that imperial motives interpreted through and justified by the mythic ideals at the core of American exceptionalism have historically motivated U.S. wars of aggression, and in the context of a number of specific contemporary events, also shaped the decision to invade and occupy Iraq.

Empire and Exceptionalism in American History

The U.S. decision to invade Iraq was the product of a presidential administration embedded in a history and ideology of U.S. imperial designs that found itself faced with opportunities and constraints created by the end of the cold war, the attacks of September 11, 2001, and a bizarre electoral outcome in November 2000. These forces intersected in ways that allowed the new administration to deploy a messianic vision of a "New American Century," crafted within the mythic idealism of American exceptionalism (Fiala 2008; Gray 2007; Hodgson 2009; Lieven and Hulsman 2006; Traub 2008), in which U.S. style free-market capitalism and electoral democracy would rule the world, with the United States as the imperial power overseeing the ongoing maintenance of this world order. It was this mythic vision, combined with specific economic and geopolitical interests, and given powerful impetus by the 9/11 attacks that served as the trigger for the commission of state crimes against the people of Iraq.

First, it is important to point out that America has been an imperial project from its earliest years (Anderson and Cayton 2005; Ferguson 2004; Iadicola 2008a, 2008b; Nugent 2008; Ryan 2007; Wright 2008), and that it has been imbued with a cultural narrative of exceptionalism from the beginning as well (Hodgson 2009; Ryan 2007). Throughout the late eighteenth and nineteenth centuries U.S. leaders sought to expand America's economic horizons through both acute and chronic applications of force, including enslavement of Africans, expropriation of native lands in the name of manifest destiny, the invasion of North African states to protect U.S. trade interests in that region, claiming North and South America as an exclusive American sphere of economic and political influence (the Monroe Doctrine), expansionist war with Mexico, and using American warships to ensure Asian trading partners (Anderson and Cayton 2005; Beard and Beard 1930; Kolko 1984; Nugent 2008; Williams 1969, 1988).

As the nineteenth century drew to a close, structural contradictions in American capitalism provoked an intensification of America's imperial reach. With the frontier expansion stalled at the Pacific Ocean and the economic infrastructure fully capitalized, surplus productive capacity in the United States began to generate significant pressures for new markets and cheaper sources of material and labor (Sklar 1988). In 1898 increased pressures for new economic frontiers motivated an imperialist war against Spain. Although it was publicly justified as bringing freedom to Spain's remaining colonies, instead of liberation the people of the Philippines and Puerto Rico were annexed and colonized by the United States, while those in Cuba were subject to a virtual colonization that did not end until the Cuban revolution of 1959 (Thomas 1971). In a foreshadowing of future American imperialism, the acquisition of these territories was not construed as expansionism; rather, it was seen through the lens of the mythic idealism of American exceptionalism as a moral duty to uplift and civilize other races by spreading the American system of business and government, what Ferguson calls "the paradox of dictating democracy, of enforcing freedom, of exporting emancipation" (2004, 54).

The United States would soon abandon its brief experiment with formal colonization as too economically and politically costly. Moreover, America's political and ideological roots were more purely commercial than European mercantile nations whose feudal history was rooted in the control of land. As a result, U.S. leaders were quicker to recognize that in the emerging commercial era "what mattered was not ownership or even administrative control but commercial access" (Bacevich 2002, 25).

Hints of this change are found in the 1899 Open Door Notes of Secretary of State John Hay. Hay promoted what Williams (1988) termed "open door" imperialism based on diplomacy among the major capitalist powers to keep foreign markets open to trade, rather than dividing the world into the closed trading blocs typical of European mercantile capitalism. Although it was based on considerable military might (by 1905 the U.S. Navy was second only to that of Great Britain), the strategy of controlling without owning became the basic design of American foreign policy in the twentieth century (Williams 1988).

Despite this early imperial history, the United States has always been, in Ferguson's (2004) apt phrase, "an empire in denial." The political and rhetorical genius of American imperialism has been to index the broader concept of freedom to freedom in the marketplace. Thus, any society that lacks an open capitalist economy that can facilitate U.S. investment, exploitation, and repatriation of profits is, by definition, unfree and therefore in need being liberated by the United States. Through this mythic ideal of American exceptionalism, two centuries of American leaders have established a political habit of heart and mind that comprehends any war or invasion as just and a noble sacrifice rather than self-interest (Fiala 2008; Hodgson 2009; Traub 2008). By limiting the conception of imperialism to the direct colonization of physical territory, the narratives of innocence and exceptionalism can be sustained (Ryan 2007). For more than a century, the open door ideology has enabled Americans to avoid recognizing that market imperialism is imperialism nonetheless, and that in the contemporary world, where favorable access to markets and labor, rather than the sovereign control of territory, is the essence of domination, it is the modal form of imperialism.

As it rose to ever greater power after World War I and then World War II, the United States clung to its self-image as a reluctant superpower, a master narrative within American exceptionalism that claims that the United States involves itself in world affairs only under duress, and then always for selfless reasons (Bacevich 2002). President Woodrow Wilson's famous claim that the United States must enter World War I "to make the world safe for democracy" exemplifies this narrative theme in action. The need to ensure the United States could play a significant role in creating a new political and economic order out of the collapse of the Ottoman and Austro-Hungarian empires was interpreted through mythic idealism as selflessness rather than self-interest (Johnson 2004, 48). Such idealism would continue to inform American foreign policy for the rest of the twentieth century and on into the next.

While isolationist sentiments would stymie Wilson's vision for a new world order, the coming of World War II helped to lift the United States out of economic depression and establish it as both the world's dominant military power and the economic hegemon in charge of the key institutions of global capitalism such as the International Monetary Fund (IMF), the World Bank, and the General Agreement on Trade and Tariffs (Derber 2002; Friedrichs 2007a, 2007b). Moreover, as Kramer and Kauzlarich point out in this volume, World War II, the "Good War," reinforced the mythic idealism at the heart of American exceptionalism and helped to reinforce the normalization of the use of state violence. Wood has argued that one of the myths of World War II is the idea that "when evil lies in others, war is the means to justice" (2006, 143). Thus, the fight against evil, such as that represented by Saddam Hussein, and the advancement of America's exceptional ideals, such as the spread of democracy and freedom to the Middle East, justifies any of the means, including invasion and military occupation, we select to accomplish our national goals.

There were two challenges to the U.S. imperial project in the post–World War II era: the threat of independent nationalism and the Soviet Union. Nations on the periphery and semiperiphery of the world system, many of them former colonies of the world's wealthy capitalist nations, were limited to service roles in the global capitalist economy, providing resources, cheap labor, and retail markets for consumer products and finance capital (Frank 1969; Wallerstein 1989). U.S. planners were concerned that "radical and nationalistic regimes" more responsive to popular pressures for immediate improvement in the living standards of the masses than to advancing the interests of foreign capital could become a virus infecting other countries and threatening the "overall framework of order" that Washington had constructed (Chomsky 2003). Another key concern for the United States in the postwar period was access to Middle Eastern oil that necessitated efforts to ensure stability in the region by defusing Arab nationalism and countering Soviet moves, primarily through covert actions and military surrogates (Bacevich 2005; Klare 2004).

Although never as powerful as American leaders made it out to be, the Soviet Union nonetheless, with its rival ideology, its own imperialistic goals, and its atomic weapons, to some extent impeded the U.S. drive to achieve global, imperial domination after World War II. However, neither the United States nor the Soviet Union seriously challenged the overall framework of power sharing established at Yalta near the end of World War II. Instead, the two superpowers pursued their global interests through client states in the less-developed world, with the Soviet Union frequently courting the favor of independent nationalist movements, and the United States working with local elites to limit the expansion of such movements. In this struggle, the Soviet Union and the United States also were able to periodically stalemate one another's interests by exercising their veto powers in the United Nations Security Council.

While it represented constraints, the cold war provided an opportunity for growth-oriented government and corporate leaders in the United States to justify expanding military budgets, establish a "permanent war economy," and strengthen the military-industrial complex (Elliot 1955). America's post–World War II imperial project began with a far-flung empire of military bases justified as necessary tools in the fight against communism, thereby linking America's imperial project to the mythic ideal of liberation rather than one of geopolitical expansion (Johnson 2004). Or in Ferguson's words, "For an empire in denial, there is really only one way to act imperially with a clear conscience, and that is to combat someone else's imperialism" (2004, 78). Thus, the cold war provided an opportunity for the United States to continue to define its imperial project within the cultural framework of American exceptionalism and the mythic ideals of freedom and democracy.

Neoconservative Ideology, the Unipolar Moment and 9/11

The fall of the Berlin Wall in 1989 and the collapse of the Soviet Union in 1991 brought the cold war to an end, presenting the United States with a new set of opportunities and challenges. With the Soviet Union out of the way and American military supremacy unrivaled, the unipolar moment had arrived (Krauthammer 1989, 1991). The goals of open door imperialism never seemed more realizable. According to one group of state officials and their ideological supporters (the unipolarists), American military power, already normalized as a primary tool at Washington's disposal to achieve global hegemony, could now be used with relative impunity, whether it was punishing small neighbors such as Panama and Grenada for their failure to fall in line with U.S. interests or using Iraq's 1990 incursion into Kuwait to establish a more overt and permanent U.S. military presence in the oil-rich Persian Gulf region (Bacevich 2005; Klare 2004).

While the end of the cold war produced demands for a "peace dividend," economic and political elites linked to the military-industrial-petroleum complex did not acquiesce to the reduction in their power that would have resulted from such a realignment of American goals. Instead, they were soon searching for new "enemies," and with them new justifications for continued imperial expansion. A sharp struggle soon emerged between rival factions over how to capitalize on the opportunities offered by the fall of the Soviet Union while deflecting threats presented by the possibility of a new isolationism. One group supported a globalist and internationalist approach typical of the administrations of George H. W. Bush and Bill Clinton. The other, which included hard-core nationalists and neoconservatives, argued for a more nationalist, unilateralist, and militarist revision of America's open door imperialism. It was this latter group that would, surprisingly, find itself in a position to shape America's imperial project for the twenty-first century.

The term "neoconservative" was first used in the early 1970s to describe a group of political figures and intellectuals who had been associated with the Henry "Scoop" Jackson wing of the Democratic Party, but in reaction to the cultural liberalism and anti–Vietnam War stance associated with the McGovern wing of the party, moved to the right, eventually joining the Republican Party (Dorrien 2004). A number of neoconservatives joined the Reagan administration, often providing intellectual justification for that administration's policies of military growth and rollback of, rather than coexistence with, the Soviet Union (Chernus 2006). As the Soviet Union began to weaken, neocons in the administration of George H. W. Bush began forcefully promoting an aggressive post-Soviet neo-imperialism. Their first concern, shared by many within the military-industrial complex, was to stave off cuts in the military budget in response to the weakened Soviet threat and popular expectations for a peace dividend.

In 1992 aides to Secretary of Defense Dick Cheney, supervised by neocons Paul Wolfowitz and I. Lewis (Scooter) Libby, prepared a draft document titled "Defense Planning Guidance" (DPG), a classified, internal Pentagon policy statement used to guide military officials in the planning process. The draft provides a first look at the emerging neoconservative imperialist agenda. As Armstrong notes, the DPG "depicted a world dominated by the United States, which would maintain its superpower status through a combination of positive guidance and overwhelming military might. The image was one of a heavily armed City on a Hill" (2002, 78). Here again we can see the historical and dialectical relationship between the mythic idealism of American exceptionalism and a hard-core nationalistic realism that concentrates on the economic and geopolitical interests of the United States.

The DPG stated that the first objective of U.S. defense policy should be to prevent the reemergence of a new rival. It also endorsed the use of preemptive (preventive) military force to achieve its goal. The document called for the United States to maintain a substantial arsenal of nuclear weapons and to develop a missile defense shield. The DPG was a clear statement of the neoconservative vision of unilateral use of military supremacy to defend U.S. interests anywhere in the world, including protecting U.S. access to vital raw materials such as Persian Gulf oil (Armstrong 2002; Bacevich 2005; Halper and Clarke 2004; Klare 2004; Mahajan 2003; Mann 2004). The aggressive tone of the DPG generated a firestorm of criticism when a draft was leaked to the press. President Bush and Secretary Cheney quickly distanced themselves from the DPG and ordered a less obviously imperialist version prepared.

The surprisingly rapid collapse of the Soviet Union ultimately revealed that the neocons had been wrong on almost every issue concerning the Soviet threat. As a consequence, neoconservatism lost much of its legitimacy as a mainstream political ideology, and these early neocons would eventually find themselves in political exile as part of a far-right wing of the Republican Party. Then, the election of President Bill Clinton removed the neocons from positions within the U.S. government, but not from policy debates. From the sidelines they generated a steady stream of books, articles, reports, and op-ed pieces in an effort to influence the direction of U.S. foreign policy. Throughout the Clinton years, the neocons continued to warn about new threats to American security, repeatedly calling for greater use of U.S. military power to address them (Bacevich 2005; Chernus 2006; Mann 2004). One persistent theme in their writings was the need to eliminate Saddam Hussein's government from Iraq, consolidate American power in the Middle East,and change the political culture of the region (Dorrien 2004). Once again, American exceptionalism was key. As Hodgson observed, "By the 1990s the background to the growing obsession with Iraq among neoconservatives was exceptionalist sentiment. Neither Saddam Hussein nor any other foreign leader must stand against the high historic mission of the United States to bring democracy to the Middle East" (2009, 171).

In many ways, the Clinton administration foreign policy was consistent with that of the previous administration. Clinton shared the elder Bush's views of America as a global leader that should use its economic and military power to ensure openness and integration in the world economic system (Bacevich 2002). In this sense, Clinton-era foreign policy remained consistent with the open door system of informal imperialism practiced by the United States since the beginning of the twentieth century, stressing global economic integration through free trade and democracy (Dorrien 2004).

Neoconservatives subjected the Clinton administration to a barrage of foreign-policy criticism, particularly with respect to Clinton's handling of the Middle East and Iraq. In early 1998, the Project for the New American Century (PNAC), a key neoconservative think-tank, released an open letter to President Clinton urging him to forcefully remove Hussein from power (Halper and Clarke 2004; Mann 2004). In September of 2000, PNAC issued a report entitled *Rebuilding America's Defenses: Strategy, Forces and Resources for a New Century*. This report resurrected core ideas in the controversial DPG, calling for massive increases in military spending, the expansion of U.S. military bases, and the establishment of client states supportive of American economic and political interests. The imperial goals of the neocons were clear. What they lacked was the opportunity to implement these goals. Two unanticipated events gave them the opportunity to do so.

In December 2000, after a botched election put the question in their lap, the Supreme Court of the United States awarded the U.S. presidency to George W. Bush, despite his having lost the popular vote by over one-half million ballots. This odd political turnabout would soon restore the neocons to power, with more than twenty neoconservatives and hard-line nationalists being awarded high-ranking positions in the new administration (Dorrien 2004). In a classic demonstration of the creation of shared understandings through differential association, the Pentagon and the vice president's office became unipolarist strongholds reflecting the long-standing working relationship between neoconservatives and hard-core nationalists like Vice President Dick Cheney and the new secretary of defense, Donald Rumsfeld (Mann 2004).

Even though a stroke of good luck had placed them near the center of power, unipolarists found that the new president remained more persuaded by pragmatic realists in his administration, such as Secretary of State Colin Powell, than by their aggressive foreign policy agenda (Dorrien 2004). This was to be expected. The PNAC (2000) report, *Rebuilding America's Defenses*, had predicted that "the process of transformation is likely to be a long one, absent some catastrophic or catalyzing event—like a new Pearl Harbor." The unipolarists needed another stroke of good luck.

The 9/11 attacks presented the neocons and the hard-core nationalists with the catalyzing event they needed to transform their agenda in to actual policy. The terror attacks were a "political godsend" that created a climate of fear and anxiety, which the unipolarists mobilized to promote their geopolitical strategy and mythic ideals to a president who lacked a coherent foreign policy, as well as to the nation as a whole (Chernus 2006; Hartung 2004). As former Treasury Secretary Paul O'Neill revealed, the goal of the unipolarists in the Bush administration had always been to attack Iraq and oust Saddam Hussein (Suskind 2004). Again, they believed this would allow the United States to consolidate its imperial power in the strategically significant Middle East and, consistent with American exceptionalism, change the political culture of the region and spread freedom and democracy (Dorrien 2004; Hodgson 2009).

On the evening of September 11, 2001, and in the days following, unipolarists in the Bush administration advocated attacking Iraq immediately, even though there was no evidence linking Iraq to the events of the day (Clark 2004; Woodward 2004). After an internal struggle between the pragmatic realists, led by Secretary of State Powell, and the unipolarists, led by Vice President Cheney and Secretary of Defense Rumsfeld, the decision was eventually made to launch a general war on terrorism and to begin it by attacking Al Qaeda's home base in Afghanistan and removing that country's Taliban government (Mann 2004; Risen 2006; Suskind 2006). The unipolarists were only temporarily delayed insofar as they had achieved agreement that as soon as the Afghanistan war was under way, the United States would begin planning an invasion of Iraq (Clark 2004; Fallows 2004). By November, barely one month after the invasion of Afghanistan, Bush and Rumsfeld ordered the

Department of Defense to formulate a war plan for Iraq (Woodward 2004). Throughout 2002, as plans for the war on Iraq were being formulated, the Bush administration made a number of formal pronouncements that demonstrated that the goals of the unipolarists were now the official goals of the U.S. government. In the January 29 State of the Union address, Bush honed the focus of the war on terrorism by associating terrorism with specific rogue states such as Iran, Iraq, and North Korea (the "axis of evil") who were presented as legitimate targets for military action (Callinicos 2003). In a speech to the graduating cadets at West Point on June 1, the president unveiled a doctrine of preventive war, a policy that many judged as "the most open statement yet made of imperial globalization" (Falk 2004b, 189), soon to be followed by the new National Security Strategy. This document not only claimed the right to wage preventive war, as previously discussed, it also claimed, again in the spirit of American exceptionalism, that the United States would use its military power to spread democracy and American-style laissez-faire capitalism around the world as the "single sustainable model for national success" (Callinicos 2003, 29). As Roy noted, "Democracy has become Empire's euphemism for neo-liberal capitalism" (2004, 56).

As noted earlier, in the marketing campaign to build public support for the invasion of Iraq, the Bush administration skillfully exploited the political opportunities provided by the fear and anger over the 9/11 attacks. By linking Saddam Hussein and Iraq to the wider war on terrorism, the government was able to establish the idea that security required the ability to attack any nation believed to be supporting terror, no mater how weak the evidence. This strategy cynically obscured the more specific geopolitical and economic motives for going to war. Concerning these motives, Schwartz notes that

> the control of oil was a prime goal of the invasion, and this control could only be assured if three intermediate outcomes were achieved: a thoroughgoing revision of the way Iraq managed its economy (so that oil could be quickly and efficiently extracted), willing participation by the Iraqi people in this transformation (no matter how much it disrupted or degraded their lives), and an ongoing, dominant military presence (to protect against domestic and foreign resistance to these and other changes that Washington hoped to implement). At the same time, control of Iraq and its oil was itself an intermediate goal in a more comprehensive foreign policy: the establishment of the United States as the preeminent power in the Middle East. (2008, 5)

The final factor to consider in understanding the Bush administration's war on Iraq is the fusion of a neoconservative imperial agenda with the fundamentalist Christian religious convictions of George W. Bush, a convergence that has been variously referred to as "messianic militarism" (*Progressive* 2003), "political fundamentalism" (Domke 2004), or "fundamentalist geopolitics" (Falk 2004b). A better description of this approach perhaps is "missionary exceptionalism" (Hodgson 2009). Bush's evangelical moralism creates a Manichean vision that views the world as a struggle between good and evil, a struggle that requires him to act on behalf of the good. In his West Point speech, for instance, Bush (2002) insisted that "we are in a conflict between good and evil, and America will call evil by its name. By confronting evil and lawless regimes we do not create a problem; we reveal a problem. And we will lead the world in opposing it."

George W. Bush was not the first U.S. president to justify his foreign policy within the ideological or moral narrative of American exceptionalism. As noted in our historical overview of the American imperial project, many presidents have rationalized the pursuit of empire on the basis of mythic ideals such as "white man's burden" or "making the world safe for democracy." But George W. Bush presents himself as more explicitly motivated by a specific religious doctrine than past presidents, and as apparently more willing to act on those convictions. As Domke observed, "The Bush administration . . . offered a dangerous combination: the president claimed to know God's wishes and presided over a global landscape in which the United States could act upon such beliefs without compunction" (2004, 116). Thus, at that moment, the leader of the global hegemon claimed to be "divinely inspired to reshape the world through violent means," a "messiah complex" that conveniently fuses with the unipolarist dream of American global imperial domination (*Progressive* 2003, 8).

The Failure of Constraints and Controls

Despite the desire of Bush administration unipolarists to invade Iraq, the military power of the United States, and the political opportunities provided by the 9/11 attacks, strong constraints and social control mechanisms could have blocked the march to war. However, the available constraints and control mechanisms failed.

At the level of the international system, the United Nations failed to provide an effective deterrent to a U.S. invasion of Iraq largely because it has little ability to compel powerful nations to comply with international law if they choose to do otherwise. There are two reasons for this. First, the use of sanctions or force to compel compliance requires a Security Council vote, and the world's most powerful nations, as permanent members of the Security Council, can and do veto any action against their own interests, just as the United States would have done in this situation. Secondly, much of the power of the United Nations rests with its ability to extract a price in terms of negative world opinion against those who would violate international law.

When a nation enjoys a hegemonic economic and military position, as did the United States in 2003, it can easily believe it need not be overly concerned with world opinion. This is precisely the understanding that informed the neoconservative vision underlying the move to invade Iraq.

Like the United Nations and world public opinion, massive antiwar protests also had little impact on the Bush administration's decision to invade Iraq. As the unipolarists pushed for the invasion of Iraq, a global antiwar movement came to life. On February 15, 2003, as U.S. military forces were poised for the invasion, over ten million people across the globe participated in antiwar demonstrations. These protests "were the single largest public political demonstration in history" (Jensen 2004, xvii). The next day the *New York Times,* seemingly in agreement with Hardt and Negri's (2004) view of the importance of multitude in the new global order, editorialized that there were now two superpowers in the world: the United States and world public opinion. The superpower of world public opinion, expressed through the antiwar movement, however, proved to be a paper tiger, exerting no deterrent effect on U.S. plans to invade Iraq. As Jensen notes, "the antiwar movement had channeled the people's voices," but it had not "made pursuing the war politically costly enough to elites to stop it" (2004, xviii).

While world public opinion was overwhelmingly against the Bush administration's war plans, within the United States public opinion shifted from initial opposition to a preventive attack without UN sanction to majority support for the war, despite a substantial U.S. antiwar movement. Two interrelated factors appear to explain the U.S. public's support for the invasion of Iraq. First, the Bush administration engaged in an effective public relations campaign that persuaded many Americans of the necessity of a war in Iraq (Rich 2006; Rutherford 2004). As we previously noted, this marketing campaign rested mainly on false claims about Iraqi WMDs, ties to Al Qaeda, and complicity in the 9/11 attacks, and was undertaken at a time when many Americans were in a wounded, vengeful, and hyperpatriotic mood as a result of 9/11.

A second factor explaining public support for the invasion of Iraq was the failure of the media in the United States to perform its critical role as watchdog over government power (Schell 2004). It is one thing to have evidence that government claims are weak; it is another to be able to insert those claims into the same high profile media where the government is promoting its public relations message. A large number of studies document that the media failed to provide the American public with an accurate assessment of Bush administration claims about Iraq, nor did they provide any useful historical or political context within which the public could assess those claims (Alterman 2003; Friel and Falk 2004; Kellner 2005; Massing 2004; Miller 2004; Moeller 2004; Nichols and McChesney 2005; O'Shaughnessy 2004;

Schechter 2006; Solomon and Erlich 2003). Most news reports promoted the administration's official line and marginalized dissenters. As Moeller concluded, most "stories stenographically reported the incumbent administration's perspective on WMD, giving too little critical examination of the way officials framed the events, issues, threats, and policy options" (2004, 3).

In addition to the institutional failure of the media, the U.S. Congress also failed to provide an effective constraint on the Bush administration's war plans. This represented a significant institutional failure of the formal system of checks and balances among the three branches of government built into the U.S. Constitution. Article 1, Section 8, Clause 11 of the U.S. Constitution grants the power to declare war to the Congress and the Congress alone. The framers of the Constitution explicitly stated their desire that the power to take the country to war not rest on the shoulders of the president, but should be reserved to the people through their representatives in Congress.

On October 16, 2002, immediately before the midterm elections, Congress abdicated its responsibility to determine when the country would go to war by passing a resolution that authorized President Bush "to use the Armed Forces of the United States as he determines to be necessary and appropriate in order to 1) defend the national security of the United States against the continuing threat posed by Iraq; and 2) enforce all relevant United Nations Security Council resolutions regarding Iraq" (Bonifaz 2003, 11). As Congressman John Conyers (2003, xi) pointed out, by taking this action, "Congress had unconstitutionally delegated to the president its exclusive power to declare war." Thus, in the aftermath of the 9/11 tragedy, Congress (including many members of the Democratic Party) voluntarily removed itself as a significant player in the unfolding events leading to the invasion and occupation of Iraq.

Sources of organizational and interactional control within the Bush administration were also ineffective. The pragmatic realists within the administration, led by Secretary of State Colin Powell, were not in full support of the unipolarist agenda. But in a struggle for control of the administration's foreign policy, Powell and the pragmatists lost out to neoconservatives pushing for war against Iraq (Dorrien 2004; Halper and Clarke 2004; Mann 2004). Among the unipolarists there is a strong "subculture of resistance" to international law and institutions (Schell 2004). According to Braithwaite, such organizational subcultures "neutralize the moral bond of the law and communicate knowledge about how to create and seize illegitimate opportunities and how to cover up offending" (1989, 346).

The group dynamics involved in the decision-making of the unipolarists also demonstrates classic characteristics of "groupthink" as described by Janis (1982). The unipolarists were a highly cohesive group with a strong commitment to their assumptions and beliefs about America's role in the world. They valued loyalty, believed in the inherent morality of their position, had an illusion of invulnerability and shared stereotypes of out groups. But most important for this analysis, the unipolarists within the Bush administration were highly selective in gathering information; ignored, discounted, or ridiculed contrary views; engaged in self-censorship; and protected the group from examining alternatives to their war plans (Dorrien 2004; Halper and Clarke 2004; Mann 2004).

THE DEMISE OF A LAW-GOVERNED APPROACH TO WORLD ORDER?

As Gwynne Dyer has noted, "The implications of the illegal invasion of Iraq for the international system are huge and entirely negative, and the fallout from that deed may blight our world for many years" (2004, 200). The major problem is that American exceptionalism has historically promoted a double standard toward international law that undermines the legitimacy of those global rules (Koh 2003), and that the neoconservative grand imperial strategy that drove so many of the critical decisions in this particular case could easily lead to the actual destruction of international law embedded in the UN Charter system. And if the illegal war on Iraq should bring about this result, it will greatly diminish the prospects for peace in the future. As Dyer (2004, 3) points out, "What is really at risk here is the global project to abolish war and replace the rule of force in the world with the rule of law, the project whose centerpiece is the United Nations." The neoconservatives and hard line nationalists detest international law because they feel, quite correctly, that international rules on the use of force and the conduct of war could at some point constrain the United States and its imperial ambitions. To head off this possibility, the Bush administration sought to thwart the application of international law to the United States in almost any arena, from preventive war, to torture, to the proliferation of nuclear weapons, to the international criminal court, to the reduction of global warming. And given the enormous power of the United States at this point in history and the lack of enforcement mechanisms under international law at the current time, no legal proceedings are likely to occur with regard to the crimes committed in connection with the war on Iraq. The United States is not a signatory to the International Criminal Court, and as permanent members of the UN Security Council the United States and the United Kingdom can veto any move to censure their illegal behavior. As the dominant state in a unipolar world order, the United States enjoys an exemption from legal accountability for its violation of the UN Charter System and other forms of international law.

Can the UN Charter System survive if the dominant state in the world refuses to adhere to its legal procedures and restraining norms? As Falk points out, "There is little doubt that the Iraq War and the American Occupation that has ensued represents a serious setback for advocates of a law-governed approach to world order, as well as to the procedural effort to give the

United Nations Security Council primary authority to mandate exceptions to the Charter prohibition on the nondefensive use of force to resolve international conflicts" (2004b, 212). While the UN successfully resisted U.S. efforts to obtain an endorsement for the invasion of Iraq, the fact that the war still took place demonstrated that the dominant global power is willing to claim that it is an exception to a law-governed world, increasing the likelihood that other nations will eventually take the prerogative to claim similar exceptions. Wars of aggression, the most destructive and destabilizing form of state crime, along with war crimes, will be far more difficult to prevent in the future if the Bush doctrine of preventive war and the Bush redefinition of torture are allowed to redefine international law. Despite the major flaws and mixed record of the UN to this point, the prospects for peace in the future will be greatly diminished if the Charter system collapses and international rules on the recourse to war and conduct during war are rendered null and void.

Therefore, the international community must once again, as it did after World War II, say "no!" to wars of aggression and "no!" to war crimes like torture. The UN-based system of international law must be strengthened in ways that impose significant costs when rogue states commit wars of aggression and violations of international humanitarian law such as the U.S. invasion and occupation of Iraq. American exceptionalism in this regard must be ended. It is critically important that Americans, as citizens of the outlaw empire, challenge empire and work toward strengthening these international rules (Bennis 2006; Jenson 2004).

The election of Barack Obama to the U.S. presidency has signaled some rollback of the criminal policies of the Bush administration. Waterboarding has been returned to its rightful place as a crime of torture (Meyer 2009). The administration has stepped back from the exceptionalist agenda of fighting a war on terror (Solomon 2009). One of the most egregious symbols of U.S. disrespect for both national and international law, the Guantánamo Bay prison camp, is slated for closure (Obama 2009). While positive, these steps are far from sufficient. Those who care about strengthening a world governed by the logic of law rather than the terror of weapons must demand that the Obama administration take aggressive legal action to hold accountable those guilty of committing war crimes and other international crimes under the auspices of the Bush administration. Without such steps, claims to a renewed commitment to a law-governed approach to world order will ring hollow on the national and international stage.

In the long run, the best hope for establishing a law-governed rather than a power-governed world order is through vocal and continuing challenges to the rhetorical and behavioral moves of governments that seek to once again make war a legitimate foreign policy tool. The Bush administration's neoconservatives and hard-line nationalists contended that a power-governed world order with the United States as its hegemon was the only path to world peace. Power and domination, however, ensure resistance, repression, and continued violence. Only when powerful nations accept that they, no less than their citizens, must abide by the rule of law will humanity be free from the scourge of aggressive war, the supreme international crime.

CHAPTER 5

Do Empires Commit State Crime?

Peter Iadicola

IF ONE REFLECTS ON THE HISTORY OF THE WORLD and focuses on those acts that have been defined by the Nuremberg Tribunal and the United Nations as the most severe crimes—genocide and wars of aggression—and combined these acts with the massive confiscation or stealing of property and resources, it would be hard to avoid the historical intersections of the actions of empires in their conquest of new territories and their efforts to control their domain. The United States' histories of empires focus on their achievements and the advancements in civilization. It is quite obvious from whose perspective these histories are written. The history of the Roman Empire is certainly not written from the perspective of the Gauls, the Celts, the Phoenicians, or any of the barbarians conquered and incorporated into the Roman Empire. Nor is the history of the Empire of the United States of America written from the perspective of the Cherokee, Apache, Mohawk, Navajo, Hawaiian, Army of the Philippine Republic of 1898, and so forth. The most severe crimes of imperial states are not highlighted as part of these histories.

Even in the area that focuses on state criminal behavior, the crimes and violence of empires are not the subject of investigation. It is as if criminologists wear blinders that limit the parameters of vision and understanding of crime as it may relate to the nature of empire and its use of violence and the usurpation of territory and resources. These blinders limit our vision of the crimes of the most powerful and largest empire in the history of humankind, the empire of the United States of America. In addition, these blinders are conceptual and ideological, defined in terms of whose perspective the field of criminology assumes in the investigation of crime, as well as the nature of understanding the United States of America. The failure of the recognition and control of crimes in the United States, as well as the overall historical pattern of failure controls and recognition of the crimes of empires of the past, determine whether or not empires commit state crime.

Defining the Terms

State Crime

To answer the question of whether empires commit state crimes, we first need to define terms. Although the field of criminology has considered crimes of governments, it is a minor area in the study of crime. It is only recently that the field of criminology has generated a significant amount of scholarly interest in this area. Chambliss's 1988 presidential address to the American Society of Criminology calling on criminologists to increase their research in this area was a particularly important historical landmark in the field's development. This call has been met with challenges, many of which have focused on defining state crime. However, there has been considerable progress in scholars reaching agreement on the recognition of crimes of states, and, like the definition of crime in general, there is sufficient agreement of the definition of the term to allow for the growing development of this area of study. Chambliss defined state crime as "acts defined by law as criminal and committed by state officials in pursuit of their jobs as representatives of the state" (1989, 184). Kramer and Michalowski (2006b) provided further specification to the definition by including activities of the state that fail to constrain criminal and dangerous behaviors.

The limitation of the legal code in the definition of state crime has been an important area of scholarly debate. It is beyond the purpose of this chapter to summarize this debate, which has been done elsewhere (Rothe and Friedrichs 2006). Alternative definitions have been advanced, from international legal codes to basic human rights precepts, and the perceptions of the state's citizens. Kramer, Michalowski, and Rothe (2005) proposed a definition that grounds the concept in a juridical framework, however, broadens it to all areas of law. Here state crime is any action that violates public international law, international criminal law, or domestic law when these actions are committed by individuals acting in official or covert capacity as agents of the state pursuant to expressed or implied orders of the state, or resulting from state failure to exercise due diligence over the actions of its agents. Rothe and Friedrichs contend that most critical criminologists studying state crime agree that the use of international law (customary, codified treaties, charters, and the newly emerged criminal law) constitutes a basic foundation for defining state crime, as this framework includes standards such as human rights and social and economic harms while providing a legalistic foundation.

Michalowski (2008) described the strengths and weakness of three approaches to defining state crime: juridical, organizational deviance, and social injury/harm. He notes that the juridical framework will tend to direct attention to high profile instances of state crime that have attracted the enforcement attention of supranational bodies. The organizational deviance perspective best represented by Green and Ward (2004) enables analysis of notable harms that have not risen to the level of law violations, but which have attracted the attention of significant audiences who would define these acts as deviant and would be willing to impose sanctions on the offenders. Lastly, a social injury model opens the door to considering the kinds of structural violence (Iadicola and Shupe 2003; Scheper-Hughes and Bourgois 2004) and harm that often is normalized as a consequence of governmentality. Michalowski notes that most would identify these harms as the unfortunate but inevitable consequences of "reality," rather than as human authored deviant acts. Michalowski claims that these different foci represent an increasing scope of harm—from the least to the most prevalent. Iadicola and Shupe (2003) make a similar point in describing the different scale of violence from interpersonal to institutional to structural forms of violence. Whether we define state crime in a restrictive, juridical framework or in a expansive, organizational deviance or social/harm framework, the crimes of empires are in the forefront. However, the prosecution of these crimes is rare and follows a pattern not so dissimilar to victor's justice. In this case, it is law and justice in the context of the power of empire.

Empire

The term "empire" is largely absent in the field of sociology as it pertains to the study of American society. There is little discussion in mainstream journals or textbooks that introduce students to the sociological study of the United States. This is also the case within the field of criminology, where there is little investigation as to how empire relates to crime patterns in the imperial center or periphery. Iadicola and Shupe (2003), in discussing state and structural forms of violence, point to the significance of empires as an important source of these more devastating forms of violence. Only recently, when the George W. Bush administration engaged in a form of "hard imperialism" with the use of military force, has there been increasing discussion about whether there is an American Empire. The multilateral character of imperialism relying on treaty organizations like NATO, SEATO, and OAS that characterized much of U.S. imperial management for the period before and just after the end of the cold war often cloaked the hard imperialism of U.S. expansionism. Nails Ferguson (2004) describes the American penchant for not recognizing the existence of this most powerful empire in the history of humankind as the "Empire in Denial." Steinmetz, in a recent article in one of the American Sociological Association flagship journals, states that "there seems to be little doubt that the United States is the controlling center of a global empire" (2005, 341). However, he laments the fact that there is little discussion of the nature of empire in American sociology.

The nature of empire has changed throughout history (Doyle 1986; Wood 2003). There are differences in the nature of the extraction of resources, whether they be defined in terms of precious metals and raw materials, access of land for settlement and agricultural production, access and surplus capital resulting from monopoly control of markets, or the access and control of labor (whether slave, bonded, or "free"). There have also been significant changes in the nature of the control systems, from direct control through the creation of colonial governing systems to the more indirect control that relies on legal and market mechanisms and political influence from the imperial center. There have also been important changes in the ideological justifications for conquest and the empire from the civilizing and Christianizing missions of earlier centuries, to the liberating, "democratizing," and nation-building missions of today.

A useful definition in providing a starting point of an investigation of empire is that an empire is "a major actor in the international system based on the subordination of diverse national elites who, whether under compulsion or from shared convictions, accept the values of those who govern the dominant center or metropole" (Maier 2005, xii). Although Maier's definition provides a description of power relations between an empire and those territories or nations that it controls, it does little to explain the function of empire, specifically the nature of imperialism. Doyle's (1986) sociological approach defines empire even more succinctly in behavioral terms as effective control, whether formal or informal, of a subordinated society by an imperial society.

The term imperialism refers to the actions of empires. Greene (1970) defines imperialism as the "economic exploitation of other peoples buttressed by military and political domination." Steinmetz (2005) refers to imperialism as the "non-territorial form of empire in contradistinction to colonialism as a territorial one. He argues that the American Empire is the former type. However, it would be too limiting to define the American Empire as only possessing one form of control. Certainly throughout its history, the United States Empire has included both colonial and noncolonial forms. During the first hundred years, the empire relied upon the outright conquest and genocide followed by the establishment of settlements that were protected by military forts and colonial governments; this is what Jefferson referred to as the "Empire of Liberty" (Williams 2007). The aftermath of the conquests included a period in which these geographic units were defined as territories that had a colonial administration in the form of a territorial governor, along with an Indian agent to negotiate the displacement of the indigenous population who were essentially not defined as legitimate users of the land. In the early empire of the United States of America, there was no place for those who were not white and of European ancestry, unless they were slaves. Locke provided the ideological structure for the essential criterion in the justification of colonial expropriation. "For Locke, America was the model state of nature, in which all land was available for appropriation, because, although it was certainly inhabited and even sometimes cultivated, there was no proper commerce, hence no 'improvement,' no productive and profitable use of the land, and therefore no real property" (Wood 2003, 96).

The colonial experience of the American system was unlike the French, Spanish, and Dutch empires and more like the British, whereby the Americans followed a policy of removal and genocide of the indigenous population and replaced them with a settler population from the imperial center or white recent migrants from Europe or their colonies (Wood 2003). The territorial system was designed during the first one hundred years of the American Empire to be a transitionary stage to the incorporation of the geographic units that were sufficiently pacified and settled by white settlers into the nation as states. This imperial strategy extended to the incorporation of the last two territories, Hawaii and Alaska, into "states." However, there were other territorial possessions that have either retained territorial or commonwealth status—as in the case of Puerto Rico, American Samoa, Northern Mariana Islands, and U.S. Virgin Islands—or were recently given formal independence but were controlled indirectly—as in the case of the Philippines. Lastly, there are large areas of the world in which the United States either militarily occupies or possess the "right" to intervene militarily if the nation-state lessens its ties and threatens its linkage to the imperial center.

Today, the American Empire, with military facilities in more than 60 percent of the world's nations, rules most of its sphere of influence indirectly through military, political, economic, and cultural dominance and control (Gardner, LaFeber, and McCormick 1973; Iadicola 2008b; Johnson 2004). As State Department Policy Planning Director Richard Haas, a member of the National Security Council and special assistant to President George H. W. Bush, stated in a paper titled "Imperial America,"

> To advocate an imperial foreign policy is to call for a foreign policy that attempts to organize the world along certain principles affecting relations between states and conditions within them. The U.S. role would resemble 19th century Great Britain. . . . Coercion and the use of force would normally be a last resort; what was written by John Gallagher and Ronald Robinson about Britain a century and a half ago, that the British policy followed the principle of extending control informally if possible and formally if necessary, could be applied to the American role at the start of the new century. (Haas 2000)

Another important term in the discussion of empire is "hegemon": the dominant power that exerts its dominance through an acceptance by lesser powers of the economic and political arrangements designed to maintain order and control. Tabb (2004) describes hegemony as one strategy of empire where there is a greater reliance on establishing the rules of commerce (the neoliberalist form of globalization) and engaging in multilateralism where it can achieve its goals. In this case, the hegemon creates the rules and abides by them. The other strategy is unilateralism, where the power of empire is naked imperial power ignores the rules and acts independently. This is the difference between soft (Wilsonian multilateralism) and hard (Teddy Roosevelt's big stick strategy) imperialism (Williams 2007). Munkler (2007) contends that the line between hegemonic supremacy and imperial domination may be fluid. "Hegemony is supremacy within a group of formally equal political players; imperiality, by contrast, dissolves this—at least formal—equality and reduces subordinates to the status of client states or satellites. They stand in more or less recognizable dependence in relation to the centre" (Munkler 2007, 7).

Other terms such as "superpower" or "hyperpower" are euphemisms for empire. The phrase "unipolar world" refers to the world hegemony by one empire. It is used to describe the current dominant political economic relationship in the world. In referring to the Empire of the United States of America, I am defining empire as an interterritorial system whereby there is a hierarchical relationship between these territorial units from an imperial center that directs the development and the nature of economic, military, political, and cultural penetration and control of the periphery. Furthermore, it is essential to recognize that empires are organized and guided by elites in the center and elites in the periphery who are in "partnership" and benefit from the nature of exploitation and control of the dominated regions. Empires may be global or regional in scale and extent of control and domination. Munkler (2007) notes that the criterion of spatial reach in the designation of world empires is not limited to physical control of territory, but may also involve near-total control of commodity and capital flows. He contends that since the end of the Soviet Union, only the United States can qualify as a world empire, and the British Empire was the predecessor to today's U.S. global empire.

Recognition and Enforcement of State Crimes

When reviewing the history of the development of international law and its prosecution as it relates to state crime, one cannot help but see a pattern of "victor's justice" and the vulnerability to prosecution of weak states (Cryer 2005; Rothe and Mullins 2006a). Cryer notes that the first case of crimes that were defined as violations of international law involving the U.S. "infant empire" was in 1812. Arbuthnot and Ambrister, two British men who were said to have encouraged the Creek Indians to fight the United States, thus levying war against it in an uncivilized manner, were tried in the United States. Cryer notes that what is most ironic about this historical case is that "there was an extraordinary level of public consternation expressed that the United States should exercise jurisdiction over British nationals for offences against international law" (2005, 27). The position of the British Empire was that this newly independent country did not have the authority under international law to challenge the British Empire or its representatives. Cryer reminds us that the current U.S. opposition to the ICC is based on the same position as the British, which was rejected by the United States at the time when it was the victim.

Some of the most famous developments in the law of war came about during the American Civil War. General Army Order 100, the Lieber Code, was influential in a number of states codifying laws of war and had an indirect effect on the 1899 Hague Conference. Courts-martial and military courts were also used for offenses committed by American and Filipino fighters involved in the war in the Philippines. However, Cryer states, regarding this period, that "there were only a few trials of US service members, and sentences, when they were imposed, bordered on derisory" (2005, 29). In all these cases, the agent was defined as to be acting not in the interest of the state. Their criminality was separated from the state, which was not found to be criminal.

The development of international law to govern warfare and state crime has been one where there has been frequent resistance from powerful empires. The initial laws that were created provided no punishment for the offenses. This was the case for the 1864 Geneva Convention, 1899 Hague Declarations, and the 1907 Hague Conventions, in particular Hague Convention IV Respecting the Laws and Customs of War on Land.

The First World War brought in a period in which the victors initially took a strong position on international criminal liability. The Commission on the Responsibility of the Authors of the War determined that there were cases of violations of the laws of war and humanity. The commission recommended the setting up of an Allied High Tribunal with members from all of the Allied countries. This tribunal was to try violations of the laws and customs of war and the laws of humanity. Cryer notes that the commission also recommended that the law applied by the tribunal ought to be "the principles of the law of nations as they result from the usages established among civilized peoples, from the laws of humanity and from the dictates of public conscience" (2005, 32). He notes that the proposals contained a clear affirmation of criminal liability directly under international law, rather than domestic legal orders incorporating such offenses. This aspect was criticized both by the American and Japanese members of the commission. The American members said that they knew "of no international statute or convention making violation of the laws and customs of war—not to speak of the laws or principles of humanity—an international crime" (Cryer 2005, 32). They would have preferred to maintain control over the process through the establishment of national military commissions, acting under domestic laws, to prosecute such offenses.

Cryer contends that if the commission's proposals had been implemented, the history of international criminal law might have taken a different route.

The first peace treaty with Turkey, the Treaty of Sevres (1920), contained a provision (Article 230) by which Turkey was obliged to hand over those responsible for the atrocities (genocide of Armenians) to the Allies. However, the treaty was never ratified and was replaced by the Treaty of Lausanne (1923), which had no equivalent provision on punishment, and was accompanied by a declaration of amnesty. All attempts of prosecution ceased in 1921.

The story of the Leipzig trials is a similar one. It started very well. The initial plans were set out in the 1919 Treaty of Versailles. Article 227 provided that the Kaiser was to be "publicly arraigned" for "a supreme offence against international morality and the sanctity of treaties" before an international tribunal (1919 Treaty of Versailles, Art. 227). However, the orders were never implemented, as the Netherlands refused to hand over the Kaiser to the Allies. Article 228 provided for the prosecution of German suspects by the Allies. The prosecutions were to be before the military tribunals of the victim states or, if the charges related to victims of more than one state, mixed military commissions made up of members from those states. Cryer notes that none of this was successful given the relatively few proceedings brought forward and the extraordinary leniency when convictions were won.

After World War I, the idea of an international criminal court regained support. In 1921 there were proposals for an international tribunal coming from a League of Nations advisory committee as a way of overcoming the problems encountered in prosecuting offenses from World War I. Cryer notes that consideration of a court then fell into the unofficial arena after the League of Nations advisory committee considered the idea premature. The International Law Association (ILA) drafted a statute for an international criminal court in 1926. The assassination of King Alexander of Yugoslavia in 1934 led to the League of Nations drafting, adopting, and opening for signature a statute for an international criminal court. The court was to enforce the (separate) convention for the prevention of terrorism. The convention remained without state support.

World War II and its aftermath provided another opportunity in the European sphere with the development of the Nuremberg International Military Tribunal. During the war, the Allies issued many statements relating to violations of the law of war and promising punishment for such offenses in Europe. The most important of these within the European sphere of the war was the Moscow Declaration of November 1, 1943, that, although not legally binding, declared that those responsible for committing criminal acts would be sent back to the countries where they committed these deeds for trial. However, the declaration did not apply to major criminals (Cryer 2005).

The Allied forces had set up the United Nations War Crimes Commission (UNWCC) to investigate war crimes and later to advise on the process for punishment. Created by the 1945 London Agreement, the Nuremberg

International Military Tribunals formed the cornerstone of the Allied prosecution policy. Cryer (2005) contends that the creation of the Nuremberg IMT was extraordinary in that it was an international criminal tribunal applying international law directly without any intercessions of domestic legal orders. However, Cryer contends that the Nuremberg legacy is a "curate's egg," something that is partly good and partly bad. He notes that allegations of victor's justice and selective justice have merit in the functioning of the tribunal.

These international tribunals were not the only or the most prevalent response to international crimes in the European sphere of the Second World War (Cryer 2005). Many more Axis personnel were prosecuted at the national level. For example, in Germany this was pursuant to Control Council Law 10. The closest followers of Control Council Law 10 were twelve U.S. trials that took place in Nuremberg known as the subsequent proceedings, which included trials of Nazi doctors and judges, extermination squads, and members of the German High Command. Cryer contends that the IMT and other proceedings were the beginning of the attempts to coordinate prosecution of offenders at the national and international levels.

There were moves to institutionalize the law identified at Nuremberg at the beginning of the cold war. The General Assembly Resolution 95(I) (1946) affirmed the principles of international law recognized by the charter of the Nuremberg Tribunal and the judgment of the tribunal. The resolution directed the International Law Commission to formulate those principles. Cryer contends that this resolution forms the backbone of the case for the contention that the innovations at Nuremberg amounted to customary law. The ILC reported with its formulation of those principles in 1950.

The cold war preempted any further development, and by 1954 the proposals were shelved pending the drafting of a definition of "aggression." However, substantive law developed during this time. Just prior to the postponement of the international criminal court project, there had been the Genocide Convention (in 1948) and the four Geneva Conventions of 1949. "Outside what might have been considered 'unfinished business' from the war crimes programmes related to the Second World War there were a considerable number of prosecutions in the United States for what amounted to war crimes, although they were prosecuted as violations of the Uniform Code of Military Justice. The best known of these were the Calley (1969) and Medina (1971) cases, both of which arose from the My Lai massacre." However, as Cryer notes, "the overall prosecutions were the exception rather than the rule, and this led some to question if there was any commitment to international law after Nuremberg" (Cryer 2005, 50).

Tribunals established by the UN Security Councils have been the next step in the trying of states and their leaders for crimes. The International Criminal Tribunal for the Former Yugoslavia (ICTY) and the International

Criminal Tribunal for Rwanda (ICTR) were creations of the UN Security Councils to address violations of humanitarian law. Both were seen as controversial. Challengers raised the point that the Security Council was not mandated by the framers of the UN Charter to create a tribunal. However, dominant legal opinion is that the UN Charter is not restrictive upon the granting of these powers by an act of the general assembly.

The most recent initiative for the creation of an international court was in 1989 in response to the request of a coalition of sixteen Caribbean and Latin American states to create a collaborative measure for enforcing national laws based on the 1988 Vienna Convention against the Illicit Trafficking in Narcotic Drugs and Psychotropic Substances. There were also concerns about the ad hoc nature and selective nature of the enforcement of international law. In 1993 the United States started to become more flexible in regard to the establishment of the court; the ILC developed a draft statute that borrowed heavily from the ICTY. The Rome Conference on an International Criminal Court met in June and July of 1998 and adopted the Rome Statute of the International Criminal Court that came into force in July 2002, shortly after the deposit of the sixtieth instrument of ratification.

The question is, given the resistance to the establishment of international controls on state crime, can they be effective as a means of social control, especially in the case of empires? Rothe and Mullins (2006a) recognize the importance of external controls such as the United Nations, the World Court, and the ICC. They note that as internationally sanctioned bodies, these organizations hold the power to apply sanctions to states that violate either international law or are overtly abusive of their own citizens. However, they note that the ability to back up sanctions with coercive force is limited to members willing to volunteer the necessary force to act in the organization's name (Rothe and Mullins 2006a, 2006b). Rothe and Mullins also note that the ICC is hindered by the limitations of jurisdiction based on issues of sovereignty. This was the central focus of the negotiations with the United States and its eventual withdrawal, opposition, and actions aimed to impede the ICC (Rothe and Mullins 2006a). "The U.S. wanted a court for the rest of the world, but insisted the jurisdiction could not impinge on the U.S., its policies, or its own state actors" (Rothe and Mullins 2006a, 76). The United States limited the ICC's jurisdiction by requiring that the court defer to the U.S. domestic courts. After Clinton signed the treaty but did not send it on to the Senate for ratification, George W. Bush rescinded the signature.

If this was not sufficient to neuter the court's prosecution of U.S. citizens and their agents, the U.S. Congress passed domestic legislation that blocked any ICC jurisdiction and limited the application of the Geneva Convention. In response to the War Crimes Acts, which defined grave breaches of the Geneva Convention, and the Hamden Supreme Court decision, which declared that the military commissions established by the Bush administration to try inmates at Guantánamo Bay were in violation of the Uniform Military Code and the Geneva Convention, the executive branch and the Republican-controlled congress passed the Military Commissions Act of 2006 and the Levin-Graham Amendment, which was attached to the McCain Antitorture Amendment. The Military Commission Act embodied in law the definition of an illegal enemy combatant as a status solely determined by the president of the United States that allows for the circumvention of the protections afforded prisoners under the Geneva Convention. It also limited Common Article 3 of the Geneva Convention by narrowly defining "grave breaches," omitting the prohibition of "outrages upon personal dignity, in particular, humiliating and degrading treatment" and of "the passing of sentences and the carrying out of executions without previous judgment pronounced by a regularly constituted court affording all the judicial guarantees which are recognized as indispensable by civilized peoples." The Levin-Graham Amendment further curtailed federal court review of detainees' cases, allowing military tribunals to rely on evidence gained from torture, and undermined vital ongoing attorney-client relations for Guantánamo detainees.

Furthermore, if there were any other question about jurisdiction of the ICC, the Service-Members Protection Act and Article 98(2) agreements, which reinforce the status of force agreements that signatory nations have with the United States, as required for U.S. forces to be present in their territories, virtually eliminated U.S. cooperation in the prosecution of any agents of the United States operating in significant portions of its imperial domain. Most of South America, Western Europe, Japan, South Korea, and Australia are ICC regions that have not signed on to the Article 98 agreements, although there are status of force agreements in place in these areas that protect U.S. military personnel from unwarranted prosecution. For most of Africa, where countries are least able to resist U.S. pressure, the George W. Bush administration was particularly aggressive in getting Article 98(2) agreements signed by using the withdrawal of various forms of aid as a threat. Forty-three of fifty-four African countries have signed Article 98(2) agreements with the United States (Georgetown Law Library 2008). The 2004 Nethercutt Amendment added to the Omnibus Appropriations Bill cuts assistance and funding for states that are signatories or party members to the ICC unless a bilateral agreement is entered into with the United States, thus granting immunity for U.S. personnel, U.S. nationals, nonnationals, and contractors from ICC prosecution.

In addition to domestic law, the National Security Doctrine of 2002 reaffirms the U.S. position regarding jurisdiction of the ICC.

We will take the actions necessary to ensure that our efforts to meet our global security commitments and protect Americans are not impaired by the potential for investigation, inquiry, or prosecution by the International Criminal Court (ICC), whose jurisdiction does not extend to Americans and which we do not accept. We will work together with other nations to avoid complications in our military operations and cooperation, through such mechanisms as multilateral and bilateral agreements that will protect US nationals from the ICC. We will implement fully the American Service-Members protection Act, whose provisions are intended to ensure and enhance the protection of US personnel and officials. (White House 2002, 31)

The George W. Bush administration also acted in other ways to protect itself and future and past administrations by elevating the level of secrecy and the restrictions on access to presidential records through Freedom of Information Act filings. The U.S. Congressional Committee on Government Reform, chaired by Henry Waxman (2004), released a comprehensive examination of secrecy in the Bush Administration that found that there has been a consistent pattern in this administration's actions: laws that are designed to promote public access to information have been undermined, while laws that authorize the government to withhold information or to operate in secret have repeatedly been expanded. Secrecy has been a very important strategy to prevent detection of state crimes. It has also been an important element in preventing prosecution within the United States. This also extends to other areas in the world that are within the U.S. imperial sphere of influence. According to a decision issued in February 2009, the High Court in Great Britain will not publish its summary of the alleged torture of Guantánamo Bay detainee Binyam Mohamed because of pressure from the U.S. government under the Obama administration (Hirsch 2009). State secrets and concerns regarding national security have been used frequently in preventing those who have been held in U.S. custody from calling on witnesses and requesting information about the evidence used against them in the secret military trials.

In reviewing the cases of state crimes that have been prosecuted in the twentieth century, they were clearly cases of victor's justice. In the clash of empires in World War I and World War II, the victors established the mechanism to try principally the vanquished in war crimes and crimes against humanity. Those states that are the weakest and not aligned with an imperial power who engage in acts of genocide or other crimes against humanity are tried initially by tribunals established by the dominant powers, in particular the United States. The first case of a conviction for genocide occurred fifty years after the passage of the UN Genocide Convention in 1998. The International Criminal Tribunal for Rwanda found the country's former prime minister, Jean Kambanda, guilty of genocide. Since these prosecutions, the

United States Empire has safeguarded itself from any prosecution in international or national courts other than its own. U.S. sovereignty and imperial defense is supreme relative to all other states in which it has the ability to violate international law.

In February 2009, the first trial of the International Criminal Court got under way, and it fits the pattern whereby it is the weak that are likely to face prosecution. Congolese rebel leader Thomas Lubanga faces charges of recruiting children as young as ten years old to become soldiers in his country's bloody internal conflicts. Lubanga denies using underage fighters in the military arm of his Union of Congolese Patriots in conducting a war to stop the plundering of Congo's rich natural resources. Although the trial of Lubanga will be important to the victims of his crimes, it will be another example whereby those who trained, equipped, and guided the actions of this warlord will not come to trial. The rape of the Congo began in the days of King Leopold. Since then, the U.S. and Belgium governments have ordered the assassination of Lumumba, and now the United States, directly through U.S. Special Forces operations and indirectly through the funding and training of forces in the region, has allowed for the exploitation of the Congo's mineral wealth (Hartung and Moix 2000; Kern 2007; Snow 2008). As Kern notes, the "civil war in Congo has cost 4 million lives over the past ten years—strife fueled by Western multinationals seeking cheap supplies of coltan [columbite-tantalite] and other minerals" (Kern 2007, 93). Mamdani claims that the actions of the ICC are part of the eventual accommodation between the world's only superpower and the struggling international system of justice. He notes that what is essentially prosecuted by the ICC are governments that are U.S. adversaries, those who interfere with the opening of resources to first-world multinational corporations, and what will be ignored are the violent actions that the United States does not oppose or commits itself, effectively conferring impunity to them (Mamdani 2008).

State crimes and violence are a principal means of empire. Sovereignty is a matter of degree as it relates to the state's position within the empire and as it relates to the power of this state relative to the center. Nevertheless, even in those areas that contain a potential economic threat of independence, the U.S. military occupies the territory or is in position to invade to change regimes. The National Security Doctrine of 2002 clearly establishes the position that the United States is to be supreme in the world. The Empire of the United States of America is the dominant force in the world today. Panitch and Gindin, in identifying a need for new theorizing on the nature of empire, describes the American Empire as characterized "by economic penetration and informal incorporation of other capitalist states, but at the same time it both permits and requires imperial policing and military intervention in 'rogue states' which have not been incorporated into the neoliberal capitalist order" (2006, 21). It is this policing function of the empire, beginning with the declaration of the Monroe Doctrine and the Roosevelt Corollary, that has often provided the justification for invasion and regime change throughout the world that will continue to fall outside of the law as defined by the ICC and other international tribunals.

CRIMES OF THE U.S. EMPIRE

The crimes of empires are the most devastating crimes, because empires have the greatest power to commit them and with impunity. Empires are also the major source of wars historically and contemporaneously, as they change regimes to maintain and expand their spheres of influence or control and as they fight the proxy wars with rival empires. They also seek to destroy or assimilate those populations that resist the transformation of their societies, which are incorporated into the world system centered in the nation-state of the imperial center. Nonstate actors who actively resist and use or incite violence to do so are seen as being the same kind of terrorists who rebelled against the Roman Empire.

Let us consider the most serious crimes that a state can commit: genocide and war of aggression. What has been the U.S. Empire's history as it relates to these acts? Genocide is certainly not foreign to imperial systems (Kiernan 2007). This is the case whether we are talking about Germany, Imperial Japan, Belgium, the Ottoman Empire, the British Empire, or the Empire of the United States of America. In 2007 the U.S. Congress deliberated on a piece of legislation that would have recognized the genocide committed by the Ottoman Empire in the early part of the twentieth century. Gregory Meeks, a Democrat representative from New York in the House Committee on Foreign Affairs, argued against recognition. Meeks wondered if it did not appear hypocritical for the United States to recognize the genocide of the Armenians without recognizing its own role in the genocide of the Native American and African slave population within the United States (Reuters News Service 2007). Although the genocide of more than four hundred Native American societies is well documented, there has been little movement nationally or internationally to recognize and prosecute the government of the United States for the harm done. This genocide occurred in the first 125 years of the empire's conquest of the societies on the North American continent. Ferguson (2004) referred to this period of imperial expansion as the empire by purchase. Those receiving the purchase price—the French, the Spanish, and the British empires—were not dependent on the land for their survival as societies. It was the estimated four hundred societies living on the land who paid the ultimate price of genocide. The Founding Fathers and succeeding leaders of the nation believed that those societies had no right to the land: "The Citizens of America, placed in the most enviable condition, as the sole Lords and Proprietors of a vast Tract of Continent, comprehending all the various soils and climates of the World, and abounding with all the necessaries and conveniences of life, are now by the late satisfactory pacification, acknowledged to be possessed of absolute freedom and independency (George Washington Circular To The States, Head Quarters, Newburgh, June 14, 1783)" (Achenbach 2004).

Those who were removed did not go peacefully. The genocidal wars began with the first Indian war in U.S. history, the American Revolutionary War. It is important to remember that this war was fought principally because the British colonial subjects were prohibited from claiming Quebec Province and the Northwest territories just recently acquired in the War for the Great Empire (also referred to as the French and Indian War) for further American colonial expansion (Van Alstyne 1960). From the perspective of Shawnee, Iroquois, Choctaw, Creek, Delaware, Mohawks, Cayuga, Onondagas, and Seneca tribes, this was a war to defend their territory from further conquest by colonial settlers. In the next fifty years, following the birth of the U.S. nation and empire, there were at least another fifteen wars or conquests to remove indigenous societies east of the Mississippi River.

The strategy of promoting settlement in lands occupied by indigenous populations and then later purchasing them from the European imperial power that claimed them was a strategy at the very beginning of the empire's history. Madison and Jefferson's empire of liberty stemmed from land ownership for white settlers only. In a letter to Archibald Stewart, penned January 25, 1786, Thomas Jefferson wrote: Our confederacy must be viewed as the nest, from which all America, North and South, is to be peopled. We should take care too, not to think it for the interest of that great continent to press too soon on the Spaniards. Those countries cannot be in better hands. My fear is that they are too feeble to hold them till our population can be sufficiently advanced to gain it from them piece by piece" (Lens 2003, 2).

The legal justification for the removal of the indigenous population was initially defined in the Washington Plan in 1782, which replicated the Proclamation of 1763 (Churchill 1997). Washington provided claims for tracts of land to war veterans, in lieu of payment, for fighting the British Empire for independence. Washington's goals were to place the former soldiers on the imperial frontier to secure control of the territory and then to gradually expand the territory with the placement of military forts and to sell the land to settlers seeking liberty. It is important to remember that Washington's profession before being the head of the military and the first leader of the infant empire was that of land speculator and surveyor, surveying land that was used by indigenous tribes of the Northwest Territory to be sold to white settlers.

President Andrew Jackson's Indian Removal Acts later in the next century further provided legal justification for the complete removal and genocide of all the indigenous societies east of the Mississippi. "It is, therefore, a duty this government owes to its new states, to extinguish, as soon as possible, the Indian title to all lands which Congress themselves have included within their limits" (Jackson 1830). There were few exceptions to this forced removal. Continued expansion west of the Mississippi led to a number of genocidal wars of conquest to remove the indigenous population from that territory that land speculators were selling to new settlers. These genocidal wars of conquest and the removal of indigenous populations from their homelands, destroying their way of life, are well documented (Brown 1970; Churchill 1997).

Glauner states that, "even though the crime of genocide remains universally condemned by the international community, the United States government, its agencies, and its personnel have been effectively granted de facto immunity" (2001, 916). She notes that piracy, slavery, slave-related practices, apartheid, crimes against humanity, war crimes, aggression, torture, and genocide are recognized as *jus congens* international crimes, and that a *jus cogens* norm holds the highest hierarchical position among all norms and principles. Furthermore, Glauner contends that these are crimes that evolved from states' universal condemnation of the prosecution of persons based solely on their minority status, as seen through the establishment of the Hague Convention and the London Charter. She also finds that the International Court of Justice in the Reservations to the Convention on the Protection and Punishment of the Crime of Genocide case in 1951 recognized genocide's status under customary international law when it stated that "the principles underlying the Convention are principles which are recognized by civilized nations as binding on States, even without any conventional obligations" (Glauner 2001, 920). The Genocide Convention (in Article 2) defines genocide as "any of the following acts committed with intent to destroy, in whole or in part, a national, ethnical, racial or religious group, as such: (a) Killing members of the group; (b) Causing serious bodily or mental harm to members of the group; (c) Deliberately inflicting on the group conditions of life calculated to bring about its physical destruction in whole or in part; (d) Imposing measures intended to prevent births within the group; (e) Forcibly transferring children of the group to another group" (United Nations 1948a). The United States required as a prerequisite to the ratification of the Genocide Convention that Congress enact implementing legislation (The Proxmire Act). On November 25, 1988, the United States deposited ratification with reservations that mandated that nothing within the text of the Genocide Convention could require or authorize legislation or action by the United States that contradicted the principles espoused in the U.S. Constitution. Furthermore, according to the Proxmire Act, the United States would prosecute a perpetrator of the crime of genocide either when the offense was committed within the United States or when the alleged offender was a national of the United States.

However, Glauner (2001) notes that the acts committed against Native Americans, such as the forced relocation (Indian Removal Act and legacy of treaty violations, including the Northwest Ordinance), the forced sterilization of 70,000 native American women (Indian Health Services 1930–1976), and the transfer of children into boarding schools, took place within the United States from 1891 to 1978, and the perpetrators of these acts were U.S. citizens. Glauner also finds that because there is not a statute of limitations for the crime of genocide, U.S. citizens can be prosecuted for these crimes at any time. Therefore, she contends that the Genocide Convention, as implemented by the Proxmire Act, can still be used as a basis to prosecute the perpetrators of the crime of genocide within the United States' borders, regardless of when the crimes were committed.

On September 9, 2000, the head of the federal Bureau of Indian Affairs apologized for the agency's "legacy of racism and inhumanity" that included massacres, forced relocations of tribes, and attempts to wipe out Indian languages and cultures. Gover stated that "by accepting this legacy, we accept also the moral responsibility of putting things right" (Associated Press 2000). Prosecutions of the U.S. government for acts of genocide against the indigenous peoples of the continent should be the next step in recognizing criminal responsibility and creating justice. However, given the power of the U.S. Empire it is doubtful that there will be sufficient international pressure and international mechanism to enforce the law.

War of Aggression and Regime Change

As part of the expansion of empire throughout the Americas and the rest of the world, the United States has been involved in a long history of regime changes (Blum 2000, 2005; Kinzer 2006). Given its imperial policing role, it has tried to establish legal justification through mutual defense treaties and claims of the extralegal right to maintain order and protect U.S. investors (Roosevelt Corollary). Rarely is this right legally challenged. However, the World Court decision in the case of *Nicaragua v. The United States of America* in 1986 did just that (ICJ 1986). The court found the United States guilty of committing several acts of state crime. It was the regime change of the Nicaraguan government under the presidency of Daniel Ortega that led to charges filed and adjudicated in the ICJ.

On June 27, 1986, a majority vote of the ICJ decided that the United States of America, by training, arming, equipping, financing, and supplying the contra forces or otherwise encouraging, supporting, and aiding military and paramilitary activities in and against Nicaragua, acted against the Republic of Nicaragua, in breach of its obligation under customary international law not to intervene in the affairs of another state. The court also decided the following:

> The United States of America, by certain attacks on Nicaraguan territory in 1983–1984, namely attacks on Puerto Sandino on 13 September and 14 October 1983; an attack on Corinto on 10 October 1983; an attack on Potosi Naval Base on 4/5 January 1984; an attack on San Juan del Sur on 7 March 1984; attacks on patrol boats at Puerto Sandino on 28 and 30 March 1984; and an attack on San Juan del Norte on 9 April 1984; and further by those acts of intervention against the Republic of Nicaragua, were in breach of its obligation under customary international law not to use force against another State. (ICJ 1986).

In addition the ICJ decided that the United States of America, by directing or authorizing flights over Nicaraguan territory, and by the acts imputable to the United States, acted against the Republic of Nicaragua, in breach of its obligation under customary international law not to violate the sovereignty of another state. Furthermore, a majority vote decided that by laying mines in the internal or territorial waters of the Republic of Nicaragua during the first months of 1984, the United States of America acted, against the Republic of Nicaragua, in breach of its obligations under customary international law not to use force against another state, not to intervene in its affairs, not to violate its sovereignty, and not to interrupt peaceful maritime commerce (ICJ 1986).

The U.S. government refused to participate in the trial, claiming that the ICJ did not have jurisdiction over the case. President Reagan withdrew American acceptance of mandatory jurisdiction of the court that had been filed forty years earlier by President Truman, with the unanimous support of the Senate. The Nicaraguan government went to the UN Security Council with a resolution calling on all states to observe international law. The United States vetoed the resolution. After this, the Nicaraguan government went to the UN General Assembly, where there is no veto power, and offered the same resolution. The resolution passed with only the United States, Israel, and El Salvador voting to oppose to the resolution. The United States responded to these actions by escalating the war against Nicaragua, and official orders were given to the terrorist forces to focus on "soft targets"—that is, civilian targets (Chomsky 2007). On September 12, 1991, after the 1990 election of Violeta Barrios Torres de Chamorro, the U.S. sponsored candidate, the government of Nicaragua informed the court that it renounced all further right of action based on the case and did not wish to go on with the proceedings. It also requested that an order be made officially recording the discontinuance of the proceedings and directing the removal of the case from the list. The U.S. government, through various foundations, including the National Endowment for Democracy, spent millions of dollars on the Chamorro campaign, in addition to the hundreds of millions spent to fund the terror campaign against the Nicaraguan citizens. This modern case certainly reveals the impotence of the law and the international judicial system in identifying and controlling the crimes of empire.

Since this time, as the U.S. Empire has grown in power following the end of the cold war and the dissolution of the USSR, it has worked to put itself above legal responsibility for its crimes. In the past twenty years it has carried out a number of regime changes, including Haiti, Afghanistan, Serbia, Somalia, and Iraq. It is not unique as an empire in its ability to do this. Throughout most of the history of empires there were little external controls other than popular resistance or warfare. However, the United States is setting a new chapter in the history of empires when it acts to neutralize the external controls that have been established to prevent the acts that are defined as most criminal, acts that it has committed in the past and continues to commit with impunity. The most recent Iraq regime change that is clearly in violation of international law as documented by Kramer and Michalowski (2005) is likely to be repeated as it has throughout U.S. history.

CONCLUSION

Can an empire commit state crime? If what we mean by state crime are those acts that are defined by law, and where there are consequences for those who violate them, then the answer is no. State crime will be defined for those states that are not the centers of empires, or those that fall outside of the imperial sphere of control, or those that are not in alliance with empires. Prosecution is more likely for states defined by the empire as rogue, meaning those outside the control of empires, or as fallen. However, in regard to fallen empires, this may not necessarily be the case. The Ottoman Empire and genocide of Armenians raises some question as to what conditions must be present for prosecution. Obviously, Turkey's relationship with the new imperial center has shielded it from prosecution. Furthermore, there seems to be little interest in the prosecution of former European empires of Germany, Belgium, and the British for their genocidal wars in Africa.

In the pattern of prosecution for state crime, one of the central axioms within critical criminology is illustrated. As critical criminology proclaims, crime is principally defined by the powerful in the interest of the powerful, and that those who are most likely to be defined as criminal are those who have the least power. This is the case within societies, and it certainly is the case in the spaces between societies that we refer to as the domain of the international. This space between nation-states is ordered, and the major force for ordering that space has and continues to be empires. International law is created and enforced to support such an order created by empires or, as in the case today, the world's most powerful empire, the U.S. Empire, in a unipolar world.

Where does this leave scholarship? It is more important than ever to investigate, theorize, and research the world of crime and violence of states and empires. This is not only for the areas where there is law and prosecutions, but even more so for where the law is not applied and there are no prosecutions. Criminologists must incorporate the concept of empire in their scholarship on crime, especially in the international arena. There is not an area of crime that does not take place in the context of empire. To ignore its existence is to be blinded to the most powerful force in the story of crime.

NOTE

This essay was presented in November 2007 at the Annual Meeting of the American Society of Criminology, Atlanta.

CHAPTER 6

Burundi

A HISTORY OF CONFLICT AND STATE CRIME

Kara Hoofnagle

IN EAST-CENTRAL AFRICA, NESTLED BETWEEN TANZANIA, the
Democratic Republic of the Congo, and Rwanda is Burundi. From the onset
of independence in 1961, Burundi has had a history of internal armed conflicts, ethnic tensions, and civil unrest in the form of crimes against humanity,
massive and systematic rape, and other gross human rights violations that
have resulted in hundreds of thousands of civilian deaths. The main civil war
began in 1993 as a response to the election of Melchior Ndadaye in 1992.
Ndadaye's victory was met with resistance by elite Tutsi and on October 23,
1993, Tutsi officers staged a coup d'état, assassinating Ndadaye, which
sparked widespread ethnic violence with hundreds of thousands of deaths. In
2008 Burundi was said to be reaping the dividends of a peace process, yet the
country continues to suffer from violence. Nonetheless, there has been relatively little attention paid to these types of offenses and/or the conflict in
Burundi by criminologists. Burundi should be of central concern, however,
given the scope and magnitude of crimes committed by the state. As others
have noted, the focus of criminologists in general still remains on traditional
street crimes, neglecting those most harmful and costly of crimes: crime by
governments.

STATE CRIME AND VIOLATIONS OF
INTERNATIONAL CRIMINAL LAW

The categorization of phenomena as crimes of the state has led to the
development of several case studies and generated additional attention to
criminology's role in understanding the worst of international crimes; yet as
Rothe and Mullins (2008a, 2009) note, such crimes do not always fit neatly
into the category of crimes of the state. In many cases, regimes are directly or
indirectly involved. In other cases studies, paramilitaries and/or militias are

not considered agents of the state, as conceptualized by state crime scholars. Furthermore, while there are cases of militias working for or with governmental support, we cannot ignore those that do not, as is the case at hand. Therefore, attempting to fit violations of international criminal law into one general typology can be problematic. Instead, the violators of international criminal law must be considered more broadly, including not only state criminality but also militias, paramilitaries, or insurgent groups. Consequentially, the author draws from Mullins and Rothe (2008a), Rothe and Mullins (2006a, 2008a) and Rothe's (2009b) Integrated Theory of International Criminal Violations to frame the analysis of the core etiological factors behind Burundi's conflict.

An Integrated Theory of International Criminal Violations

Drawing off of the theoretical framework by Kramer and Michalowski (1990) and Kauzlarich and Kramer (1998), Mullins and Rothe (2008a), Rothe and Mullins (2006a, 2008a, 2009), and Rothe (2009a, 2009b) have presented an Integrated Theory of International Criminal Violations. Because international crimes involve a multitude of social forces, as well as actors, it is necessary to examine a variety of factors on different levels of analysis. As such, these modalities are explored on four levels: the international level, macro level (i.e., the state-structural), meso level (i.e., organization), and interactional level (i.e., individual). Noting that singular societies are not atomistically separated from each other and that institutional arrangements and forces do not cease their influence at the arbitrary political boundaries on maps, Rothe and Mullins (2006a, 2008a) maintain that any theory of international criminal law violations must be able to address the larger structure that states interact within. The culture of a state—its economic, political, cultural, and historical environment—is distinct from and often in contradiction to those at the international level. In this way, Kauzlarich and Kramer's (1998) theory was not sufficient to address the cultural, economic, political, and historical environment of both the international realm and a particular state (Rothe and Mullins 2006a, 2009). Thus, Rothe and Mullins revised and expanded the original framework to address the additional and equally significant international level of analysis in order to incorporate the increasingly international nature of state criminality. This includes international relations, controls, political pressures, overarching ideological and political interests, economic and military positions of the particular states involved (Rothe and Kauzlarich 2010).

This integrated theoretical model also considers four modalities of international criminal law violations: motivations, opportunities, constraints, and controls. Motivation is the coming together of the general and specific drives that both attract and coax an organization or an individual organizational actor toward offending (Rothe and Mullins 2009). Motivation is the element

Table 1

An integrated theory for international criminal law violations

	Motivation	Opportunity	Constraints	Controls
International Level	Political interests	International relations	International reaction	International law
	Economic interests	Economic supremacy	Political pressure	International sanctions
	Resources	Military supremacy	Public opinion social movements	
	Ideological interests	Complementary legal systems	NGOs and INGO	
			Oversight/ economic institutions	
Macro Level	Structural transformations	Availability of illegal means	Political pressure	Legal sanctions
	Economic pressure or goals	Control of information	Media scrutiny	Domestic law
	Political goals	Propaganda	Public opinion	
	Ethnogenesis	Ideology/ nationalism	Social movements	
	Anomie	Military capabilities	Rebellion	
Meso Level	Organizational culture and goals	Communication structures	Internal oversight	Codes of conduct
	Authoritarian pressures	Means availability	Communication structures	
	Reward structures	Role specialization	Traditional authority structures	
Micro Level	Strain	Obedience to authority	Personal morality	Legitimacy of law
	Socialization	Group think	Socialization	
	Individual goals and ideologies	Diffusion of responsibility	Obedience to authority	Perception of reality of law application
	Normalization of deviance	Perceived illegal means	Informal social controls	
	Definition of the situation			

Source: For previous versions, see Mullins and Rothe (2008a); Rothe (2006a, 2009b); Rothe and Mullins (2006a, 2008a, 2009).

that drives an organization or actor toward offending. Motivating forces can be specific, such as the enhancement and/or maintenance of political power, personal or organizational economic gain, access to valuable natural resources, religious factors, or revenge (Rothe 2009b). They can also be general, such as oppressing a certain ethnic group or governmental party. Opportunities come in many different forms and are largely situational in nature. It is important to recognize that opportunities are not the same as motivations, as without the opportunity to commit a crime, the motivation would not be put into action (Rothe and Kauzlarich 2010).

Constraints and controls are the key components that act as possible deterrents to the crime. While undoubtedly different, they each serve as a curbing mechanism. Constraints are those social elements that stand to potentially make a crime either riskier or less successful; offenders must navigate around them. These can take several forms, including what other scholars have defined as controls: international reactions; political pressures; public opinion, international social movements, oversight from agencies such as the United Nations; political pressures; media scrutiny; and socialization (see also Ross 1995a, 2000a). By definition, they serve as potential barriers before or during an act (Rothe and Mullins 2006a).

Conversely, controls are formal institutions that have the capability to formally punish and hold the offender(s) criminally liable for their actions. Unlike constraints, controls are defined as institutions that have the ability to stave off or prevent entirely the criminal action or to ideally address such violations as an after-the-fact mechanism in the form of accountability. Controls can be conceptualized then as formal social controls that provide accountability, punishment, and/or a range of sanctions (Rothe 2009b).

In sum, the integrated theory incorporates international variables, including but not limited to, factors associated with noncapitalistic endeavors of corporations and/or states, international relations, the international legal system, and components of social disorganization. Additionally, as indicated in table 1, they propose other features that allow for the adaptation of catalysts that may be unique to specific cases (e.g., paramilitary groups, insurgencies, militias, postcolonial conditions, and weakened or illegitimate governments) (Rothe and Kauzlarich 2010). Prior to exploring the crimes committed in Burundi from a theoretical perspective, an understanding of the history of the country and subsequent waves of conflicts is necessary. As such, the following section provides a brief overview of Burundi's history as well as the events surrounding the 1993 civil war and subsequent years of violence.

Historical Background

Dating back to 1890, the region known today as Burundi was attached to colonial rule, beginning with Urundi and neighboring Rwanda all being incorporated into what was then called German East Africa. In 1916 Belgian troops occupied the Ruanda-Urundi territory, and in 1923 the League of Nations granted Belgium the mandate to administer the territory. Belgium typically ruled its colonial holdings indirectly, and this region was no different (Mullins and Rothe 2008a). Specifically, Belgium focused on the distinction between the Tutsi and the Hutu, subsequently capitalizing on the division and establishing it as the basis of their colonial system, giving economic and social preferences to one group over the other. As with neighboring Rwanda, the ethnic divide of the population comprised Hutu (85 percent), Tutsi (14 percent) and Twa (1 percent). The ethnic groups were further stratified, dividing the Tutsi into two groups, the Hima and Baganwa, which facilitated the ethnic polarization of Burundi. Henceforth, the Tutsi-Hima became the elite group, and governmental power rested in their hands (Uvin 1999). The class divides in Burundi were characterized by the ownership of cattle, which denoted power: the Hutu could not own cattle, as such ownership denoted power and prestige in society (yet they could be granted forms of usufruct by their labor and political fealty) (Loft 1998).

Society in Burundi was stratified into a sociopolitical hierarchy with a king at the top, Tutsi in the middle, Hutu at the lower level, and Twa at the bottom (Uvin 1999); land tenure was the main means of surplus production (Loft 1998). As in Rwanda, the colonial administration reserved the higher levels of education and jobs for the Tutsi and acted according to the "incorporation of native authority into a state enforced customary order to benefit the colonial power" (Mamdani 1996, 42). Colonization did indeed change the nature of the political rule. The power of the Tutsi increased, while political, social, and economic relations became more unequal and biased against the Hutu (Uvin 1999). The increase of power, and subsequent wealth into the hands of the Tutsi, left the Hutu marginalized.

Rwanda (or Ruanda, as it was called at this time) suffered more unrest than the Urundi territory, and in 1957 Hutu leaders published the Hutu Manifesto, which fueled the fire between the Tutsi and the Hutu by preparing Hutu supporters for a political conflict based on ethnic lines. By 1959 there were intense localized anti-Tutsi sentiments that resulted in fighting, framed by ethnic differences. Thousands were killed and an influx of Rwandan refugees into Urundi territory occurred (Uvin 1999). This marked the beginning of the turmoil in Burundi and played a critical role in fostering an environment of conflict.

Postcolonial Independence

Ruanda-Urundi colony gained independence on July 1, 1962, despite pressure from the United Nations to form a single country. The Urundi territory became a constitutional monarchy and changed its name to Burundi. In neighboring Rwanda, the rise of Hutus into political positions influenced many of their kinsman in Burundi to share their political objectives, which increased fear among the Tutsi that the Hutu may intensify their desire to dominate society (Lemarchand 1998). Many Rwandans sought refuge in Burundi, bringing with them their ideologies regarding the ethnic divisions. In essence, the ethnic conflict in Rwanda bled over to Burundi.

Various political parties also began to form, including the UPRONA (Union for National Progress), a royalist and biethnic party led by Prince Louis Rwagasore, who initially held office as the ruler of Burundi. Soon after taking office, Rwagasore was assassinated by the opposition (Uvin 1999). Competition for power was intense, primarily between the Tutsi-Hima, the Tutsi-Banyarugur, and a small percentage of emerging Hutu elite (Uvin 1999). In 1965 King Mwambutsa refused to appoint a Hutu prime minister despite the Hutus' victory in parliamentary elections. This resulted in an attempted coup led by Michel Micombero and the Hutu police that was brutally suppressed, leading to the deaths of an estimated five thousand Hutu (International Crisis Group 2008). Mwambutsa fled the country and was replaced by his son Ntare V. In all, during 1965 four key political actors were assassinated, including Prime Minister Ngendandumwe (which intensified the ethnic division between the Tutsi and Hutu). Additionally, the Hutu were excluded from virtually all key political, social, and economic institutions (Brachet and Wolpe 2005). Hutu power was feared greatly by the Tutsi, and Ngendandumwe's assassination served to intensify fears within both ethnic groups. As the conflict in Rwanda intensified, fear, hatred, and racial sentiments increased in Burundi, most significantly attributed to the stories told by Rwandan refugees. The division between the Tutsi and Hutu widened and the socially constructed perspective of ethnic differences became entrenched even deeper within civil society.

In November of 1966 a second, and successful, coup resulted in Micombero declaring himself as president of Burundi. Over the next seven years unrest defined Burundi. The government struggled to maintain power, and opposition forces fought to destroy the current government apparatus. By late 1971 the struggle for power between the Tutsi-Hima from the south and the Tutsi-Banyaruguru from the north escalated, and rumors of plots and coups resulted in arrests and questionable trials of scores of Banyaruguru politicians (Lemarchand 1998).

April 1972 marked another period of atrocity after the death of Ntare V that resulted in roughly 150,000 Hutus being massacred. Hutu and Mulelists operating in groups of ten to twenty people armed with small automatic weapons, machetes, and spears proceeded to kill every Tutsi they came in contact with, as well as Hutu who refused to join them (Lemarchand 1998). On April 30, the Tutsi-dominated army and *jeunesses* youths (i.e., a collection of secondary-level students, school dropouts, and unemployed) were called upon by governmental leaders to exterminate all individuals suspected of being involved in the Hutu assassination, a task that resulted in a two-month-long rampage. As the army moved from the capital to the southern province, they rounded up, jailed, or killed cadres of Hutus, including local administrators, skilled workers, chauffeurs, clerks, and students. For example, at the University in Bujumbura a multitude of students were physically assaulted and beaten to death (Lemarchand 1998). Soldiers and *jeunesses* youths entered classrooms and called Hutu students by name. Those identified were removed, and few, if any, returned. This practice was not unique to the University in Bujumbura, but rather took place across the territory. No sector of society was left untouched. It is estimated that at least 100,000 Hutu were killed and an approximately 150,000 more fled the state (Uvin 1999).

In 1976 President Micombero's tenure as head of state came to an end as a result of yet another military coup. He was replaced with Jean-Baptists Bagaza. As is typical in countries ridden with histories of coups and counter-coups, the replacement head of state often reacts to their newfound political power with efforts aimed at ensuring its legitimization and maintenance (Mullins and Rothe 2008a). In 1981 a new constitution was put into effect making Burundi a one-party state, formally wiping out political opposition. Just over a decade later, September 1987, Bagaza found himself victim to yet another coup d'état, under the rule of Major Pierre Buyoya, which resulted in additional outbreaks of violence (Reyntjens 1993).

In August of 1988, during an operation aimed at restoring order, the armed forces randomly killed thousands of Hutu civilians in the northern municipalities (e.g., Ntega and Marangara). It is estimated that in excess of 15,000 were killed, while another 60,000 fled into Rwanda (Reyntjens 1993; Uvin 1999). Hutu farmers in the northern provinces rebelled and killed approximately 3,000 Tutsi. In response, President Buyoya, in October of 1988, set up the National Commission to Study the Question of National Unity, which led to the Charter of National Unity. Despite Buyoya's rhetoric of reconciliation, the military was much less willing to change and remained Tutsi dominated.

From 1966 to 1993, power was in the hands of three primary military regimes (Micombero 1966–1982; Bagaza 1982–1987; Buyoya 1987–1993). The presidents had all been Tutsi-Hima, originating from the same village in the Bururi region. As previously noted, through the 1970s and 1980s there were several instances of Tutsi using their power to repress Hutu populations, some events genocidal in nature. Consequentially, several Hutu rebel groups formed, dissolved, and split apart during the course of the various conflicts— for example, PALIPEHUTU (Parti pour la Libération du Peuple Hutu, or Party for the Liberation of the Hutu People), PALIPEHUTU-FNL (Parti pour la Libération du Peuple Hutu–Forces Nationales de Liberation, or Party for the Liberation of the Hutu People–Forces for the National Liberation), FROLINA (Front pour la Libération Nationale), CNDD (Conseil National pour la Défense de la Démocratie, or National Council for the Defense of Democracy), and CNDD-FDD (Conseil National pour la Défense de la Démocratie–Forces pour la Défense de la Démocratie, or National Council for the Defence of Democracy–Forces for the Defence of Democracy).

The PALIPEHUTU and CNDD have been the central rebel actors, with many of the other groups splitting off in various processes of factionalization. PALIPEHUTU was established in 1980 among Hutu within refugee camps in Tanzania. While it strongly advocated armed struggle as the primary tool to gain Hutu rights, it took eleven years before it began launching attacks directed at the Burundi government. Factionalization and splits within the group reduced its military capabilities early in the conflict. FROLINA broke away in 1990, with its military branch FAP (Forces Armées Populaires) launching its first raids in August of that year. Another splinter group, PALIPEHUTU-FNL—which had a stronger impact on the fights—organized in 1991 in response to the PALIPEHUTU military failures. As political factions continued to split while others grew, and civil, political, and economic unrest remained a constant, another trigger sparked an additional era of conflict, violent crimes and gross human rights violations.

The onset of the civil war of 1993 began almost immediately after the election of Melchior Ndadaye, the first president of the country to be democratically elected and the first Hutu president. In October 1993, less than a few months after his installation as head of state, Tutsi officers staged a coup d'état assassinating Ndadaye. This event can be seen as the trigger to the current conflict, though grievances historically run deep. Ndadaye's assassination and the Tutsi coup sparked widespread ethnic violence, with estimates ranging between 25,000 to 300,000 deaths.

The 1993 Civil War and Subsequent Years of Violence

The year 1993 had the look of change and hopes for a unified society, yet with the executions of President Ndadaye, speaker and deputy speaker of the newly elected *assemblee nationale*, and several high government officials, the reality was that a new violent period was setting the course of Burundi's history, causing severe economic disruption and dislocation. In response to the assassination of Ndadaye, FRODEBU party members began massacring Tutsis. In response, the army initiated reprisals, killing thousands of Hutu. In all, approximately 50,000 to 100,000 persons (both Tutsi and Hutu, many of which were women and children) were killed in the three months following the coup; one million more fled the country and hundreds of thousands were displaced internally by the time the FRODEBU government regained control (Uvin 1999).

In January 1994 Cyprien Ntaryamira was elected as president, though his presidency was also cut short when he and Rwandan President Habyarimana were killed in a plane crash on April 6 of that year. While this was the onset of the Rwandan genocide, for Burundi it only marked a slight increase in the violence. Sylvestre Ntibantunganya was named as new head of state, but this new regime did not hold much legitimation as the security situation in the country continued to deteriorate. As noted by the U.S. State Department (1995, 3),

> In addition to extrajudicial killings by the armed forces, armed groups perpetrated unlawful, politically and ethnically motivated killings of that group's ethnic counterpart or political opponent. The armed forces frequently committed abuses in government-approved operations to disarm civilians. On May 9 troops in pursuit of armed civilians killed 52 unarmed civilian residents in the nearby Gashorora region of rural Bujumbura province. . . . In July, military forces removed approximately 30 male refugees from a U.N. High Commissioner for Refugees (UNHCR) transit point in Kabarore, Ngozi province, without prior notification to UNHCR. The group never returned and a mass grave for a similar number of persons was found across the provincial border. . . . Also in July, men in military uniforms gathered approximately 45 refugees, mostly women and children, into a deserted church in Cendajeru, Ngozi, threw a grenade into the church and fired on those who survived the blast. . . . In June civilians—with some degree of complicity by unidentified military forces—separated about 100 Rwandan Hutu refugees from their families near Kiri, in Kirundo province, removed them to another location, and killed them.

In roughly two years' time, another coup replaced Ntibantunganya with Major Pierre Buyoya, who stated he was intervening to prevent an expansion of ethnic violence. Since then, however, the armed forces of Burundi have continued to engage in massive violations of human rights. For example, soldiers and their civilian allies continued to slaughter innocent victims daily. The army, still composed largely of Tutsi, "operated at the command of radical Tutsi leaders rather than under the orders of the ineffective civilian government, nominally controlled by FRODEBU . . . [using a] combination of violence, intimidation, and political blockage, Tutsi-dominated factions re-appropriated the political control they had lost at the polls in June 1993" (Human Rights Watch 1996, 2). The FDD—the military faction of the CNDD, began fighting in 1994, taking advantage of Hutu refugees fleeing Rwanda's civil war. CNDD-FDD established itself as its own faction within the CNDD in 1998.

Civil war between the Tutsi led government and Hutu rebel groups continued in 1998 as the two groups targeted and aimed to displace civilians from their homes by executing, torturing, and raping those of the opposing group. The year 1999 saw more than 500 people being killed. As noted by Feller (2001,16), in the fall of 1999,

> the Tutsi-dominated army and government of Burundi started to forcibly move from their homes up to 80% of the population living in the province of Rural Bujumbura forcing most of them into over 50 re-assembly camps. [At the end of 1999] more than 350,000 people were displaced in Rural Bujumbura province alone. Elsewhere in the country, hundreds of thousands of people were internally displaced or forcibly relocated . . . In some cases, the army allegedly killed people if they did not obey their orders quickly enough. The displaced population suffered multiple and systematic abuses of their human rights, ranging from overcrowding, poor sanitation and inadequate medical care in the camps to extra-judicial killings, rape and torture of the displaced population by the soldiers.

As is typical in most conflict situations, especially those where women are subordinate within the culture, rape has been systematically used as a strategic weapon of war.

By 2001 two groups joined forces to rebel against the Tutsi government: the FDD, with an estimated 10,000 fighters, and the FNL, with an estimated 3,000. In 2001 the FDD split into two camps; in 2002 the FNL likewise was sundered in leadership infighting (Rothe and Mullins 2008a). As with other Great Lakes conflicts, the Burundi civil war was quickly intertwined with other regional conflicts. The government had drawn aid from the Rwandan army, the Ugandan government, and the RDC in the Democratic Republic of Congo (DRC). Rebel factions have allied with Rwandan insurgents, the DRC government, and the Mayi-Mayi in the DRC. Both FDD and FNL forces had bases of operation in the DRC. Further, both former members of the Armed Forces of Rwanda (FAR) and Interhamwe joined the Burundian rebellion. Tanzania provided both succor, in allowing bases to be established in their territory, and military aid to the FDD throughout the conflict. Early in the conflict the United States and France assisted the sitting government. Later, the African Union put a peacekeeping force on the ground, which was later taken over by the UNSC and was present in the country until 2007. Additionally, Human Rights Watch (2000) divulged detailed evidence of Rwandan Hutu participating in the uprisings in Burundi. In fact, they stated that approximately half of the combatants in some of the rebel groups in Burundi were Rwandans—many of which were soldiers of the former Rwandan government responsible for the 1994 Tutsi genocide in Rwanda.

During 2000, the signing of the Arusha Peace Accords by seventeen political parties provided a framework for peace and postconflict reconstruction, including a power-sharing agreement between factions. However, neither the FDD nor FNL were party to these talks. Two years later in October, the main fighting forces of the FDD and the FNL signed treaties with the government. In December of that year the smaller FDD faction signed an agreement; the faction of the FNL led by Agathon Rwasa refused to enter into an agreement. While the 2002 ceasefires were often broken, they did establish a mutual understanding that allowed more talks in 2003. The 2003 Pretoria Protocol, an internationally brokered agreement, established a cease-fire, a general amnesty, and the blueprint for a power-sharing government and integrated military force. Yet, even with peace accords and a tentative power-sharing agreement in place, the disorder and violence had not ceased. The FNL again rejected the Pretoria agreement and continued to fight against the government and the FDD. In 2003 and 2004, CNDD-FDD forces established their own institutional control over territories in Burundi, establishing and carrying out de facto governance despite existing agreements with the government. FDD forces have been implicated in numerous violations of human rights and of international criminal law (i.e., assault, rape, looting, political intimidation, and extrajudicial executions). The record of the government forces and those of the FNL are not better in the region.

Despite several peace talks between 2000 and 2006, hundreds of citizens continued to be killed. In 2005 a new constitution was enacted and general elections were held with numerous parties vying for power. The CNDD-FDD won, with their leader Nkurunziza installed as the new head of state. As many international commentators and nongovernmental organizations have noted, the Nkurunziza government continues to have a poor human rights record and presides over a less than stable state (Rothe and Mullins 2008a). For example, over thirty Burundian civilians were killed between June and August 2006 by National Defense Forces. The victims were suspected of supporting the rebel party for the liberation of the Hutu people and were subsequently arrested by local administrative officials and agents of the intelligence service. The National Defense Forces transported the victims from the Mukoni military camp to Ruvubu National Park, where they were killed, their lifeless bodies tossed into the river.

In 2007 the FNL stated that they were recommitted to the peace accords. However, their involvement in violence continued: "Fighters of Burundi's last active rebel group have for the second time in one week attacked a position occupied by a break-away faction, forcing villagers to flee their homes. The evening raid by combatants of the Front National de Liberation (FNL), led by Agathon Rwasa, took place on a site where the so-called FNL "dissidents" have gathered in the Gakungwe village of Kabezi commune in Bujumbura Rural province" (IRIN 2007, 1).

Further, the actions of the FNL and their withdrawal from peace talks with the government resulted in a new governmental program initiation that was cited on many occasions for torture and illegal detentions. In 2007 the commissioner general of the Internal Security Police (PSI) developed the GMIR (Groupements Mobile d'Intervention Rapide). GMIR officers were dispersed throughout communes, focusing namely in the Rutegama Commune. It was reported that officers of the GMIR beat, tortured, and carried out unwarranted searches. Several residents were targeted for arbitrary arrests by the local police chief (Nestor Niyokuri) and the Rutegama communal administrator (Josias Ndikumagenge). Human Rights Watch (2008a, 6) interviewed eleven former detainees, all of which were beaten, and intimated into giving information—even if false. "He asked me if I was a member of the FNL. I said that I used to be, but that I haven't been a member for a long time. The OPJ wrote a statement and made me sign it, saying I used to be a member of the FNL but that I no longer was involved." Another victim stated, "I was beaten on my hands, face, buttocks, backs of my legs, and my back. I still have problems walking and I have scars on my legs. When I was freed, they told me to quit the FNL and not to help the FNL when they ask for help." GMIR officers also subjected detainees to false executions and death threats. While sporadic, violence continued into 2008 despite several attempts to resolve the ongoing conflict.

THEORETICAL APPLICATION

Here the Integrated Theory for International Criminal Law Violations is used in an effort to draw out the etiological factors behind this violence. Such an endeavor is especially important to understanding that when the causal mechanisms are not addressed, the likelihood that state and/or internal paramilitary groups will continue to commit massive crimes against the civilian population is significantly higher than had such conditions been addressed, as we continue to witness with Burundi.

As the theoretical model highlights, variables within motivation, opportunity, constraint, and control have been operationalized as core etiological factors when combined in specific fashions. As such, the following analysis is divided amongst the catalysts of motivation, opportunity, constraints, and controls.

Motivation

Several variables, including political and economic interests, external to the state facilitated motivational drives. For example, political and ideological interests of neighboring countries resulted in support for both Hutu and Tutsi regimes in Burundi and the various political factions or insurgency groups. Recall that the government had received political and economic support from the Ugandan government and the Rwandan armed forces, of which support was tied to their own political and economic self-interests. Further, rebel factions allied with Rwandan insurgents as well as with the DRC and the Mayi-Mayi in the DRC. Such interstate support fueled motivational drives behind the conflict. This was further evidenced by the direct involvement and support of the Rwandan FAR and Interhamwe, which provided additional ideological motivation. Such networks resulted in an isomorphic relationship where shared ideological, political, and economic interests fueled the tensions between the Hutu and Tutsis, as well as the belief in their cause. In many ways, the genocide in Rwanda tapped into the extant motivations of the various factions and civil society, including but not limited to fear, prejudice, and revenge.

There were also economic interests embedded within policies initiated at the international level that prompted motivation at the interactional level. For example, the International Monetary Fund (IMF) structural adjustment programs in Burundi were suspended following the outbreak of violence in 1993. This coupled with the many bilateral embargoes resulted in additional poverty and worsening state economic conditions. This in turn enhanced ethnic polarization. Burundi's economy dropped 21 percent (gross domestic product) and it experienced a sharp rise in inflation. As noted by the World Bank, "rural poverty increased by increased 80 percent between 1993 and 1999 with a 50 percent increase in urban poverty" (1999, 6). Goods prices increased due to higher import prices and the embargoes. "Since the imposition of the embargo there has been a further drop in external aid" (6).

As state crime literature and the theoretical model used here suggests, global and state economic conditions are central to criminogenic environments (Friedrichs and Friedrichs 2002; Rothe, Mullins, and Sandstrom 2009). When drastic fluctuations occur, economically weak states find themselves in dire conditions. This in turn may result in overall instability, coups, genocides, or additional forms of state repression to offset the chaos or disorder brought about by the larger economic conditions (Rothe 2009b). Further, contending groups generally make rival claims to the state authority, creating further instability, leading to conditions of additional oppression and targeting of opposition groups. Simply, the consequences of policies at the international level impacted the state level (larger structural conditions), the organizational level (governmental political and economic support as well as economic and ideological support for the various faction groups), and the interactional level where such conditions motivate individuals.

Historically, it has been the Tutsi who have dominated the government and military, thus having primary access to resources and their allocation. When social and economic conditions worsened, so did the economic and political marginalization of the Hutu population, resulting in increased ethnic tensions and resentment. This was in turn internalized, resulting in individual level motivational drives. For the government, maintaining control over resources, continued regime legitimacy, and its political and economic goals facilitated motivation. This was evident in the violence of 1972 when a two-month rampage resulted in mass deaths of the most educated and most skilled Hutu—those who posed the most threat to the extant power structure.

Military coups in Burundi have often been instigated as a response to a corrupt regime, ethnic hostility and disenfranchisement. As discussed, they usually result in a one-party state under the control of a single, populist leader and their ethnic kin. Newly empowered regimes typically lead to their own deposal by subsequent coups that generally set up yet another one-party state, or they maintain a military junta rule (Rothe 2009b; Rothe and Mullins 2008a). This upheaval fuels tensions as well as an environment of social disorganization and/or anomic conditions ripe for violence.

Common enactment procedures include the use of ethnocism or racism, propaganda, militarization, and/or fear of creating or enabling an environment conducive to violence by states as well as militias. In the case at hand, ethnogenesis was core to motivational factors. As previously noted, ethnogenesis was enhanced with international policies, intrastate involvement of insurgents and governments, and the Rwandan tensions and subsequent genocide, which had an immediate impact on Burundi given the influx of refugees. Scholars of genocides and other war crimes have long pointed toward the "otherizing" effects of ethnic polarization and dehumanization as facilitating violence in general and widespread lethal violence in particular. This otherizing has typically been manifested through constructed ethnic or racial divisions. After all, a central element within atrocity-producing environments is a set of intense ethnic rivalries and tensions often focused on capital attainment, be it political, social, or economic (Rothe 2009b).

Such ethnic divisiveness comes to bear on the use of rape as a tool of warfare. As in other conflicts (e.g., Rwanda, Serbia, Sierra Leone, and Uganda), rape has been used as a tool of terror in Burundi. A key motivation for mass rape is the humiliation of community members, including, and perhaps more specifically, male members. Derogation and identity spoilage of the rape victims also plays a role, especially so when ethnic divisions are so deeply entrenched and one of the more visible forces facilitating the violence (Mullins 2009; Mullins and Rothe 2008a; Rothe and Mullins 2008a).

Where ethnic cleavages are deeply ingrained within the population and reflected by a portion of society marginalized and victimized, hatred, revenge, and fear become powerful emotions that often translate into violence. Fear is a tool that can be used not only at the cultural and organizational levels to ensure complicity, hatred, and/or obedience, but also at the individual level. This intense fear explains why people can engage in mass violence that under other conditions they would not be capable of. It also explains how some can become bystanders. The culture in Burundi, like Rwanda, has a traditional practice of obedience, especially toward authority. This is also driven by a fear resulting from blackmails or threats (Gourevitch 1998; Prunier 1995). Fear can also act as a powerful motivating factor that is translated into larger security issues of a particular ethnic group. Fear serves to motivate to kill the other so that the other either does not kill or continue to oppress the self.

Opportunity

While I have discussed the impact of international relations and subsequent policies on motivational drives, such relationships also provide opportunities. Indeed, Tanzania provided both succor and military aid to the FDD throughout the conflict (Rothe and Mullins 2008a), which increased the opportunity structure for such violence to be carried out. Early in the conflict, the United States and France assisted the sitting government financially and through military support. In 1997 a report from a New York–based watch group, Stoking the Fires, named China, France, North Korea, Russia, Rwanda, Tanzania, Uganda, the Democratic Republic of Congo, and the United States as the most significant suppliers of military aid.

As in Rwanda, thousands of refugees fled Burundi for the DRC, which served as a safe haven for both Rwandan and Burundian Hutu rebel groups. In exchange for allied participation in the Congolese war, the Congolese army provided training, arms, and funding to the groups. Armed, the groups returned to their respective countries to continue fighting against the regimes and civilians. Similarly, the Tanzanian government provided support to the Hutu that fled to Tanzania.

Additionally, during times of political turmoil, opportunity structures are often present in the chaos and/or disorganization (Rothe and Mullins 2009). The 1993 assassination of Ndadaye provided an opportunity for the Front Democratique du Burundi (FRODEBU). As noted by Lemarchand (1998, xv), "What happened in our county is not accident, but a catastrophe engineered by the Frodebu." The involvement of organizations operating within the apparatus of the state provided additional opportunities to engage in criminal behavior. As Mullins and Rothe contend, "When there are multiple organizations involved, one being the state, the relationship of the secondary organization to the regime provides additional opportunity and impunity for criminogenic behaviors" (2008a, 213). This was the case with several factions in Burundi, specifically FRODEBU and UPRONA and their respective relationships with paramilitary forces. The relationship between the GMIR and the internal policing organization also provided legitimized opportunities.

Intensive propaganda was distributed using the media. Extremist newspapers and radio stations, in particular the radical newspaper Radio Libre des Mille Collines and Kangura, spread hateful propaganda about the Tutsi. This included explicitly inciting murder, using verbal attacks, publication of individuals' names to be killed, and threats to anyone having affiliation with the Tutsi (Uvin 1999). The media was also a means in which counterhegemony could be suppressed. As an example, shortly after Nikundanda interviewed Alain Mugabarabona on the radio station Isanganiro, and Mugabarabona made allegations that the alleged coup of 2006 was propaganda, the CNDD-FDD determined that the story was false. Nikundanda was arrested and charged with belonging to the opposition army and broadcasting enemy propaganda in a time of war. Such actions also served as a public statement to independent broadcasters in an effort to ensure their self-censorship.

While stated as a protective measure, the state mandated displacements and subsequent camps provided opportunity for much violence. As noted by Feller, "most of the displaced population felt more secure before being displaced. It seems, rather, that the army wished to have greater military control over the population and to create a free zone where anyone outside the camps would be considered a member of the armed opposition and, as such, a military target" (2001, 23).

The structure, or lack thereof, of the military also provided opportunity for crimes to be committed with plausible deniability. For example, the lines of command and authority in the newly integrated military were not clear. The government officers insist that former FDD troops are under the direct control of former FDD officers; while FDD officers point out that the governmental forces constitute the true military authority. This has been made even more problematic by the nature of the integration committee, which Human Rights Watch points out existed only to discuss logistics of force combination and decommission, not on-the-ground issues of command and control of forces.

The opportunity to use rape as a tool of the war is obvious in many ways, yet, under certain cultural conditions, such ability is enhanced. The culture and traditional relationships of men and women, including their subsequent legal rights, facilitated the opportunity for women and children to be victimized. In Burundi, women suffer from discrimination based on a belief in male superiority and the cultural and social subordination of women. Burundi law institutionalizes this subordination: men are the head of the family, women cannot inherit land, and women's participation in the governmental decision-making processes is very limited. Women retain a position more closely aligned with property; as such, the raping of a woman is akin to taking or vandalizing a man's property without any real fear of reprisal or legal punishment. This, coupled with the motivation for rape in times of conflict, made a powerful connection that became actualized on a massive scale.

Constraints

There have been several mechanisms at the international level put in place to constrain the civil war in Burundi, including political pressure, nongovernmental organizations, oversight and economic institutions, and interstate relations in the form of embargoes. Several of these not only failed to constrain the ongoing violence but also provided additional motivation and opportunity, thus aggravating rather than constraining conditions. Recall the discussion of the embargoes and subsequent results that intensified dire economic conditions, facilitating anger, fear, resentment, and other motivating forces. Additionally, the international finance institutions' ending of support for several years added to growing economic and social upheavals. In this case, they were not only failed constraints as perceived by the theoretical model, but also mechanisms that facilitated the war.

In an effort to constrain the ongoing war, on August 29, 1995, Resolution 1012 was approved by the United Nations Security Council (UNSC) requesting the establishment of an international commission of inquiry. However, the International Commission of Inquiry failed to provide any meaningful headway. Following the death of Tanzanian President Nyerere, former South African President Nelson Mandela assumed the lead role in the process that resulted in the Arusha Peace Agreement. In 2000 seventeen political parties signed the Arusha Accords, which provided a framework for peace and postconflict reconstruction, including a power-sharing agreement between factions. As previously noted, neither the FDD nor the FNL were party to these talks. In 2002, the main fighting forces of the FDD and the FNL signed treaties with the government. In December of that year the smaller FDD faction signed an agreement, but an off-shoot of the FNL led by Agathon Rwasa refused to enter into an agreement. While the 2002 cease-fires were often broken, they did establish a mutual understanding that allowed more talks in 2003, which resulted in the Pretoria Protocol.

The Pretoria Protocol, an internationally brokered agreement, established a cease-fire, a general amnesty, and the blueprint for a power-sharing government and integrated military force. Yet, even with peace accords and a tentative power-sharing agreement in place, the disorder and violence had not ceased. In part, this is because the implementation of the protocol's provisions have been haphazard, piecemeal, and with little in the way of a firm authority structure to oversee enactment. Also, the FNL rejected the Pretoria agreement and continued to fight against the government and the FDD (Rothe and Mullins 2008a).

A disarmament, demobilization, and reintegration (DDR) program was created to integrate and address the immediate needs of child soldiers and former combatants (namely the FNL). The first was initiated during 2003 under the auspices of the government, with implementation support from UNICEF. Under the 2004 Security Council Resolution 1545, United Nations Operation in Burundi (ONUB) was mandated to carry out the disarmament and demobilization portions of the national DDR program (S/RES/1545).

Yet, the commission responsible for managing the program was not established until 2005. Since May 2004 approximately 6,000 UN peacekeepers have been involved in the ONUB. In 2006 they left Burundi, to be replaced by the civilian United Nations Integrated Office in Burundi (BINUB), tasked with the mission to support the consolidation of the peace and to act as a liaison between UN agencies in Burundi.

Controls

International laws are indeed a control; after all, the foundation of law is to deter. When that fails, ideally law would be used as a control in the form of accountability. In the case of Burundi, there are several applicable international laws covering the vast numbers of crimes (including crimes against humanity, torture, rape, and displacement) committed by the Tutsi army and insurgency groups. These include both customary law and international humanitarian law. For example, Article 3 of the 1949 Geneva Conventions and the 1977 additional Protocol II serve as controls in the case of the noninternational armed civil conflicts occurring on the territory of a state party. Furthermore, Article 3 outlines several provisions that each party involved in the conflict must abide by, including, but not limited to, the prohibition against violence against life and person, the taking of hostages, and humiliating and degrading treatment. The application of the 1977 Additional Protocol II has a higher threshold than Article 3 of the Geneva Convention, yet it can be applied given the effective control of certain territory by the FNL. As a party to the UN Convention against Torture and other Cruel, Inhuman or Degrading Treatment or Punishment (CAT), perpetrators could be held accountable for their acts of torture and other relevant crimes.

While nonbinding, international human rights laws have been violated as well. Burundi is a party to the International Covenant on Civil and Political Rights and the African Charter on Human and People's Rights and is supposed to ideally guarantee protection for freedom of expression. Undoubtedly, the extant body of international law, as a control, is problematic given its complementary nature and lack of enforcement mechanisms. Impunity has and will most likely continue for most of the perpetrators of the crimes committed during the long civil war. Nonetheless, the lack of effectiveness cannot negate the presence of these laws and their potential to be used to hold those violators accountable.

In 2005 the government of Burundi approved a Truth and Reconciliation Commission, a component of the Arusha Peace Agreement that also included a general amnesty and a transitional power-sharing government. Resolution 1606 established a partial truth commission and special court to prosecute war crimes and other violations committed during the past decades of the conflict. The commission would fall under the Burundi's judicial system, with three international and two Burundian commissioners. In May 2007 an agreement was reached by the UN high commissioner for human rights and Burundi to set up the truth commission and a special court with the understanding that the government would not grant amnesty for war crimes, genocide, crimes against humanity, and other serious violations. To date, no real progress has been made in the implementation of the Truth and Reconciliation Commission or accountability.

CONCLUSION

Since gaining independence in 1962, Burundi has been trapped in an unending cycle of violence. The main cause of incompatibility between parties is rooted in a power struggle, embedded in ethnic divisiveness. As with most of the conflicts in Sub-Saharan Africa, such divisions and ethnic polarization can be traced back to the colonial authority's preferential treatment, in this case the Tutsis (Mullins and Rothe 2008a). Constructed or not, the ethnic nature of the conflict is real in its consequences. In this case, it is tied heavily into capital accumulation, where the Tutsi have maintained the power and resources of the state, especially the military, representing Tutsi interests, and empowerment and the rebel groups representing Hutu interests, reducing Hutu submission and exploitation by the Burundian state. However, this is not simply a clear-cut ethnic conflict. Radical Hutus expressing an ethicist ideology and radical Tutsis, primarily in the armed forces, have driven the conflict toward extreme violence, preventing more moderate elements from establishing stable political systems and institutions.

Research has shown that countries that experience a pattern of coups and countercoups are often vulnerable to violence, one-party states, and continued marginalization of a significant portion of the population. Burundi is no exception. Operationalized constraints not only failed to work in the case at hand but facilitated motivation and opportunity structures. This was evidenced not only by the sanctions, or embargos. Additionally, while the media is seen as a potential constraint, it failed at the international level, as Burundi was overshadowed by the Rwandan genocide and other conflicts in the region, and the domestic media was used to incite violence, hatred, and fear.

Indeed, the atrocities and the surrounding conditions do not exist in a vacuum or operate independently, nor do the motivations, opportunities, constraints, and controls. Structural and regional cleavages play a vital role as well. As interstate conflicts have spilled over the border, refugees have fled into and out of Burundi. Economic conditions, embargoes, structural adjustment aid, arms trade, and military support all come together to affect in some form the decision-making processes at the individual level. Fear, self-interest, revenge, hatred, and a host of other emotions, whether born out of propaganda, relationships, subjugation, or obedience, each can be essential given a particular moment in time; yet agency is as central as the conditions that come together.

Perhaps the most disheartening conclusion is that the many efforts to achieve peace and to hold those responsible accountable have been ineffective on many levels, due to factors ranging from lack of political will to actualized resources. Undoubtedly, the conflict in Burundi is complex, which contributes to the difficulty of implementing effective peace-making policies. Additionally, having underscored the primary etiological factors that undergird the conflict, and having witnessed the multiple failed attempts to end the conflict, I suggest that unless these conditions are addressed, the road to sustainable peace is rocky at best.

CHAPTER 7

Legal Precedent, Jurisprudence, and State Crime

PINOCHET AND CRIMES AGAINST HUMANITY

Dawn L. Rothe and Michael Bohlander

WITH THE 1973 MILITARY COUP OF Chilean President Salvador Allende, General Augusto Pinochet began a seventeen-year dictatorship founded on fear, oppression, intimidation, and violence. According to the *Report of the Chilean National Commission on Truth and Reconciliation*, 3,200 people were killed or forcibly disappeared, with more than 28,000 victims of torture and hundreds of thousands of civilians who were exiled or left the country in fear for their lives (Human Rights Watch 2006a; Chilean National Commission on Truth and Reconciliation 1991). While the crimes committed by Pinochet and his regime were horrific, they were not unlike atrocities committed by other authoritarian heads of state (e.g., Idi Amin and General Museveni of Uganda, Mobutu Sese Seko of the Congo, and Hissene Habré of Chad). What makes this case of particular importance is the legal precedent set with the first acting head of state being charged with international criminal law violations by another state. As stated by Sugerman, "Pinochet's arrest and 'the Pinochet precedent' reflected and strengthened a new international movement to end impunity for the worst abuses of human rights. Since the Pinochet case, several former and even serving heads of state have found themselves in the dock for massive violations of human rights" (2008, 1).[1]

THE REIGN OF TERROR, 1973–1990

The onset of seventeen years of oppression and intermittent crimes against humanity began September 11, 1973, as the armed forces attempted to bring Chile under their control, eliminating any resistance of the deposed Allende regime supporters. In what was to become a common pattern, officials from the deposed regime, the main leaders, and social and political supporters were detained. As noted by the *Report of the Chilean National Commission on Truth and Reconciliation*:

> During these months mistreatment and torture were an almost universal feature of detentions. . . . Beating and humiliation were common when people were being arrested . . . Torture was also usual during interrogation. Their families were waiting outside these places. They knew or had been told that their relatives had been arrested, that they were here—or over there—at some prison site. . . . Then on some fateful day . . . their loved ones were no longer there. Sometimes families were told that they had never been there. Or that they had been transferred somewhere else—where it was then denied. Or that they had been released. Other times the answer was ridicule, a threat, a sinister hint. In some cases their loved ones would never come back. As a rule, those killed were already in custody, and the killing took place in isolated areas and at night. Some of the shootings happened at the moment of detention . . . [or] were executed in the presence of their families. (Chilean National Commission on Truth and Reconciliation 1991)

These events resulted in the first wave of victims. Once the junta had effective control, they unified and centralized their power through Decree No. 8, published in the national newspaper September 12, 1973. This included consolidating power under the Code of Military Conduct (Article 77), which mandated that military law was now binding on armed forces and civilians, essentially replacing civilian criminal and civil law. This allowed the junta to effectively treat the population as if they were in an occupied territory in a time of war. The decree was deemed a practical measure due to the time limitations for drawing up a comprehensive piece of legislation that would have granted the armed forces the necessary power the junta deemed necessary to legitimize their position and remove any and all opposition (Fruhling 1983). The decree included installing top-ranking military officers acting as governors and military judges of the providences.

Around October 1973 a tougher approach was taken in an effort to ensure legitimacy and governmental support, and to end any resistance by civilians, social and political activists, or former regime supporters, which resulted in approximately seventy-two people killed.[2] According to the Chicago Commission of Inquiry (1973), this tougher approach resulted in a grand total of nearly 80,000 Chileans being detained, a documented 250 more listed as disappeared, and over 400 individuals killed "while attempting to escape" within the first six months of the Pinochet junta control.

Economic sanctions were also used to bring ensured conformity in the population. For example, approximately 160,000 Chileans were expelled from their jobs, and many of those were barred from other employment. This

tougher approach was grounded in the idea that political and economic transformation was necessary.[3] As noted by Fruhling, "The aim became one of
building a market economy in an authoritarian state, and a change in the political values of the society was needed. To implement this, large doses of coercion
were required. It was necessary to modify democratic values at every level of
society in such a way that the past would be forgotten . . . thus the repression
was aimed at the twin goals of heading off any possibility of socialist resurgence
and of implanting a new social structure" (1983, 511). As Pinochet stated,
"Every so often, democracy has to be bathed in blood. There is not a leaf in this
country which I do not move" (1987, 6). Pinochet, with counsel of U.S. econ-
omists and international financial institutions, implemented laissez-faire, free-
market, neoliberal, and fiscally conservative policies, where market forces
guided most of the economy's decisions (Klein 2007).

These economic policies led to increases in unemployment, decreases in
salaries, and social services that created further conditions of oppression.
During the month following the military coup, Pinochet set up a task force,
known as the caravan of death, where scores of prisoners were removed and
executed. Those gathered for detention included individuals who appeared
before authorities after having found their names in the Diario Oficial, as
mandated in Decree 81 (November 1973). As an example, a seventeen-year-
old pregnant high school student turned herself in after hearing her name
announced on the radio. She was detained and tortured: electric currents
were applied to her genitals during interrogation, which resulted in massive
brain damage to her child. Others were tortured and then killed. Disposal of
the bodies included mass graves or dumping the bodies in rivers.

The following three years, 1974–1977, saw continued violence. As noted
by the Chicago Commission of Inquiry, "the campaign of terror developed
by the junta assumed a systematic and organized character" (1973, 60). This was
accompanied by generating fear throughout the country. Fear-mongering is
often a key mechanism used to legitimate and/or overshadow illegal or illegitimate governmental action (Rothe 2009a). Rose Styron states, "the real
purpose of the torture seems to be not so much to extract confessions as to
induce conformity by terror, dehumanization, and the destruction of the will
by prolonged pain" (1974, 79).

In 1974 Pinochet closed down the Chilean parliament and appointed himself as president. Like other authoritarian regimes (e.g., Obote in Uganda), following his self-appointed position as head of state Pinochet banned all political
activity. It was during this period that the Dirección Nacional de Inteligencia
(National Intelligence Directorate, DINA) began a systematic centralized pattern of political repression. The institutionalization of the DINA brought an
important change in the organizational structure of the newly formed repressive government and in the means in which the oppression and crimes against

the population were carried out. The regime began selectively targeting political groups perceived to represent a threat, including, though not limited to, the Socialist Party of Movimiento de Izquierda Revolucionaría (the Revolutionary Left Movement, MIR), and the Communist Party (Fruhling 1983). The result was mass disappearances and other means of elimination, with the goal of eliminating all perceived politically dangerous civilians.

In November 1975 Operation Condor, a joint intelligence operation headed by the Chilean military with other neighboring countries (e.g., Argentina, Brazil, Bolivia, Paraguay, and Uruguay), was initiated (Human Rights Watch 2006b). The purpose of the operation was to track and kill any dissidents that fled Chile after the military coup and were living abroad (Chilean National Commission on Truth and Reconciliation 1991).

In August 1977, Decree Law No. 1876 officially dissolved DINA and inaugurated the Third Wave, a new period of repression and series of the human rights violations that lasted through 1990. Decree Law No. 1878 created the National Center for Information (CNI) , which took over as the repressive arm of the Pinochet regime, continuing the political repression, forced disappearances, and murder the country had been subjected to periodically since 1973 (Chilean National Commission on Truth and Reconciliation 1991). During this period, containment became a popular means of removing political opposition. The levels fluctuated with the perceived and real mobilization of other political parties and insurgencies. This period came to be seen as the progressive legal institutionalization of the use of force (Fruhling 1983). The CNI continued the practice of the DINA to use force and violence. Yet use of torture was more systematic by the CNI than that of the DINA, "which tortured practically everyone who passed through some of its secret facilities . . . The main torture methods continued to be the use of electricity, especially on the sensitive parts of the body, all kinds of beatings, and plunging the person's head down into water to the brink of asphyxiation, and then doing it again," often to the point of death (Chilean National Commission on Truth and Reconciliation 1991, 840).

In 1978, Pinochet declared a state of emergency, allowing the government additional tools and power, including some that had been granted with the state of siege, which was declared over at this same time. This was but one of the many changes in the legal system aimed at providing extensive powers, maintaining repression, and appearing legitimized in the regime's actions to outsiders. For example, the military junta ensured their impunity through Decree Law 2.191, granting amnesty for military and police personnel who committed human rights violations between 1973 and 1978. During this same year, political opposition parties began preparing for an armed struggle. As noted in the *Report of the Chilean National Commission on Truth and Reconciliation*, "The MIR began its return in 1979 and did so more systematically from 1980 onward.

Activists who had been living outside the country and had received weapons training returned secretly to prepare for armed struggle against the military government. Subsequently, the FPMR was organized in Chile and later yet came the group known as MAPU Lautaro or 'Lautaro.' Under several directors, the CNI responded to these developments with much more intense repression" (Chilean National Commission on Truth and Reconciliation 1991).

The response by the government not only included containment and violence, namely torture, but forced exile. For example, during 1980 over one hundred individuals were exiled to remote areas in Chile in an effort to quell the growing resistance efforts by opposition groups. Police were often assisted by plainclothes agents, *qurkas*, wielding brass knuckles, ready to contribute to the oppression and violence and aid in the containment effort. Those contained continued to be tortured, and others were victims of forced disappearances, though these acts were now being concealed from the public. Common torture practices included "sexual abuse, including rape using animals, burns from cigarettes, welding torches and acid, ripping off fingernails with pliers, immersion in water, cooking oil or petroleum, and being forced to watch other detainees, often family members, being tortured, mock executions, lengthy detentions with blindfolds or hoods, electric shock to the genitals, as well as the bursting of eardrums using loud noises" (Gonzales 2004, 1). Torture was directed toward fear-mongering, public intimidation, and extracting information "as a matter of priority" (Amnesty International 1999, 1). A family member of one such victim stated that "he was missing one eye, his nose was torn off, one ear was separated and hanging, there were marks of deep burns on his neck and face, his mouth was very swollen" (*Boston Globe* 1991, 4).

A state of siege was enacted in 1984 and remained in effect until 1985. This gave rise to increased detentions, raids, torture, and death. As noted by the Vicaria of Solidarity report, 39 percent of all the deaths between 1973 and 1989 occurred in the last six years of Pinochet's rule. As noted by Derechos Chile (2008, 1), "Abuse of power, as in the notorious case of the military patrol which poured kerosene over Rodrigo Rojas and Carmen Gloria Quintana and set them on fire, accounted for about half of all deaths in 1986. In that same year, when demonstrations and protests increased considerably, more than 35,000 human rights violations were reported. Executions were used during ambushes, others were individually direct and included kidnapping followed by execution style gunshot deaths or throat slitting." Such acts of violence, oppression, and repression continued through the 1980s, waning and/or increasing with perceived threats to the regimes political power, legitimacy, and larger economic plans. The goal, as with most cases of state crimes by authoritarian regimes, was to eliminate opposition while simultaneously generating fear in its citizenry to enhance compliance and obedience, as well as to ensure a level of secrecy, ensuring immunity (Rothe 2009a).

The information in figure 1, taken from the *Report of the Chilean National Commission on Truth and Reconciliation* reflects a partial account of the totality of victimization that occurred during Pinochet's time as head of state. In 1989 Pinochet received a significant blow to his time in power with his defeat in a plebiscite that was intended to legitimize and sustain his autocratic rule. The following year he lost the presidency. Consequently, his seventeen-year reign of terror came to an end. Yet, he held his post as army commander in chief until 1997 as a result of part of the constitutional, legislative, and legal changes he instituted during the early 1980s (Human Rights Watch 2006a, 2006b). In

Decisions Made by the Commission	
Victims of human rights violations	2,115
Victims of political violence	164
Total number of victims	2,279
Cases in which the commission could not come to conviction	641
Total number of cases	2,920

Victims of Human Rights Violations	
Victims of government agents or persons at their service:	
A. Killed	
In war tribunals	59 (2.8%)
During protests	93 (4.4%)
During alleged escape attempts	101 (4.8%)
Other executions and deaths by torture	815 (38.5%)
Total killed	1,068 (50.5%)
B. Disappeared after arrest	957 (45.2%)

1. Partial account of the totality of victimization while Pinochet was head of state. *Source*: Chilean National Commission on Truth and Reconciliation (1991, app. 1).

1998 Pinochet received a lifetime seat in the "Chilean Senate, giving him additional parliamentary immunity from prosecution." In 2000 the Chilean Congress "granted yet another layer of immunity to all former Presidents of the Republic" (Jonas 2004, 38). Nonetheless, with his loss of position as president and with Chile under the effective control of President Patricio Aylwin, Pinochet's ability to commit atrocities ended. His enjoyment of impunity remained, however. Efforts to hold him accountable resulted in international precedents with far-reaching impact. According to Jonas, "The 1998 detention of former Chilean dictator Augusto Pinochet in London and the subsequent legal proceedings against him marked one of the most important events in international law since Nuremberg. Although Pinochet's release was a blow to the struggle to end impunity for human rights violators, five years later, it is clear that the case against him has had lasting political and legal impacts in Chile and other countries around the world" (2004, 36). There has indeed been a ripple effect with the move to hold Pinochet accountable for the vast victimization and crimes committed during his reign.

LEGAL PRECEDENT AND JURISPRUDENCE

It has been pointed out that, "until recently, it seemed that if you killed one person, you went to jail, but if you slaughtered thousands, you usually got away with it. Times change" (Human Rights Watch 1998a, 1). There have been international criminal tribunals that have held accountable top-ranking military and political personnel for massive crimes. For example, the Nuremberg Trials resulted in the conviction of eighteen Nazi officials under the Nuremberg Charter for war crimes, the highest ranking member of the German government being Hermann Goering. Former president of Serbia and Yugoslavia, Slobodan Milosevic, was brought to stand trial at the International Criminal Court for the former Yugoslavia. Former top-ranking government officials in Rwanda were brought before the International Criminal Tribunal for Rwanda, including the former president of MRND, Mathieu Ngirumpatse; the vice president, Edouard Karemera; the secretary general of MRND, Joseph Nzirorera; and the former minister of education, Andre Rwamakuba. Yet, the case of Pinochet differs in that a head of state was indicted and his extradition was approved by another state. Because there was "no real prospect of Pinochet being tried in Chile or any international tribunal, Spain's extradition request was the only vehicle for the emplacement of the rule of law in these matters" (BBC 1999, 1). The case opened up new possibilities for the exercise of universal jurisdiction, in that the Spanish court sought to judge crimes alleged to have been committed by a former head of state in his own country, against his own population. The court verdicts establishing the lawfulness of Pinochet's arrest and extradition were a dramatic lesson in the implementation of international public law and the recognition of the principles of universal criminal jurisdiction for domestic courts. While Pinochet died in December 2006 at age ninety-one, escaping justice and accountability for his crimes, the legal precedent will have a lasting impact.

A MOVE TOWARD ENDING IMPUNITY?

One month after Patricio Aylwin became the new head of state in Chile in 1990, Supreme Decree No. 355 was instituted, creating the Chilean Commission on Truth and Reconciliation (TRC). The Rettig Commission's mandate was limited to the following:

1. To establish as complete a picture as possible of the human rights violations that occurred under the Pinochet regime
2. To gather evidence to allow for victims to be identified
3. To recommend reparations
4. To recommend legal and administrative measures to prevent a repetition of past abuses

The commission was allowed to investigate only crimes resulting in death. Additionally, as noted in Article 2 of the Supreme Decree: "In no case is the Commission to assume jurisdictional functions proper to the courts nor to interfere in cases already before the courts. Hence it will not have the power to take a position on whether particular individuals are legally responsible for the events that it is considering."

Further hampering the commission's investigative abilities was the limited scope of time awarded: nine months to accomplish its mandate (Brahm 2005; Ensalaco 1994; Hamber 1998). Having completed its mandate with the limitations imposed upon it and through the limited cooperation it received, a brief six-month period of declared reconciliation was ended. While there were active nongovernmental organizations and other groups of concerned citizens and/or victims that continued to press for accountability, Chile failed to move beyond truth to trial. Nonetheless, the TRC eventually turned over the collected evidence after Pinochet's detention in London.

It was only through the external intervention of Spain and their efforts to hold Pinochet accountable that a window of opportunity and a legal accountability momentum occurred within Chile. As a result, the Chilean Supreme Court ruled in 1999 that the 1978 amnesty law did not apply to disappearances (Brahm 2005). Additionally, domestic trials began occurring in Chile in an effort to hold others in the regime accountable for their role in the crimes. In 2001 Pinochet was charged in connection with the Caravan of Death policy that resulted in the deaths or disappearances of over seventy-five people. After an appeal to the Supreme Court, the proceedings ended with the court's ruling that Pinochet was mentally and physically unfit to stand trial. Then on December 13, 2004, Chilean Judge Juan Guzmán Tapia ruled that Pinochet was indeed competent to stand trial and immediately charged him with nine counts of kidnapping and one murder, though Pinochet never stood trail.

As previously noted, efforts to hold Pinochet and other top-ranking officials accountable can only be contributed to Spain's attempts to bring him to trial and end his twenty-five years of impunity. The account (see overview by Brody and Ratner 2000) begins with a criminal investigation triggered in July 1996 for the murder or disappearance in Chile of seven Spanish citizens by the Association of Progressive Prosecutors. The legal foundation of the case was derived from the "Bilateral Extradition Treaty between Chile and Spain, and International Criminal Law ratified by both States" (Garcas 1999, 1). From the initial accusation, limited to disappearances and murder, the prosecution's allegations expanded into indictments to genocide, murder, and the torture of thousands of Chileans, which are essentially crimes against humanity. A letter by Amnesty International News Service, acting as amicus curiae, states that "the widespread and systematic human rights violations in Chile during the military government amount to crimes against humanity" (1998, 1). Yet, it was the 1984 torture convention that was used in the decision for the applicability of Spain to try Pinochet and for the House of Lords' decision for extradition. As noted by Dame Rosalyn Higgens, the president of the International Court of Justice, "Both issues of jurisdiction and of immunity were involved. As to the former, the question was whether alleged acts of torture could qualify as extradition crimes under the UK Extradition Act 1989 . . . [and] whether universal jurisdiction meant that torture committed outside of the UK was already a crime punishable under UK law" (2006, 2).

In October 1998, upon hearing that Pinochet was in England, a petition was filed with the Investigating Court of the Spanish National Criminal Court asking the court to interrogate Pinochet about his role in Operation Condor and requesting that he and other Chilean military be charged for the disappearance and kidnappings of civilians.[4] Another group of Chilean relatives of the disappeared asked the judge to charge Pinochet and other leaders with genocide, terrorism, and torture. On October 16, Judge Baltasar Garzón issued a provisional arrest warrant for Pinochet charging that he was responsible for the murder of Spanish citizens in Chile while acting head of state. That same day, the London Metropolitan Police, acting on the request of Judge Garzón, arrested Pinochet while he was recovering from back surgery in a private London clinic. The following day, the Chilean Foreign Ministry entered a protest to Pinochet's detention, claiming diplomatic immunity. Nevertheless, on October 29, 1998, the Spanish court rejected a challenge to the jurisdiction of the Spanish judiciary to try Pinochet, and on November 3, Judge Garzón issued an extradition order for Pinochet, setting a worldwide precedent. This was followed by the House of Lords magistrate's rejection of Pinochet's claim to immunity. Nearly one year to the date, October 1999, Magistrate Bartle upheld Spain's request for Pinochet's extradition: "Accordingly I find that the information before me relating to allegations constitute a course of conduct amounting to torture and conspiracy to torture for which Senator Pinochet enjoys no immunity" (Judgment of the English Court Allowing the Extradition of Pinochet 1999, 4).

This decision was appealed and for nearly two years, Pinochet continued to enjoy a level of impunity. This was enforced further by UK Home Secretary Jack Straw's decision not to extradite Pinochet based on a disputed health report claiming he was mentally unfit for trial (Brody and Ratner 2000, 447). Nonetheless, due to the House of Lords' rejections of Pinochet's claim of entitlement to immunity, there was some progress in ending head-of-state immunity. With the Lords acknowledging that a former head of state enjoys immunity for acts committed in his functions as head of state, international crimes such as torture and crimes against humanity were not functions of a head of state, and that due to Britain and Chile having ratified the United Nations Convention against Torture, Pinochet was not entitled to immunity.

As previously discussed, these proceedings and the initial attempts by Spain to hold Pinochet accountable resulted in accountability of a few military leaders in Pinochet's regime and several domestic attempts to end Pinochet's impunity. As such, the proceedings had an immediate impact beyond the borders of Spain and the UK, where Pinochet was arrested and served roughly 530 days of incarceration. The legal initiation taken by Spain also had a ripple effect back to Chile and far beyond. As stated by Higgens, "the events surrounding this litigation were at the time regarded as momentous. These types of cases are now arising thick and fast, and in different forms" (2006, 4).

RIPPLE EFFECT

This Spanish case was only the beginning of what would come to be a number of cases instituted in domestic courts against Pinochet. The Swiss government also sent an extradition request to the UK to try Pinochet for the death of a Swiss citizen killed in Chile while Pinochet was acting head of state. Other requested extraditions came from Belgium and France. As stated by Hitchins, "The Netherlands, Switzerland, Denmark, and Germany have all recently employed the Geneva Conventions to prosecute war criminals for actions committed against non-nationals by non-nationals. . . . The British House of Lords' decision in the matter of Pinochet has also decisively negated the defense of 'sovereign immunity' for acts committed by a government or by those following a government's orders" (2001, 1). The Pinochet effect caused ripples far beyond the confines of crimes in Chile. Using the same principles that were applied to charge and extradite Pinochet, a Senegalese court indicted Hissene Habre, Chad's former head of state, in February 2000 on torture charges.

In 2004 a complaint was filed on behalf of four Iraqis in the German courts against Donald Rumsfeld and other military officials over the torture at Abu Ghraib. While the prosecutor failed to take the case, it is nonetheless yet another example of attempts by civilians and nongovernmental organizations to use national courts to try high-ranking state officials for crimes that would otherwise not be tried.

In 2005 Heshamuddin Hesam and Habibulla Jalalzoy, two Afghan officials, were tried and convicted in the Hague under Dutch law.[5] The court held that the Geneva Conventions of 1949 constitute a basis for universal jurisdiction with the obligation to penalize grave breaches. In June 2006 a case was opened accusing seven Chinese leaders, including the former president and prime minister, of genocide, crimes against humanity, and torture in Tibet during the 1980s. A 2006 Supreme Court decision in France also ruled that a lawsuit alleging genocide against Zhou Yongkang, the Chinese minister in charge of public order, could proceed (Higgens 2006). In 2007 Spain's Supreme Court ruled that Ricardo Cavallo, a former Argentine junta officer, should stand trial in Madrid for crimes against humanity (REDRESS and FIDH 2007).

Other former heads of state have also been held accountable recently. Consider the arrest of former Liberian president Charles Taylor, currently at trial at the Special Court for Sierra Leone, as another example of efforts to end regimes long enjoyed impunity. Most recently, in July 2008, the International Criminal Court announced it would seek an arrest warrant for Sudanese president Omar al-Bashir for charges of genocide and crimes against humanity (Rothe 2009a). While the latter two examples are not directly related to the precedent set by the Pinochet case, they do represent the ongoing trend to end impunity.

THE IDEOLOGY GUIDING THE USE OF STATE PROSECUTIONS

The Pinochet case reaffirmed the principles of international law that a country can judge the crime of torture no matter where the acts were committed, and that not even a former head of state has immunity from prosecution. Yet, what exactly are these principles of international law founded on? There is little dispute to the fact that the case of *Kingdom of Spain v. Augusto Pinochet* set precedent for the application of universal jurisdiction. As noted by Human Rights Watch, "the most striking feature of the Pinochet case was that a Spanish judge had the authority to order Pinochet's arrest for crimes committed mostly in Chile and mostly against Chileans" (1998b, 1). The ideology of and principle behind universal jurisdiction is that every country has an interest and obligation in bringing to justice those that commit crimes of an international concern. The crimes of international concern are per- ceived as the gravest of crimes, no matter where the acts were committed and regardless of the nationality of the victims or those accused for the sake of international peace and justice.

In the case of Pinochet, and the more recent case against Habre, the 1984 United Nations Convention against Torture and Other Cruel Inhumane and Degrading Punishment has been applied as both *jus cogens* and *erga omnes* (meaning it was a binding obligation on all states), with the attendant obliga- tion of all states to prosecute violators. Article 7.1 of the convention, under which Pinochet was ruled subject to extradition, states that the state party in the territory under whose jurisdiction a person alleged to have committed any offense, referred to in Article 4, is found, shall in the cases contemplated in Article 5, if it does not extradite him, submit the case to its competent authorities for the purpose of prosecution. As Lord Browne-Wilkinson stated in his opinion in *Pinochet III*, "the purpose of the Convention was to introduce the principle *aut dedere aut punire*—either you extradite or you pun- ish" (Brody and Ratner 2000, 268).

There are also obligations of states to prosecute those that commit inter- national crimes deemed as universally prohibited under customary international law. The principle of universal jurisdiction allows every state to "exercise jurisdiction over a limited category of offences of universal concern, irrespective of the *situs* of the offence and the nationalities of the offender and the offended" (Higgens 2006, 3). However, the reach and precise nature of universal jurisdiction as a general legal principle and its practical implications are far from clear. While the applicability of conventions such as the torture convention provides for universal jurisdiction and, to a limited degree, the inapplicability of immunity for certain crimes, there had been little to no implementation of these principles. It is for this reason that the case against Pinochet was such a significant mark in ending immunity for crimes commit- ted by heads of state and other high-ranking governmental positions. After all, it has been suggested that "in the related fields of jurisdiction and State immunity—as in almost no other field of international law—the role of national courts and legislation has a very particular significance" (Higgens 2006, 5). Nonetheless, there is reason to remain skeptical over future applica- tions, as well as the idea that impunity may be nearing an end. This may be out of concern over the legal developments after Pinochet and because of problems arising out of politics.

The Ripple Effect Stops: The Congo v Belgium
Arrest Warrant Case before the ICJ

In 2002 the International Court of Justice (ICJ) handed down one of the most far-reaching and possibly one of the most morally disappointing decisions since its inception.[6] The case concerned an international arrest warrant issued by a Belgian court for the foreign minister of Congo for serious international crimes. Congo argued that the minister was protected by immunity from prosecution by the authorities of another state. After Pinochet, everyone expected the ICJ to gut the vexing principle of immunity once and for all. Yet, the ICJ declared that immunity applied even for the most serious international crimes, and, more to the point, the court did not follow the equation of "unlawful = not official" that underlay so much of the initial Pinochet rhetoric in the United Kingdom. The salient paragraphs from the majority opinion bear reproducing:

55. In this respect, no distinction can be drawn between acts performed by a Minister for Foreign Affairs in an "official" capacity, and those claimed to have been performed in a "private capacity," or, for that matter, between acts performed before the person concerned assumed office as Minister for Foreign Affairs and acts committed during the period of office. Thus, if a Minister for Foreign Affairs is arrested in another State on a criminal charge, he or she is clearly thereby prevented from exercising the functions of his or her office. The consequences of such impediment to the exercise of those official functions are equally serious, regardless of whether the Minister for Foreign Affairs was, at the time of arrest, present in the territory of the arresting State on an "official" visit or a "private" visit, regardless of whether the arrest relates to acts allegedly performed before the person became: the Minister for Foreign Affairs or to acts performed while in office, and regardless of whether the arrest relates to alleged acts performed in an "official" capacity or a "private" capacity. Furthermore, even the mere risk that, by travelling to or transiting another State a Minister for Foreign Affairs might be exposing himself or herself to legal proceedings could deter the Minister from travelling internationally when required to do so for the purposes of the performance of his or her official functions.

58. The Court has carefully examined State practice, including national legislation and those few decisions of national higher courts, such as the House of Lords or the French Court of Cassation. It has been unable to deduce from this practice that there exists under customary international law any form of exception to the rule according immunity from criminal jurisdiction and inviolability to incumbent Ministers for Foreign Affairs, where they are suspected of having committed war crimes or crimes against humanity. . . .

61. Accordingly, the immunities enjoyed under international law by an incumbent or former Minister for Foreign Affairs do not represent a bar to criminal prosecution in certain circumstances.

First, such persons enjoy no criminal immunity under international law in their own countries, and may thus be tried by those countries' courts in accordance with the relevant rules of domestic law.

Secondly, they will cease to enjoy immunity from foreign jurisdiction if the State which they represent or have represented decides to waive that immunity.

Thirdly, after a person ceases to hold the office of Minister for Foreign Affairs, he or she will no longer enjoy all of the immunities accorded by international law in other States. Provided that it has jurisdiction under international law, a court of one State may try a former Minister for Foreign Affairs of another State in respect of acts committed prior or subsequent to his or her period of office, as well as in respect of acts committed during that period of office in a private capacity.

Fourthly, an incumbent or former Minister for Foreign Affairs may be subject to criminal proceedings before certain international criminal courts, where they have jurisdiction.

Pinochet's effect on interstate immunity would seem to be history given the above scenarios. Yet, there are real-world implications that should be considered.

The Question of Political Will and Realpolitik

International criminal justice has indeed made great strides post–World War II and impunity is increasingly being viewed as unacceptable by international political leaders, NGOs, and the international civil realm. Consider that in 1971 the United Nations General Assembly (UNGA) adopted a resolution on war criminals that reaffirmed a state's obligation to cooperate in the arrest, extradition, trial, and punishment of individuals accused of war crimes and crimes against humanity. The resolution states that a state's refusal to do so is contrary to the UN Charter and to the generally recognized norms of international law. Two years later, in 1973, another resolution was adopted by the UNGA, Principles of International Cooperation in the Detention, Arrest, Extradition, and Punishment of Persons Guilty of War Crimes and Crimes Against Humanity, yet no international convention followed and "therefore the duty to prosecute or to extradite, while argued for by scholars, must nonetheless be proven part of customary international law in the absence of a specific convention establishing such an obligation" (Bassiouni 1996, 16). Consequently, the ideological support to end impunity by states supporting accountability was said to be present, yet the reality of such relations remained absent. There is a difference between the stated support for an ideology of and the realpolitik involved in the implementation for ending impunity for all, regardless of the accused's position as head of state or high-ranking official. The political will of the prosecuting and/or extraditing country remains a critical factor in the potential prosecution of former heads of state and other high-ranking state officials who have committed crimes against humanity, genocide, and/or war crimes. There is the realpolitik of individual state interests that all too often outweigh the need for that country to step in and provide a realm for accountability. These interests include political, economical, military, and, to a lesser degree, social, in the context of other states and with the international status quo that has remained dominant. Simply, we have not achieved a level world wherein ending impunity is universally recognized and supported as a commonly shared value and practiced by states. As noted by M. Cherif Bassiouni, "There is hardly anything to be said of an international community other than an international community of interests. . . . You don't see an international community having responsibilities deriving from commonly shared values . . . . you do not see an international community that feels a sense of social responsibility or social solidarity . . . or share resources . . . or even a community that is willing to intervene to assume the responsibilities of intervention that the community knows is likely to commit genocide or crimes against humanity" (2008b).

There have also been setbacks in state courts exercising their right and obligation to prosecute, try, and/or extradite, especially if the case involves a current head of state where it is still believed that immunity is a given so long as the individual(s) are currently serving regardless of the crimes committed. As noted by Higgens, "In 2004, a private application for an extradition warrant against the President of Zimbabwe, Robert Mugabe, was refused by the Bow Street Magistrate's Court. That Court stated that 'whilst international law evolves over a period of time, international customary law, which is embodied in our Common Law, currently provides absolute immunity to any Head of State'" (2006, 12).[7] In another example, Higgens noted that in a recent decision issued by the U.S. Court of Appeals in a civil suit filed against Jiang Zemin, former president of the People's Republic of China, alleging genocide, torture, and other human rights abuses, "the US Government intervened to argue that as he was Head of State at the time of filing, Zemin was entitled to absolute immunity from jurisdiction. . . . The Court held the Government's suggestion of immunity was conclusive and must be accepted" (2006, 13). As such, it is evident that the reality of immunity for heads of state remains. While legally grounded in arguments, there is the hint of realpolitik at work as well. As case in point, consider the last example, where the U.S. government's intervention on behalf of Zemin, as with Mugabe, may well have been grounded in self-interest and future insurance of their own impunity. Recall that there have been attempts to hold the George W. Bush administration accountable for crimes of aggression, war crimes, and crimes against humanity committed in the grander war on terrorism by certain groups in Germany and Belgium. As such, there should remain a level of skepticism where it is touted that we have a common desire and belief in ending impunity and achieving international social justice. It is an ongoing problem that requires diligence, commitment, and a change in ideology, praxis, and relations to continue the momentum and precedent set in the Pinochet case. Hopefully, in the future, as states continue prosecuting those enjoying impunity we can move beyond the observation once made by Jean-Jacques Rousseau in *The State of War*: "Well instructed as to my duties and my happiness, I close the books, leave the lecture room, and look around me. There I see a miserable people groaning under an iron yoke, the whole human race crushed by a handful of oppressors, and an enraged mob overwhelmed by pain and hunger whose blood and tears the rich drink in peace. And everywhere the strong are armed against the weak with the formidable power of the law" (Rousseau 1990, 185). Indeed, we have a long way to go, yet "the saga of the Pinochet Case remains a historical milestone in the pursuit of accountability over atrocity" (Kornbluh 2004, xii).

Notes

1. Due to the legal and ideological changes that occurred, the focus of this chapter is unlike the previous case studies in that the analysis is not focused on the etiological factors or enactment procedures of the crimes committed by a particular regime, in this case Chile, but instead on the legal precedent to end Pinochet's impunity. For a detailed analysis and report of the conditions and crimes committed by Pinochet and his regime, see Ensalaco (2000), Roht-Arriaza (2005), and *Chile: Under Military Rule* (1974). For a detailed analysis of U.S. involvement, which facilitated both motivation and opportunity, see Dinges (2004) and Kornbluh (2004).
2. "Four executions in Cauquenes (October 4), fifteen in La Serena (October 16), thirteen in Copiapó (October 17), fourteen in Antofagasta (October 19), and twenty-six in Calama (October 19)" (Chilean National Commission on Truth and Reconciliation 1991).
3. One cannot ignore the complicit role of the U.S. government, U.S. economic advisors, and U.S. corporations in pushing this economic transformation for self-interests, as Chile was seen as the perfect location for trials of this economic shock doctrine. For more details of the U.S. role, including those of the economic advisors, see Dinges (2004) and Kornbluh (2004).
4. Juzgado Central de Instrucción, attached to the trial jurisdiction of the Audiencia Nacional in Madrid.
5. Case against Heshamuddin Hesam and Habibulla Jalalzoy, Hague District Court, October 14, 2005, Case No.09/751004-04.
6. Arrest Warrant of April 11, 2000, *Democratic Republic of the Congo v. Belgium* (Merits) Judgment of February 14, 2002.
7. Application for a Warrant for the Arrest and Extradition of Robert Gabriel Mugabe, president of the Republic of Zimbabwe, on charges of torture under Section 134 of the Criminal Justice Act 1988, before Bow Street Magistrate's Court, January 7 and 14, 2004, decision of Judge Timothy Workman, January 14, 2004.

PART TWO

◆ *Controlling State Crime*

CRIMINOLOGY IS NOT just focused on explaining the etiological factors behind crime commission; ultimately the goal is to find and
empirically assess policies to control it. A criminology of the state is no different. While explaining the causal mechanisms and common enactment procedures of state crime are important in themselves, at core, the goal is to
control such actions and end the long-standing impunity enjoyed by high-
ranking officials and heads of state who violate domestic law, international
criminal and humanitarian law, or human rights. Nonetheless, one can reasonably argue that the majority of the research on state crime has focused less
on issues of controls. Further, unlike street crime, accountability mechanisms
for those who orchestrate crimes of the state are far more complex and difficult to achieve for a variety of reasons, including resources, economic costs,
lack of political will by the international community, the sheer numbers of
those involved in the crime commission, failed and/or weakened governments, plausible deniability, and realpolitik. Over the course of the past two
decades, a growing number of scholars of state crime have devoted attention
to and research on these issues; yet as we have noted, there have been
relatively few articles and/or books that solely focus on and analyze extant
controls.

One of the earliest attempts to focus on controls of state crime can be
traced back to Jeffrey Ian Ross's two edited anthologies, *Controlling State
Crime* (1995a) and *Varieties of State Crime and Its Control* (2000b). As Ross
notes, "Unlike the voluminous literature in individual and organized crime,
there is little material that addresses and systematically analyzes methods for
abolishing, combating, controlling, decreasing, minimizing, and/or resisting
state crime" (1995a, 7). In these works, the issues of controls are delineated
into internal and external. Internal controls are those created by the state to
effectively govern itself, such as domestic laws and self-regulation. They can
be tangible (e.g., the firing of an agent) or symbolic (e.g., an official statement
of denial or a promise to investigate). Internal controls are broadly viewed as

restrictions placed on state agencies by themselves or by other state agencies in the wake of publicity generated by various criminal state practices—most of which involved the abuse of power by state-run intelligence agencies against their own citizens (e.g., the United Kingdom's 1977 establishment of a Royal Commission on Police Procedure and the campaign finance reform laws in Japan). Ross suggests that external controls can be localized either within or outside of a state's own territory. External controls within the state have included media organizations, interest groups, and domestic nongovernmental organizations (NGOs). Those outside of the country include organizations such as the World Bank or International Court of Justice.

As noted in the introduction, in 1998 David Friedrichs published a mass two-volume work on state crime. Volume II is divided into key chapters that examine not only acts of state crime but also research on policing state crime, the role of international law in responding to such acts, including the adjudication of state violators, and a section dealing with potential long-term prevention. For example, the Nuremburg trials are drawn on to illuminate the applicability of international law in response to crimes by state agents as well as the role of international law in South Africa's struggle for liberation. Other chapters focus on international criminalization of internal atrocities, the genocide treaty, and the adjudication of perpetrators from Nuremburg to Bosnia for war crimes. While not limited to scholars of state crime, this classical work stands as one of the earliest efforts to address controlling state crime.

The following year, Ron Kramer and Dave Kauzlarich (1999) published "The International Court of Justice Opinion on the Illegality of the Threat and Use of Nuclear Weapons: Implication for Criminology." Here the focus is not solely on the International Court of Justice, per se, but the relevance of international law's applicability for many, if not most, state crimes and the relative lack of attention given to controlling such acts.

In 2004 the first article was published by scholars of state crime dealing solely with the issue of controls. Mullins, Kauzlarich, and Rothe's (2004) piece, "The International Criminal Court and the Control of State Crime: Problems and Prospects," provided a discussion on the relevance of the newly formed International Criminal Court (ICC) in terms of its potential to act as a control of crimes committed by states—in this case, genocide, war crimes, and crimes against humanity.

Less than two years later, Dawn L. Rothe and Christopher Mullins (2006b) published an article looking at the U.S. opposition and efforts to delegitimize the ICC in "The International Criminal Court and United States Opposition: A Structural Contradictions Model." In it they suggest how the U.S. withdrawal and legislative undermining of the ICC not only reflects the state's ambiguous relationship with international law but also reveals some of the inherent limitations placed on the ICC as an international institution of formal social control. At the same time, their book, *Symbolic Gestures and the Generation of Global Social Controls: The International Criminal Court* (2006a), was released. They note that while the ICC has been touted as a major break-through in the potential control of genocide, crimes against humanity, and war crimes, there are several barriers to the reality of such an ideal. They first explore the historical origins of the court and provide an overview of its basic structure and functioning, which is followed by a more detailed critique of procedural, conceptual, and practical elements of the ICC, including some problems with the implementation of the court's jurisdiction and enforcement. Critics of the court maintain that such an institution threatens state sovereignty and advocate further limitations of its jurisdiction while proponents of the institution view the court as a potential deterrent and as a tool to empower and provide legal proceedings to victims of the gravest breaches of international law. While the volume concludes that the court is hindered by underlying contradictions existing within the international system, the authors see the ICC as highly valuable in contributing to the goal of ending impunity and holding those most responsible for the commission of state crimes accountable. Nonetheless, Rothe and Mullins (2006a) suggest that attempts to control or block state criminality can and have resulted in state actors finding illegitimate means to achieving their goals, thus sidestepping legitimate control mechanisms. While these are not the deterrence effects desired by the control modalities, they do show that state actors engage social agency as they navigate legal and organizational environments.

It was with this in mind that Jeffrey Ian Ross and Dawn L. Rothe (2008) published "The Ironies of Controlling State Crime." Ross and Rothe suggest that while social controls against state criminality are important, the results often lead to unintended consequences for the attempted controllers. Additionally, they highlight the fact that victimization of state crime extends beyond the harms of the crime itself and that state responses to control mechanisms can create secondary victimizations. Drawing on examples of U.S. criminality, they proposed eight catalysts used to negate attempts by controller(s): censure, scapegoating or obfuscation, retaliation, defiance/resistance, plausible deniability or improving the agency's ability to hide and/or explain away crimes, relying on self-righteousness, redirection/misdirection, and fear mongering. By implication, attempts to control state criminality may have consequences that are unintended and actually frustrate our ability to control state crime or, in other cases, may well result in additional victimization.

As discussed, through the initiative of Catrien Bijleveld, Uwe Ewald, Roelof Haveman, and Alette Smeulers, European and U.S. scholars interested in international criminal law violations such as war crimes, crimes against humanity, torture, genocide, and other gross human rights violations were brought together for an expert meeting in Maastricht to discuss not only the practicality of a supranational criminology but also issues of controlling such acts. This resulted in the 2008 edited anthology by Smeulers and Haveman, *Supranational Criminology: Towards a Criminology of International Crimes.* Here, the importance of controls is brought out by several scholars discussing issues ranging from the *Gacaca* in Rwanda to the problems of international tribunals constructing regimes of truth in terms of prosecution and accountability. Specifically, Jennifer Balint's chapter, "Dealing with International Crimes: Towards a Conceptual Model of Accountability and Justice," examines the parameters of international crime, including legal approaches to its use and civil liability. Stephan Parmienter, Kris Vanspauwen, and Elmar Weitekamp extend their long interest in and research on restorative justice with their chapter "Dealing with the Legacy of Mass Violence: Changing Lenses to Restorative Justice." Here the focus is on not just critiquing extant retributive mechanisms but also on showing how in the face of mass violence, post-conflict justice mechanisms must be more inclusive to extend to searching for truth, accountability, reparations for victims, and promoting reconciliation. Roelof Haveman then analyzes the *Gacaca* as a mechanism of control in response to the Rwandan genocide in "Doing Justice to Gacaca." As will be presented in the following chapters, Haveman views these quasi-traditional modalities of justice as misunderstood and essential given the complexities and massive numbers of perpetrators and victims. Additionally, Uwe Ewald continues his research, which is drawn from his practical experience at the International Criminal Tribunal for the Former Yugoslavia, by critiquing the processes of finding truth, the use of expert witnesses, and the construction of evidence in "Reason and Truth in International Criminal Justice."

Most recently, in Rothe's 2009 book, *The Crime of All Crimes: An Introduction to State Criminality*, issues of control are given extensive attention, with chapters focusing solely on various types of domestic and international constraints and controls, their effectiveness and/or lack thereof, as well as a closing chapter that looks at the potential to reduce or control state criminality. For example, chapter 8 introduces the extant international institutions of control, specifically the institutions of international law, the United Nations, the International Court of Justice, the International Criminal Tribunals for Yugoslavia and Rwanda, and the International Criminal Court. The chapter concludes with a summary of their potential and the critique of such institutions that are said to be based on retribution versus social justice and reconciliation. Chapter 9 then examines domestic controls, including those that were created to act simultaneously with the international systems, including the *Gacaca*, the hybrid tribunal for Sierra Leone, truth and reconciliations commissions, amnesty projects, and the countries' own domestic laws and criminal justice systems. The following chapter then provides an overview for potential or real barriers to state crime by describing the fundamental mechanisms associated with constraints: international citizen's tribunals, the media, political pressure from states, and public movements. Rothe concludes the book with a discussion of future directions and policies for controlling crimes of the state and ending impunity in the face of the realpolitik of international relations, human nature, and power. After all, as the body of state crime and postconflict justice literature has shown, enhancing accountability and minimizing impunity are important elements for peace; yet, both are typically absent for the majority of state crimes. As noted by Bassiouni, "between 1948 and 2008, some two hundred ninety-five conflicts have taken place whose total victimization fluctuates, depending on the estimates, between seventy to one hundred seventy million casualties. Surprisingly, not to say shockingly, the overwhelming majority of these conflicts have resulted in total impunity for the perpetrators of large scale victimization" (2008a, 11).

While the field of state crime is no longer in its infancy, criminological research on controls for the worst of worst crimes is indeed still lagging. The following section of this book addresses some of the issues raised by efforts to control state crime and the impunity long enjoyed by most perpetrators.

CHAPTER 8

Reinventing Controlling State Crime *and* Varieties of State Crime and Its Control

WHAT I WOULD HAVE DONE DIFFERENTLY

Jeffrey Ian Ross

IN 1995 MY EDITED BOOK *Controlling State Crime* was published (Ross 1995a). Five years later, not only was my follow-up edited book, *Varieties of State Crime and Its Control*, released (hereafter *Varieties*), but so too was the second edition of *Controlling State Crime* (Ross 2000a, 2000b). In between the time that the two books were published, and since the release of *Varieties*, the once nascent field of state crime, interchangeably labeled governmental crime, illegality, lawlessness, official deviance, or misconduct, has evolved. Old and rudimentary ideas have either been abandoned or modified, and numerous subject-relevant essays and case studies have accumulated. Some scholars of the subject of state crime have produced a steady flow of research, while others have moved on to different criminological/criminal justice subjects. Then again, new and emerging young scholars have entered the field carrying the banner of this cross-disciplinary field.

One aspect that has been central to the subject of state crime, the one that most intrigued me and still appears to be relevant, is the matter of control. Those familiar with my work might recall that I was initially influenced by Gregg Barak's edited book, *Crimes of the Capitalist State* (Ross 1992). Gregg showed considerable vision for the field. Perhaps more than anyone else, Gregg was and continues to be one of the biggest catalysts for the academic respectability of state crime. But I felt that the bigger question of control had been ignored (Ross 2002). I wanted to correct this imbalance, and this is what led to *Controlling State Crime* and *Varieties*.

Personal history aside, the following sections attempt to give the reader a sense of the major arguments from the original *Controlling State Crime*, followed by a review of *Varieties*, and then a review of what scholarly research has been produced since then to answer the proverbial question of what I would have done differently had I had to do it again. This is not an easy question to answer. As a relatively introspective scholar, I frequently question my agency and actions, and no ox is too sacred to gore, particularly if it is an edited book.

CONTROLLING STATE CRIME: AN INTRODUCTION

In order to understand the control of state crime, it is wise to look at the wider literature in which the concept exists. In general, state crime tended to fall under the subject of political crime. Of the books focusing on political crime, the majority (e.g., Bassiouni 1975; Ingraham 1979; Roebuck and Weeber 1978; Schafer 1974; Turk 1982) primarily concentrate on oppositional political crimes, whereas a minority (e.g., Barak 1991a; Comfort 1950; Proal 1973; Tunnell 1993a; Ross 2002) address, to some extent, state political crimes.[1] Still other works occupy a middle ground. Turk (1982), for example, discusses political policing and outlines the activities that police may take to manipulate the public order. He stops short, however, of labeling these actions as state crimes. Others (e.g., Ingraham 1979) fail to consider oppositional political crimes as such and focus the bulk of their discussion on crimes against the state.[2] Some of these works (e.g., Sink 1974) simply serve as manuals to aid professionals responsible for defending individuals charged with political crimes.

Since the original publication of *Controlling State Crime*, few additional books on political crime have been published. For example, Hagan's *Political Crime: Ideology and Criminality* (1997) deals with state crime in the context of human rights and genocide and illegal surveillance; and Kittrie's *Rebels with a Cause* (2000), in a disproportionately theory-laden treatise, looks at oppositional political crime.

The Control Agenda

Many criminologists have concluded that certain types of crime require better control than currently available (e.g., Pepinsky 1980, 4). A minority (e.g., Berkman 1971; Pepinsky 1980) oppose current crime control efforts on ideological (Berkman 1971) or empirical grounds (Pepinsky 1980; Walker 1985). Those opposed to crime control methods on empirical grounds cite our inability to specify what exactly we should be controlling; the inadequacy of data on and methods to study conventional crime; and the means utilized to deter or reform criminals. Those opposed to controlling crime on ideological grounds believe that since crime is a manifestation of a criminal (or illegitimate) state, we are only furthering the power of that country by controlling those actions that the entity deems illegal. Both of these types of critiques have been made in the context of conventional crime; however, they fail to consider controlling state crime as a separate issue.

Others are pessimistic about the possibility of controlling the state on structural grounds. Wilson and Rachel (1977) suggested that it is easier to control private rather than public institutions because governmental organizations in particular have at their disposal more resources. Although this may be the case, it should neither serve as a signal for failure nor imply that we automatically abandon the controlling state crime agenda. Controlling state crime can be accomplished through sound theoretical conceptualization; carefully identifying the illegal actions committed by the state as well as the mechanisms that sustain them; and devising methods to control them and hence minimize the abuse of coercive power.

The controlling state crime agenda assumes that, much like the search for the causes of traditional crime in general (e.g., property, occupational, violent, public order, white collar, organized, etc.), the search for causes of state crime may have limited utility in the ability to control state crime. As with the study of conventional crime, we do not have good measures of state crime. The problem is compounded because there is considerable debate over a definition of state crime, identifying perpetrators, processes, and rates. For example, organizations like Amnesty International and databases on specific types of state crime, such as genocide, have been criticized for their accuracy, validity, and reliability (Stohl and Lopez 1984).

Criticism, while important, is not enough (e.g., De Bonno 1979, 35–39), or an end in itself; we need to go beyond this approach to salvage what is good and offer suggestions to improve the state of affairs. Moreover, even though proposing solutions is relatively easy, suggesting those that are realistic and practical for minimizing state crime are not simple. Whichever mechanisms for control are instituted, they must be implemented so that they do not unnecessarily frustrate the state organizations' original mission. In other words, we must be careful about not throwing the baby out with the bath water.

Nevertheless, missing from most analyses of state crimes has been a model or theory of control that might help us understand how to minimize the amount, frequency, and intensity of state crime. The book was divided into thirteen chapters. The introductory part of the book included a number of seminal chapters, including one by Sharkansky (1995) that has served as a foil for many of those doing research in this area. The other was a definitional essay written by Friedrichs (1995). An integral part of this research should be to look at victims' methods to control state crime. Victims of state crime can be divided between individuals and classes on the one hand, and organizations and processes on the other. This, distinction, however, is not clear–cut; rather it recognizes that there is a certain amount of interdependence amongst these actors.

Causes and Perpetrators of State Crime

At the core of each state are a number of powerful individuals and organizations capable of or actually engaging in a considerable and disproportionate amount of crime against their own citizens and external adversaries, sometimes as part of their policy and other times as a consequence of their mission. Comfort (1950, 13) explains how these perpetrators were either in the "legislative position" or work in an enforcement capacity.

The police, the military, and national security/intelligence organizations—the principal state criminogenic organizations (Tunnel 1995)—have been criticized for violating criminal laws, constitutional protections, as well as fundamental civil and human rights. Regardless of the political system, the police, national security agencies, and the military in many countries have broken the law or engaged in practices that can be considered state crimes (e.g., Gill 1995; Menzies 1995; Ross 1995b). Several mechanisms have been advocated, many of which have been introduced, to control law enforcement, the armed forces, and national security agencies in general and these organizations' ability to engage in these types of crime in particular.

Another influential actor on state criminogenic organizations is large corporations. Corporations and states routinely forge mutually beneficial relationships because they pursue the same objectives, oftentimes engaging in criminal actions to achieve mutual goals (Aulette and Michalowski 1993). Indisputably, this relationship should be controlled when it transgresses criminal laws. A number of practices, including boycotts, lobbying, and legal recourse, have been used by the public, interest groups, social movements, other corporations, and by states including regulatory bodies/agencies and advisory boards to control such actions.

Although many organizations transcend state borders, controls that are instituted against government bureaucracies generally can be found both inside the state and outside. The effectiveness of these controls is difficult to determine in light of government's self-preserving policies and practices. Ultimately, most states want to preserve their integrity at home and in the international community and try to utilize their internal organizations and structures for control before external ones can get involved. Alternatively, they engage in public relations exercises.

Internal Controls: State Organizations and Processes

Most educational systems and processes are tragically flawed and hence demand improvement. As Cabrera argues (1995), our educational system reproduces the social order by reinforcing the meritocratic myth and appealing to an instrumentalist approach to literacy. The development of critical thinking is an important approach to controlling state crime. Building on the work of Freire (1985), Giroux (1983), and others, a critical literacy is one of the most effective ways of ending the "pedagogy of the oppressed," a process whereby successive leaders behave the way their rulers treated them.

To address these criticisms, governments have at their disposal a number of mechanisms external to state criminogenic actors to reactively influence and in some cases control state crime. Some of the processes are freedom of information legislation, colored papers, advisory councils, commissions of inquiry, ombudsmen, oversight, legislative committees, watchdog organizations, and courts.

External Controls: State-Sponsored and Private Organizations and Processes

The doctrine of *raison d'état*, (i.e., sovereignty) holds that under normal circumstances outside states are exempt from international intervention into their affairs. It implies that governments are above the law because by their very nature they are law-making, not law-breaking, institutions. However, many political philosophers, human rights advocates, and political activists argue that states should be held responsible for their actions. To facilitate this process, international law and related organizations have been established in order to monitor selected state crimes.

Several state-sponsored organizations and documents (e.g., United Nations resolutions) to control state crime have been created. In recent years, one of the most important international bodies is the International Court of Justice, which has been established to adjudicate International and State Transnational Crimes (e.g., Yarnold 1995). Alternatively, a number of external nongovernmental agencies attempt to assist the process of resisting state crimes.

Summary

The excerpt above is drawn from my previous work of 1995. In an effort to continue to focus research and policy on controlling state crime, I embarked on another edited book. The goal of *Varieties of State Crime and Its Control* was to take this research agenda to the next step; to provide analyses that examined the methods that public and private organizations have used to control domestic and international state crime caused by individual countries and their respective criminogenic agencies.[3] One way to achieve this objective, I argued, was by compiling case studies written by country experts who analyze attempts to control state crime.

A systematic analysis of state crime in particular countries provides a contextual approach to the subject of state crime. By seeing how states compare against each other we can observe what deters or facilitates state crime in particular settings. Research of this nature represents the basis of theory development, hypothesis testing, analysis, and, perhaps more important, policy formation, implementation, and evaluation. In short, this type of inquiry is an important building block in the emerging study of state crime and in the broader area of political crime.

It must be acknowledged that although there have been comparative studies of political violence, juvenile delinquency, and crime (e.g., Gurr 1988), rarely is state crime, whether we are talking about causation or control, treated comparatively. *Varieties* was an attempt to redress this imbalance.

VARIETIES OF STATE CRIME AND ITS CONTROL

As the second edition of *Controlling State Crime* was being printed, *Varieties* was released. It was intended to be the first of a series of edited books that provided case studies of controls in context.

Why focus on advanced industrialized democracies? Because data on state crime and measures to control it are unavailable, unreliable, too costly to collect, and plagued with jurisdictional and mandate vagaries among different countries, those studying the control of state crime should select a sample of the total population of countries that exist in the world. Although there are several possible systems and countries to study, the most similar systems design offers many advantages.[4] Although communist, authoritarian, totalitarian, and/or lesser developed states have been routinely identified as having a greater incidence of state crime than first world countries, data from these former types of states are often the most problematic. Adding to this problem is the fact that state agencies in these countries differ substantially in mandates and organization within and between them.

For these reasons, *Varieties* focused on first-world advanced industrialized democracies. As compared to those countries in other political systems, government bureaucracies of advanced industrialized democracies are relatively open to outside observers. Often these state crimes are revealed to the public by the media when scandals and/or crises of legitimation occur. Consequently, access to information on state crimes in advanced industrialized democracies is easier than in authoritarian or totalitarian states.[5] Their governments usually have a high degree of legitimacy, and their coercive organizations usually are bounded (but not necessarily or always properly controlled) within the rule of law. It is recognized by scholars, politicians, policy makers, the public administration, and activists alike that in democracies, politicians, governments, and the bureaucracy are accountable to the citizenry. This is accomplished through a variety of control mechanisms or processes.[6]

Moreover, during the twentieth century, democracies have spread throughout the world. During the 1970s many of these countries experienced so-called crises of capitalism (O'Conner 1973). Governments in these jurisdictions have adopted a plethora of legal and parliamentary mechanisms to stay in power. It is interesting to discover how controls on state crime can fail when they are utilized in such a manner as to protect and hide those that are really responsible for such crimes. Not only are some of the actions and omissions of politicians criminal, but they also violate the mandate of representation that they have received.

Reexamining Control

In an attempt to develop our notions of control, *Varieties* spent some time reviewing deeper understandings of control. In any organization, the principle of control arises from the need for members to perform their duties in accordance with some set of standards. Such control should be an ongoing process, not simply a response to some specific wrongdoing. Regardless of the organization, control mechanisms may be either internal or external. Internal controls include hiring policies, training, supervision, hierarchy, disciplinary codes, policy manuals, collective agreements, internal review boards, and intra-agency competition. External controls include external review boards, legislation, and extra-agency competition. Both kinds of control mechanisms may include powers of review or sanction. Control may also differ on an inclusivity/exclusivity dimension. According to Bayley, "Civilian review boards in the United States, for example, deal single-mindedly with police; legislatures, on the other hand, regulate the police as part of a larger mandate to regulate governmental processes generally" (1990, 161).

Internal and external types of control may be further classified as "institutional/formal" (e.g., legislation, legislative oversight, congressional committees, courts, advisory boards, review boards, ombudsmen, ethics committees, commissions of inquiry, governmental regulation, monetary appropriations, prosecutors, inter-agency competition, etc.) and "informal" (e.g., public opinion, media attention, public protest, educational activities, lobbying, critical international attention, etc.). The former are bureaucratic solutions, while the later appear to be more unstructured and spontaneous. Informal controls are often the last resort for citizens and usually have some influence on other forms of control. Conterminously, these control mechanisms (both formal and informal) can be ordered along a continuum from low intensity (e.g., letters to elected officials) to high intensity (e.g., riots, armed attacks, assassinations). In sum, institutional controls are primarily conventional and legislated, whereas informal controls are mostly unconventional and nonlegislated.

Most state criminogenic agencies in advanced industrialized countries are subject to the previously mentioned types of control. The relative influence of these mechanisms, however, varies with the state criminogenic agencies, units in the organization, state agents, and the many different actions the state agents engage in. This process, a subject of recent scholarship, is often referred to as the power of state capabilities, a subject of recent scholarship (e.g., Migdal 1988; Migdal, Kohli, and Shue 1994). When intolerable levels of state crime come to public attention, there is often public and governmental indignation. Moreover, the nature of these political systems, unlike the nondemocratic states, facilitates the expression of public discontent, which often leads to calls, if not the implementation, of greater control. Finally, information on the incidence of state crime and its effects in first world countries is easier to obtain and more reliable.

Advanced industrialized countries are where much of this research is grounded. For example, Barak's *Crimes by the Capitalist State* began with an introduction to state criminality in advanced capitalist states, and *Varieties of State Crime and Its Control* is one of the natural follow-ups to this research agenda. Understandably, there is considerable diversity (e.g., cultural, ethnic, and developmental) among the plethora of states subsumed by the advanced industrialized democracies label.[7] Three groupings falling under this rubric can be identified: western states, nonwestern states, and Anglo-American democracies. States covered in this book range from the nonwestern Japan (Potter 2000), to the Anglo-American democracy of Great Britain (Ross 2000b), to Israel (Miller 2000). Some are relatively new democracies, such as Japan and Israel. Others have had a long philosophical tradition of democracy and accountability (e.g., Great Britain, France, and the United States). This diversity, however, does not preclude generalization.

During the 1970s and 1980s all of these countries were affected by belt-tightening policies and practices situationally referred to as Reganism, Thatcherism, or Mulronyism. This has led to a decline in the provision of social services and in many cases an increase in public security functions. This situation has created the conditions for a variety of injustices including state crimes.

Summary

Contributors to the book reviewed the most frequent types of state crime occurring in each state. State crimes take particularly unique forms in advanced industrialized democracies. Eight principle state crimes were covered in the countries analyzed. From least to most frequently occurring, they are military violence (2 countries); human rights violations (3); tax evasion by politicians (3); torture (3); illegal domestic surveillance (4); illegal police violence (5); corruption/bribery (6); and cover-ups (7).

Chapters demonstrated historical depth and covered events and processes connected to overt and covert causes that may otherwise be overlooked. The genesis of these state crimes as well as the success or failure, if any, of solutions implemented to control such crimes are an integral component of the book. The contributions were not content to simply use anecdotal, hearsay, or undocumented evidence. Instead they used empirical data; in other words, the marshaling of historical examples, case studies, and statistics where appropriate. Each chapter includes a brief historical treatment of the subject, but the bulk of the discussion covers the past thirty-five years (i.e., since 1960), a period coterminous with what some researchers label the postindustrial phase.

I closed the book with a call to those interested in the subject, particularly doing research on the field of state crime. Specifically, I asked what we have learned, what the next step is, and what the controls are that have been found. In answering these questions, I emphasized the need for case studies in other advanced industrialized democracies, theoretical work, policy work, and moving the discussion toward lesser developed and nonadvanced industrialized countries. I argued that now that we have examined the control of state crime in advanced industrialized countries, we are in an ideal position to counsel the less developed countries in their efforts to create more democratic societies. This is not to suggest that we should impose some sort of government structure on them, or be insensitive to their own indigenous cultures, or processes, but only that the west has made many mistakes and perhaps can help the less developed countries.

WHAT DID I MISS OUT ON? RECOGNIZING THE IRONY OF CONTROLLING STATE CRIME

Since the publication of *Controlling State Crime* and *Varieties of State Crime and Its Control*, a growing body of literature on state crimes has focused on documenting and explaining the etiological factors of the worst atrocities known to humanity. By the late 1990s and early twenty-first century, researchers and writers had developed a significant amount of literature on crimes of the state (Ross 1995a, 1995b, 2000a, 2000b; Friedrichs 1995, 1998; Kauzlarich and Kramer 1998; Kramer, Michalowski, and Rothe 2005; Kramer and Michalowski 2005; Mullins, Kauzlarich, and Rothe 2004; Mullins and Rothe 2007, 2008a, 2008b; Rothe and Friedrichs 2006; Rothe 2009a, 2009b; Rothe and Mullins 2006a, 2007, 2008a, 2009; Ross et al. 1999). This last decade has also been witness to a growing body of literature on state crime controls (Ross 1995b, 2000b; Rothe and Mullins 2006a, 2006b). While a significant portion of this work has focused on international and/or foreign domestic controls, I and Dawn L. Rothe have focused on the literature most relevant to controls and/or constraints specifically addressing the United States.

To date, in most of the research on controls of state crime, internal controls continue to be perceived as those created by the state to effectively govern itself. Generally, they are attempts to assuage public criticism over government and bureaucratic actions. They often are limited to specific types of offenses that have already occurred (often taking the form of investigative commissions), quickly circumvented by new procedures or new depths of secrecy (i.e., the FOI acts in Japan's campaign finance laws), or left underfunded and/or understaffed (i.e., OSHA and the EPA) (Aulette and Michalowski 1993; Ross 2000a; Rothe and Mullins 2006b). Internal controls such as domestic laws and self-regulation arise within the state and are directed against itself. These mechanisms can be tangible (i.e., the firing of an employee) or symbolic (i.e., an official statement of denial or a promise to investigate). Internal controls are broadly viewed as restrictions placed on state agencies by themselves or by other state agencies. Examples of such internal controls include the United Kingdom's 1977 establishment of a Royal Commission on Police Procedure and the establishment that same year of a Police Complaints Board in response to police brutality (Ross 2000c); the passage in 1984 of the Canadian Security Intelligence Service Act (Corrado and Davis 2000); the Zorea, Blatman, and Karp Commissions in Israel (Miller 2000); and the campaign finance reform laws in Japan (Potter 2000). All of these mechanisms were established in the wake of publicity generated by various criminal state practices—most of which involved the abuse of power by state-run agencies against their own citizens (Ross 2000a; Rothe and Mullins 2006a).

External controls lie outside of a specific state apparatus (i.e., elected and appointed politicians and the bureaucracy) and are imposed on the state. To be effective, such controls actually have to exert some form of pressure and/or ability to penalize after the fact (i.e., in a political, economic, legal, or military way) on the state. External controls can be localized either within or outside of a state's own sovereign territory. External controls within the state have included media organizations, interest groups, and domestic non-governmental organizations (NGOs). Rothe and Mullins (2006a, 2007, 2008b) and, more recently, Ross and Rothe (2008) refer to these external agencies as constraints versus controls. The core problem with the efficacy of these types of constraints is the fact that they are not expected to act as an after-the-fact formal control in legal accountability or to fully block state or organizational criminogenic behaviors. Instead, by definition (Rothe and Mullins 2006a, 2007), they serve as potential barriers during an act or in response to an incident.

Such pressures from these external constraints (e.g., media, citizenry, and interest groups) raise inherent contradictions within the United States and other countries. Simply put, while many reactions are supposedly citizen driven, they operate in a more elite-orientated fashion (Bacharach and Baratz 1962). As such, there is a contradiction between the ideal of modern democracy and the efficacy of these types of constraints. When media or other agencies specifically address these contradictions in a public sphere, the state feels compelled to respond through actions that are typically symbolic in nature and often involve the erection of new veils of secrecy (Edelman 1971). Moreover, constraints such as the media, popular opinion, and/or internal state obstacles can often be ignored or manipulated via hegemonic discourse, symbolic political gestures, or altering policy to immediately appease while continuing in a covert direction (Rothe and Mullins 2006b).

The notion of the negative effects of controls has a long history. Some authors have suggested that there are limits of control (Peters 1989). According to Peters, "Aside from the average, garden-variety problems of administrative accountability and control, there are a number of more specialized problems and considerations that also deserve attention. In these cases the conventional mechanisms for public control and accountability are strained to their limits and are often exceeded" (276). In this context, he cites how the power of the professions, nationalized industries, unions, political structure, culture, and nonadministration can frustrate the ability of control efforts. In 1981 Gary Marx wrote a much-cited and reprinted article, "Ironies of Social Control: Authorities as Contributors to Deviance through Escalation, Nonenforcement and Covert Facilitation." Marx describes the process and contexts whereby "authorities may play a role in generating deviance" (221). In particular, he outlined how law enforcement officers, as state agents, can frustrate legitimate attempts by citizens to fight for social justice by engaging in confrontation, failing to enforce the law, and using surreptitious methods to force state opponents to break the law and thus become subject to arrest or pacification. Similarly, Rothe and Mullins (2006a) noted that attempts to control or block state criminality can and have resulted in state actors finding illegitimate means to achieve their goals, thus sidestepping legitimate means of control. Indeed, efforts to control or confront government wrongdoing may not have the intended chilling effect one hoped for: All too often, controls on state criminogenic agencies and practices can have unintended and undesirable effects.

Nonetheless, few scholars have outlined what happens to those who confront state crime. Turk (1982), in the context of explaining political policing, for example, outlined a series of state efforts against individuals and organizations that the state perceives as threatening to its stability: intelligence gathering, information control, neutralization, and specific and general deterrence.[8] Churchill and Vander Wall (1990) also reviewed seven major outcomes to individuals and organizations that confronted the Federal Bureau of Investigation and the Chicago Police Department in their extralegal actions against the American Indian Movement and Black Panther Party activities. State agencies' responses included eavesdropping, false letters/mail, black propaganda operations, disinformation or gray propaganda, harassment arrests, use of infiltrators and agents provocateurs, pseudo-gangs, black jacketing, fabrication of evidence, and assassinations. Although Turk, Churchill, and Vander Wall produce relevant categories, they are much too small in scope to provide a general framework for examining adverse effects of attempts to constrain or control government criminality, especially given the varieties of additional victimization that can occur.

Building on earlier research (Barak 1991a; Ross 1995b, 2000a; Kauzlarich and Kramer 1998; Rothe and Mullins 2006b), Ross and Rothe (2008) proposed a continuum that explains the irony of controlling state crime and provides a model for contextualizing the forms of additional victimization that can intentionally or unintentionally occur. These practices are listed from least to most common in frequency: censure, scapegoating or obfuscation, retaliation, defiance/resistance, plausible deniability or improving the agency's ability to hide and/or explain away crimes, relying on self-righteousness, redirection/misdirection, and fear mongering. Ross and Rothe have argued that while social controls against state criminality are important, the results often lead to unintended consequences for the attempted controllers. Additionally, they highlighted the fact that the victimization of state crime may well be more than the result of primary crimes of omission or commission. Victimization can occur as a secondary factor that results in state responses to attempts of control. By implication, it is prudent for those intent upon controlling state crime to acknowledge that we must recognize that attempts to control state criminality may have consequences that are unintended and actually frustrate our ability to control state crime or result in additional victimization.

Conclusion

Despite the election of what appears to be a progressive democrat, the problems of controls will not magically evaporate. As long as people are human beings and organizations are allowed free reign to do what they need or want to do to accomplish their goals, state crimes and the need to monitor and control them will not disappear. We need to be constantly vigilant and realize that state crimes may morph, particularly as new mechanisms for circumvention appear.

Notes

Special thanks to Dawn L. Rothe for comments on this chapter.
1. An alternative but complementary distinction involves "political crimes against the state," "domestic political crimes by the state," and "international political crimes by the state" (Beirne and Messerschmidt 1991, chap. 8).
2. For a content analysis of the coverage of political crime by criminology and criminal justice texts, see Tunnell (1993a).
3. There is some appreciation that states can be not only domestic contributors to crime but also transnational criminals (Chambliss 1989). Some, but not all, contributors explore this part of the state crime question. Many of the advanced industrialized countries have supported and also exploited lesser developed countries. This phenomenon, usually characterized by dependency theory, has led a number of development and dependency theorists to suggest that what the advanced industrialized countries are doing is a subtle form of state crime.

4. See Almond (1956) for an introduction to different types of political systems.
5. Although there is an appreciation that we could look at the newly industrialized countries (e.g., Taiwan, Singapore, Malaysia), which have different historical and economic circumstances, most of them can hardly be called democracies. Consequently, the focus here is clearly on the advanced industrialized democracies. It is also recognized that the term "democracy" is difficult to define and consists of various dimensions and types (Lange and Meadwell 1985; Lijphart 1984).
6. For an excellent addition to the research on democracy that explains the actors and instruments of this process, see, for example, Diamond (1995).
7. For a review of different types of democracies, see, for example, Lange and Meadwell (1985).
8. These actions can take place before and after a citizen actually engages in some sort of political action.

CHAPTER 9

Complementary and Alternative Domestic Responses to State Crime

Dawn L. Rothe

OVER THE PAST TWO DECADES a growing body of literature on state crime has focused on documenting and explaining the etiological factors of the worst atrocities known to humanity. One can reasonably argue that the majority of this research on state crime has focused more on description and less on issues of controls of state crime. In general, when criminologists do address these controls, their findings can typically be categorized as theoretically grounded and policy oriented with an international focus (Ross 1995a, 2000a; Mullins and Rothe 2008a, 2008b; Rothe and Mullins 2006a, 2006b, 2007), and embedded within an analysis of a particular institution (Ross 1995b, 2000b; Kauzlarich and Kramer, 1998). Controls have been conceptualized as external and internal (see Ross 1995a, 1995b, 2000a, 2000b; Ross and Rothe 2008; Rothe and Mullins 2006a, 2008a). For example, Ross suggested that external controls are those that lie outside of the state apparatus and are imposed on the state itself, and internal controls are those that arise within the state and are directed against itself (e.g., domestic laws and self-regulation).

External controls provide powers of review or sanction by organizations both domestic (e.g., external review boards) and/or international (e.g., the World Court of Justice and the United Nations). Rothe and Mullins (2008a) note that controls over state crime are the strongest at the international level. This is in part due to the very position of the state: its power, resources, and ability to avoid accountability. After all, a regime that has committed criminal acts is unlikely to govern, regulate, or penalize itself. Consequentially, regulation or controls may not only be absent in particular countries, the criminal actions may be legitimized or made ineffective. Additionally, the idea of domestic controls implies that there are similar and/or consistent forms in all or most countries. However, as Rothe and Kauzlarich (2010) and Rothe

(2009a) have noted, there are vast differences in controls between countries. For this reason, one cannot propose or suggest broad-based policies to address state criminality at the national level.

For example, domestic laws and sanctions vary from state to state, and as such, any internal responses to past or occurring forms of state criminality would necessarily have to take into account the specific country's needs, especially those in transitional capacities (Rothe and Kauzlarich 2010). Additionally, effective responses need to be varied enough to incorporate the wide variety of crimes. For example, international prosecution for the Rwandan genocidaires was highly problematic when considering the scope of participants. The vast numbers of offenders created massive infrastructure problems for the state. In response, gacaca courts have been set in place to address the crimes (Haveman 2008). States may often need to incorporate systems of amnesty and/or truth and reconciliation commissions, or rely on traditional cultural or spiritual redresses to address offenders in certain cases. For example, the Lord's Resistance Army's long-standing use of abducted child soldiers in Uganda's decade's long civil war presents a challenge for addressing the atrocities they have been forced to commit. Kidnapped and pressed into service, these children do not bear the same level of legal or social culpability as their adult counterparts. Yet, as they are returned to their communities, tensions remain over the actions they committed. Here, reintegration is more important than punitive formal controls. Additionally, one form of domestic control (e.g., state-level prosecutions) may not provide the best or sole solution for the local level or communities. After all, in postconflict situations peace is the most desired commodity. However, peace depends "not only on the absence of war but also on the existence of both justice and truth, with both justice and truth dependent on the other" (Amnesty International 2007). As such, responses may need to be more than what is typically thought of as systems of accountability. For this reason, this chapter explores core domestic controls and various formal responses to crimes of genocide, war crimes, crimes against humanity, human rights abuses, and/or extensive corruption aimed at reconciliation, accountability, and restoration.

Domestic Laws

As with any social phenomena, the social construction of what constitutes a criminal act is continuously redefined; behaviors are either legitimized or delegitimized in public and legal discourse arenas. As many scholars have pointed out, these processes are influenced by existing politico-social power structures. When the state commits acts they would view as intolerable or illegal by others (crimes against humanity, repression, war crimes, or corruption), they generally label them "legitimate," a "positive" violence, or justified by the greater good. The state can also, due to its very position, legitimize certain violence as a means of social control. In other words, the process of defining values and norms in the legitimation (or lack thereof) of behavior is a key role of the state political apparatus. Simply, while a state's domestic laws ideally can serve to control its actions, due to the unique position of a government as a self-regulator and lawmaker, it is in the position to create or nullify laws governing it. Nonetheless, most all international treaties, charters, or statutes require that states' domestic laws conform through legislation or constitutional changes to the international standard a state has agreed to comply with (Rothe 2009a).

For example, the U.S. War Crimes Act of 1996 and the Expanded War Crimes Act of 1997 were created and passed in response to the development of the Rome Statute of the International Criminal Court being developed during the early and mid 1990s. The U.S. Torture Statue (18 USC 2340) is the domestic codification of the Convention against Torture and Other Cruel, Inhumane or Degrading Treatment of Punishment (ratified by the U.S. in 1994). The Uniform Code of Military Justice (UCMJ) is the code that subjects all military personnel to criminal responsibility for acts such as Article 93—Cruelty and Mistreatment. The above were all legislated to bypass potential international legal responsibility (especially from the ICC) by ensuring the domestic procedures and laws were in place. This does not mean they need be used, but the state can argue that, as a sovereign, it has the means and legislation to prosecute those accused, thus negating the need or ability of international intervention. Simply, the legislation enforced the state's position that, as a sovereign state it could and would domestically prosecute its own citizens for breaches of international war crimes that were to be included in the Rome Statute of the International Criminal Court.

On the other hand, states, due to their unique position, can ensure impunity at the local level for participants of state-sanctioned violence and criminality. For example, during the ongoing genocide in Darfur, the Sudanese government ensured the Interim Constitution for Sudan (Article 60), ratified July 6, 2005, contained a provision granting immunity from prosecution to the president and vice president of the Republic of Sudan. Similarly, Article 92 granted immunity to members of the National Legislature. Again, this was a strategic move to ensure impunity for the genocidaires, complicit and implicit, at the state level. Thus, if the regime were overthrown or dismantled, the constitution afforded them legal protection from prosecution.

Likewise, after decades of widespread violence and disorder in Burundi, the government created the Immunity Law granting temporary immunity to political leaders who returned from exile. This piece of domestic legislation has come under much scrutiny by international leaders, organizations, and citizens of Burundi, as it contradicted the Arusha accord for peace and reconciliation law. Moreover, it grants amnesty for those who planned the crimes, while those who executed the orders were to remain in custody.

This is not to say that a country should never consider or implement amnesty or immunities. It can indeed be one mechanism that achieves reconciliation and restoration; nonetheless, when such laws are put in place to grant impunity for state leaders without the larger goal of restoration or support of the peoples, such acts are an additional abuse of political power and become a legalized tyranny or create the legal criminal. Further, it is this type of action by state leaders that has reinforced the need for an international institution of control that can indeed intervene in cases where states either cannot or are unwilling to prosecute those accused of violating international criminal law.

DOMESTIC LAW AND CIVIL REMEDIES

Most governments have similar laws that govern traditional street crimes such as murder, kidnapping, and larceny, and many of them treat any offender from any country as the same as one of their citizens. As such, these laws act in a way to allow a citizen of another country to seek redress in the offenders' state(s) of citizenship. For example, in the United States there is the Alien Tort Claims Act (ATCA). Its origins date back to the first Judiciary Act of 1789, which created the U.S. court system. It provides that "the district courts shall have original jurisdiction of any civil action by an alien for a tort only, committed in violation of the law of nations or a treaty of the United States" (National Law Journal 2004, 1). The ATCA grants U.S. courts jurisdiction in any dispute where it is alleged that the law of nations, or international laws, are broken (Rothe 2006). As an example of the Tort Act for noncitizens to use as recourse against U.S. citizens, in June 2004 a Supreme Court ruling upheld the core principles of the 1789 Alien Tort Claims Act (ATCA). As such, potentially, individuals abused and tortured at Abu Ghraib (and in the war on terrorism in general) would be entitled to bring a civil suit against the United States for alleged abuses. This would include being able to sue corporations whose employees took part in the systematic abuses and torture. Such is the case with CACI International and Titan, who are named as defendants in a suit filed in Federal District Court in Washington, D.C., under the Alien Tort Claims Act, on behalf of four Abu Ghraib detainees. The Center for Constitutional Rights (CCR) and the Philadelphia law firm of Montgomery, McCracken, Walker and Rhoads filed a second lawsuit (a class action suit) on June 9, 2004, in a federal court in San Diego. This action also utilizes the Alien Tort Claims Act (ATCA), along with the Fifth, Eighth, and Fourteenth Amendments to the U.S. Constitution (Rothe 2006).

Another component of domestic laws is their ability to try noncitizens for crimes committed within their territory or, in some cases, committed in one country by a national of another country, with enforcement by a third country. Within this volume, chapter 7 uses the Pinochet case as an example of state-sponsored terrorism that later established international legal precedent. This was the result of enforcement by a third country, most notably Spain. Baltasar Garzón, the Spanish judge who initiated the successful prosecution of General Pinochet, also secured the detention in Mexico of the Argentine torturer Ricardo Miguel Cavallo, who is now awaiting extradition to Spain for his trial. Additionally, the Belgium parliament empowered Belgian courts to exercise jurisdiction over war crimes and breaches of the Geneva Convention committed anywhere in the world by a citizen of any country (Hitchins 2001). According to Hitchins, "The Netherlands, Switzerland, Denmark, and Germany have all recently employed the Geneva Conventions to prosecute war criminals for actions committed against non-nationals by non-nationals. . . . The British House of Lords' decision in the matter of Pinochet has also decisively negated the defense of "sovereign immunity" for acts committed by a government or by those following a government's orders. This has led in turn to Pinochet's prosecution in his own country" (1).

Yet, this is another case where we must be cognizant of states' interests in using their authority to pursue foreign nationals, citizens, or even heads of state. For example, in September 2000 Zimbabwe's president, Robert Mugabe, visited the United States to attend the UN Millennium Summit. Prior to his arrival, he had been served with summons of appearance for a lawsuit alleging that he had organized assassinations, torture, rape, terrorism, and other acts of violence to reduce or control his political opposition. Yet, the U.S. State Department submitted an official "suggestion" to the court claiming that Mugabe was entitled to head-of-state immunity in U.S. courts. Further, they noted that putting President Mugabe on trial would be incompatible with U.S. foreign policy goals and interests—an example of the realpolitik involved in the implementation of laws and justice. Nonetheless, domestic law and civil remedies can act as enforcement mechanisms or controls for those beyond its borders as well as for those within. Such types of recourse are indeed an alternative to the newly formed ICC or to relying on the long and arduous task of creating an ICT through the United Nations. Moreover, they afford protections to the accused typically not provided in domestic military tribunals.

Beyond this, there are generally laws within each state's legal system that prohibit these types of behaviors, some stronger than others, especially given the position of a state to legitimate or even decriminalize its actions. Luckily, such cases are not the dominant ones. Again, we are talking about the presence of laws, not the enforcement of them. Due to the vast array of domestic laws, it would be beyond the scope of this chapter to identify and discuss them in detail. Nonetheless, as an example, consider the following: Sweden criminalized genocide with a special domestic law in 1964, and war crimes are penalized through a legal norm. On the other hand, Finland and Poland cover genocide and war crimes within the general Finnish and Polish penal codes. In Finland and Sweden, crimes against humanity can be punished only as ordinary offenses. In order to prosecute war crimes in Finland, Poland, and Sweden, a reference to international treaty and customary law is deemed necessary. Austria has a special national provision covering only the crime of genocide. Croatia, Serbia, and Montenegro penalize not only genocide but also war crimes as special offenses; yet, crimes against humanity are not codified separately and are prosecuted as ordinary criminal offenses. When looking at domestic laws in Spain, Ivory Coast, France, and Italy, national prosecution systems also differ. Canada, on the other hand, has enacted an independent Crimes against Humanity and War Crimes Act, which penalizes the worst of the worst state crimes—acts of genocide, crimes against humanity, and war crimes—and relies on customary international law. In Israel and the United States, crimes against humanity can be punished only as an ordinary criminal offense, while acts of genocide are explicitly covered. In China, violations of international criminal law can be prosecuted only as ordinary offenses. The legal situation in domestic jurisdictions is quite heterogeneous and the prosecution of international crimes is very limited in many countries' legal systems (Ambos and Stegmiller 2008).

Military Tribunals

Domestic military tribunals are not to be confused with the international tribunals. The war crimes trials at Nuremburg and Tokyo were not military tribunals; they were ad hoc tribunals like the International Criminal Tribunals for the Former Yugoslavia and Rwanda. Moreover, domestic military tribunals have been called, often interchangeably, military commissions, tribunals, courts-martial, war courts, courts of inquiry, and common law war courts. To give an idea of the history behind these types of courts, consider that British precedents for using them date back to around 1650. They were used in the United States during the Civil War by President Lincoln; in this case, the tribunals were also used for civilians in the spring of 1865. They were also used during the Indian Wars to try Native Americans. Throughout history, the support for and/or criticism of use of military tribunals has waned and waxed according to different political and ideological stances of administrations. The current George W. Bush administration has reinstituted using the courts to address civilians as well as those they deem enemy combatants, which has been a highly controversial decision. Interestingly, the United States has consistently criticized other countries for using the same type of redress (e.g., Burma, China, Colombia, Egypt, Malaysia, Peru, Russia, and Turkey).

With these caveats in mind, it is important to note that military tribunals can serve as a last resort mechanism when a country will not prosecute its own people that have committed atrocities in that country or another. For example, the trials against Argentinean and Chilean leaders in Spain were instituted for this very reason. The Derechos News Service noted that "in 1996 the Progressive Union of Prosecutors decided to file criminal complaints against the Argentinean and Chilean military for the disappearance of Spanish citizens in those countries. . . . On June 28th, [1996] Judge Garzón ruled that the court had jurisdiction to investigate the facts denounced by the popular action and to prosecute any of the crimes committed by the accused and others responsible for the crimes" (1998, 2).

In October 1998, upon hearing that Pinochet was present in England, the popular action asked the court to interrogate Pinochet about his role in Operation Condor and requested that he and other Chilean military be charged for the disappearance and kidnappings of civilians. Another group of Chilean relatives of the disappeared asked the judge to charge Pinochet and other leaders with genocide, terrorism, and torture. On October 16, Garzón ordered the arrest of Pinochet, issuing an international arrest order. On November 3 of that year, Garzón issued an extradition order for Pinochet, setting worldwide legal precedence for a military tribunal for a head of state by another state, thus showing universal jurisdiction for the crimes of genocide. As noted by the BBC, because there was "no real prospect of Pinochet being tried in Chile or any international tribunal, Spain's extradition request was the only vehicle for the emplacement of the rule of law in these matters" (1999, 1). The power of this mechanism to be an effective control is direct but also indirect, through the perception of those that have committed such atrocities and violated international criminal law that a military tribunal could be initiated to prosecute their actions. For example, fear of military tribunal prosecutions was formally discussed within the U.S. State Department. The FBI has warned several former U.S. officials not to travel to some countries, including some in Europe, "where there is a risk of extradition to other nations interested in prosecuting them" (Rothe 2006, 248). Henry Kissinger is sought for extradition for violations of international law, and as such he does not leave the United States without assurances of not being extradited. Moreover, "Secretary of State Colin Powell demanded that Belgium change its war crimes legislation in order to halt a case against Powell, George Bush senior, Vice President Dick Cheney, and former U.S. army commander Norman Schwarzkopf for committing war crimes during the 1991 Gulf War. Washington fears a similar lawsuit is about to be made against George W. Bush for human rights violations and civilian deaths in the current war" (Michaels 2003, 1).

Other examples include countries prosecuting Rwandese genocide suspects under their national jurisdictions: a Swiss military court arrested a genocide suspect in 1996 and tried him between July 1998 and April 1999; a Belgium Cour d'Assises (Crown Court) tried four individuals for war crimes and human rights violations from April to June 2001; the Canadian government used two federal immigration tribunals to try a Rwandan accused of genocide, but the federal court halted his deportation proceedings in April 2001 (Amnesty International 2002). It is with this in mind that military tribunals can produce positive results and can act as a much larger control than a country's own military forces or individuals caught committing such crimes on the soil of another state.

SPECIAL DOMESTIC COURTS

Beyond a state's existing criminal justice institutions, temporary special courts have also been convened to address violations of international criminal law by agents of the state (or post heads of state administrators). The use of these special courts can provide an alternative to or act as a complement to international tribunals (e.g., East Timor, Kosovo, Bosnia, Serbia, and Croatia). These local justice mechanisms operate under state law, although there can be an international component. Nonetheless, they are considered domestic courts and differ from other hybrid forms of domestic/international, as in the case of Sierra Leone, that will be discussed later in this chapter. For example, there has been a transfer of cases from the ICTY to local Bosnian courts. In this case, the temporary or ad hoc court serves as an internationalized war crimes chamber of the Bosnian state court system. The War Crimes Chamber, established in Sarajevo in March 2005, handles cases of serious war crimes transferred from the ICTY, as well as war crimes cases initiated locally (Human Rights Watch 2006c). Additionally, it will continue to handle war crimes cases after international involvement has been phased out. According to Almiro Rodrigues, judge at the War Crime Chamber in Bosnia and Herzegovina,

> The Chamber is vital for the process of reconciliation in Bosnia . . . the prosecution of war crimes suspects on home soil has a far more positive effect on reconciliation than the dispensation of "distanced" justice in a forum such as the ICTY. It is important the perception of justice being done in accordance with the traditional maxim "justice must not only be done, but seen to be done." Such a perception becomes far more prevalent if a domestic, rather than an alien, judicial mechanism, dispenses justice. Moreover, it forces Bosnian society to confront the truth of its recent past in a very practical and real sense. (2006, 3)

Similar initiatives have been carried out in Serbia and Croatia to help alleviate the financial and economic burden on the ICTY.

In response to the atrocities committed in the Kosovo conflict during 1999, Regulation 64 Panels were instituted to adjudicate war crimes cases.

At the time of this writing, the Regulation 64 Panels have conducted more than two dozen war crimes trials, which resulted in the indictments of Milos Jokic and Dragan Nikolic for genocide. Additionally, the trial for Milorad Trbic began in November 2007, in which he was charged with genocide. In March 2000, the UN Transitional Authority for East Timor created a judicial system of district courts, which included Serious Crimes Panels. In the case of East Timor, the Dili District Court has exclusive jurisdiction over genocide, war crimes, crimes against humanity, murder, sexual offenses, and torture for crimes committed between January and October 1999 (UN 2008). Similarly, an Extraordinary Chambers was created in Cambodia to address the crimes committed by the Khmer Rouge between 1975 and 1979. The chamber is mandated to try those responsible for genocide, crimes against humanity, and other crimes defined by Cambodian law: murder, torture, religious persecutions, destruction of cultural property in armed conflict, and violations of the Convention of Vienna on the protection of diplomats. Nonetheless, as with other special courts, the chamber has been unable to hold accountable those who orchestrated the atrocity. For example, Pol Pot, the regime's leader, died in 1998, and Ieng Sary is politically protected against prosecution through his self-proclaimed 1996 amnesty. Successful indictments, however, do include two senior Khmer Rouge leaders: Ta Mok, seventy-five, alias "The Butcher," and Kang Kech Eav, widely known as Duch, who managed the S-21 prison where many of the executions occurred (UN 2008).

While these types of specialized courts have contributed to accountability in cases that would have been yet another example of impunity, they do have many practical barriers to their success. Additionally, in some cases these special courts are convened by a government in response to international political pressures and serve as nothing more than a symbolic, hollow gesture. For example, on June 14, 2005, Sudan opened a Special Court to try alleged war criminals in the ongoing genocide campaign against the Darfurians; however, as Amnesty International (2005) noted, the establishment of such a court was reminiscent of past governmental inquiries into the atrocities and represented a tactic to avoid prosecution of regime members by the ICC. After all, the announcement of the creation of Special Courts came one week after the prosecutor of the ICC announced the opening of investigations into the war crimes and crimes against humanity committed in the Darfur region. Under the constitution, a provision was implemented granting immunity from prosecution to the president and vice president of the Republic of Sudan, as well as members of the National Legislature. To date, the Special Criminal Court has handed down several verdicts; however, none of the cases were related to the conflict in 2003 or 2004, nor did any verdicts convict any high-level officials. Thus, it remained a symbolic gesture by the el-Bashir regime (Mullins and Rothe 2007).

HYBRID SYSTEM: SIERRA LEONE

The middle ground between international tribunals and wholly domestic courts has been called "hybrid tribunals." The special courts mentioned in the previous section are often grouped in this category; however, I view them as separate since they are able to continue without international involvement and rely heavily on domestic law and participation of local prosecutors and other agents of a criminal justice system. On the other hand, the hybrid tribunal, in the case of Sierra Leone, consists of international and domestic judges and an international prosecutor, Desmond de Silva, appointed by the UN secretary general (May 2005). As such, the hybrid system for Sierra Leone is a jointly administered court by the United Nations and the Sierra Leone government (UN Resolution 1315, August 14, 2000). The court was created by a treaty between the United Nations and the Sierra Leone government in response to the devastating conflict that occurred between 1991 and 2002, which was characterized by massive human rights abuses by all warring factions. It is mandated to try only those who bear the greatest responsibility for war crimes and crimes against humanity committed in the territory of Sierra Leone between 1996 and 2002, leaving the rest of those that committed such acts to the country's Truth and Reconciliation Commission (UN 2008). As of January 2008, eleven people have been indicted by the Special Court via three separate trials; they were charged with war crimes, crimes against humanity, and other serious violations of international humanitarian law (rape, sexual slavery, conscription of children into an armed force, and attacks on UN peacekeepers, among others). Although individually charged, they have been grouped into three separate trials: the Revolutionary United Front (RUF) trial, begun in July 2004; the Civil Defense Forces (CDF) trial, commenced in June 2004; and the Armed Forces Revolutionary Council (AFRC) trial, begun in March 2005. According to the Office for the Coordination of Humanitarian Affairs, "The single most well known person indicted by the Special Court is the former Liberian President, Charles Taylor, accused of backing the civil war in Sierra Leone by providing arms and training to the RUF in exchange for diamonds" (UN 2008, 1).

The advantages of a hybrid system of justice, as used in Sierra Leone, include the following: it tends to avoid allegations that it is partisan, as the judicial body is composed of a mixture of domestic judges and international ones; it is less costly than "pure" international ad hoc tribunals; it is more transparent than a domestic military tribunal; there is less of a cost burden on the state involved, which is often going through massive reconstruction efforts (political, economic, and social); it is international enough that head of state immunity would not apply; and it has the ability to carry out an extensive outreach to disseminate information about the court through video, radio, and discussion. Nonetheless, such tribunals are often unable to hold accountable all individuals involved and are often seen as incompatible with larger restorative justice measures.

SYSTEMS OF ACCOUNTABILITY, RESTORATION, AND SOCIAL JUSTICE

In the aftermath of state crimes that leave countries ripped apart, accountability is only a small part of the countries' needs. A state is often in need of transitional justice mechanisms that can provide restorative aspects. The best examples include the Truth and Reconciliation Commission in South Africa, the gacaca court in Rwanda, Amnesty in Mozambique, or a combination of nonformal or ad hoc judicial mechanisms of conflict resolution. Villa-Vicencio 2000). Such mechanisms are a valuable and complementary tool to civil or state or international criminal courts because of their strong emphasis on truth, reparation, and reconciliation (Christie 2001; Vanspauwen, Parmentier, and Weitekamp 2007, 2008).

Gacaca Trials: Rwanda

In response to the 1994 genocide, the Rwandan government wanted to hold accountable the massive numbers of genocidaires through prosecution in an effort to end the impunity that had long characterized the Rwandese political culture. To do so, it passed special domestic legislation: Organic Law No. 08/96 (1996), which established specialized genocide chambers in the Courts of First Instance and Organic Law No. 40/2000 (2001) for the creation and implementation of the gacaca (Amnesty International 2002). The gacaca is a hybrid system that merges customary practice with a Western, formal court structure (see Haveman and Muleefu, this volume, for additional details). Historically, the gacaca were a customary system of community hearings that were used to resolve community disputes such as land or inheritance rights or marital disputes. These were informal, ad hoc in nature, and led by community elders (*inyangamugayo*). By creating approximately 10,000 gacaca throughout the country, the Rwandese government transformed this traditional mode of conflict resolution in order to try the more than 800,000 to 1 million genocide suspects overfilling the country's prisons. Thus, the new tribunals are legal judicial bodies that hear three of the four categories of genocide and crimes against humanity. The categories are meant to distinguish between the various degrees of individual responsibility and they carry different penalties:

> The first category includes leaders and organizers of the genocide, persons who abused positions of authority, notorious killers who distinguished themselves by their ferocity or excessive cruelty and perpetrators of sexual torture [to be heard at the ICTR]. Category 2 includes the perpetrators of or accomplices to intentional homicides or serious assaults against

individuals that led to their death. Category 3 contains persons guilty of other serious assaults against individuals, while category 4 covers persons who committed property crimes. (Amnesty International 2002, 2)

The gacaca courts hear charges only for crimes that fall into categories 2, 3, and 4. These courts are located in the local communities and try those persons alleged to have participated in the genocide within the regions where the offenses occurred. The government claims that these community-style hearings, where the members themselves serve as witness, judge, and party, more effectively ventilate the evidence, establish the truth, and bring about reconciliation than what had been achieved previously by either the specialized genocide chambers of the Rwandan courts or the ICTR. As noted by Fatuma Ndangiza of the National Unity and Reconciliation Commission, "Most of the perpetrators who have confessed, when they are taken to the communities to tell what they did, they ask for forgiveness" (Walker 2004, 1). The estimated cost of the gacaca system totaled approximately US$1.03 million by the end of 2007. Yet, as of January 2008, approximately 1 million people accused of involvement in the 1994 genocide had appeared before the courts, where more than 800,000 were tried. Apart from a legal system, gacaca is much more. It is a social process: "It is a cultural phenomenon with historical roots; it is a psychological phenomenon as part of a complex of ways to overcome the mental aftermath of the genocide; it is a political phenomenon, bridging gaps (or widening them) between political opponents, or as an alleged mechanism for the minority in power to suppress the majority of the population, to give just some examples of ways to approach the gacaca. Maybe the least important therefore is to consider the gacaca as a legal system" (Haveman 2008, xx).

When these types of courts are convened and trials are carried out in a fair manner, and when judges exclude themselves from personal cases, they can be an effective alternative for delivering justice to the victims and survivors of the genocide, as well as to the perpetrators. Yet, as with any other system of control, when they fail to deliver justice fairly, they lose legitimacy and weaken efforts to end impunity. Nonetheless, they are strong alternatives to impunity and, in many cases, a practical solution in transitional situations.

Truth Commissions

Since the 1974 Commission of Inquiry in Uganda, there have been nearly two dozen truth commissions in various regions around the world with varying degrees of structure and success: Uganda 1974; Argentina 1983–1984; Uruguay 1985; Uganda 1986–1995; Philippines 1986; Nepal 1990–1991; Chile 1990–1991; Chad 1991–1992; El Salvador 1992–1993; Sri Lanka 1994–1997; Haiti 1995–1996; Burundi 1995–1996; South Africa 1995–2000;

Guatemala 1997–1999; Nigeria 1999–2001; Uruguay 2000–2001; Panama 2001–2002; Sierra Leone 2002; Ghana 2002 (U.S. Institute of Peace 2008).

Generally, these commissions are established to report on human rights abuses over a certain period of time in a particular country or in relation to a particular conflict. The overarching goal is allow victims, their relatives, and perpetrators to give evidence of human rights abuses, providing an official public forum for their accounts and a historical record of the atrocities that occurred. Additionally, there has been a concerted move, headed by the United Nations, toward establishing truth commissions as a complementary tool together with restricted amnesty limited to those least responsible for crimes.

SOUTH AFRICA TRUTH AND RECONCILIATION COMMISSION. The Truth and Reconciliation Commission (TRC) was established by the 1995 Promotion of National Unity and Reconciliation Act to investigate crimes committed during the apartheid era in South Africa, from March 1960 until May 1994. Specifically, the commission was charged with finding the extent of and recording human rights violations committed by the state and the insurgent groups as a part of the institutionalized apartheid, recommending reparations and overseeing the amnesty given to those who admitted their crimes. The amnesty component was limited to those who made full disclosure of all the relevant facts relating to acts associated with a political objective committed in the course of the conflicts of the past. Chaired by Archbishop Desmond Tutu, hearings began in April 1996. Upon completion of the TRC in July 1998, the commission received over 7,000 applications for amnesty and rejected more than 4,500 of the applications, granting approximately 125 amnesties. It heard testimony from over 21,000 victims of apartheid. Findings include that "the state, in the form of the South African government, the civil service and its security forces, was, in the period 1960–1994 the primary per-petrator of gross violations of human rights in South Africa and, from 1974, in southern Africa" (Truth and Reconciliation Commission Final Report, Section 5, 2003). This included the head of state and chair of the State Security Council, Botha, for facilitating a climate in which gross violations of human rights "could and did occur and as such is accountable for such actions." The charges brought by victims included the deliberate, unlawful killing and attempted killing of persons opposed to the policies of the gov-ernment; the widespread use of torture and other forms of severe ill treat-ment; and the forcible abduction of individuals who were residents in neighboring countries.

In the cases where amnesty was denied or not sought by the defendants, prosecution could be considered wherein evidence found by the commission could be handed over to prosecutors. The hope of the commission was to contribute to reconciliation in South Africa's divided society by providing a venue for truth. Nonetheless, very few political leaders or leading white civilians came forward to apologize or accept responsibility for their role. Mathatha Tsedu, the political editor of South Africa's most popular black newspaper, the Sowetan, said, "Black people are the sufferers here . . . they saw the TRC as a mechanism to try to deal with that pain . . . White people have so much to hide about what they have been doing all along and they saw the TRC as some kind of witch hunt and therefore didn't go" (BBC News 1998: 2).

Additionally, many victims and their accounts were not taken into consideration or heard because they were not "victimized enough," according to the mandate. Only victims of gross human rights violations were defined as victims in the TRC Act. As such, the victims omitted from this process felt their rights and feelings had been neglected and justice was not gained. In this respect, it is important to consider the distinction between individual and collective victimization, direct and indirect, to better address the needs of both groups without sacrificing one over the other (Vanspauwen, Parmentier, and Weitekamp 2007, 2008). This may well mean using a combination of mechanisms to reveal truth, accountability, community restoration, and social justice.

SIERRA LEONE TRUTH COMMISSION. Beyond the hybrid court of Sierra Leone, the country created a truth commission under the auspices of the National Forum for Human Rights for the purpose of creating an impartial historical record of violations and abuses of human rights and international humanitarian law related to the armed conflict in Sierra Leone, from the beginning of the conflict in 1991 to the signing of the Lomé Peace Agreement. Its purpose was to address impunity, to respond to the needs of the victims, to promote healing and reconciliation, and to prevent a repetition of the violations and abuses. The commission was composed of seven commissioners, four Sierra Leoneans (selected through a process managed by the special representative of the UN secretary general) and three international commissioners. The commission was composed of four units: legal and reconciliation, administrative, information management, and public outreach. The commission was to report on the nature and extent of the violations and abuses; the context in which the violations and abuses occurred; and whether those violations and abuses were the result of deliberate planning, policy, or authorization by the government, group, or individual. This was to contribute to helping the victims restore their dignity and promote reconciliation by providing the victims an opportunity to give an account of their victimization, giving special attention to the subject of sexual abuses and to the experiences of children within the armed conflict. Further, the truth and reconciliation commission worked alongside the international criminal tribunal and the Special Court for Sierra Leone.

In all, the commission collected 7,706 statements of Sierra Leoneans living in Sierra Leone and/or as refugees in Gambia, Guinea, and Nigeria. This significantly contributed to the understanding of the scope of atrocities that had occurred during the conflict and the involvement of the various fraction groups.

TRUTH AND RECONCILIATION COMMISSION OF CHILE. In 1988, President Augusto Pinochet lost a referendum that triggered democratic elections for the first time in decades. Once Patricio Aylwin was named the new head of state in 1990, the government created a truth commission, known as the Rettig Commission, which was composed of representatives from both Pinochet supporters and his opponents. The primary task was fourfold: to establish a complete picture of human rights violations that had been committed under the Pinochet regime, to gather evidence and victim identifications for the purposes of possible reparations, and to recommend legal measures in an effort to ensure deterrence and end the impunity that had long served the previous regime. Specifically, it was to investigate and provide a written record of "disappearances after arrest, executions, and torture leading to death committed by government agents or people in their service, as well as kidnappings and attempts on the life of persons carried out by private citizens for political reasons" (Brahm 2005, 1). Despite the severe political restraints placed upon it (e.g., limited mandate and stifled cooperation), the commission investigated 3,400 cases of death, and reached definitive conclusions on all but 641, and investigated 2,920 cases of disappearances and identified 2,298 victims of military abuses during Pinochet's rule. It attributed 95 percent of the crimes to the military. While the commission did not name perpetrators, provisions were made that they would be publicly available in 2016 (Quinn 2001). Once the commission had completed its work, it submitted the findings to the government. The report called on the state and all of society to acknowledge and accept responsibility for past crimes. The commission's report made a significant contribution to the finding of facts for Spain's request for extradition and charges against Pinochet.

NATIONAL COMMISSION ON THE DISAPPEARED OF ARGENTINA. As with the other truth and reconciliation commissions, the National Commission on the Disappeared for Argentina (CONADEP) was created in 1983 as a tool for truth-telling and to chronicle the events and cases that occurred. As such, the commission's report would not determine responsibility of those named as having had a part in the mass numbers of disappeared. The commission was structured with five departments: depositions, documentation and data processing, procedures, legal affairs, and administration. The commission presided over hearings of thousands of cases of abduction, disappearance, torture, and executions in which they compiled over 50,000 pages of documentation. As a result, they recommended that the Argentina courts process the investigation and verification of the depositions received by this commission for potential prosecutions. CONADEP was able to present evidence comprising 1,086 dossiers that proved the existence of secret detention centers and provided a partial list of the disappeared as well as a list of members of the Armed Forces and Security Forces mentioned by victims as responsible for the serious crimes. This resulted in nine members of the former junta being prosecuted in trials. Without such a process, quite possibly the junta members would have escaped accountability in any form. Additionally, the historical record of the numbers of victims and their voices were documented at a time the public needed a collective recognition of the past events (U.S. Institute of Peace 2008).

THE COMMISSION ON THE TRUTH EL SALVADOR. The conflict in El Salvador lasted twelve years (1980–1991) and resulted in a mass number of deaths and other violations of human rights. During July 1992 the secretary general for the United Nations began an effort to create the Commission on the Truth for Salvadorians. The commission was charged with examining the systematic atrocities committed by the state armed forces and members of insurgent groups that inflicted individuals and the communities as a whole. The mandate of the commission defined their function as to "have the task of investigating serious acts of violence that have occurred since 1980 and whose impact on society urgently demands that the public should know the truth. The Parties recognize the need to clarify and put an end to any indication of impunity on the part of officers of the armed forces, particularly in cases where respect for human rights is jeopardized. To that end, the Parties refer this issue to the Commission on the Truth for consideration and resolution" (Commission on the Truth for El Salvador 1992). The commission was given two specific powers: the power to make investigations and the power to make recommendations. The latter power is particularly important since, under the mandate, the parties should attempt to carry out the commission's recommendations. Unlike other truth commissions discussed, the Salvadorian commission comprised only international staff, due to the ongoing involvement of the UN in the peace process, as well as the domestic legal, political, and economic conditions that were the result of the conflict.

The commission registered more than 22,000 complaints of serious acts of violence. Of those, nearly 60 percent were for extrajudicial executions, over 25 percent involved victimization through enforced disappearances, and nearly 20 percent were complaints of torture (U.S. Institute of Peace 2008).

Of these reported cases, the commission found that approximately 85 percent of the cases of violence were attributed to agents of the state, paramilitary groups working with or for the state, and death squads. On the other hand, of all the complaints registered, only 5 percent were attributed to the insurgent group Frente Farabundo Martí para la Liberación Nacional (FMLN). With the numbers of complaints that had been heard and verified, the commission was limited in its recommendations for prosecution. As noted by a 1993 TRC report: "The question is not whether the guilty should be punished, but whether justice can be done. Public morality demands that those responsible for the crimes described here be punished. However, El Salvador has no system for the administration of justice which meets the minimum requirements of objectivity and impartiality so that justice can be rendered reliably" (U.S. Institute of Peace 2008). Consequently, they were limited to naming the accused. Furthermore, five days after the report was issued, the government passed legislation granting amnesty to those named in the report. The end result of the nine-month work of the commission and involvement of the mass victims was the revelation of some truth but no accountability for perpetrators.

Amnesties

States have used a wide variety of types of amnesty to address crimes of the state and other violators of international laws (e.g., paramilitaries and/or militia groups). These are often combined with truth and reconciliation commissions, as in the case of South Africa, where amnesty accompanies only full truth disclosures or conditional amnesty. In other cases, such as the Democratic Republic of Congo, the amnesty covers political assassinations but not war crimes committed during specific times. In other cases, amnesties are used for political purposes to achieve peace, as in the case of Mozambique, or as a means to allow impunity after individuals have been named as perpetrators by truth commissions (e.g., El Salvador). Amnesty laws may be a precondition for peace negotiations by one or more of the forces involved in a conflict or may form the central corpus around which a fragile peace is built. In other situations, they serve as a form of reintegration into the community, often through a combination of culturally specific traditions. For example, in Mozambique, traditional healing mechanisms, such as purifying those involved in a civil war, made it possible, after the purification, for links to the past to be severed and the individual to be reintegrated back into the community. Additionally, in Mozambique the term "reconciliation" is used to refer to forgetting the past and being tolerant. Together, the fact that Mozambique experienced a civil war along with these community-level traditions allowed the blanket amnesty to succeed to the degree it did. In other cases, such as Uganda, amnesty is being used to reintegrate child soldiers that have escaped and are returning to their communities. Here again, traditional rituals are used to purify the child's sins at the same time informal amnesties are granted.

While amnesties are generally frowned upon by Western models of criminal justice and/or nongovernmental organizations promoting accountability, they can serve as a tool for collective forgiveness in cases where entire communities were victimized and in situations of large-scale participations of atrocities. However, when amnesties are used for the purposes of granting impunity to a select few or regime leaders, they serve no grander function as a mechanism for reintegration or restoration. In these cases, amnesty allows a state to judge its own case, violating the general principle forbidding self-judging, and is unlikely to be considered a valid mechanism of control under international law (Naqvi 2003).

Impeachment

Impeachment is a process of removing heads of state that hold security of tenure; the official cannot be removed from his or her office except in exceptional and specified circumstances. It is a formal process governed by nearly every country's constitution or laws and is equivalent to a criminal indictment. Typically, impeachment serves to remove the person(s) from office; however, this may not always be the case. While all laws, regulations, and other systems of controls are politicized, impeachments are particularly vulnerable to misuse and manipulation by other or competing party members. Nonetheless, it is a control mechanism that can be used to address crimes committed by a regime and/or parts of an administration. While less tenable than other forms of control, it is a viable mechanism for reacting to and controlling state criminality.

Impeachments are not a new phenomenon, though they are rather rare. The United States has had two presidents impeached: Lyndon Johnson (for violating the Tenure of Office Act) and Bill Clinton (for perjury and suborning perjury), though neither was removed from office. The process of impeachment against President Nixon by the House Judiciary Committee was ended when he resigned before the house voted. In 1992 the Peruvian Congress voted to impeach President Fujimori and to remove him from office, naming the second vice president as new head of state. Fujimori's impeachment was in response to a general fear of dictatorship rule due to his attempt to dissolve Peru's congress, to suspend the constitution, and to detain lawmakers that were primarily the opposition Apra Party. During 2004 South Korea experienced the country's first presidential impeachment when President Roh Moo-hyun was removed from office on the grounds of illegal electioneering and incompetence. Other examples include President Banisadr of Iran, who was impeached during 1981 by the Iranian parliament, Brazil's

President Collor de Mello in 1992, President Pérez of Venezuela in 1993, and President Grau of Paraguay in 1999.

Impeachments can be an effective means for removing or shaming leaders' behaviors; yet, they are limited in addressing the scope of many state crimes. They cannot address larger structural problems that often accompany or predate the more widespread and atrocious forms of criminality, nor are they effective for addressing entire governmental structures that participate in these forms of crime. It is the latter that has been addressed through processes of lustration.

Lustration

The term "lustration" is derived from Latin, meaning to purify ceremonially. As a control mechanism, it is a tool created by special legislation to effectively remove a segment or political party from holding political and/or civil offices that committed abuses under a past regime. States that undergo extreme transitional circumstances are often facing multiple challenges for restoration and some form of justice for past abuses. This is especially the case for state crimes that are the result of systematic or institutionalized abuses by vast bureaucracies, where a significant portion of the population is implicated through acts of omission or commission rather than direct actions of regimes. The various forms lustration has taken have been dependent on a state's history and the nature of transitions, ranging from soliciting information to investigating, trying, and disqualifying from office those most complicit with the past regime. Lustration has most notably been used in countries that have dealt with a legacy of abuse under communism in post-Soviet Eastern Europe. In these cases, states have adopted some form of practice of lustration that for various timeframes excludes from political offices former Communist Party functionaries and collaborators with secret police forces (Brahm 2004). Nonetheless, lustration has occurred in other contexts, including the U.S.-led de-Baathification in Iraq after the 2003 invasion and occupation.

Out of the context of communist countries, postcommunist countries adopted lustration laws, with Czechoslovakia as one of the first. In October 1991 former party officials, members of the People's Militia and members of the National Security Corps were barred from holding a range of elected and/or appointed positions in state-owned companies, academia, and the media for five years. In 1990 Hungary held its first free elections in forty years, in which the Communist Party, the Hungarian Socialist Party, was defeated. In March 1994 the Hungarian parliament adopted a lustration law subjecting 12,000 "officials" to a screening process to determine whether they had collaborated with the former secret police (e.g., members of parliament and government, ambassadors, army commanders, chiefs of police, career judges, and district attorneys). If found to be collaborators, they were barred from political or state-owned civil jobs. Albania also practiced lustration against former Communist Party members. In Lithuania, the government declared in 1991 that former KGB employees and collaborators could not hold local or national government posts until 1996.

The few cases listed above illustrate how lustration is commonly used to remove a political, ethnic, or religious party that oppressed other segments of society during its rule. Nonetheless, lustration practices do not come without their own political ramifications and abuses. Some observers have suggested that while there is nothing wrong with this practice in principle, it has often been implemented in a subpar fashion by entangling the innocent (Brahm 2004). Furthermore, it is not a magic panacea for addressing past abuses or attaining social equilibrium—nor is it necessarily effective for restorative justice. Such a move, as is the case with most attempts to use lustration, is guided by the assumption that former officials and collaborators would undermine a new democratic system, which may not be the case at all (Boed 1999). This can be seen with the U.S. initial (Coalition Provisional Authority) implementation of a de-Baathification program. A formal policy and law was then implemented by the new Iraqi government barring all Baathists from holding government, military, and police positions. Since that time, however, the United States has demanded that the former members of Saddam Hussein's Baath Party, whom the U.S. military recruited into Iraq's internal security forces, keep their positions. In the case at hand, lustration efforts, which targeted numbers of innocent civilians as well, were supported primarily because of political and economic interests for a new regime and may have contributed to the ongoing civil strife and ethnic divisions occurring in Iraq.

Summary

This chapter provided brief reviews of domestic controls, including some of the hybrid or innovative ways states have attempted to address massive past crimes. Undoubtedly, some are more problematic than others. For example, domestic laws do little in the form of deterrence for state actors when or if they can redefine their behaviors as legitimate, necessary, or for the greater good. For this reason, except for mechanisms such as coups, criminal heads of states or leaders of agencies within regimes most often must be held accountable by external controls, typically other states, as was the case with the increased use of domestic courts or by international institutions. Other forms of control have looked beyond just accountability to try to address issues of restoration or restorative justice. This has included efforts such as the hybrid tribunals, truth commissions, and, in some cases, conditional or blanket amnesties as a means of social healing. Controls at this level must take into account the specific country's needs, especially those in transitional capacities. Additionally, effective responses and postcontrols need to be varied enough to incorporate the vast types of crimes and the extent of the type of government that is in place. As a closing thought, we must also be cognizant that most all types of social control have risks and can pose latent consequences. This is no different at the domestic level than it is for international controls where issues of power, politics, and intervening states' interests often come to bear on the effectiveness or ineffectiveness of responses. Additionally, in every case no mechanism of social control can serve as a form of justice for all. In other words, there will always be underlying factors to each system that can be easily critiqued, and there will be those victims and perpetrators who feel that whatever control was enacted did not succeed in a justice for all.

NOTE

This chapter is a revised excerpt from previous work including Rothe (2009b).

CHAPTER 10

The Fairness of Gacaca

Roelof H. Haveman and Alphonse Muleefu

IN 1994, FOR ONE HUNDRED DAYS, Rwanda lost more than one million lives of innocent men, women, and children. In the aftermath of the genocide that killed mostly Tutsi and moderate Hutu, the country was laid in shambles: bodies were generally strewn everywhere in the country, some floating in rivers and a few buried in shallow graves. The country's population was unstable: a large number of perpetrators fled the country seeking refuge in other countries, while others returned who had left the country as refugees in previous conflicts. The genocide left behind a large number of orphans and widows, traumatic stress and grief, mental disorder, and physical disability; destroyed the country's social fabric; desolated the population; compromised unity among Rwandans; and tarnished the image of Rwanda in general. Unlike the past regimes, the postgenocide government of national unity concluded that they would not tolerate the culture of impunity, an idea that was strongly shared by the international community. However, keeping this promise turned into a nightmare because important government institutions, including the justice sector, were completely destroyed. The judicial system, already weak before the genocide, was left with no adequate personnel and resources to effectively prosecute the suspects. The challenges mounted when the number of arrested suspects grew to over 120,000 for a prison system designed for 15,000. A solution through the classical justice system (Organic Law No. 8/96 of 30/8/1996) proved inadequate; by 2000, only 6,000 cases had been tried by the Rwandan ordinary courts, while the United Nations International Criminal Tribunal for Rwanda (UN-ICTR) was to focus on only a very small number of those held most responsible. This implied that neither the system in Rwanda nor the ICTR in Arusha were in a position to handle the volume of suspects in prison, not forgetting that justice concerned also those suspects still living in the community and in exile, hence the need to look for an alternative solution. After pondering ways in which to deliver a speedy and fair trial to the population at large, gacaca became a viable option and finally started in 2005.[1] It is expected that the gacaca trials will end by July 2010; by then more than a million people will have been tried. It is important to note that the credibility of the whole work completed by gacaca courts partly depends on judging its standards of fairness or fair trial rights.

THE QUESTION: FAIR OR UNFAIR?

One question at the core of discussions about gacaca is whether it is fair—that is, does the gacaca system function according to the fair trial standards that have been developed over at least the past sixty years with regard to the traditional penal systems? Fair trial rights are part of the core elements of the rule of law, which bind all state judicial/legal institutions in order to protect, respect, and ensure that there is fair and equal treatment of citizens. The right to a fair trial or due process is guaranteed by the Rwandan constitution and by regional and international human rights instruments, some of which Rwanda is a party to.[2] However, mere existence, with little or no mechanisms in place to ensure effective enforcement, renders the whole system flawed. Fairness should be seen in practice rather than as a statement on paper.

Immediately after the introduction of the gacaca courts, many scholars from all over the world showed an interest in the phenomenon. However, despite a general acknowledgment that the gacaca could play an important role in achieving justice that would be impossible to reach through either the classical penal system or the international penal system, gacaca faced much criticism from the start. The main criticisms of gacaca are that there is no right to legal representation, there is no independent and impartial judiciary, confessions play too important of a role, and witnesses are obliged to testify.

The question whether the gacaca system is fair is only one of the questions to answer when assessing the value of gacaca (Clark 2009; Haveman 2008). At the same time, it is one of the most difficult questions to answer. There are very few people who unconditionally state that the gacaca system is fair. To be honest, it would be strange if anyone did say as much, as no penal system in the world can unconditionally be said to be fair. Very few, if any, jurisdictions in practice apply all rules and principles on human rights. This may explain why organizations such as Human Rights Watch in general have such a negative opinion about the fairness of the penal system in Rwanda: they compare the practice of the Rwandan system with a nonexistent ideal. Fairness of a penal system is not a question of black and white; it has to do with shades of gray. Hence, the question should not be "Is the gacaca system fair or unfair?" but rather "To what extent can the gacaca system be considered fair?"

The assessment as to whether a particular system is fair or not is a relatively subjective assessment, for which one tries to find more or less objective arguments, but the final ordeal is a rather subjective conclusion. Some rights are more serious than others. Torture to get a confession is a deadly sin and will stop the whole process in any serious penal system. Other rights are less heavy and can be put aside—for instance, in the interest of national security—or can be counterbalanced by other measures. The assessment of fairness depends on the system in a particular country, common or civil law, or, in a penal context, adversarial or inquisitorial. In the inquisitorial system, it is less important that all witnesses are heard in the courtroom in front of the judges, parties, and jury, as some checks and balances have been incorporated as a guarantee against abuse of power that do not exist in the adversarial system. The same pertains to the use of anonymous witnesses: in some countries it is categorically refused as being the worst violation of human rights possible; in other countries it is accepted, although with systematic guarantees against abuse. This shows that it is very tricky to criticize one element of a penal system without placing it in the wider context of the system as a whole. That this is most often not done is one of the reasons that in general adversarial lawyers/jurists consider the inquisitorial system unfair and vice versa. Interesting in this regard is the observation by Schabas, who attended the first genocide trials before regular courts in Rwanda:

> Some of the harsh initial judgments about the shortcomings in the trials were made by lawyers trained in common law jurisdictions, who misunderstood some of the aspects of the "civil law" approach that Rwanda had inherited from Belgium and France. They were shocked, for example, at the relative brevity of the trials, and the reliance on written evidence, and the lack of cross-examination. By contrast, trial observers who came from "civil law" traditions were relatively sanguine and even rather impressed with the proceedings. (Schabas 2002)

This again may strengthen the negative opinion of organizations such as Human Rights Watch, which not only compare practice with a nonexistent ideal situation but also compare practice in an inquisitorial country (such as Rwanda) with the theory in an adversarial country (such as the United States), instead of with the practice in another inquisitorial country.

Last but not least: without a doubt, the context in which the gacaca system has been developed and functions is an important factor when assessing fairness. This context is rather different from the context in which the fair trial standards have been developed over the years. For instance, the gacaca system was created as a quasi-judicial post-Tutsi genocide management system with the intention of providing solutions to the challenges faced by the ordinary Western-style classical criminal justice administration. If the classical penal system could have dealt with the aftermath of the genocide, the reinvention of gacaca would not have been necessary.

Keeping these considerations in mind, it would be an interesting topic for a dissertation to rethink the concept of fairness within the context of nontraditional penal approaches such as the gacaca in postconflict situations. We see at least two questions, in line of each other, that can lead to some answers. The first question is whether one accepts that a postconflict society can be so different from ordinary societies that rules and principles written for ordinary societies do not fully apply—that is, in all aspects and unconditionally. Do all ordinary standards apply in a situation in which 10 percent of the total population is tried for its involvement in a genocide after having killed another 10 percent of the population? What about in a situation where not only the physical infrastructure, including the justice sector, has been destroyed but also the mental infrastructure, the social tissue of the society?

> Despite research showing the unique harms inflicted by interethnic violence, little attention has been paid to the fact that people who once saw each other as the enemy must learn to live together again on a daily basis—in shops, the market, in schools, playgrounds, concerts and coffeehouses. . . . We know surprisingly little about how neighbors who have tortured neighbors, looted their homes or fired them from jobs can learn to live together again. . . . It is the interpersonal ruins, rather than the ruined buildings and institutions, that pose the greatest challenge for rebuilding society. (See Halpern and Weinstein 2004)

Does this extraordinary context influence the way we have to assess a legal system that has been developed to cope with this extraordinary situation and to rebuild the society, not only its buildings and institutions but also its social fabric, because the ordinary system proved to be unfit for the extraordinary situation? The answer to this question is clear for human rights organizations that stay outside this society, but it is much more difficult to answer for those human rights organizations that actively take part in finding a solution (e.g., Chakravarty 2006). Practice may limit the possibilities of acting in a theoretically best way. The mere fact that one does act, however, may be a huge step forward. We would not be amazed if Rwanda scores very low on international indexes on the rule of law, negatively influenced as it will be by the way genocidaires are tried through gacaca. But when one accepts that human rights may be reconsidered in a situation such as in Rwanda, maybe the conclusion would be justified that, on the contrary, this country should rate very high, as at least it seriously tries to deal with the huge number of alleged perpetrators in the best way possible considering the circumstances of the country.

If one accepts that human rights standards do not always apply in full and unconditionally, the question remains how to determine what the standard should be to assess whether what is happening in practice is acceptable. Is there a bottom line? Where does the relative nonapplication of a particular right turn into a violation of fair trial as a whole? Where does the fairness of the system as a whole become so faint that the overall conclusion should be that the system is not sufficiently fair? The answer to these questions could be that we step back from the rules and return to the principles that underlie a specific rule, such as the rule that everybody has the right to legal counsel of his or her own choice. Human rights principles, the overarching concept of fair trial or due process rules, have been developed as safeguards against abuse of power by state organs.[3] The rules, moreover, seem mainly to have been developed from the principles with a view to relatively formal penal systems. Are all these rules unconditionally applicable to a relatively informal penal system based on broad participation of the population? Would not we be overdogmatic when doing so, especially in cases where the underlying principle is met?

With these considerations in mind, the following paragraphs discuss some fair trial issues regarding gacaca. The fair trial rights will be divided into pretrial rights (detention, counsel, and interrogation), trial rights (e.g., courts established by law, independence and impartiality, and undue delay) and post-trial rights (e.g., sentencing, execution, *ne bis in idem*, appeal). However, before starting we have to pose one caveat: the scope of this chapter limits us from going really into depth and details. Nonetheless, we hope to stimulate thinking about fair trial in the context of postconflict alternative mechanisms to deal with the consequences of conflict by giving some considerations that have to be taken into account when looking at the fairness of an institution—in this case, the gacaca.

THE PRETRIAL PHASE

There are three different levels of gacaca: the gacaca courts of the cell, the gacaca courts of the sector, and the gacaca courts of appeal (Art. 3 and 4 of Organic Law No. 16/2004 of 19/6/2004 as amended by Art. 1 and 2 of Organic Law No. 28/2006 of 27/6/2006). Each court is made up of a general assembly, a bench, and a coordination committee (Art. 5 of Organic Law No. 16/2004 of 19/6/2004). Apparently, there are also gacaca established in prisons by prisoners themselves, according to the cells where suspects come from, although not officially; the information gathered there may be used in the official gacaca. The general assembly on the lowest level, that of the cell, consists of all the cell's residents of eighteen years and older, at least two hundred persons (Art. 6 of Organic Law No. 16/2004 of 19/6/2004 as amended by Art. 3 of Organic Law No. 28/2006 of 27/6/2006). The general assembly for the sector is composed of judges of the cell gacaca in that sector, together with the sector judges and the judges of the appeals gacaca (Art. 7 of Organic

Law No. 16/2004 of 19/6/2004). Each bench consists of seven persons of integrity—the so-called *inyangamugayo* (judges)—and two substitutes. The members of the bench elect out of their midst the coordination committee that serves as sort of a daily management team. The pretrial phase of the gacaca consists of three steps: the process of collecting information, the validation, and the making of files and categorization of suspects.

Collection of Information

On June 19, 2002, the pilot phase of collecting data started in 12 sectors, to be increased within five months to 118. Due to the insignificant participation of the population from the beginning—in some places it was viewed as something to be carried out by only survivors, victims, and inyangamugayo—it was identified that this exercise would not get enough information without involving local leaders. With this perception, *nyumbakumi* (heads of ten households, the smallest administrative unit) were mobilized to lead the process of collecting information based on questionnaires to ensure that the information gathered was written in a uniform manner. During this phase, information is collected regarded the preparation and implementation of the genocide, the role of each suspect, the consequences of the genocide, and many other aspects that happened during the genocide in a particular cell, including the identification of the victims.

Being at the nyumbakumi level ensured that the information collected represented what happened in the villages. At this level, neighbors know each other, and so whenever someone raised partial information or there was confusion over an issue, other members could supplement on how events of the genocide unfolded in their cell. This process aimed at documenting as much information as possible on how the genocide was carried out. Difficulties could arise if someone present was mentioned as a perpetrator and hence would want to defend him or herself, which could result in a de facto minitrial. Such situations were avoided during this pretrial phase since the collection of information was not a platform where the accused could deny allegations; the accused person would be advised to wait until trial commenced to provide witnesses and fully challenge the case against him or her. The accused person would not be allowed to defend a specific case against him- or herself. However, the accused person, like any other member of the community, was allowed to give his or her version on how the genocide took place in the cell and could also confess.

Validation

After registering all information at nyumbakumi level, judges of the gacaca court of the cell preside over the process of validation through the General Assembly by bringing together residents of different nyumbakumi—a cell made up of about twenty different nyumbakumi, with a population of about two hundred inhabitants. This process aims at verifying whether information provided to local leaders was correctly documented. At this level, inyanga-mugayo (judges) read out all the information to the general assembly of the gacaca court of the cell. Participants confirm to the judges that the information gathered by the local leaders at nyumbakumi either properly represents their views or alters the information given. Where necessary modifications are made for clarity.

Much criticism against the pretrial phase indicated that the process was political rather than judicial because of the role of local administrators being involved in filing the forms at the nyumbakumi level. However, these critics seem to forget an important part of the whole exercise: when local authorities completed the information gathering, they handed over the record books to the president of the gacaca court of the cell, who convenes the general assembly to confirm the information contained therein. After the validation phase, judges proceed with the making of the files (*actes d'accusations*), and categorizes the suspects.

Categorization of Suspects

At the final stage of the pretrial phase, judges focus on drawing files and categorizing suspects according to the crimes allegedly committed by each suspect as found in the information collected. To this end, the crimes are grouped into three categories (Art. 11 of Organic Law No. 10/2007 of 01/03/2007). Initially there were four categories (Art. 2 of Organic Law No. 8/96 of August 30, 1996, on the organization of the prosecution of offenses constituting the crime of genocide or crimes against humanity; Art. 51 of Organic Law No. 40/2000 of 26/01/2001). But the four categories have been refined and, broadly speaking, have been brought back to three categories by combining the initial second and third category.

The first category is formed by "*les planificateurs, les organisateurs, les incita-teurs, les superviseurs et les encadreurs*"—that is, those who allegedly committed crimes as high-ranked officials within religious or state institutions or in militia, or incited to commit crimes, and those who allegedly committed rape and (sexual) torture. Until Organic Law No. 10/2007 of 01/03/2007, the first category entailed also those who distinguished themselves by the zealousness or excessive wickedness with which they took part in the genocide, torturers and violators of corpses. At the end of the information phase of the gacaca, this category turned out to be too big—about 70,000 to 80,000 suspects—to be tried by the regular courts within a reasonable amount of time (as first category cases were); therefore, the first category was diminished, and these three groups were shifted to the second category. The second category entails those who allegedly distinguished themselves by the zealousness or excessive wickedness (*"le zèle (. . .) ou la méchanceté excessive"*) with which they took part in the genocide, torturers, violators of corpses (*"les actes dégradants sur le cadaver"*), those who "just" killed someone else, and those who acted with the intention to kill but did not succeed, and other criminal acts against persons without the intention to kill. The third category is formed by those who allegedly committed acts against property. All these categories include the accomplice—that is, the person who has, "by any means, provided assistance to commit offences with persons" who committed the said acts themselves (Art. 53 of Organic Law No. 16/2004 of 19/6/2004). Superiors are criminally responsible for the acts of their subordinates "if he or she knew or could have known that his or her subordinate was getting ready to commit this act or had done it, and that the superior has not taken necessary and reasonable measures to punish the authors or prevent that the mentioned act be not committed when he or she had means" (Art. 53 of Organic Law No. 16/2004 of 19/6/2004).

Having categorized the suspects, the judges at the cell level transferred files within the first category to competent ordinary national courts.[4] Files in the second category were sent to the gacaca courts of the sector. Suspects in the third category were retained by the gacaca courts of the cell and tried there at the first and last resort. However, in this third category, if the perpetrator and the victim have agreed on an amicable settlement on their own or before the public authority or witnesses, the perpetrator cannot be prosecuted; instead the gacaca court of the cell requires the parties—the victim and the offender who reached an understanding—to make a written declaration and sign or fingerprint it; then inyangamugayo sign it for filing purposes.

PRETRIAL RIGHTS

Pretrial rights regard the rights of a suspect before the trial against him or her starts. These rights are protection from arbitrary detention, the right to remain silent, and the right to counsel. The right to be protected against prohibited forms of interrogation will not be discussed here, as it is not a serious criticism of the gacaca.[5]

Protection from Arbitrary Detention

Article 9 of the Universal Declaration of Human Rights states that "no one shall be subjected to arbitrary arrest, detention or exile." In the first years after the genocide many suspects were arrested. By the end of October 1996 a total of 86,200 prisoners were incarcerated in nineteen Rwandan detention centers (among them 3,000 women and 2,000 adolescents), an increase of 23,000 people since the beginning of 1996 (report of the UN Human Rights Field Operation in Rwanda (HRFOR), as mentioned in IRIN Emergency Update No. 56). This number further increased over the years. About 125,000 of those suspects were still incarcerated in 2004, ten years after the genocide, awaiting trial within prisons built for about 15,000 people. A substantive part of these suspects were held imprisoned without a reasonable—that is, traceable—basis; in some cases dossiers were lacking.

This may indeed be considered a big flaw in the judicial system of Rwanda. However, at least until the start of the gacaca it has little to do with the gacaca system as such but with the lack of a properly working state judicial system in general, one of the reasons to establish the gacaca. In 2003 about 25,000 suspects were released in order to diminish the number of prisoners to reduce the costs for the state and to answer international pressure due to excessively long preventive incarceration. In mid-2005 another 36,000 suspects were released. In early 2007, 8,000 suspects were released. As a result of the gacaca trials since 2005, quite a number of suspects were released from prison when their case was acquitted or ended in a sentence less than the years spent in prison. Approximately 20 percent of the cases brought before the gacaca were acquitted. The conversion of part of the prison sentence of those who confessed into community service, later the conversion of part of the prison sentence left into a conditional sentence, and starting the execution of sentences with the community service and conditional part of the prison term further emptied the prisons.

During the gacaca pretrial procedures all suspects named during the collection and validation of information for having participated in the genocide in one way or another were left in their ordinary status: those already in preventive detention stayed in prison, and suspects still living in their communities remained free until sentenced. Like in any other penal system, pretrial detention is only possible if a suspect is likely to flee justice, if there is an indication the suspect will damage evidence, and/or if there is serious evidence that the suspect threatens the security of witnesses, victims, and inyangamugayo; because of these reasons the prisons were filled again with new suspects when the gacaca procedures started.

The process of making dossiers, hence providing a reasonable basis for pretrial detention, in gacaca has been criticized. Human rights organizations have mentioned the absence or small role of the accused during the process of validation of information, categorization or recategorization of suspects. In general, however, one cannot say that the mere fact that the accused does not play a role in this respect is a sign of unfairness. In an inquisitorial system this is in fact quite normal. The prosecutor formulates his indictment on the basis of the dossier, which contains all evidentiary material gathered during the pretrial investigation phase. This difference can also be captured in the procedures of the international criminal justice systems. The confirmation of indictments at the International Criminal Tribunal for Former Yugoslavia (ICTY) and the International Criminal Tribunal for Rwanda (ICTR), for instance, is different from the procedures at the International Criminal Court

(ICC). Unlike the confirmation of charges at the ICC, which is an adversarial procedure where parties present their evidence, ICTR/ICTY's confirmation of indictments is done *ex parte*—that is, it is conducted in the absence of the defendant. To challenge the Trial Chamber's decision, this process allows an accused to submit a defense motion showing defects in the indictment during the accused's appearance before the court (*Prosecutor vs. Pauline Nyiramasuhuko*, Case No. ICTR-97–2-T). The recategorization of suspects in gacaca courts, either in the general assembly or by inyangamugayo of the sector or appeal court of the sector, can be compared with the amendment of indictments at the ICTR/ICTY. Unlike the ICC prosecutor, who can only amend charges before the trial, the ICTR/ICTY prosecutor may amend the indictment before and during trial (Rule 50 of the Rules of Procedure and Evidence ICTY/ICTR; Article 61(9) of the ICC Rome Statute).

Right to Remain Silent

The right to remain silent is an important right, not only during the pretrial phase but also during trial. No accused can be forced to speak; if an accused speaks, no one can force him or her to say everything he or she knows. It should be noted here that this is not the same as the right to lie. One may remain silent or decide to tell only part of the story, but if one speaks one has to tell the truth. In practice, this means that a judge cannot make inferences on the basis of the accused remaining silent, but the judge can make inferences on the basis of the accused lying. It also should be clear that this right only applies to an accused, not to witnesses; a witness can be forced to speak.

The right to remain silent is often linked to confessions in the gacaca system. As from the start, confession, guilty plea, repentance, and apology play an important role in the proceedings, in order to encourage confessions, apologies to victims, and cooperation with the judicial system.[6] A special procedure has been introduced in the law to which every person who has committed one of the three categories of crimes has recourse. Whether or not the suspect/offender has confessed, pleaded guilty, repented, and apologized is an important determining factor in sentencing: in that case the punishment is substantially diminished. First-category offenders, however, only benefit from the procedure when they confess before the cell gacaca make up the list of offenders at the end of the information phase; it does not benefit offenders who confess only during the appeals proceedings (Art. 55–58 of Organic Law No. 16/2004 of 19/6/2004, Art. 58 amended by Art. 12 of Organic Law No. 28/2006 of 27/6/2006). To be accepted as confession, guilty plea, repentance, and apology, the law determines that the defendant must do the following:

1. Give a detailed description of the confessed crime, how (s)he carried it out, where and when, witnesses to the fact, the persons victimized, where (s)he threw their dead bodies and the damage caused

2. Reveal the co-authors, accomplices and any other information useful to the exercise of the public action;
3. Apologize for the offences that (s)he committed (Art. 54 of Organic Law No. 16/2004 of 19/6/2004)

The confession, guilty plea, repentance, and apology have to be done before the bench of the gacaca, the judicial police officer, or the public prosecution officer in charge of investigating the case. The apology is made orally during the gacaca session or is presented in a written statement (bearing the apologizer's signature or fingerprint). An apology, however, is made publicly to the victims, if they are still alive, and to the Rwandan society (Art. 59–63 of Organic Law No. 16/2004 of 19/6/2004).

Criticism of the confession procedure is that by offering a lower sentence in exchange for a confession, a person might be compelled to confess in order to be released from pretrial detention or to at least avoid a long prison sentence. In assessing this criticism, it is important to know more about the reasons behind the confession procedure. It may also be interesting to compare this procedure with similar existing procedures in classical penal systems.

The importance of the guilty plea in gacaca courts can be captured in the way the system favors suspects who confess before they are denounced by their neighbors. The guilty plea process is administered at two levels: before the cell gacaca makes up the list of offenders at the end of the information phase and after the list but before the case is examined in substance. To better understand this trade-off between getting the truth and punishing perpetrators of genocide, an example is taken from Article 73 of the gacaca organic law (Article 73 of Organic Law No. 16/2004 of 19/6/2004, as modified and complemented by the Organic Law No. 10/2007 of 01/03/2007), which provides different penalties for notorious killers, those who committed acts of torture, and those who committed dehumanizing acts on dead bodies, depending on a confession:

> An accused found guilty who refused to confess or who pleaded guilty but whose guilty plea was rejected is punished with a minimum sentence of 30 years to life imprisonment.
>
> Those who pleaded guilty *after* being put on the list of suspects—that means: after having formally been accused by the community—are sentenced to imprisonment between twenty-five and twenty-nine years. However half of the sentence (1/2) is commuted into community service, one sixth (1/6) of the prison sentence is suspended, and one third (1/3) is served in prison.
>
> The accused who pleaded guilty *before* being formally accused is sentenced from twenty to twenty-four where half (1/2) of the prison sentence is commuted into Community Service, one third (1/3) is suspended and only one sixth (1/6) is served in prison.

By distinguishing the punishments on the basis of confessions, a clear message is sent to the public in general that reconciliation is only truly possible through voluntary confessions. Hence, whoever committed the crime of genocide is asked to come forward and enter the process of guilty plea, most preferably before others start pointing an accusing finger to her or him. Practice proves that guilty pleas in gacaca courts have played an important role in revealing the truth on genocide. This is due to the fact that a lot of things that happened during the genocide are much better known to the perpetrators than to the victims who survived the genocide, as most of the time the latter were in hiding and in total fear that thwarted their attention. When suspects genuinely confess, it helps in finding the truth. This approach has greatly helped victims to find the dead bodies of their relatives, making a decent burial possible, which has contributed to the process of reconciliation and healing.

When criticizing the gacaca guilty plea procedure, it may be revealing to compare the gacaca with the guilty plea and plea bargaining tradition within regular criminal justice systems. Pleading guilty, hence cooperating with the prosecution, in exchange for leniency in pretrial detention and sentencing is common practice in the U.S. criminal justice system. It may be interesting to see whether the gacaca practice in this respect is more acceptable to American common law lawyers than for civil law trained lawyers in, for instance, Europe. One may object, of course, to the practice of confessions in exchange for leniency in sentencing, but one should realize that this is not particular for gacaca—one objects to criminal practice in a large part of the world.

Right to Counsel

During the pretrial phase no right to legal council exists. Where possible, the process of collecting information, validation, and categorization of suspects in the gacaca pretrial phase includes information for the defense. During the validation phase, the general assembly of the gacaca court of the cell unanimously concludes whether the information collected is accurate and whether such information should be removed. If the conclusion is not arrived at unanimously, the information is challenged during the trial phase.

THE TRIAL PHASE

On the basis of the categorization in the pretrial phase, suspects are subsequently tried by the gacaca courts. In order to fulfill these tasks they must summon persons to appear in court, order and carry out searches, take temporary protective measures against the property of the accused, and issue summons to the alleged authors of crimes and order detention or release on parole (Art. 39 of Organic Law No. 16/2004 of 19/6/2004). Gacaca meet once a week, if the quorum is present—five of the seven members of the bench and one hundred members of the general assembly—and the meetings are public except when decided differently (Art. 17 and further of Organic Law No. 16/2004 of 19/6/2004, Art. 23 amended by Art. 5 of Organic Law No. 28/2006 of 27/6/2006). Decisions are made in consensus. If this is impossible, then an absolute majority of members is required (Art. 24 of Organic Law No. 16/2004 of 19/6/2004). Decisions and deliberations of judges are made *in camera*. Judgments must be motivated (Art. 21 and 25 of Organic Law No. 16/2004 of 19/6/2004). The sole exception to the public character of the gacaca are (first category) acts of sexual torture and rape, which cannot be confessed and tried in public but must take place behind closed doors. Victims of these acts (or in case of death or incapacity of the interested party) choose one or more members of the seat to submit a complaint to, either in words or in writing, or if the person does not trust the members of the seat, the complaint is submitted to the public prosecution (Art. 38 of Organic Law No. 16/2004 of 19/6/2004).

The steps to be taken during the gacaca court proceedings have been laid down in law and are separate for the cell gacaca and the sector and appeals gacaca. The cell gacaca, only dealing with property crimes, starts with a determination of the damaged property, linking this to the owners, then to those accused of having damaged the property. The latter can present their defense, followed by a response of the owner of the property, upon which the list of property, victims, and defendants is adopted. Subsequently, the bench explains to the defendants the modalities for granting the compensation by asking each defendant to decide on his or her means and the period of payment, in case of conviction (Art. 68 of Organic Law No. 16/2004 of 19/6/2004).

The sector and appeals gacaca deal with the actual killing and similar crimes, starting, in case of a confession, with the identification of the defendants and the plaintiff. All charges against the defendant are read out loud, as well as the minutes of the defendant's confession. Each defendant may comment on the accusation. Then any interested person takes the floor to testify in favor or against the defendant and responds to questions put to him or her. Every person taking the floor to testify takes an oath to tell the truth by raising his or her right arm, saying, "I take God as my witness to tell the truth." The plaintiff describes all the offenses suffered and how they were committed, upon which the defendant responds. Then the bench of the gacaca establishes a list of the victims and the offenses each of them suffered, upon which the defendant can respond. The minutes of the hearing are read out loud, and when all agree the parties to the trial, all who took the floor and the bench, put their signatures or fingerprints on the statement of the hearing. Finally, the hearing is closed or postponed if deemed necessary to obtain further information (Art. 64 of Organic Law No. 16/2004 of 19/6/2004). When there is no preceding confession, the defendant gets the opportunity to confess during the hearing (Art. 65 of Organic Law No. 16/2004 of 19/6/2004).

The judgment contains, apart from information on the proceedings and identity of parties, the damaged property that requires reparation and the defendants responsible (cell gacaca) or the charges against the defendant (sector and appeals gacaca), the facts presented by the parties, the motives of the judgment, and the modalities and period for reparation (cell gacaca) or the offense of which the defendant is found guilty and the penalties pronounced (sector and appeals gacaca). The judgment is given at the same day of the final hearing or at the subsequent hearing, in public, the date and time of which all present in the hearing are informed (Art. 67, 69–70, 83 of Organic Law No. 16/2004 of 19/6/2004).

TRIAL RIGHTS

During the trial an accused possesses various rights: Access to a court established by law, independence and impartiality of judges, a public trial without undue delay, the right to defense counsel, the right to ask witnesses *à charge and à décharge*, and a trial in the defendant's presence if possible.

Access to Courts Established by Law

Gacaca courts were created by Organic Law No. 40/2000 of January 26, 2001, setting up and organizing the prosecution of offenses constituting the crime of genocide and crimes against humanity committed between October 1, 1990, and December 31, 1994. This law was modified by Organic Law No. 33/2001 of June 22, 2001, to be replaced three years later by Organic Law No. 16/2004 of June 19, 2004, Establishing the Organization, Competence and Functioning of Gacaca Courts, Charged with Prosecuting and Trying the Perpetrators of the Crime of Genocide and Other Crimes against Humanity committed between October 1, 1990, and December 31, 1994. This 2004 gacaca law was subsequently modified and completed in 2006, 2007, and 2008.

It is clearly indicated in the preamble that among other reasons considered was the need to eradicate the culture of impunity in order to achieve justice and reconciliation in Rwanda. This required adopting provisions enabling rapid prosecutions and trials of perpetrators and accomplices of genocide, whose number was too big to be tried through the ordinary penal system. The aim was to provide punishment but also to reconstruct the Rwandan society by providing a system that allows convicted persons to amend and favor their reintegration into the communities.

Independence and Impartiality of Judges

According to the law, inyangamugayo are persons who have not participated in the genocide, are "free of the spirit of sectarianism" and from genocide ideology,[7] are of high morals and conduct, truthful, honest, and characterized by a "spirit of speech sharing." Government officials, politicians, soldiers, policemen, and magistrates cannot be elected as inyangamugayo (see Art. 14 and 15 of Organic Law No. 16/2004 of 19/6/2004 as amended by Art. 3 and 4 of Organic Law No. 10/2007 of 01/03/2007).

The independency of the inyangamugayo is provided in Article 30, paragraphs 1, 2 and 3 of the gacaca law, which stipulates the following:

> Anyone who exercises pressures, attempts to exercise pressures or threatens . . . the Seat members of the Gacaca Court shall incur a prison sentence from three months to one year. In case of repeat offence, the defendant risks a prison penalty from six months to two years. Is regarded as an act of exercising pressures on a Court, anything aiming at coercing the Seat into doing against its will, translated into actions, words or a behaviour threatening the Seat, and clearly meaning that if the latter fails to comply with, some of its members or the entire Seat may face dangerous consequences. However, when the pressure is performed, provisions of the penal code of criminal procedure are applied by ordinary courts. Is considered as an attempt to exercise pressures on a Court, any behaviour translated into words or acts, showing that there has been an attempt to coerce a Court into taking a decision in a way or another.

Of course then it has to be seen how these rules are applied in practice. Independence and impartiality of the judiciary is an issue with many aspects, and again more complex than many critics of the gacaca tend to think. It is not easy to find an answer to the impartiality and independency of the gacaca judges without thorough research. Some remarks can be made, however.

Concerning independence and impartiality with regard to the population and accused, one may raise the question as to whether lay judges are less independent and impartial than career judges. Are judges that live close to the place and the persons who committed the crimes less independent and impartial? Are Tutsi judges—if it is at all known what the ethnic background of the inyangamugayo is, *quod non*—less impartial toward Hutu defendants? It may be interesting to compare the role of the gacaca lay judges with the jury system in many countries all over the world—for instance, in the way they are trained and get instructions on their role in the trial. It may show that these practices are less strange than thought at first hand and may be less unfair.

Concerning independence of the gacaca judges from the executive, as challenged by, for instance, Human Rights Watch, it is difficult to say more about practice at this moment without a thorough study of the allegations.[8] It is interesting to note, however, that during the information phase more than 45,000 local authorities were identified as suspects of genocide. Sarkin criticizes the fact that "the more educated, intelligent and potentially more able stratum of society" has been excluded by law to serve as judges in the gacaca (see also Sarkin 2001, 163–164). This exclusion regards "heads of government administrations whether centralized or decentralized with the cell level; politically active persons; active military personnel; active members of the national police or the local defence force; career magistrates, unless they are used as legal advisors; members of the managing bodies of political parties, religious sects, or non-governmental organisations" (163–164). Sarkin also criticizes the "Tutsisation" of public functions, including the army, police, politics, and administrative functions all over the country (Sarkin 2001, 151–152). Which makes one wonder: What would his conclusion have been if these people were not excluded to serve as judges?

Additionally, one of the criticisms on the gacaca is that about 20 percent of the cases were acquitted, which as such would be firm proof of the unfairness of the gacaca. That is an interesting inference. But the question is which presuppositions underlie this statement. At least for an inquisitorial penal system, conclusions more favorable to gacaca are possible, which may (or not) be different for an adversarial system. In an average inquisitorial system, with indictments based on thorough pretrial investigations, it would mean that either the judges are partial and dependent in favor of the accused or the pretrial investigations are not properly performed. In case of the gacaca, the latter seems the case; one of the justified criticisms on gacaca is that of many accused there have no dossiers speaking against them.

That a relatively great number of inyangamugayo were suspected themselves and had to be replaced is proof of a failing system for some, showing the partiality and dependency of the judges.[9] But it may well be considered an example of a perfectly working, self-cleaning system; after all, it would be worse for the inyangamugayo to stay untouched as persons of integrity.

Trial without Undue Delay

That suspects are detained too long before their trials is definitely a problem. However, this is not a result of the gacaca; on the contrary, it is exactly the reason for the establishment of the gacaca. In the late 1990s it was estimated that trying all suspects—then about 120,000 persons—in regular criminal courts would take more than one hundred years. Considering the speed of the ICTR—thirty to fifty suspects tried in ten years—it would take the international tribunal 15,000 to 20,000 years to try all the suspects. Therefore, nationwide more than 12,000 gacaca were established, with about 250,000 persons elected as inyangamugayo. Together with the release of tens of thousands of prisoners between 2003 and 2007, this should have emptied the prisons considerably. And it did. However, because of the many new accusations during the gacaca, which started in 2005, the prisons refilled with new suspects between 2005 and 2007. Considering the fact that the vast majority of these cases were handled by the gacaca before mid-2008, resulting in the release of many of the accused either because they were acquitted or (conditionally) released, one could say that the gacaca has functioned to empty prisons rather than keeping prisoners from being tried.

One could of course argue that everybody should have been released a long time ago. One should realize, however, that during the 1990s, and maybe even in the twenty-first century, when the fight against impunity was the buzzword and the idea that everybody had to be tried dogma, this was no option: "individuals who commit genocide, crimes against humanity, and war crimes are to be treated as *hostis humani generis* (an enemy of all humankind). . . . This preclusion [from impunity] extends from the most junior soldier acting under the orders of a superior to the most senior government officials, including diplomats and heads of states" (Bassiouni 2002a, 257–258).

We are amazed that this dogma is still popular. It is not often acknowledged that it may be impossible or unrealistic to prosecute everybody involved in a genocide (Schabas 2002). Holding on to this dogma and subsequently criticizing a country that indeed tries to do what the dogma tells it to do but does not fully succeed due to exceptional circumstances is too unrealistic to be taken serious.

Public Conduct of the Trial

In principle all gacaca trials have been conducted in public, with one exception, notably the approximately seven thousand first-category sexual violence and sexual torture cases. The amendment of the gacaca law in 2008 addressed the possibility of trying some category 1 suspects behind closed doors, heretofore unknown in gacaca, which led to fierce criticism from international NGOs. In their letter of May 19, 2008, addressed to the Rwandan Judicial Authorities, Avocates sans Frontières (ASF), Penal Reform International (PRI), and Human Rights Watch (HRW) explicitly criticized trying rape and sexual torture related cases in gacaca courts, indicating how the system could infringe on the victims' rights to privacy and dignity. In their opinion, it is inappropriate to have such cases heard "on the hills," even if behind closed doors. Moreover, in 2008 HRW stated, "Nearly 90 percent of these 9,300 cases [category 1] involve sexual violence and will be heard behind closed doors, a policy meant to protect victims but which also prevents monitoring the performance of judges, who are minimally trained and who can impose penalties up to life imprisonment in solitary confinement" (100). This is a fine example of the damned-if-you-do, damned-if-you-don't dilemma. Judging these cases in the open would not be good, nor would be hearing them behind closed doors. One might also wonder whether it makes a difference, since these cases are likely to be heard by state courts all over the country, either in public or behind closed doors. It is also possible that the sexual violence and sexual torture cases could have not been tried at all. The criticism would have been the same in all cases. Of course, *in camera* proceedings are quite common all over the world, particularly in inquisitorial penal systems, and are accepted by various human rights instruments.

Right to an Adequate Defense

Accused persons do not receive legal assistance from a defense attorney. Nor do victims testifying in the process have the right to legal assistance. This is an important point of criticism against the gacaca. However, in proceedings in which the whole population takes part—or at least is expected and able to—one might say that the role of the defense is taken over by the population. Some say that it is not so much the accused as it is the victim who needs legal support in a situation where the majority of the population is in the hands of the perpetrator. Kirkby states that it may be a conscious "trade-off between retributive and restorative aims" and therefore "criticism should instead focus on the judges' role in both ensuring survivors' expectations are met and facilitating the integration of those confessing to or convicted of crimes back into society" (Kirkby 2006, 108).

Right to Examine Witnesses à Charge and à Décharge

Another one of the criticisms on the gacaca regards the duty to testify, as laid down in the law. Every citizen is obliged to take part in the gacaca (Art. 29 of Organic Law No. 16/2004 of 19/6/2004). This is less strange than it seems at first glance when read in conjunction with the duty to testify. Already in the preamble to the law establishing the gacaca, it is made clear that every Rwandan citizen is obliged to testify on what he or she has seen or knows. The first substantive consideration reads that the crimes were "publicly committed in the eyes of the population, which thus must recount the facts, disclose the truth and participate in prosecuting and trying the alleged perpetrators." The second one is of the same character: "Considering that testifying on what happened is the obligation of every Rwandan patriotic citizen and that nobody is allowed to refrain from such an obligation whatever reasons it may be."[10]

Every citizen is obliged to take part in the gacaca, as all having been witnesses to the crimes. Persons who omit or refuse to testify on what they have seen or know, as well as persons who make a slanderous denunciation, face a prison sentence of three to six months.[11] A similar fate faces those who exercise pressures "anything aiming at coercing the Seat into doing against its will, translated into actions, words or behaviour threatening the Seat, and clearly meaning that if the latter fails to comply with, some of its members or the entire Seat may face dangerous consequences or attempt to do so or threaten the witness or the members of the bench: three months to one year imprisonment" (Art. 30–32 of Organic Law No. 16/2004 of 19/6/2004).

Who criticizes this should realize that many criminal codes all over the world provide for a duty to testify for witnesses of crimes. So does the Rwandan Code of Criminal Procedure, threatening the person who does not want to appear or testify with a penalty of one month in prison and/or a fine of fifty thousand Rwandan francs (Law No. 13/2004 of 17/5/2004 relating to the Code of Criminal Procedure, Art. 54–57). As the preamble states, "the crimes were publicly committed in the eyes of the population, which thus must recount the facts, disclose the truth and participate" in the prosecution and judging of suspects. Many people participated in the genocide within their own neighborhoods, and afterwards still many people, whether perpetrators, survivors, or bystanders, reside in the same neighbourhood as where they lived during the genocide. A general obligation to participate in the gacaca is therefore less strange than it seems at first glance. This may be true in general, but it does not, per definition, pertain to Kigali, where many people, both survivors and perpetrators, retreated to after the genocide. Those people are not participating in the gacaca at the place where they were living during the genocide. It is therefore not amazing that the information phase in Kigali took more time than in rural parts of the country, and that participation in some sectors has been enforced by measures such as giving the population cards signed by the authorities when the person attended a gacaca. Inability to provide this signed card could lead to services not being rendered to the person. Criticizing this aspect without realizing that the practice is quite common in many jurisdictions in the world is no more than neo-legal colonialism. It becomes entirely ridiculous when it is linked to *umuganda*, the monthly obligation of the population to perform public services, presented as precolonial communal work, which "the Belgian colonizers and the postcolonial Habyarimana regime exploited . . . to conscript forced labourers for public works projects" (Tiemessen 2004).

Amnesty International issued a press report on November 2, 2007, urging countries not to extradite suspects to Rwanda. One of the reasons mentioned is that victims and witnesses are not sufficiently protected. This led to many comments, including one of a survivor of the genocide, Yolande Mukagasana, author of several books, who wrote the following in an open letter to Amnesty International: "En tout cas, moi je vous demande une chose, c'est de ne plus jamais me suivre sur ma route de lutte contre la mort des hommes par les mains des autres. C'est de ne plus mettre les pieds là où je vais témoigner du génocide tant que la mort ne veut pas de moi. Attendez lorsque je ne serai plus là et faites ce que vous êtes habitués de faire. Ne me poursuivez plus. Tout homme peut tomber, l'essentiel est de pouvoir se relever. Vous aussi, faites votre examen de conscience. Arrêtez de faire la politique destructrice, faite une politique plus humaine." (Mukagasana 2007). This communication shows, among other things, the gap between abstract notions of an outsider human rights organization and the concrete opinions and needs of those directly involved.

Trial in Presence, in Absence

Trial in absentia is possible in the gacaca system. For those suspects known to have died in their villages, their files/dossiers are classified without trial; but for those who died outside their neighborhood or outside Rwanda to classify their dossiers requires witnesses to confirm their death. At least three members of their families or relatives must sign or fingerprint the declaration before judges. If there is no proof that someone died, the person is tried in absentia.

Criticism of trials in absentia does not regard the gacaca in particular but the practice in at least half of the world. A trial and conviction in absentia may be abhorrent for an adversarial-educated lawyer, but it is accepted in an inquisitorial process model. The person who rejects this has to acknowledge that he or she not only rejects gacaca but an important part of the world penal systems.

POSTTRIAL RIGHTS

The rights of the accused do not stop at the end of the trial and after conviction. One might say that an accused has the right to a motivated and justifiable decision, sentencing, and punishment. The accused has the right to an appeal (or revision) and should be shielded against a second prosecution on the basis of the same facts (*ne bis in idem*).

Decision, Sentencing, Punishment

The measure for punishments after a genocide is a difficult discussion. It seems as if the extraordinary is measured against a new standard, which would by no standards be acceptable in ordinary circumstances. The ICC statute provides for a maximum penalty of thirty years imprisonment, and a lifelong sentence can only be imposed "when justified by the extreme gravity of the crime."[12] Compared to national context, however, every case that is and will be tried by the ICC and the ad hoc tribunals falls within the category of extremely grave cases. When applying the national standard to these cases, one could not decide anything other than maximum penalties: lifelong imprisonment (if not the death penalty). On the supranational level, however, one has made, within the category of cases that from a national perspective without exemption can be regarded as belonging to the most severe cases ever, a new hierarchy between grave cases and extremely grave cases, with a new hierarchy of sentences. It may very well be that the same pertains to the sentences as pronounced by the gacaca, in particular when taking the recent law on suspended sentences into account. In normal circumstances the crimes committed as prosecuted by gacaca may have led to heavy penalties, probably heavier than under the gacaca regime.

This brings us to another criticism ventured against the gacaca, regarding the ever-changing punishments in the law and the execution thereof since the establishment of the gacaca and the first convictions and executions:

> In 1998, a total of twenty-two people have been brought to death in public execution ceremonies. Since then more than five hundred first category offenders have been convicted to the death penalty, but no one has been executed;
>
> June 2004: prison sentences have partly been commuted into public service;
>
> March 2007: the remainder of the prison sentences has partly been made conditional;
>
> July 2007: the death penalty has been abolished;
>
> May 2008: the execution starts with the community service, then the conditional sentence, then the unconditional; after serving the community service and conditional sentence well, the unconditional part is commuted into community service;
>
> Part of the prison sentences will probably even be remitted in the (near) future.

This is no sign of arbitrary or inconsequential governmental behavior, as Kirkby (2006, 109–110) points out when discussing the possibility of an amnesty of convicted persons in the future. This is no weakness but the logical consequence of a changing context.

The goals of an approach to atrocities change overtime. Where it starts with the idea that everybody has to be punished severely—fight against impunity—after some time also more general societal considerations pop up, such as whether a country can develop with the majority of the population living for a very long period of time with at least one member of the family in prison, for whom they have to earn food, and without this person contributing to the subsistence of the family. These kinds of questions were overshadowed by more pressing issues immediately after the genocide.

There were also constraints imposed on the execution of the punishments, given the huge number of individuals found guilty of participating in genocide. The capacity of the penitentiary services in Rwanda has been and still is overworked; prisons have to be emptied. However, the legislature has not been lenient to suspects in community service or in suspension of their sentence who commit another crime. The law stipulates the following:

> If a person is serving a community service sentence or is on a suspended sentence and is convicted of another crime, the period the offender had

served on community service or on suspended sentence, shall become void and the offender shall serve the remaining sentence in prison and shall also serve the punishment for the new committed crime.

[Le sursis équivalent à toute la période de ces travaux encourus est de nul effet et le concerné rentre dans la prison pour y purger la totalité de la peine lui infligée . . . et il est puni pour la commission de la nouvelle infraction; meaning that the convicted person has to return to prison to serve the whole initial prison sentence, including the time that had been commuted into a suspended sentence and into community service.]

However, when a person is not found guilty of the new offence, he/she shall be released to serve the remaining period of community service sentence or suspended sentence taking into consideration the time spent in prison (Art. 74 of Organic Law No. 16/2004 of 19/6/2004 as amended by Art. 18 of Organic Law No. 13/2008 of 19/05/2008).

This kind of a provision can to some extent be understood as a postgenocide society management strategy. Sending thousands of allegedly dangerous individuals back into their communities with little or no measures to ensure safety and security for victims, witnesses, and inyangamugayo against reprisals at local community level requires putting in place some harsh measures to deter any genocide suspects who pleaded guilty for the sake of having lesser punishment without genuine acceptance of the wrongs they committed.

Appeal and Review

Similar to the ordinary penal system, there are three legal remedies against gacaca decisions and sentences: opposition, appeal and review of judgment. Opposition is the remedy against a judgment *in absentia* and is brought before the court that passed judgment in the first instance. An opposition is only admissible if the party who was absent pleads a serious and legitimate reason for his absence during the trial. Opposition can be made within fifteen calendar days from the day of notification of the judgment passed *in absentia*. Cell, sector, and appeals gacaca deal with opposition against their own judgments *in absentia*.[13]

An appeal—a request to a higher court of law to reconsider a decision rendered by a lower court—can be lodged against all decisions of cell gacaca—except judgments—and sector gacaca, at the sector gacaca and appeals gacaca respectively. Hence, the sector gacaca serve as the appeals court for sentences by the cell gacaca on perjury and unlawful pressure and threats on witnesses and judges, and for other decisions in general—not sentences in third-category cases—of the cell gacaca. The gacaca courts of appeal serve as the appeals court for sentences pronounced in first instance by the sector gacaca in second-category cases. An appeal has to be lodged by the defendant, plaintiff, or any other person acting in the interest of justice, within fifteen calendar days after the decision or sentence to be appealed against has been pronounced (Art. 41–43 of Organic Law No. 16/2004 of 19/6/2004, Art. 23 amended by Art. 7–9 of Organic Law No. 28/2006 of 27/6/2006; Art. 89–92 of Organic Law No. 16/2004 of 19/6/2004, Art. 90 amended by Art. 19 of Organic Law No. 28/2006 of 27/6/2006).

Review is possible in cases of contradicting sentences—acquittal and convictions alike—between gacaca and ordinary courts when after a judgment has been passed by a gacaca court new evidence turns up contrary to the initial judgment, and thirdly when a person has been given a sentence that is contrary to legal provisions of the charges. A review can be lodged by the defendant, the plaintiff, or any other person acting in the interest of justice (Art. 93 of Organic Law No. 16/2004 of 19/6/2004, amended by Art. 20 of Organic Law No. 28/2006 of 27/6/2006).

The criticism of the review of the gacaca court's decision is that the decision to accept that a case be reviewed is decided by the general assembly, which is composed of judges who tried the case at either first or appeal level. So, the judges who tried the case in first instance and the judges that will review the case could be influential in taking a decision on whether someone's case should be reviewed or not. However, this criticism forgets that the general assembly consists of about hundred inyangamugayo; therefore, this influence is minimal.

Some critiques have been raised against transfer of cases to gacaca courts that initially were in ordinary and military courts—after referral by the cell gacaca at the end of the information phase before the gacaca trials started. The 2008 gacaca law stipulates (Art. 26 of Organic Law No.13/2008 of 19/05/2008) that genocide-related cases that come within the jurisdiction of gacaca courts, which initially had been referred to ordinary and military courts for prosecution before publication of this 2008 law in the official gazette of the Republic of Rwanda, shall be tried by gacaca courts. These cases include those before the High Court, Military High Court, and Supreme Court, where there is no final decision and in which the period to appeal to a higher court has not expired. The criticism is that a gacaca court should not be allowed to rule against a decision of the ordinary court. It is important to note that cases subject to this article are those without a conclusive decision, since the judge of the higher court could take a different decision. Additionally, these are cases that originally formed the part of gacaca competence; the transfer was delayed by Article 100 of the 2004 gacaca law, which stated that "the cases already forwarded to the courts before the publication of this organic law in the Official Gazette of the Republic of Rwanda, shall remain handled by the same courts. Provisions provided for by the ordinary laws shall apply thereto, without prejudice to special provisions of this organic law. As for the subject of the action, those courts shall apply provisions of this organic law." However, due to an enormous backlog of cases in ordinary courts, it seems unrealistic to keep these cases in ordinary courts without any hope for expeditious trials.

Ne Bis in Idem/Double Jeopardy

Initially the law made it possible that a decision by an ordinary court or military court was reviewed by a gacaca court. This anomaly has been repaired in the 2008 gacaca law, stating that "a case determined at least an appellate level by an ordinary or military court may also ["also" would suggest that still the gacaca courts were authorized to review these cases; again the French text is more clear, leaving out this "also"] be reviewed by the same court" (Art. 24 of Organic Law No. 13/2008 of 19/05/2008).

CONCLUSIVE REMARKS

The criticism on gacaca has been fierce from the start. Part of that criticism regards the fairness of the gacaca system. The question whether the gacaca system is fair is only one of the questions to answer when assessing the value of gacaca, but it is not the least important. At the same time, it is one of the most difficult questions to answer. In this article we have tried to make a start of thinking about fair trial in the context of postconflict alternative mechanisms to deal with the consequences of the conflict by giving some considerations that have to be taken into account when looking at the fairness of an institution without denying that the gacaca system has—at times, serious—flaws.

The gacaca system was created as a quasi-judicial post-Tutsi genocide management system with the intention of providing solutions to the challenges faced by the ordinary Western-style classical criminal justice administration. If the classical penal system could have dealt with the aftermath of the genocide, the reinvention of gacaca would not have been necessary. It is an extraordinary penal system to cope with an extraordinary situation. This is not to say that all fair trial requirements are not applicable, but it makes an assessment difficult.

In terms of penal systems, the gacaca system, based on Rwandan customary law but transformed into a more formal written law system, has developed into a peculiar mix of the adversarial and inquisitorial penal systems, with more focus on the trial than the pretrial phase, which makes it difficult to compare the gacaca with the well-known Western-style classical penal systems and therefore difficult to assess in terms of the well-known traditional systems.

Although the gacaca has traditional roots, never before has it had to deal with crimes as acts of genocide, and never on this scale. As a result, the gacaca has been a work in progress from the first moment the idea was put on the table. One of the unforeseen circumstances is the number of suspects to be tried, which range from 125,000 to over 1 million persons at the end of the process. Certainly, the way alleged genocidaires have been treated since 1994 is not ideal. However, to blame the gacaca for all wrongs would not be fair. On the contrary, one might say that with the gacaca Rwanda has tried to cope with an unfair situation caused by a rather indiscriminate incarceration of suspects and a lack of well-functioning legal apparatus, due in part to the genocide, the legacy of the former regime, and judges without authority.

As one scholar rightly remarks about justice in the context of responses to the Rwanda genocide: "Any response Rwanda develops not only must be consistent with principles of justice but also must be pragmatically feasible. Justice that exists only in theory is no justice at all" (Daly 2002, 367). Gacaca has been finding a balance between justice in theory and extraordinary circumstances, resulting in as much justice in practice as possible. We would not be amazed if Rwanda scores very low on international indexes on the rule of law, negatively influenced as it will be by the way genocidaires are tried through gacaca. But when one accepts that human rights may be reconsidered in a situation such as in Rwanda, maybe the conclusion would be justified that, on the contrary, Rwanda should rate very high, as at least it seriously tries to deal with the huge number of alleged perpetrators of genocide in the best possible way considering the circumstances of the country.

Notes

1. "Gacaca" refers to a soft kind of grass/herb, *umucaca*, on which traditionally a community came together to discuss conflicts within or between families or inhabitants on a certain hill. After the genocide, it was revised and adopted as a viable option to address the scope of genocide participants and victims. As such, gacaca is a legal system born out of a local tradition.
2. Some of the international instruments ratified by Rwanda include the 1948 Universal Declaration of Human Rights, the 1986 African Charter on Human and Peoples' Rights, the 1966 International Covenant on Civil and Political Rights, the International Convention on the Elimination of All Forms of Racial Discrimination, the Convention on the Rights of the Child, the Convention Relating to the Status of Refugees, the Four Geneva Conventions, the Protocol Additional to the Geneva Conventions of August 1949, and Relating to the Protection of Victims of International Armed Conflicts (Protocol 1), Protocol Additional to the Geneva Conventions of August 1949, and Relating to the Protection of Victims of Non-International Armed Conflicts (Protocol II), and the African Charter on the Rights and Welfare of the Child.
3. Only recently has it been accepted that human rights can also be invoked when the state does not do enough to protect an individual against another individual, but this is not uncontested, particularly when used to curtail the rights of individuals—for instance, in order to "protect" citizens against possible terrorist acts by other citizens.
4. Modified by the Gacaca Law No. 13/2008 of May 2008. Suspects who committed the crime of rape or sexual torture, who incited or supervised, and ringleaders and

others at the leadership level at the sub-prefecture and commune, together with their accomplices, were, under the competence of ordinary courts, originally to be tried by gacaca courts.

5. HRW in its 2008 Rwanda report mentions some cases of "torture and cruel treatment" in relation to interrogations, but remarks that, "given the scarcity of information, it is impossible to assess the extent of torture by state agents" (81).

6. Already the first law dealing with the trials of alleged genocidaires contains special provisions. See Organic Law No. 8/96 of August 30, 1996, on the Organisation of the Prosecution of Offences Constituting the Crimes of Genocide or Crimes against Humanity, Articles 4–16.

7. "Ideology of genocide consists in behaviour, a way of speaking, written documents and any other actions meant to wipe out human beings on the basis of their ethnic group, origin, nationality, region, colour of skin, physical traits, sex, language, religion or political opinions" (Art. 3 of Organic Law No. 10/2007 of 01/03/2007).

8. Regarding the independence of the regular state court judges, see the decision of the Appeals Chamber of the ICTR, *Prosecutor v. Yussuf MUNYAKAZI*, Case No. ICTR-97-36-R11bis, Decision on the Prosecution's Appeal against Decision on Referral under Rule 11bis, para. 29: "The Appeals Chamber therefore finds that, based on the record before it, no reasonable Trial Chamber would have concluded that there was sufficient risk of government interference with the Rwandan judiciary to warrant denying the Prosecution's request to transfer Munyakazi to Rwanda." Not less interesting is the decision of the English judge in an extradition case, discussing the alleged partiality and dependency of the Rwandan judiciary: "examples . . . were pre 2004 and the greater majority of the others were from the late 1990s. . . . These were of historical interest only"; "The brief from HRW, which I am sure, reflects the views of other NGOs working in Rwanda does not quote any other examples, only anecdotal evidence"; "on the basis of the evidence put forward in this case I am not satisfied that the defence has shown that the independence of the judiciary is now so compromised that it would support their argument in respect of Article 6 [of the European Convention on Human Rights]." Decision of the City of Westminster Magistrate's Court between the *Government of Rwanda v. Vincent Bajinya* [and 3 others], June 6, 2008, considerations 380/381 and 400, 477/478, 525.

9. There were 45,396 judges suspected, according to results from information collected countrywide from January 15, 2005, to June 30, 2006. See "Gacaca Process: Achievement, Problems and Future Prospects," at http://www.inkiko-gacaca.gov.rw/.

10. The preamble of the 2001 law reads: "Considering that the duty to testify is a moral obligation, nobody having the right to get out of it for whatever reason it may be."

11. Article 29 of Organic Law No. 16/2004 of 19/6/2004, doubled in case of a repeated offense. The previous Organic Law No. 40/2000 of 26/01/2001 did contain a similar provision in Article 32, with a prison sentence of one to three years maximum.

12. "and the individual circumstances of the convicted person" (Art. 77.1, ICC Statute).

13. Art. 86–88 of Organic Law No. 16/2004 of 19/6/2004. It seems reasonable to assume that the regular criminal procedural rules apply here—that is, that this notification must be personal or otherwise within fifteen days from the day when the sentenced person received the notice personally, and hence when he or she becomes aware of the judgment to be opposed against.

CHAPTER 11

Assassination of Regime Elites
versus Collateral Civilian Damage

Michael Bohlander and Dawn L. Rothe

THE U.S.-LED AGGRESSION AGAINST IRAQ IN 2003 makes one wonder why it was that thousands of Iraqi civilians would have to die because the George W. Bush administration and their allies thought it prudent to bomb the country's cities before they risked the lives of their own ground troops, beginning with the well remembered "shock and awe" mission. As the intense bombing continued, hundreds of civilian casualties occurred without any discernable military gains. There was widespread use of cluster bombs, deployment of napalm-like Mark 77 firebombs, the indiscriminate use of depleted uranium munitions, and numerous attempted decapitation strikes targeting senior Iraqi government officials. Iraqi civilians have indeed been victim to significant collateral damage. None of these civilians had given any cause to be so treated. More to the point, why did the cities have to be bombed at all? Why did the United States gamble on the very real dangers of destabilization and ensuing sectarian violence, not to speak of the effects a destabilized Iraq would have on the whole region, and the ensuing risk of more civilian loss of life? Could not the United States have employed the services of its "black-ops" specialists and simply assassinated Saddam Hussein and his top aides as the real root of the problem? After all, the United States has led covert actions, directly and indirectly aimed at assassinating and/or overthrowing regimes that conflicted with its political, economic, or military interests many times throughout its history. Many will say that even if it could have been done, who would have guaranteed that killing the regime would have resulted in a more peaceful and stable Iraq? One cannot eradicate a government and then simply leave a leaderless people to its own devices; there needs to be a strategy of institution-building and pacification for the time after the change. The value of the argument seems to be of minor importance as the invasion and occupation, or the preemptive war of the United States, has not resulted in conditions of stability or peace five years past.

If killing a head of state can put a definite end to a serious danger to international peace and security caused by that head of state, how can it be proportionate to respect international comity toward him but to prefer killing thousands of his innocent subjects to achieve the same aim? One must, of course, remember that as long as the head of state is not a member of the armed forces, he will count as a civilian and will enjoy the protection meant for civilians. But does it really make a decisive difference whether he is a part of the operational chain of command, as Thomas Wingfield (1998) has suggested, or is it not enough that he holds de facto political power over the military? Even if he is, do the actual circumstances of the assassination matter—that is, whether it was done openly or treacherously or in a situation that did not (yet) warrant the initiation of hostilities in the conventional military sense?[1] Are the traditional aversions against clandestine targeted operations based on an outmoded code of chivalry from a time when the use of highly destructive weapons and the risk-free means of their delivery were not as widespread as they are today? Can, for example, national resistance movements, legitimately following the right to self-determination, be held at all to conventional methods of fighting, if by doing so they have to engage a superior enemy on a vastly uneven playing field? If certain states use methods such as extraordinary renditions and highly orchestrated transnational torture networks based on an interpretation of operative necessity to counter Islamist terrorism, what claim do these countries have to expect chivalry from others? Do we not foster resentment among the have-nots of the latest military technology, based on the double standards created by the haves? Is the contention really adequate any longer that armed conflicts are collective-based and not between individuals, when it is more often than not individuals, even in the context of an organization, who stir up their citizenry into collective violence?

In the age of the often bemoaned asymmetric warfare and the war on terror, is there not a much more immediate moral asymmetry: if murdering a dangerous head of state by using stealth or deception is the only practicable method, but is unacceptable under international law, does that not leave us with the conclusion that the people whom much of the humanitarian law of war is meant to protect in the first place, the "ordinary" civilians, are at the end of the day the ones who have to suffer the consequences after all? Is it really better that thousands of innocent citizens die for the sake of one person, who may even be oppressing them? If the very people whom to liberate is the aim of a humanitarian intervention can become the victims of the ideology of collateral damage in a campaign of area bombing? Is it not time that the war was brought, preemptively or not, home to those who *cause* it rather than those who merely have to *fight* it or cannot escape the theater of operations?

While some will be able to develop some sympathy for these emotionally charged questions, most will probably say that this is the way of the world. What purpose would it serve if we allowed assassination? Admittedly, there is the realpolitik of international relations behind the questions we raise. Would it not again be one of those international rules that apply in practice to a multitude of smaller, weaker, poorer, or, to put it bluntly, "inconsequential" countries, but not to the few powerful ones, and, even among those, not to each in equal measure? *Homo homini lupus—Hobbes locutus, causa finita?*

Indeed, there are those who will accuse us of proposing the unthinkable by tinkering with a fundamental legal principle that prohibits the assassination of heads of state by other states, and of allowing the use of the crime of murder to become an acceptable, if *ultima ratio*, instrument of international politics. These objections must be taken very seriously. Yet, we do know that intentional killing (and thwarted attempts) by black-ops missions has been used throughout history by many states, including the United States, as a means for regime change when it suited the interest of that state or its business community (see Kinzer 2004, 2007). Considerations of the wider consequences of these missions have very often been notoriously absent in the decision-making process.

The final question posed here, should not war—preemptive or not—be brought home to those who *cause* it rather than those who merely have to *fight* it, highlights a deeper legal, ethical, and criminological issue, and that is the one we wish to address in this contribution. The questions we have to ask ourselves are these: If we could do it, would we be allowed to do it? Would it be morally acceptable or justifiable? In certain situations would we be compelled to do it? If we were to answer yes, what would this mean given the realpolitik of international relations, the current state of impunity, states' self-interests, and unequal distribution of power and resources? As noted by Michael Walzer: "Characteristically (and not foolishly), lawyers have frowned on assassination, and political officials have been assigned to the class of non-military persons, who are never the legitimate objects of attack. But this assignment only partially represents our common moral judgments. For we judge the assassin by his victim, and when the victim is Hitler-like in character, we are likely to praise the assassin's work" (2006, 199).

To begin to untangle the moral and yet practical quagmire of this subject, we first turn to a brief discussion of the traditional, ethical, and legal positions. From this we offer a discussion that includes a criminological perspective based on state crime research. For reasons of space, we will not address the use of assassination by a state against nonstate-related actor (i.e., the targeted killing practice of Israel vis-à-vis Palestinian resistance group leaders recently and succinctly circumscribed and analyzed by the Supreme Court of Israel, sitting as the High Court of Justice, in the case of *The Public*

Committee against Torture in Israel and others v. The Government of Israel and others, decided on December 11, 2005, Case No. HCJ 769/02). We will look merely at the assassination of foreign heads of state by another state.

THE DEVELOPMENT OF THE LAW AND ETHICS OF ASSASSINATIONS: A BRIEF OVERVIEW

The history of the ethics of war and especially the question of the suffering of noncombatants or civilians fills entire libraries. We will only attempt a very brief chronological outline of the ideas professed through the centuries. We are moving in an area of overlap of the *ius ad bellum* (when may a state attack another one by using force, or by proxy, its head of state) and, more to the point, the question of preemptive self-defense, and the *ius in bello* (which methods can a state use in an otherwise lawful attack—that is to say, may the head of state be targeted at all). The whole question rests on the acceptance of some form of just war theory (Walzer 2006), the idea that the formula *inter arma silent leges* is no longer representative of common international opinion. Further, there is the question as to whether or not any war can be justified, given its costs.

In the age of asymmetrical warfare with resistance movements, insurgents, and terrorist groups intentionally targeting the civilian population or using them as cover, this consensus is being called into question. It is becoming more and more difficult to maintain the traditional just war standards and be effective in reaching a military goal against targeted enemy groups (Reynolds 2005). Not least, the reason for this is that those rules were drafted and pronounced with a classical war between sovereign states in mind.

Those have become more the exception than the rule, leaving aside the attendant issue that hardly ever are attacks by states accompanied or even preceded by a declaration of war. Consider that between 1945 and 2008 there have been 295 armed conflicts, of which 157 have been classified as civil wars, 61 as the result of state terror or state repression, 20 as territorial conflicts, and 57 as external wars in the more traditional sense of warfare (Bassiouni 2008b). In other words, of the 295 armed conflicts spanning sixty-three years, only 5.17 percent are categorized as international armed conflicts. Seventy-seven percent of the conflicts are of an internal nature.

A look at the Bush Doctrine on preemptive strikes and the rather lukewarm criticism by the international community may serve as an example (Hofmeister 2005). The guerrilla tactics used by resistance groups against their government's troops and occupying armies exact a high death toll among the regular troops, and, consequently, states embarking on such an enterprise will have to weigh the need to protect their own soldiers from harm, on the one hand, and the compliance with proportionality as well as targeting requirements, on the other. Of course, this presumes the government would be in its "right" to respond. As recent cases have shown, such groups often form in response to heavily corrupt and violent authoritarian regimes and, having experienced massive oppression, leave the option of an insurgency as one of the few remaining. As the recent campaigns by the United States and its coalitions of allies since the first Gulf War in 1991 have shown, the approach tends to be better safe than sorry, or as a German proverb literally translated would say: Caution is the mother of the porcelain chest. Almost every campaign has begun with the massive use of cruise missiles, extensive and prolonged aerial bombing, and heavy artillery shelling.

When one talks about just war theory, the references are almost exclusively to schools of thought developed by thinkers in Western and, more to the point, Christian value systems. In some parts of the world, the use of treacherous surprise tactics and targeting of individuals were part of the code of warfare and expected of successful warlords. Karl Friday has shown that the medieval Japanese warrior's codex or *Bushido* had little time for ideas of chivalry as we would understand them; in fact, he states that while *bushi* did sometimes announce certain times and places for battles, "such promises were honored far more often in the breach than in the event" (Friday 2006, 169).

The sources that deal with tyrannicide and its attendant problems do not always distinguish between internal resistance (sedition) and external attack, although very often they will be seen in the context of an armed conflict, but the underlying ethical approaches are at the end of the day similar. They all center around the issues of chivalry vis-à-vis the use of treacherous means, and the avoidance of casualties among the innocent population, namely of collateral damage. Cicero, for example, said after the assassination of Caesar: "There can be no fellowship between us and tyrants . . . on the contrary there is a complete estrangement . . . and it is not contrary to nature to rob a man, if you are able, whom it is honourable to kill. Indeed, the whole pestilential and irreverent class ought to be expelled from the community of mankind" (Reichberg, Syse and Begby 2006, 59).

In a letter to St. Boniface, St. Augustine, while emphasizing that promises given to an enemy must be kept and the victor should show mercy to the vanquished enemy, made it clear that he did not view it as illegitimate to use ruses and ambushes, as long as the war they were meant to further was legitimate: "Such things as ambushes are legitimate for those who engage in a just war. In these matters the only thing a righteous man has to worry about is that the war is waged by someone who has the right to do so because not all men have that right. Once an individual has undertaken that kind of war, it does not matter at all, as far as justice is concerned, whether he wins victory in open combat or through ruses" (Reichberg et al. 2006 79, 83).

This view of St. Augustine was adopted by Gratian and the decretists in the *Decretum divi gratiani* and the glosses thereto after the twelfth century

(Reichberg et al. 2006, 113). Another writer of the twelfth century, John of Salisbury, in his treatise *Policraticus* addressed the issue of tyrannicide at length. Although he, too, noted that promises under an oath or an obligation of fealty must be honored even when made to a tyrant, that the use of poison was deplorable and not permitted, and that he was somewhat wary about leaving the decision in the hands of just any individual, he was fairly straightforward as to what fate should generally befall a tyrant: "To kill a tyrant is not merely lawful, but right and just . . . [T]he tyrant, the likeness of wickedness, is generally to be even killed. The origin of tyranny is iniquity, and springing from a poisonous root, it is a tree which grows and sprouts into a baleful pestilent growth, and to which the axe must by all means be laid . . . [I]t has always been lawful to flatter tyrants and to deceive them, and . . . it has always been an honourable thing to slay them if they can be curbed in no other way" (Reichberg et al. 2006, 129–130).

The view that promises certain conventions must be honored even against the worst and cruelest enemy can also be found in medieval Muslim war tradition; a telling example is the famous incident related to Saladin's treatment of Reynald de Châtillon, Lord of Karak and a ruthless crusader bent on destroying the fragile peace previously kept until the death of King Baldwin IV of leprosy in 1085, and that of his six-year-old nephew Baldwin V in 1186, and of the new King of Jerusalem, Guy de Lusignan, after defeat at the battle of Hittin on July 4, 1187. As the biography of Saladin, written by his confidant and army judge advocate 1188–1193, Ibn Shaddad, tells us, Saladin had offered Guy a cup of water, which Guy passed on to Reynald without the consent of Saladin. Saladin, who had previously vowed to kill Reynald and later did, is reported to have said to his interpreter: "Say to the king, 'You are the one who gave him the drink. I give him no drink, nor any of my food.' What he meant was 'If anyone eats my food, chivalry would demand that I harm him not'" (Shaddad 2002, 37–38).[2] Saladin allegedly also told Guy that "kings do not kill each other" (Shalabi 1983, 28; Shaddad 2000, 62).[3] Killing their subordinates was, however, apparently acceptable.

St. Thomas Aquinas, writing in the thirteenth century in his *Summa theologiae* made a distinction between an ambush based on false pretenses or breach of a promise, which he declared illicit, and the mere concealment of one's intentions, which was a legitimate tactic of war in his view (Shalabi 1983, 28; Shaddad 2000, 62), an approach which has survived to this day as the so-called ruse-perfidy distinction. He also approved of sedition against a tyrannical government unless such a course of conduct brought about even greater suffering for the people (Reichberg et al. 2006, 186). According to his *Commentaries on Lombard*, obedience to tyrants or rulers in general was based on the question of whether lawfully acquired authority was merely abused (presumption in favor of obedience), or whether authority was not even lawfully acquired (no obedience owed) (Reichberg et al. 2006, 194–195). As far as tyrannicide was concerned, St. Thomas Aquinas, in his *On the Governance of Rulers*, entertained the possibility of tyrannicide but warned at the same time against the dangers arising from unsuccessful attempts or from the ensuing power vacuum, which may be usurped by even worse people, resulting in deteriorating circumstances. In general, he appeared to favor a presumption against action by force (Reichberg et al. 2006, 195–198).

The ruse-perfidy distinction is again clearly mirrored in the writings of Christine de Pizan from the fourteenth and fifteenth centuries, which in part refer to the teachings of her mentor, Honoré Bonet (Reichberg et al. 2006, 219–220) and are structured as a kind of dialogue between Christine and him. She also advocated the keeping of promises—for example, of safe conduct to Saracens, as Muslims were called at the time, and which apparently was not a uniformly accepted custom in her days (225).

Niccoló Machiavelli appeared to disagree with the evolving ideology of making moral judgments the basis for political decisions in peace or wartime. Accordingly, the ruse-perfidy rule meant nothing to him in moral terms. Famously, in his *Discourses* he presents necessity and political expedience as the main factors of his approach: "For when the safety of one's country wholly depends on the decision to be taken, no attention should be paid to either justice or injustice, to kindness or cruelty, or to its being praiseworthy or ignominious. On the contrary, every other consideration being set aside, that alternative should be wholeheartedly adopted which will save the life and preserve the freedom of one's country" (Reichberg et al. 2006, 257).

Thomas More, a contemporary of Machiavelli, would seem to have agreed with the latter on a rather pragmatic view of warfare, although his attitude was driven by an almost economic cost-benefit analysis combined with just war ideas of proportionality. In *Utopia* he explains how the inhabitants of his perfect world set about the business of going to war:

> And so, immediately after declaring war, they see to it that many notices certified by their official seal are put up secretly and simultaneously in the most conspicuous places in the enemy's territory promising a huge reward to anyone who does away with the enemy's prince; they also assign lesser, but still very substantial, sums for the deaths of those individuals they list in the same notices. These are the persons who, apart from the prince himself, were responsible for the plotting against the Utopians. . . . Other nations condemn this practice of bidding for and buying off an enemy as a barbarous, degenerate crime, but the Utopians think it does them great credit: it shows them to be wise, since in this way they win great wars without fighting at all, and also humane and compassionate, since by

killing a few malefactors they spare the lives of many innocent persons who would have fallen in battle, both their own soldiers and those of the enemy; for they pity the rank-and-file of the enemy's soldiers almost as much as their own citizens because they know they do not go to war of their own accord but are driven to it by the madness of princes. . . . They offer amnesty to cities that surrender and even those taken by siege they do not sack; instead they execute those who prevented the surrender; they enslave the rest of the defenders, but the civilian populace they leave unharmed. (Reichberg et al. 2006, 262–264)

The ideology espoused by Thomas More's perfect civilization in theory comes close to what caused this chapter to be written in the first place: A desire to hold only those accountable, to differing degrees that they are responsible. However, as we will see, this idea was not successful in the course of history, and as later philosophers such as Alberico Gentili pointed out, the expected result may also have been far from certain.

Martin Luther, the Protestant reformer, seemed to recognize the appeal of a concept that allowed oppressed people, or by proxy those bent on humanitarian intervention, to depose or even kill a tyrant; yet he warned against the dangers of the slippery slope:

Furthermore, such conduct has bad results or sets a bad example. If it is considered right to murder or depose tyrants, the practice spreads and it becomes a commonplace thing arbitrarily to call men tyrants who are not tyrants, and even to kill them if the mob takes a notion to do so. The history of the Roman people shows us how this can happen. They killed many a fine emperor simply because they did not like him or he did not do what they wanted, that is, let them be lords and make him their fool. This happened to Galba, Pertinax, Gordian, Alexander, and others. (Reichberg et al. 2006, 270)

The other Protestant reformer, Jean Calvin, would appear to have altogether rejected the idea of any aggressive action against tyrants from a Christian point of view that postulated obedience, even to those who blatantly abused their God-given office, to the point where obedience would have meant disobeying the commands of God. Calvin took a very individualistic Christian view by referring to the example of Christ who preferred unjust suffering to righteous resistance (*Institutio christianae religionis*, Book IV, 22–32). Calvin's approach brings out in sharp contrast the question of whether the Christian faith can be made the basis of any aggressive course of conduct at all. Both Luther and Calvin, the former famously by his motto *sola scriptura*, did not put any similar weight on non-Christian philosophers as the protagonists of scholasticism and Catholicism had previously done.

The doubts about deposing, let alone assassinating, princes were shared by Francisco de Vitoria. He appeared to allow such a course of action only in circumstance when the prince had been a tyrant, causing enormous suffering or harm, or if security and peace could not otherwise be restored (Reichberg et al. 2006, 331). Balthazar Ayala, in his *Three Books on the Law of War* of 1582, approved of St. Augustine's view that the use of trickery was as such irrelevant for deciding on the justice of military operations, but made it clear that he, like St. Thomas Aquinas, wanted to distinguish treacherous means, which he called "fraud and snares" from mere trickery (Ayala 1912, 84–87). Francisco Suárez, whose writings had a large influence on the course of modern philosophy, in reference to St. Thomas Aquinas also supported the ruse-perfidy distinction as to which sort of tricks a party to a conflict is allowed to employ to further its own cause (Reichberg et al. 2006, 367).

Alberico Gentili, while approving of the actions of Pepin, the father of Charlemagne, who slew one of his enemies in his sleep, criticized the approach taken by Thomas More by calling the use of assassinations shameful, contrary to justice and honor, and in contravention of the laws of nature and God. He also thought that More's hopes of keeping the casualties down to a minimum by targeting those who carried the greatest responsibility and power were mistaken, as the use of treacherous means could have the unwanted effect of strengthening the solidarity of the enemy's troops or even of the whole population (Gentili 1933, 167–168). However, Gentili was more progressive on the idea of preemptive attacks, which he accepted were a reasonable course of action of anticipatory defense before surrounding states became too powerful (61–66).[4] Johannes Althusius, writing in the seventeenth century in his *Politica*, reluctantly approved of killing a tyrant: "When his tyranny has been publicly acknowledged and is incurable: when he madly scorns all laws, brings about the ruin and destruction of the realm, overthrows civil society among men as far as he is able, and rages violently: and when there are no other remedies available" (Reichberg et al. 2006, 384).

Hugo Grotius, in his monumental work *De iure belli ac pacis*, joined Gentili in his positive view of the course of action taken by Pepin, saying, "Not merely by the law of nature but also by the law of nations . . . it is in fact permissible to kill an enemy in any place whatsoever; and it does not matter how many there are that do the deed, or who suffer. . . . According to the law of nations not only those who do such deeds, but also others who instigate others who do them, are considered free from blame" (Schmitt 1992, 614). Grotius did, however, also adhere to the distinction between treachery and mere ruses, saying that treacherous killings may result in reprisals: "In general a distinction must be made between assassins who violate an express or tacit obligation of good faith, as subjects resorting to violence against a king, vassals against a lord, soldiers against him whom they serve, those also who have been received as suppliants or strangers or deserters, against those who have received them; and such as are held by no bond of good faith" (615). He also disagreed with any ideology that allowed a war to be waged for the mere purpose of regime change, even with the best of intentions, such as, for example, the promotion of democracy and human rights (Reichberg et al. 2006, 411).

Returning to the issue of stealth and trickery, Samuel von Pufendorf in 1673 tried to push the envelope of the ruse category by stating, "The most proper form of action in war are force and terror. But one has equal right to use fraud and deceit against an enemy, provided one does not violate one's pledged faith. Hence one may deceive an enemy by false statements or fictitious stories, but never by promises or agreements" (Reichberg et al. 2006, 458).

Emmerich de Vattel, the Swiss scholar, despised any ideas that favored the use of assassinations but restricted the meaning of the word to situations of treachery:

> But in order to reason clearly on this question we must first of all avoid confusing assassination with surprises, which are, doubtless, perfectly lawful in warfare. When a resolute soldier steals into the enemy's camp at night and makes his way to the general's tent and stabs him, he does nothing contrary to the natural laws of war, nothing, indeed, but what is commendable in a just and necessary war . . . If anyone has absolutely condemned such bold strokes it was only done with the object of flattering those in high position who would wish to leave to soldiers and subordinates all the danger of the war . . . Hence I mean by assassination a murder committed by means of treachery, whether the deed be done by persons who are subjects of him who is assassinated, or of his sovereign, and who are therefore traitors, or whether it be done by any other agent who makes his way in as a suppliant or refugee, or as a turncoat, or even as an alien; and I assert that the deed is a shameful and revolting one, both on the part of him who executes it and of him who commands it. (De Vattel 1916, 287–288)

He further argued on the respect due to a head of state:

> In former times he who succeeded in killing the King or general of the enemy was commended and rewarded; we know the honours attending the *spolia opima*. Nothing could have been more natural than such an attitude; for the ancients almost always fought for the very existence of the State, and frequently the death of the leader put an end to the war. At the present day a soldier would not dare, ordinarily at least, to boast of having killed the enemy's King. *It is thus tacitly agreed among sovereigns that their persons shall be held sacred.* It must be admitted that where the war is not a violent one, and where the safety of the State is not at stake, such respect

for the person of the sovereign is entirely commendable and in accordance with the mutual duties of Nations. In such a war, to take away the life of the sovereign of the hostile Nation, when it could be spared, would be to do a greater injury to that Nation than is, perhaps, necessary for the successful settlement of the dispute. But it is not a law of war that the person of the enemy's King must be spared on every occasion, and the obligation to do so exists only when he can easily be made prisoner. (De Vattel 1916, 290; emphasis added)

Immanuel Kant, the German philosopher, took a very clear stance on assassination in his treatise on *Perpetual Peace*: No state at war with another shall permit such acts of hostility as would make mutual confidence impossible during a future time of peace. Such acts would include the employment of assassins . . . or . . . poisoners . . . breach of capitulation, the instigation of treason within the enemy state (Reichberg et al. 2006, 521). From the context it would appear clear that Kant also subscribed to the ruse-perfidy divide; yet it is curious why the excessive suffering inflicted on the civilian population does not merit explicit mention, too. One might safely assume that with the pervasive public dissatisfaction with the political class in a vast majority of countries and the horrendous potential for severe civilian collateral damage, the people of almost any given nation would prefer to see their leaders killed rather than see them spared and their own children slaughtered. De Vattel came very close to the real reason for the ubiquitous aversion to aiming higher up the chain of command.

This is not really surprising, and it becomes especially clear if one looks at the whole issue in the light of Carl von Clausewitz's famous dictum, commonly rendered as "war is the continuation of politics by other means," whereas the accurate quotation is, "We see, therefore, that war is not merely an act of policy but a true political instrument, a continuation of political intercourse, carried on with other means . . . The political object is the goal, war is the purpose of reaching it, and means can never be considered in isolation from their purpose" (Reichberg et al. 2006, 556).

Moving into more recent times, we see the first attempt at codifying the rejection of assassinations in Article 148 of the so-called Lieber Code of 1863:

The law of war does not allow proclaiming either an individual belonging to the hostile army, or a citizen, or a subject of the hostile government, an outlaw, who may be slain without trial by any captor, any more than the modern law of peace allows such intentional outlawry; on the contrary, it abhors such outrage. The sternest retaliation should follow the murder committed in consequence of such proclamation, made by whatever authority. Civilized nations look with horror upon offers of rewards for the assassination of enemies as relapses into barbarism.

This has very much been the publicly stated stance in the international political community ever since, at least as far as the law was concerned and has become part of customary international law. Looking only at a few examples, such a position is also evident in the Hague regulations, additional protocols, military manuals, and peacetime treaties, such as the 1973 New York Convention, and the perceptive article by Michael N. Schmitt (1992) and the more recent and comprehensive ICRC study on customary international humanitarian law, especially chapter 18 on deception (Henckaerts and Doswald-Beck 2005, 203). Rule 65 of that study states that "killing, injuring or capturing an adversary by resort to perfidy is prohibited." "Perfidy" is defined in the study using the language of Additional Protocol I, Article 37(1), as "acts inviting the confidence of an adversary to lead him to believe that he is entitled to, or obliged to accord, protection under the rules of international law applicable in armed conflict, with intent to betray that confidence" (223). This does, of course, leave the interesting question open of whether it is perfidious to exploit a misunderstanding one has not invited or at least not with intent to betray at the time the invitation was made.

In his above-mentioned magisterial treatment of the law and practice of targeted killing, Nils Melzer (2008) sets out the conditions and moralities that he thinks should guide the discussion of whether targeted killing should be permitted as a method of conducting hostilities:

> In order to be lawful . . . a particular targeted killing must, cumulatively
>
> - constitute an integral part of the conduct of hostilities in a situation of international or non-international armed conflict;
> - be likely to contribute effectively to the achievement of a concrete and direct military advantage without there being an equivalent non-lethal alternative;
> - be directed against an individual not entitled to protection against direct attack;
> - not be conducted by undercover forces feigning non-combatant status or otherwise by resort to perfidy;
> - not be conducted by resort to poison . . . or other prohibited weapons.
>
> . . . In terms of concept and principle, and despite their limited quantitative scope, targeted killings must be located at the extreme end of the scale of methods permitted under the normative of [sic] paradigm of hostilities. (426–427)

This approach does not leave much room for effective assassination projects. It implicitly states that highly foreseeable and massive collateral damage to civilians, who are after all entitled to protection against *direct* attack, is to be preferred to direct and intentional covert attacks against the persons responsible for the conflict in the first place. The innocent civilian who has seen his family bombed to smithereens over some people's political or economic ambitions might ask why that should be so. He would have a point, in our view. We now turn to a discussion of heads of state assassinations from a criminological state crime perspective.

WHAT WOULD THE IMPLICATIONS OF LEGITIMIZED ASSASSINATIONS MEAN FROM A STATE CRIME PERSPECTIVE?

The concept of legitimized state sponsored assassinations of another head of state presents several dilemmas from a criminological perspective. Namely, state crime research has (1) accepted that the assassination of a head of state by another state is a crime; (2) accepted that crimes of aggression and civilian casualties are also considered grave offenses; (3) recognized that the level of impunity enjoyed by heads of state that commit crimes upon their own population (those most likely to be targets of state-sponsored assassinations) as well for those that sponsor or facilitate the assassination, wage war, and/or sacrifice a civilian population in the name of a greater good needs to end; (4) noted the extensive problem with controlling state crimes and the level of realpolitik involved in accountability, prosecution, or even adherence to the rule of law and; and (5) shown that deterrence, though highly problematic at the level of street crime, could hold more promise with those in high positions, heads of state and high level officials, given certainty and swiftness. Simply, assassinating a head of state is criminal, yet, on the same note, military humanitarian intervention to stop atrocities (e.g., genocide, crimes against humanity, general oppression, and violence) that result in massive segments of the population being killed and/or harmed is also viewed as criminal.

If both are too inconceivable to condone from an abstract argumentative position, then the only alternative is to do nothing. Yet, this too is criticized as a lack of political will, guilt by proxy or nonaction-bystander guilt, or as yet another example of the international political community allowing impunity to reign over the rule of law. Yet, the fundamental concern of criminologists who specialize in crimes of the state is ending impunity and holding those guilty of the worst crimes accountable. How then does one reconcile the contradictions between intervention, assassinations, civilian death tolls, ending impunity, and/or inaction?

As noted, state crime literature has produced case study after case study documenting the illegalities of state-sponsored assassinations. For example, Rothe (2009b) suggests that the U.S. links to and involvement in the assassinations of Rafael Trujillo, Patrice Lumumba, Ngo Dinh Diem, and

Mossadegh of Iran constitutes a crime of the state. In August 1960 the U.S. administration carried out planning and preparations for the assassination of Patrice Lumumba, the leader of the Congolese independence struggle and critic of colonial oppression of Africa. "Investigations uncovered ample proof that the assassination of Lumumba was the direct result of orders given by the Eisenhower Administration, acting through the Central Intelligence Agency (CIA) and local clients financed and 'advised' by Washington" (Vann 2002). In 2002 the state released material that included an interview with Robert Johnson (the White House minute-taker under the Eisenhower administration), giving a recorded a discussion wherein Eisenhower ordered the CIA to "eliminate" Lumumba. Other allegations of the United States' involvement in assassination plots include Cuba, Vietnam, the Congo, the Dominican Republic in the 1960s, and Chile in the 1970s (Rothe 2009b).

Similarly, other scholars of state crime claim that most cases of conflict and subsequent civilian deaths constitute a crime of the state—recognizing the agentic force and criminality of individuals occupying positions within that government. For example, Kramer and Michalowski (2005, 2006a) have stated that the U.S. invasion and occupation of Iraq was itself illegal, and that war crimes were committed through the use of indiscriminate bombing and civilian deaths. Similar arguments have been lodged against NATO on the basis of its bombing campaign against Yugoslavia for failing to minimize civilian casualties. Beyond the issue of undue collateral damage, the realization that military humanitarian interventions are prey to realpolitik of states' interests comes to bear.

For instance, humanitarian intervention has long been criticized in different cases as being politically driven. This is even more problematic when states use humanitarian intervention as pretexts for fulfilling their own economic, military, or political interests. There is the issue of state selectivity. This is evident with the current situation in Darfur, where neither the international political community nor empowered states have used forced interventions; instead, hundreds of thousands of civilians have died (Rothe and Mullins 2007). There is the critique of *hegemonic* change from above and beyond the region. Dating back to research on colonialism, neocolonialism, and the dependency models of international relations, there is the questioning of the right of the international political arena or external states to impose Westernized hegemonic values. This has brought into question the moral right to change these types of regimes and conditions; the issue of state sovereignty, which frames international relations, statehood, and states' rights to self-govern; and the ethical dilemma of unseating a head of state or regime for the stated purposes of a greater good. Further state crimes scholars have long recognized the lessons learned from state intervention based on economic, political, or military self-interests, realpolitik, and political will.

Nonetheless, if interventions, such as NATO's actions or the United States' unilateral aggression in the guise of military humanitarian interventions and state sponsored assassinations, all ultimately can be claimed as or result in cases of state criminality, can there be any other alternatives or a common ground? After all, the larger goal of criminology, as well as international institutions of social control, is accountability and general deterrence. The whole idea behind the rule of criminal law is to deter violators. As noted in the separate opinion of Judge Schomburg: "I also fully accept, within the margin determined by the Appellant's individual guilt, the special emphasis on general deterrence . . . in particular when it is to prevent commanders in similar circumstances from committing similar crimes in the future" (2004, xiv, 260).

Given that, if the political objective is deterrence and accountability, and if the means to achieve that is the assassination of a head of state responsible for vast atrocities, then is this not a better means of reaching the goal than war? After all, the means can never be considered in isolation from its purpose. Perhaps the answer to this contradiction lies in the belief in the potential of general deterrence for heads of state coupled with the international political community's publicly stated goal and ideology for ending impunity. This of course assumes there can be a time when the ideal is the real: when the extant realpolitik of international relations is no longer the dominant ideology.

Deterrence and Ending Impunity

Deterrence is indeed a model of obedience, the very cause of social order itself: to punish now to prevent future offenses by example of the offender. The earlier statement by Judge Schomburg affirms that a key goal of these international criminal proceedings is to act as a general deterrence, focused on reducing the probability of deviance in the general population—in this case, the international political population, namely other heads of state. Indeed, as street crime research has shown, social location and position strongly influences deterrence (Paternoster and Piquero 1995; Paternoster and Simpson 1992; Piquero and Paternoster 1998; Stafford and Warr 1993). Simply, the more individuals had at stake to lose, the greater the likelihood was they would desist and/or reject additional criminal activity. Life-course criminologies have shown that while aging out of crime is a factor at the street level, social position and relationships are also factors in desisting criminal activity. Scholars of corporate crime have shown that the threat of losing social position is even more relevant for corporate offenders (Braithwaite and Makkai 1991; Makkai and Braithwaite 1991, 1994a, 1994b, 2007). As such, the belief in effective deterrence can be carried over to assume that those actors most likely to be involved in state crimes discussed here would seem to be those most susceptible to legal sanctions and/or other forms of perceived punishment given what they have to lose—social position. This, of course, is premised on the *ideal* rule of law, which includes certainty.

Additionally, deterrence theories locate the real general deterrent function of law and potential punishment not at the macrolevel of society but at the microlevel of *perception*. Even the earliest rational choice models (e.g., Bentham and Beccaria) focused not simply on the intensity of certainty, celerity, and proportionality of punishment but rather the individual's perception of these elements. Most committers of atrocities do not perceive international law or a given country's law as legitimate and/or a real threat, especially given the past history of impunity. We have seen this in recent cases, including the United States' use of torture and renditions, Sudan's support of the Joseph Koney and the Lords Resistance Army, Joseph Koney's regrouping and escalation of abductions of child soldiers after the International Criminal Court's warrant issued for his arrest (Kramer and Michalowski 2005, 2006a; Rothe and Mullins 2008a). Additionally, high-level commanders will not necessarily be deterred from criminal action if they can sacrifice mere individual subordinates to stand trial in their place before a court.

It is these types of actions by leaders that have reinforced the need for an international institution of control that can indeed intervene to disabuse the practice and belief in impunity. Yet, such advancements are complicated and remain selective. Furthermore, empirical studies of general deterrence have found the component of certainty to be the most effective factor. When the issue of certainty is weakened or put into question, as has been the case to date, general deterrence has little to no empirical support. Yet, if we were to argue that the issue must become more than just the moral or ethical decision of legitimizing assassinations, and must include the need to ensure certainty of punishment, providing the greater cost, would this not then serve as a general deterrent to others, and if that failed, then as a specific deterrent to assassination? Given the high levels of impunity, selective accountability, and the greater costs of waging war and the untold deaths of civilians, is it really so far of a stretch to argue that if assassinations were legitimized, allowed, and consistently enacted in the most extreme cases to avoid war and/or to save a populace from a tyrant's violence, that such assassinations would not serve as the much needed general deterrent?

Concluding Thoughts

Indeed, arguing for the assassination of a head of state by another state to reduce the costs of civilian casualties is not a simplistic matter. "The ethical dimensions of policy have an obvious claim to be taken seriously" (Coady 2002, 4). So where does that leave us with regard to avoiding unnecessary civilian deaths by targeting those who are politically responsible and killing them if nothing else will help? What, other than the tacit and mutual agreement of the lords of this world, who, after all, are the ones who sign and ratify such conventions and who make international law, can justify the existing absolute ban on assassination and the comparatively easy acceptance of collateral damage among those who have no choice or say? Possibly the objection that the use of such methods will result in much worse conditions, that we would set foot on a slippery slope, especially given the realpolitik of international relations and accountability. Yet are we sure that such an outcome would be the foreseeable result in any given case?

The answer has to be very skeptical, both in law and even more so in practice. Yet, even if we accept the difference in importance and power of states, is it such an unthinkable idea that if the heavyweights *have* to go after the weaker countries, then they should at least go after the people who are to blame, rather than leave them alone in the interests of possible future reestablishment of commerce and bomb their innocent citizens to death instead?

NOTES

This paper is drawn from another recent study by one of the authors, namely the domestic use of military force against civilian airplanes hijacked by terrorists in 9/11 scenarios. The (utilitarian) conclusion was that under an argument based on the principle of necessity, shooting down the planes was justified, even if there were hundreds of innocent passengers on board, as long as that served to save a greater number of innocent lives on the ground. Taken together with the state's duty to protect its citizens, one might even arrive at a duty of the state, or an individual for that matter, to choose a course of action that is made legitimate, and even lawful, by a defense of necessity in combination with the principle of collateral damage. Similar considerations, we think, may apply on the international law level under the headings of discrimination and proportionality. An earlier version was published in Bohlander (2009).

1. Michael N. Schmitt (1992) makes this distinction, stating that under existing principles peacetime assassinations are forbidden if they happen for political reasons, in armed conflict if they are committed by treacherous means; he acknowledges, however, that other rules of international law may forbid acts of intentional homicide even if they meet the threshold for assassinations as such.
2. See also Maalouf (2006, 193–200) on the events after the Battle of Hittin and the reconquest of Jerusalem by Saladin.
3. I wish to thank Justice Professor Adel Ibrahim Maged, Egyptian Court of Cassation, Cairo, for providing me with the original sources.
4. With which Hugo Grotius strongly disagreed (see Reichberg et al. 2006, 405).

CHAPTER 12

How to Restore Justice in Serbia?

A CLOSER LOOK AT PEOPLES' OPINIONS
ABOUT POSTWAR RECONCILIATION

Stephan Parmentier, Marta Valiñas,
and Elmar Weitekamp

SIXTEEN YEARS AFTER the beginning of the disintegration of Yugoslavia and the conflicts that ravaged the whole region, most intensely Croatia, Bosnia and Herzegovina, Serbia, and Kosovo, each of the countries is still struggling to find the best way(s) to address the atrocities that occurred in the past, realize their consequences, and rebuild trust among its citizens.

The debate on how to deal with the past in Serbia is an ongoing one. Since 1993 the International Criminal Tribunal for ex-Yugoslavia has indicted 161 persons, of which 120 have been tried in eighty-six cases (June 2009) of international crimes in the territories of the region. In the country itself, new criminal justice mechanisms have been created, such as the War Crimes Chamber in the Belgrade District Court. Other transitional justice approaches, such as a truth commission or reparation programmes, continue to be discussed. The debate about dealing with the international crimes of the past thus remains of high relevance to the people, organizations, and institutions of Serbia. In this context, international crimes as a relatively new concept cannot be seen as simply identical with the older concept of state crimes (Friedrichs 1998; Kauzlarich, Mullins, and Matthews 2003). On the one hand, state crimes constitute a wider category than international crimes, as they also involve behavior that is not traditionally regarded as violent, such as instances of treason, espionage, or corruption; on the other hand, state crimes are to be seen as narrower than international crimes, as they are committed by institutions or persons entrusted with state powers, while international crimes can also be committed by nonstate actors, such as guerrilla groups or private individuals. The central question of this contribution is how to understand the restoration of justice for international crimes, mostly committed for political reasons, in Serbia.

All in all the Yugoslav and the Serbian cases are similar to other debates about dealing with the past or transitional justice, as they are taking place between or among elites—political, economic, and from civil society—both in the country concerned and at the international level. Likewise, the views and expectations of the local populations in any given country are very rarely taken into account. To do so, however, is to provide an additional source of information about the strategies and the mechanisms for dealing with the crimes of the past and for reconstructing the future. Population-based research still constitutes the exception; nonetheless, it is true that the last years have seen a rapid development of empirical research being conducted in postconflict situations and sometimes in ongoing conflicts (see ICTJ 2004, 2006, 2007).

In this contribution we report, for the first time, on the findings of a population-based research carried out by our research team in Serbia in 2007, by means of a quantitative survey across the country on several issues of postconflict justice. We will only focus on one such issue here, namely reconciliation between individuals and between sectors in society. The main objectives of our contribution are twofold: to demonstrate the value of empirical research on postconflict justice with the local populations and to highlight these findings for the broader theoretical framework of restorative justice.

A Population-Based Survey on Postconflict Justice in Serbia

What do people in Serbia think about the crimes committed during the war and about the strategies and mechanisms to deal with the horrors of the past? These were the two leading questions that led us to design and to conduct a quantitative survey with the Serbian population in 2007. The survey constituted part of the broader research project titled "Mass Victimization and Restorative Justice," in search of the position of restorative justice in an integrated approach to mass victimization in postconflict situations. Case studies in Bosnia and Herzegovina and Serbia, were carried out at the Leuven Institute of Criminology, Catholic University of Leuven, Belgium, between 2004 and 2008. While the research focus was on restorative justice, it should be clear that the surveys themselves addressed many more issues in both postconflict situations.

Objectives and Survey Design

The aim of the survey was to inquire about the attitudes and opinions of individuals about the process of dealing with the past (or transitional justice) in Serbia, with a particular focus on the "possibilities" (or opportunities) and the potential of a restorative approach to such process. To analyze these attitudes and opinions, we made use of the heuristic model developed by Parmentier, the TARR model (Parmentier 2003; Parmentier and Weitekamp 2007). This model is composed of four building blocks that correspond to key issues in the process of dealing with the past by new regimes—namely, to search for truth about the past (T), to ensure accountability of the offenders (A), to provide some form of reparation for the victims (R), and to promote reconciliation between former enemies (R). This model arguably provides a useful framework to analyze the various relations between two or more of its building blocks, it allows us to examine specific institutions and mechanisms of dealing with the past in relation to each of these issues, and it suggests that transitional justice approaches will result from the interplay between these four building blocks (Weitekamp et al. 2006). The survey was designed to include questions related to each of these four core issues. All figures presented in the following paragraphs are the result of this four-step process of data gathering and data analysis.[1]

The Questionnaire

Being aware of the impact that each person's experiences during the war have in their current opinions and attitudes toward issues of postconflict justice, we have tried to understand what had been the type and the extent of victimization suffered by the respondents. The first part of the questionnaire therefore asked questions about forms of direct (e.g., physical injuries on the respondent) and indirect victimization (e.g., having lost family members). Moreover, the respondents were asked about their perceived suffering in three categories—physical, material, and psychological—and in two time periods—during and after the war. The responses allow us to conclude that among our sample, individuals have suffered mostly in emotional terms, both during and after the war; secondly they suffered material harm; and thirdly they suffered physically. These results are completely in line with the results of the survey conducted in Bosnia in 2006. It should be noted that the respondents in the Serbian survey reported victimization in relation to three main violent conflicts: first the war in Croatia 1991–1995 (36 percent), secondly the NATO bombings in 1999 (24 percent), and thirdly the war in Bosnia and Herzegovina (20.8 percent). Moreover, some respondents reported victimization related to the war in Kosovo from 1998 onward (15 percent) and a small number to the conflict in Slovenia in 1991 (4.2 percent).

The second part of the questionnaire asked various questions under four different headings (seeking truth, establishing accountability, providing reparation, and promoting reconciliation). Before looking into the most salient findings, it is important to emphasize that all questions were asked to all the respondents in the survey, not only to those who might be legally or sociologically qualified as "victims," thus going beyond a specific victim survey and extending into a broader population-based survey. The reason is that in violent conflicts like Yugoslavia, it is virtually impossible to make such clear-cut distinctions between those who are only perpetrators and those who are only victims, since individuals can and sometimes do assume different roles, even reverse roles, in different phases of a conflict.[2]

MAIN RESEARCH RESULTS: WHAT DO SERBIANS THINK OF RECONCILIATION?

Reconciliation has been a highly controversial term and concept in the former Yugoslavia since the end of the violent conflicts. Reconciliation has been regarded by many as a threat to criminal accountability and for that reason it has encountered strong resistance, from individuals and organizations (national and international). A minimalist approach to reconciliation has at best been defended by some. One of the observations from previous field research was that in the discourse on dealing with the past, trust was much better accepted than reconciliation. While reconciliation seemed to entail some form of impunity or an acceptance that the two sides had become involved in conflict in the same way and with the same degree of responsibility, rebuilding trust suggested that social relationships had been broken and now needed to be mended. Reconciliation may take place at different levels—individual, interpersonal, community, national, and (in the case of former Yugoslavia) regional. In our survey reconciliation was analyzed from a bottom-up as well as a top-down approach. Accordingly, both the individuals' views on interpersonal processes of reconciliation and the factors that, at the macro level, have been fostering or hampering the process of reconciliation in the former Yugoslavia were inquired.

Inquiring about reconciliation in Serbia is not an easy task. In fact, in most cases those fighting against each other during the war do not live in the same country (in this case, Serbia) nowadays. Instead, many of those from Serbia actively participating in the war were fighting outside the borders of Serbia against others who remained outside these borders. Similarly, many of those who were victimized outside the borders of Serbia today live in Serbia. For these reasons—and setting aside for the moment the many social tensions among the different social groups—it can be argued that in Serbia there are no clear categories of victims and perpetrators in the classical sense. As a result, we formulated our questions on reconciliation in terms of the relations between different ethnic groups involved in the conflicts in the former Yugoslavia (see table 1). On the possibilities of reconciliation between the different ethnic groups, the relations between Serbs and Slovenians stand out as having the largest number of positive answers. The relations between (Kosovo) Serbs and Kosovo Albanians also stand out but as the ones where

Table 1

Do you think it is possible for the members of the following ethnic groups to reconcile with each other?

	Percentage		
	Yes	No	I don't know
Serbs and Slovenians	76.9	7.9	15.3
Serbs and Croats	54.0	22.4	23.6
Serbs and Bosnian Muslims (or Bosniaks)	54.	19.4	25.8
Croats and Bosnian Muslims (or Bosniaks)	54.2	13.2	32.5
Serbs (from Serbia) and Kosovo Albanians	32.8	39.6	27.6
Kosovo Serbs and Kosovo Albanians	31.9	40.7	27.3

Note: Missing values: option (a) 4.8, (b) 5.7, (c) 5.7, (d) 6.6, (e) 6.8, (f) 6.7.

Table 2

Do you think you would be able to reconcile with the persons who did to you the things described above?

	Frequency	Valid Percent
Yes	86	23.6
No	147	40.3
I don't know	132	36.2

Note: Missing values: 7.4%.

there is less hope for reconciliation, especially in the case of Kosovo Serbs and Kosovo Albanians. In these two cases, there is a relative majority of respondents who say that reconciliation is not possible. In the case of the relations between Serbs and Croats, Serbs and Bosniaks, and Croats and Bosniaks, over half of the respondents believe that reconciliation is possible, followed by considerable amounts that are not sure and then by slightly fewer respondents who do not think it is possible.

When the question on reconciliation is formulated in more personal terms and respondents are asked whether they would be able to reconcile with the persons responsible for their victimization, the percentage of those answering "no" rises. This question was formulated in general terms, without specifying the ethnic group of the victim and/or perpetrator (see table 2). In any case, it is possible to see that the percentage of respondents who answered

TABLE 3

Do you think you would be able to reconcile with the persons who did to you the things described above?

Ethnicity	Albanian	Bosniak	Croat	Hungarian	Roma	Serb	None	Other
Yes, within ethnicity (%)	9.5	10.0	20.0	33.3	27.6	16.7	–	–
No, within ethnicity (%)	100.0	59.5	30.0	20.0	33.3	37.5	45.5	33.3
I don't know, within ethnicity (%)	31.0	60.0	60	33.3	34.9	54.5	50.0	–

Note: Missing cases: 7.4%.

"no" in this question is higher than in all the cases where respondents answered negatively to the possibility of reconciliation in abstract terms between the different ethnic groups—except in the case of Kosovo Serbs and Kosovo Albanians where 40.7% said that it will not be possible for them to reconcile. Of course, these results should be interpreted with caution, as only one-third of all respondents actually filled out this question.

Concerning ethnic distribution of these responses (see table 3), Albanian respondents said they would not be able to reconcile and that the majority of Bosnian respondents said "no" (although a considerable number said they did not know). Among Croats, most said they did not know. Serb respondents appear again as the ones most divided: a relative majority of 37.5% said 'no,' 34.9% said they did not know and 27.6% answered 'yes.'. In comparison to the other groups, Serbs (proportionately) were more ready to reconcile. Again, given the limited numbers of persons who responded to this question, the results should be interpreted with the necessary caution.

We also rephrased the issue of reconciliation in terms of trust between the various groups, and the respondents were asked to rate how much certain factors had helped or hampered the process of rebuilding trust between these groups in the former Yugoslavia. From the results, it appears that the main obstacles ("Has not been helping at all" and "Has not been helping") respondents saw in the process of rebuilding trust were the following:

1. The trauma that individuals still suffer from the war (52%)
2. The attitudes and strategies of politicians (50.6%)
3. Criminal prosecutions at the International Criminal Tribunal for the former Yugoslavia (49.5%)
4. The schools (46.1%)
5. Criminal prosecutions at the national courts (44.4%)

On the contrary, the factors that respondents thought had helped ("Has help-ing very much" and "Has been helping") this process the most are the fol-lowing:

1. The positive memories people have from the times before the war (66.3 percent)
2. The time that has already passed since the war ended (60 percent)
3. The acknowledgment of each other's suffering (53.9 percent)
4. The role of nongovernmental organizations (53.1 percent)

Various interesting observations arise from these percentages. First, the factor concerning which respondents were most divided in their opinions was the media. While 42.9 percent said the media was an obstacle in the process of rebuilding trust, 41.2 percent believe it has fostered the process. Similarly, the presence and role of the international community sparked divided reactions: 40.8 percent of the respondents said it was an obstacle, while 39.3 percent said it helped. Also noteworthy is that trauma is recognized as the major obstacle in this process, which supports the interpretation of emotional trauma as well as the fact that it is often highly neglected in the public discourse and in the poli-cies of the government and donors. Another important observation is that prosecutions are seen as contrary to the process of rebuilding trust, especially those taking place at the ICTY but also those taking place in national courts. Finally, a point of reflection that these results prompt is the fact that the two factors seen as helping the most in rebuilding trust are not related to any pol-icy or mechanisms; they have a more spontaneous and psychological nature. This triggers the question of whether the rebuilding of trust cannot be induced from the outside, or whether this simply means that the policies and mecha-nisms adopted so far are not seen to be helpful in this regard.

The above results make clear that figures, while interesting, are some-times difficult to interpret without further contextual information. In order to dig deeper into the understanding of reconciliation in the survey, we found it essential to ask respondents the term "reconciliation" means to them. We opted to use the open-question method to ensure we were not limiting or inducing the answers given, an approach that seems to have increased the value of the data collected in this question. Nonetheless, in order to analyze this qualitative data in statistical terms and in relation to the other questions asked in the survey, we had to combine qualitative and quantitative methods of analysis. The final result of this exercise was that the following concepts were most often expressed by the respondents when asked to describe reconciliation: peaceful coexistence (21.9 percent), forgiveness (12 percent), respect/tolerance (11.9 percent), acceptance of responsibility (8.8 percent), and truth (6.2 percent). These were followed by prosecution (3.4 percent), forgetting (3.3 percent), trust (3.1 percent), and remembrance

(2.9 percent). These percentages refer to the times when this concept was mentioned on its own as well as when it was mentioned in combination with other concepts.

THE RELEVANCE OF RESTORATIVE JUSTICE FOR INTERNATIONAL CRIMES OF THE PAST

The survey aimed at exploring the possibilities of applying restorative justice principles in the process of dealing with the past in Serbia to better understand how respondents viewed the key issues in postconflict, with particular attention to the potential of a restorative approach in such processes. In other words, when confronted with searching for truth, accountability, reparation, and reconciliation, this survey explored the importance given by respondents to elements of a restorative approach by asking them about some core elements in restorative justice theories and practices.

One of these elements is encounter. According to the process-oriented definitions of restorative justice, the different parties to a conflict should "resolve collectively" that same conflict.[3] This formulation can be deconstructed into the following principles: inclusion, active participation, and encounter.[4] Encounter, in a more or less mediated form, has been considered central to restorative justice processes. Experiences of encounters between those responsible for the violence and those who were victims of it have taken place in other postconflict settings such as South Africa, East Timor, and Northern Ireland.

In this survey the respondents were asked whether they would like to meet with those who had victimized them (the so-called direct perpetrators) (table 4). A relative majority (42.4%) of the respondents said "no." 35.1% said 'yes' and 22.6% said 'I don't know.' What we see again here—as in many other of the more controversial or sensitive questions in the survey—is that, although there is an absolute majority that is not ready for such an encounter, it is far from being a sweeping majority. It might be important to mention

TABLE 4

Would you like to meet with those who did to you the things described above (i.e., the persons who victimized you)?

	Frequency	Valid Percent
Yes	129	35.1
No	156	42.4
I don't know	83	22.6

Note: Missing values, 6.6%.

here that out of all respondents 79.9% did not know personally the people who victimized them and only one out of five personally knew the person who victimized them. Once again, when we look at the ethnic distribution of these answers, we see that Serbians' answers are most divided: 40 percent say they would not like to meet their perpetrator, 31 percent say they would like to, and 29 percent say they do not know what to answer. Croats also seem to be quite divided in this question, while Bosniaks seem to be more certain of not wanting to have such an encounter (while 45.5 percent of Croats says "no," 51.8 percent of Bosniaks say "no"). Furthermore, among those who said they would like to meet their perpetrators, there is a slight majority of men (55.3 percent of those who said "yes"). But of course the numbers of respondents are not very high on this question.

The respondents who answered they would like to meet those who victimized them were asked the reasons for their answers. Here are the reasons given, from the most to the least important: "to ask them why they did what they did," "to have a chance to tell them what I have suffered," "to see if they regret what they have done," "to see if they would apologize," "to ask them to repair the damage I have suffered," and "to ask them info about my missing relatives and friends." The two primary reasons given by respondents as to why they would like to meet those who caused them harm are quite common in other instances of encounter between victim and offender. Trying to make some sense out of the suffering one has been caused and having a chance to voice that suffering and to make the perpetrator aware of it are said to be part of the healing process and are, thus, a common feature of such meetings. The two other reasons given by respondents—to see if the perpetrators would feel regretful or would apologize—are also predictable and understandable motivations for such encounters. However, they may pose greater difficulties, as they indicate that there might be unrealistic expectations on the side of the victims, which may lead to frustration and disillusionment during and after the encounter.[5] It is quite surprising to see that the respondents did not attribute a great importance to the issue of reparation in this question. This seems to suggest that the respondents victimized are primarily seeking psychological and emotional repair when they think of an encounter with the perpetrator. One of the possible explanations is that the postwar scene in Serbia and the former Yugoslavia is highly characterized by a persistent denial and a lack of acknowledgment of what happened in the past. It should, however, be noted that the respondents' understanding of the word "reparation" in this question is more likely to be associated with material reparation, despite recent developments to widen the concept and to include additional categories.[6]

The respondents who answered that they did not want to meet with those people who had victimized them were also asked why not. The reasons adduced, in the order chosen by respondents (from the one most chosen to the one least chosen) are as follows: "I do not want to see that/those person/s again *and* I want to forget about what happened," "it would make me suffer again," "I do not know," "I hate him/her/them," and "I am scared of him/her/them." It seems that for the respondents avoiding contact or meeting with the perpetrator is associated with avoiding renewed suffering (namely, by recalling the past) or at least feelings of discomfort. These feelings are linked to psychological processes (or defense mechanisms) that victims go through when dealing with extreme pain or suffering, and they might not be so easily changed or influenced from the outside. This is the group of people that do not feel ready to have such an encounter. Interestingly, however, the two stronger feelings presented as possible reasons to refuse such an encounter, fear and hate, are actually the reasons less frequently chosen by respondents.

Forgiveness is a recurrent and controversial topic in the debate on reconciliation and also in the literature of restorative justice. Many have argued that in order to have reconciliation, one needs to have forgiveness and the associated rejection of feelings of revenge. Although reconciliation as a concept per se is not frequently mentioned in restorative justice theories, the process of dialogue and exchange that the parties engage in is regarded as potentially fostering empathy between them, and ultimately forgiveness from the victims. Forgiveness has, however, become a highly controversial issue in societies in transition facing a past of gross human rights violations. It has been many times associated with disguised impunity. But even when it accompanies a process of accountability, such as in South Africa, forgiveness has been criticized by many as the imposition of a new burden on those already seriously victimized. Despite the controversy, forgiveness continues to be a central issue in countries struggling to come to terms with horrendous atrocities and to move on. The respondents who said they would be ready to meet with those who victimized them were asked whether they would be able to forgive their perpetrator(s) if during such encounter the perpetrator(s) would acknowledge and show regret. An equal amount of respondents said that they would be able to forgive and that they did not know, with fewer saying they would not be able to forgive (see table 5).

On top of the low numbers who responded in the first place there were many respondents who did not know what to answer, given the highly sensitive nature of the issue, which makes it very hard to think about in hypothetical terms. On the other hand, one must note that this question contemplated what one could call a conditional forgiveness—that is, only if certain conditions are fulfilled. In this case, conditional forgiveness would require the perpetrator to acknowledge and show regret. Taking into consideration that we know these conditions are difficult to fulfill and that the respondents had in

Table 5

*If in such an encounter (between the respondent and
perpetrator), the person who did to you the things described
above would acknowledge and show regret, do you think you
would be able to forgive him/her?*

	Frequency	Valid Percent
Yes	73	39.4
No	78	21.3
I do not know	116	39.4

Note: Missing values, 1.6%.

previous questions given a great deal of importance to apologies, regret, and admission of guilt, one can say that there is still a high percentage of those who say they either did not know or would not be ready to forgive. Combined with ethnic background, the ones who seemed to be more ready to forgive are Serbs (41.7 percent of the Serb respondents in this question said they would be able to forgive), while Albanians are the least ready to forgive (50 percent say they would not be able to, and the other 50 percent do not know the answer). Croats are very divided in their opinions given that half of them do not know what to answer, and the other half is equally split between "yes" and "no." Bosniaks are also divided, although a relative majority of them (41.7 percent) say they would not be able to forgive.

Conclusion

Through this survey we aimed at contributing to a better understanding of the opinions and attitudes of individuals residing in Serbia on how the past could and should be dealt with and particularly whether and how a restorative approach could be part of such process. It has become clear that the issues of forgiveness, trust, and reconciliation are among the most controversial topics discussed in the survey. In this sense, it was very important to look at the divisions of the survey answers, but also to take into consideration the group of respondents whose opinions were mixed or uncertain—those who opted for "I don't know." Another important observation is that opinions on these subjects, particularly on reconciliation, do change when placed at a more abstract or at a more personal level. Moreover, although reconciliation is currently given a negative connotation in Serbia because of its trivialization in the public discourse, it is probably seen as more likely to become a reality than the rebuilding of trust. And in the process of rebuilding trust there is consensus about the negative role played by politicians and trauma.

The readiness and conditions for forgiveness were further analyzed in the context of encounters between the conflicting parties that remain divided along the lines of separation created by the war. Encounter has been a central element of restorative justice programs, and it has also been integrated into certain mechanisms that are close to a restorative philosophy in contexts of transition after large-scale conflicts. It must be made clear that such encounters imply a degree of preparation and involvement of all parties that we can not ensure were contemplated by the respondents in this survey. Perhaps because of that, more respondents answered that they were not willing to meet with those who victimized them, and a great majority preferred not to know personally those who victimized them. Observations of this nature have also been made in other processes where forgiveness became part of the national strategy and rhetoric of dealing with the past, sometimes sparking harsh reactions from those who felt that forgiveness could only be a difficult, long, individual, and private process dependent on a multitude of circumstances and conditions.

What this survey suggests is that more than sixteen years after the beginning of the disintegration of Yugoslavia many key issues in dealing with the past are still very present in the current debate on how to move forward. This debate might benefit from putting in question certain assumptions on how accountability can be ensured and reconciliation achieved. The question of what approach to take in the process of dealing with the past—either a primarily retributive or restorative one—seems to be very timely and necessary in the current context of Serbia. For that reason only it was crucial to ask a representative part of the population for their opinions and attitudes. The Serbian survey has demonstrated that many interesting results are emerging from such an endeavor, as well as hypotheses for further investigation.

Notes

The authors gratefully acknowledge the financial support of the Research Fund of the K. U. Leuven for the four-year research project of which the Serbian survey was a part, and of the Flemish Academic Centre, Royal Academy for Science and the Arts in Brussels, for providing the perfect academic environment to finalize this manuscript. The team also wishes to express its sincere thanks to Professor Vesna Nikolic-Ristanovic (University of Belgrade) and to Professor Johan Goethals (K. U. Leuven) for their insightful comments on earlier versions of the empirical part of the survey.
1. Details of survey and methods are available from the authors on request.
2. On the concept of role reversal, see Friday et al. (2007).
3. Following Marshall's concept, "Restorative justice is a process whereby all the parties with a stake in a particular offence come together to resolve collectively how to deal with the aftermath of the offence and its implications for the future" (Marshall 1996).
4. For a theoretical framework, see Valiñas and Vanspauwen (n.d.).

5. A combination of showing regret and apologies for the deeds of the past coming from the perpetrator would probably represent the greatest form of acknowledgment to the victims and bear the greatest reparative potential, but such an ideal outcome cannot be guaranteed to the victims. Some restorative justice experts have warned that regret and apologies should not be expected outcomes of a restorative encounter but welcomed as very important side results, and that it is enough if the offender agrees to provide reparation to the victim without necessarily having to show any repentance or apologizing (see Walgrave 1994). This was also the line of thought followed by the South African TRC's Amnesty Committee, where full disclosure of the facts was a prerequisite to granting amnesty, while regret, remorse, or apologies were not (see Parmentier 2001; Parmentier and Weitekamp 2005).

6. The Van Boven and Bassiouni reports led to the Basic Principles and Guidelines on Reparation that conceives of reparation as a wide concept to include restitution, compensation, rehabilitation, satisfaction, and guarantees of nonrepetition (see UN 2006; for a scholarly analysis, see Shelton 2005).

CHAPTER 13

The Current Status and Role of the International Criminal Court

Christopher W. Mullins

THE TWENTIETH CENTURY saw a number of attempts to create a permanent court to adjudicate cases involving the worst sorts of crimes people commit—genocide, war crimes, and crimes against humanity. From the Leipzig trials after World War I, through Nuremburg and Tokyo, to the International Criminal Tribunals for the former Yugoslavia and Rwanda, international society created institutions designed to bring those responsible for mass harms to justice. These and other ad hoc tribunals (i.e., the hybrid court in Sierra Leone, the Cambodian tribunal established to investigate the crimes of the Khmer Rouge, and the East Timor Tribunals) were created in response to horrific events. Their charters and missions are tied directly to the series of crimes they were created to investigate and prosecute as well as the locale of atrocities. While they are indeed meaningful and important components of international justice, there are far more instances that require tribunals than have received them. Such piecemeal endeavors do little to create a real sense of deterrence attached to international criminal law and leave open the common criticism that courts merely represent victor's justice and are driven more by political concerns than justice itself.

As these tribunals have carried out their mandates, there was a slow process of the development of a permanent court designed to try such crimes as were being dealt with by these ad hoc tribunals.[1] This drive culminated in the creation of the first permanent court designed to try violations of international criminal law, the Rome Statute of the International Criminal Court (ICC) in 1998. The ICC was constructed to prosecute those most responsible for widespread and systematic violations of International Humanitarian Law. With its ratification by sixty countries, the Rome Statute went into force July 2002. As of March 2010, 111 countries are states parties to the statute (30 African, 15 Asian, 17 Eastern European, 24 Latin American and Caribbean, and twenty-five Western European, including the cultural descendent states of Australia, Canada, and New Zealand).

The court's early actions suggest that it is starting to make good on its promise to end impunity for such acts. While limited by jurisdictional and resource concerns, the court's first cases are concrete steps toward fulfilling its stated goals. In 2004 Mullins, Kauzlarich, and Rothe published the first criminological examination of the ICC. Soon thereafter, Rothe and Mullins (2006a) published their book-length examination, *Symbolic Gestures and the Generation of Global Social Control*. Both of these works examine the ability of the court to act as a body that can both reduce impunity and potentially generate deterrence. A number of other works have been published in international legal studies examining the court as well (see especially Broomhall 2003; Politi and Nesi 2001; Sadat and Carden 2000). Much of the legal writing has been on the history and various interpretive elements of the Rome Statute itself. Save for the former pieces mentioned above, little criminological work has been done on the court. This chapter intends to draw on and revisit some of the major points of Mullins, Kauzlarich, and Rothe (2004) and Rothe and Mullins (2006a). It begins by providing a brief summary of the structure and functioning of the court as outlined in the Rome Statute. It then discusses the current cases the court is either investigating or prosecuting. From there it discusses key critiques of the court and closes with an exploration of ongoing possibilities for the control of criminal violations of international criminal law.

THE STRUCTURE AND FUNCTIONING OF THE COURT

As an independent judicial body, the ICC represents a unique structural and organizational position. It is the only court in existence that is not directly tied to some form of governmental or quasi-governmental (i.e., United Nations or European Union) body. Thus, while other courts are staffed, supported, and organized via existing governmental bodies, the ICC is self-contained. Oversight and management of the court is conducted by the Assembly of State Parties, which is composed of all states that have ratified and acceded to the Rome Statute. State parties, through the assembly, nominate and elect judges (Art. 36) and the prosecutor (Art. 42), and set up and manage a trust fund for victims (Art. 79).[2] The other organizational aspects of the ICC are handled by the court itself through its four organs, which are the presidency; separate judicial chambers, including appeals, trial, and pretrial divisions; the Office of the Prosecutor; and the registry (Part 4, Article 34, Rome Statute). The presidency is an elected office with a term of three years and holds responsibility for the administrative duties of the court, excluding those under the purview of the Office of the Prosecutor (Art. 38).[3] The presidency is comprised of three judges of the court, elected by the other judges for three-year terms.

The Office of the Prosecutor is a separate organ of the court that takes responsibility for the investigation of referrals on crimes covered by the ICC. The prosecutor has full authority over the administration of the prosecutorial organ (Art. 42) and is designed to function independently of the judicial organs. The office has wide discretion in opening investigations, pursuing cases, and filing warrants. A state or the United Nations Security Council may refer cases to the prosecution; the prosecutor can also independently initiate the investigation based on information of a crime being committed within the jurisdiction of the court (Art. 14–15). Individuals and other organizations can also submit information and requests for the opening of an investigation. Yet, the decision to pursue any investigation ultimately rests with the Office of the Prosecutor.

The judiciary consists of eighteen judges, divided into three divisions: pretrial, trial, and appeals. Each division is further subdivided into chambers that conduct the actual court proceedings at each stage. Judges are assigned to divisions based upon their unique experiential skill sets. Per the Rome Statute, judges are selected in a manner that ensures equal representation in the court in terms of gender and geography. Each of these chambers is responsible for adjudicating separate aspects of the trial process.

The pretrial chambers hear issues relating to preliminary case processing. They rule on any motions brought forth by the defense regarding issues that arise once a suspect is in custody. They further validate (or invalidate) the prosecutor's request for the issuance of an arrest warrant. As early cases have shown, the pretrial chambers have in no way been a rubber stamp for the Office of the Prosecutor. Once a suspect has been taken into custody on an arrest warrant, the pretrial chamber then holds a hearing to confirm the charges presented to the court by the prosecutor. As with warrant requests, to date, the pretrial chambers have been highly active in this process, refusing to confirm charges where they felt the evidence was thin and suggesting that crimes other than those listed by the prosecutor are the more appropriate charges for a given case.

The trial chambers are responsible for conducting the trial proper. As with any court, the judges of the trial chambers are to ensure appropriate and efficient conduct of the presentation of evidence, argument, etc. Trial chambers are also empowered to find a defendant guilty or innocent and to set sentence. There are currently two cases at this stage before two different trial chambers. Neither has been completed as of this writing.

The appeals chamber is composed of five judges who hold all appellate powers. As with appellate courts in general, the primary focus of the appeals chamber is to review procedural decisions to ensure that decisions made in pretrial or trial chambers followed the rule of law as established within the Rome Statute, specifically, and customary international law, generally, where there are interpretive disagreements. The appeals chamber can hear an appeal from a convicted person if new evidence is produced after the trial that the court determines would have had a meaningful outcome in the case at hand. The chamber has the power to revise a judgment or sentence if it determines that a harmful error was made. The chamber is also responsible for sentence review once handed down, and every three years thereafter until completion of said sentence (Art. 81–84).

The registry is solely responsible for the administrative and nonjudicial aspects of the court under the guidance of the registrar, elected by the court judiciary to five-year terms (Art. 43). Since its creation, the registrar has created two semiautonomous offices—the Office of Public Counsel for Victims and the Office of Public Counsel for Defense—oversees the victim's trust fund established by the Assembly of State Parties. The Office of Public Council for Victims, established September 2005, provides legal representation to the victims of crimes brought before the court. This is an innovation in Western criminal procedures and represents the court's attempts to address widespread criticisms particularly of the International Criminal Tribunals for the Former Yugoslavia and Rwanda. In extant cases, the victim's advocate has played an important role in proceedings (i.e., the Dyilo case). The Office of Public Counsel for the Defense supplements any private defense counsel a defendant may select. The office provides assistance and support to externally acquired defense counsel, represents the rights of defendants before they acquire counsel, and acts as a mediator in any dispute between defendants, their counsel, and other organs of the court.

Crimes

Article 5 of the Rome Statute lists the crimes within the jurisdiction of the ICC: crimes of genocide, crimes against humanity, and war crimes. Additionally, the court will hold jurisdiction over crimes of aggression, once the Assembly of State Parties arrives at an agreed-upon definition consistent with the Charter of the United Nations.

Crimes of genocide refer to "acts committed with intent to destroy, in whole or in part, a national, ethnical, racial, or religious group" (Art. 6). Killing, bodily and mental harm, inflicting of deleterious life conditions, birth prevention, and forcible transfer of children are all components of genocide under Rome. As of this writing, this article has been invoked one time by the prosecutor. In his request for an arrest warrant for Omar al-Bashir, president of Sudan, the prosecutor listed a series of counts in violation of Article 6. However, the pretrial chamber rejected these counts.

Article 7 defines crimes against humanity as acts that are widespread or systematically directed against a civilian population. This includes acts of torture, intentional causing of great suffering to body or mental health, murder, and attacks directed against civilian population. Crimes against humanity are not as inclusive as previously recognized human rights law (HRL). The HRL applies in times of peace or war but is primarily concerned with protecting people from governmental transgressions of their recognized civil, political, economic, social, and cultural rights (United Nations 1948b).

War crimes are defined as breaches of the Geneva Conventions of 1949 (Art. 8), including torture or inhumane treatment, biological experiments, extensive destruction and appropriation of property, and willfully denying a prisoner of war or other protected persons the right to a fair and regular trial. In addition to general *actus reus* concerns, to activate this portion of the Rome Statute the court must deliberate upon and issue findings of facts regarding the existence and nature of a conflict during the times in which the alleged breeches occurred.

As was the intent of the state parties, these four categories of crimes are the most serious and gravest violations of international law. The ICC has an express hierarchy of these crimes that it uses to prioritize its investigations and prosecutions. Genocide is seen as the most serious, followed by crimes against humanity, and then war crimes. The ICC was never envisioned as a global clearinghouse of minor violations or other treaties and statutes. It was designed to end impunity for the most severe violations of existing law and to try those most responsible for these acts.

There are also factors relevant to prioritizing and case selection, which is central to the court's limited abilities to pursue all cases brought forth by states and nongovernmental organizations. This includes trying only those cases that are widespread patterns of atrocities and gravity of allegations when compared with other situations facing the court. After all, as of 2008, more than two thousand incidents have been referred to the court from various organizations (states and nongovernmental agencies) (Rothe 2009b).

There are numerous other international crimes that could have been included within the ICC's mandate (i.e., drug or human trafficking, etc.). However, with its limited financial, human, and political capital, there is only so much the court can do. As it stands as of this writing, there are numerous grave and severe breeches of law that the court does not have the resources to deal with at this given time.

Temporal and Geographic Jurisdiction

The court's jurisdiction is not unlimited. It can only try cases dealing with crimes that have occurred since the Rome Statute's entry into force (July 2002) or those after a state's ratification of said statute, thereby avoiding the common critique of ad hoc tribunals that it represents post hoc victor's justice. Further, in order for a case to fall under its jurisdiction, one of three conditions must be met in terms of location of the crimes (Art. 12).

The first geographic criterion is that the crimes in question must have occurred within the territory (or territory controlled by), vessel, or aircraft of a state party or have been committed by nationals of a state party (i.e., uniformed military). Thus, as of this writing, that includes the 108 state parties to the Rome Statute. Secondly, a state may agree to accept the jurisdiction of the court without being a state party. For example, in relation to its civil war, the government of Cote d'Ivoire submitted itself to the jurisdiction of the court (ICC-CPI-20050215–91). While the state signed the Rome Statute in 1998, it had not yet domestically ratified it and was thus not a state party. Thirdly, the United Nations Security Council can recommend a case to the court and authorize the court's jurisdiction in the matter if neither of the above conditions is met. This is what occurred in the Sudan-Darfur case.

The ICC was devised as a complementary court (Art. 1), one which would activate only if the state responsible for those that committed the criminal acts was unable or unwilling to engage in prosecution on its own. Thus, the court would have no power nor seek jurisdiction over crimes being tried by other sovereign nations. However, as the Sudan-Darfur case has shown, the court has not accepted symbolic or show trials as adequately fulfilling this requirement.

Investigation and Policing Authority

The ICC is severely limited in its investigative reach, being unable to subpoena any state or their records. While the court may request a warrant or subpoena, the prosecutor and the court lack an empowered policing agency to ensure the fulfillment of either request (Art. 54–58 statute). The prosecutor is limited to requesting the presence of persons being investigated, victims, and witnesses. It must rely on the compliance of a state or state party to relinquish any evidence, suspects, or witnesses relevant to the ongoing investigations carried out by the prosecutorial branch. It is completely dependent upon state parties and allied organizations to bring fugitives into custody.

As established in the Rome Statute, state parties are obligated under the treaty to cooperate with the court in its requests for evidence, apprehension, and extradition of fugitives (Art. 86–93). Additionally, as the court relies upon evidence or other information obtained by states and non- or quasi-governmental agencies, it must enter into cooperation agreements with them to preserve national security interests (Art. 72) or consent of the providing agency to disclose information for use by the court (Art. 73). Conflicts over disclosure had occurred within the Dyilo case that caused the pretrial chamber and appellate chambers to rule on the admissibility of evidence wherein the providing body seeks to maintain a level of confidentiality of informants and investigators.

The dependence upon cooperation, especially in terms of securing fugitives, is problematic. In fact, most individuals who have warrants issued against them by the court remain at large due to the inability to secure them. However, in light of the organizational, financial, and political needs of creating a policing agency with global authority, the reliance on state cooperation will remain central to the court's functioning.[4]

CURRENT CASES

Central African Republic

On December 21, 2004, the government of the Central African Republic (CAR) referred to the ICC crimes committed after July 1, 2002, arising out of a protracted civil war involving state troops, a rebel group led by the former army chief of staff Francois Bozize, Chadian mercenaries, and the Congolese Mouvement de Liberation du Congo (MLC) (ICC-OTP-20050107–86). In June of 2005 the CAR government submitted evidence to the prosecutor relating to acts committed during the conflict. On May 10, 2007, the prosecutor opened a formal investigation.

THE CASE AGAINST JEAN-PIERRE BEMBA GOMBO. On May 21, 2008, the court issued an arrest warrant for Jean-Pierre Bemba Gombo, leader of the MLC, for crimes related to their participation in the protracted conflict in the CAR. Specifically, acting in support of the CAR national army and at the request of President Patasse between October 25, 2002, and March 15, 2003, the prosecutor claimed that Bemba's MLC forces committed war crimes against civilians, including acts of rape, torture, outrages upon human dignity, and pillage during attacks on the villages of Bossangoa, Mongouba, Bangui, Damara, Bossembele, Sibut, Bozoum, Kabo, Batangafo, Kaga-Bandoro, Bossemptele, and the localities referred to as PK 12 and PK 22 (ICC-01/05–01/08–1-tENG).

Pre-Trial Chamber III issued the warrant May 2008, enumerating six counts: rape as a crime against humanity (Art. 9(1)(g)); rape as a war crime (Art. 8(2)9e)(vi)); torture as a crime against humanity (Art. 7(1)(f)); torture as a war crime (Art. 8(2)(9)(i)); committing outrages on personal dignity as a war crime (Art. 8(2)9ii)); and pillaging as a war crime (Art. 8(2)(e)(v)) (ICC-01/05–01/08–1 para 21). On June 10, 2008, Pre-Trial Chamber III amended the arrest warrant to include two further counts: murder as a war crime (Art. 8 (2)(c)(i)) and murder as a crime against humanity (Art. 7(1)(a)) (ICC-01–05/01/08–15 para 10).

Though a member of the seated government, Bemba was not in the DRC when his arrest warrant was issued: he had fled to Europe claiming health concerns and did not return to his native country due to security concerns. On

May 24, 2008, Bemba was taken into custody outside of Brussels by Belgian authorities and transferred to ICC custody on July 3. He made his initial appearance before the court on July 4. A hearing to confirm his charges was held on January 12–15, 2009. On June 15, 2009, the pretrial chamber asserted its jurisdiction to hear the case. It confirmed that charges for seven counts of murder as a crime against humanity, one count of rape as a crime against humanity, six counts of murder as a war crime, two counts of rape as a war crime, eight counts of pillaging as a war crime. But it declined to confirm the charges of torture as a crime against humanity, torture as a war crime, and outrages of personal dignity as a war crime (ICC-01/05-01/08-424).

Democratic Republic of Congo

The protracted multiparty conflict in the Democratic Republic of Congo (DRC) has produced widespread violations of international criminal law. In 2004 the president of the DRC requested the ICC prosecutor investigate any crimes committed in the territory since the entry into force of the Rome Statute, July 2002 (ICC-OTP-20040419–50). This constituted the ICC's first investigation. As of early 2009, three cases are ongoing related to the DRC situation.

THE CASE AGAINST THOMAS LUBANGA DYILO. Thomas Lubanga Dyilo, founder of the Union des Patriotes Congolais (UPC) and the Forces Patriotiques pour la Liberation du Congo (FPLC), was the first individual arrested under an ICC issued warrant. Pre-Trial Chamber I issued a warrant on February 10, 2006, listing three counts of war crimes involving child soldiers: the enlistment of children under fifteen in armed forces, the conscription of children under fifteen in the armed forces, and the use of children under fifteen to participate actively in hostilities (Art. 8(2)(b)(xxvi) or Art. 8 (2)(e)(vii) (ICC-01/04–01/06–2-tEn)). Congolese authorities arrested Dyilo on March 17, 2006, and he was transferred to the Hague the next day. In January 2007, Pre-Trial Chamber I confirmed the charges against him, and his trial began on January 26, 2009.

Dyilo's trial has produced the first set of procedural appellate issues within the ICC's jurisprudence. As allowed by Article 54(3)(e), the prosecutor relied upon information submitted to him by the United Nations Security Council and nongovernmental organizations in formulating charges, here interviews with former child soldiers. The defense argued that the prosecutor failed to disclose potentially exculpatory evidence contained within the interviews as the prosecutor protected the confidentially of the informants, as per his agreement with the information providers. Specifically, 207 items of evidence (156 originating from the UN) were not disclosed to either the defense or the ICC Chamber due to providers seeking to protect the identities of individuals and organizational bodies. The prosecution admitted that 95 of the items contained potentially exculpatory materials and 112 were material to Dyilo's defense preparation (ICC-01/04–01/06–1401 para. 63). The defense suggested this violated Dyilo's right to a fair trial. Trial Chamber I agreed, ruling that disclosure of exculpatory evidence is fundamental to a right to a fair trial; that the prosecution had incorrectly used Article 54(3)(e) protections; and that, as it could not review the evidence in total (or even in part), the chamber had been prevented from exercising its jurisdiction in determining whether or not the nondisclosure violated the defendant's right to a fair trial. Thus, on June 13, 2008, the chamber imposed a stay on the proceedings. July 2008 Trial Chamber I ordered the release of Dyilo (ICC-01/04–01/06–1401). While rejecting a defense submission that the arrest warrant was unlawful (ICC-01/04/01/06–1418), it found that as the chamber had indefinitely suspended the proceedings, the accused could not be held to ensure his appearance at a trial that may not resume. Thus, his unconditional release was ordered, pending a delay for the appeals chamber to consider the issue (ICC-01/04–01/06–1401).

The appeals chamber reversed the trial chamber ruling, arguing that the warrant of arrest was not invalidated and that, if released, Dyilo would return to the DRC and would not in all likelihood be returned to custody if the stay was lifted (ICC-01/04/01/06–1487 OA 12 para. 38). Further, since the trial chamber ruling, the UN had made documents available to the trial chamber under specific conditions; therefore, there was an expectation of the stay being lifted. On January 23, 2009, Trial Chamber I lifted the stay of proceedings and Dyilo's trial resumed (ICC-01/-04–01/06–1644).

THE CASE AGAINST GERMAIN KATANGA. On July 2, 2007, Pre-Trial Chamber I issued a warrant of arrest for Germain Katanga, commander of the Force de Resiustance Patriotique en Ituri (FRPI). The warrant focuses on actions committed during a joint attack by the Front des Nationalistes et Integrationnistes (FNI) and FRPI on the village of Bogoro, which occurred February 2003, as well as other actions committed during the joint campaign occurring between January and March 2003. The warrant contains nine counts: murder as a crime against humanity (Art. 7(1)(a)); willful killing as a war crime (Art. 8(2)(a)(i)); inhumane acts as a crime against humanity (Art. 7(1)(k)); inhumane treatment as a war crime (Art. 8 (2)(a)(ii)) or cruel treatment as a war crime (Art. 8(2)(c)(i)); using children under fifteen to participate actively in hostilities as a war crime (Art. 8 (2)(b)(xxvi) or Art. 8(2) (e) (vi)); sexual slavery as a crime against humanity (Art. 7(1)(g)); sexual slavery as a war crime (Art. 8(2)(e)(vi)); intentionally directing acts against civilians as a war crime (Art. 8(2)(e)(vi) or Art. 8(2)(e)(i)); and pillage as a war crime (Art. 8(2)(b)(xvi) or Art. 8(2)(e)(v)) (ICC-01/04–02/07–1-US-tEng).

Katanga was arrested by Congolese authorities in March of 2005 and was surrendered to the Hague on October 17, 2007. On September 30, 2008, Pre-Trial Chamber I released its ruling on the confirmation of charges in this case. It unanimously confirmed that enough evidence was properly presented to proceed with: murder as a crime against humanity; willful killing as a war crime; using children to participate actively in hostilities as a war crime; intentionally directing attacks against civilians as a war crime; pillage as a war crime; and destruction of property as a war crime. By majority vote it confirmed the charge of sexual slavery as a crime against humanity; the charge of sexual slavery as a war crime; rape as a crime against humanity; and rape as a war crime. Judge Anita Usacka dissented on these counts, arguing that while she had no doubt that the rapes happened and that troops serving in the FRPI and FNI were responsible for them, she concluded that the prosecution did not sufficiently establish evidence suggesting that Katanga and Ngudjolo had knowledge of them or had planned them as part of the operation. Usacka points to the fact that Katanga and Ngudjolo disciplined troops who raped Hema women as counterevidence suggesting that he was trying to maintain order and had not ordered or approved systematic sexual assaults as part of the campaign (ICC-01/04–01/07–717). It declined to confirm the charges of inhuman treatment as a war crime and outrages upon personal dignity as a war crime. Again, Usacka dissented on the inhuman treatment as a war crimes charge. Specifically, she argued that Katanga and Ngudjolo ordered deliberate and indiscriminate attacks on civilians and therefore knew that severe bodily injuries would occur, making them criminally culpable. She also notes that even if the evidence was lacking on inhumane treatment, the chamber could have adjourned and requested that the prosecutor file the charges, attempted murder as a war crime (ICC-01/04–01/07–717).

THE CASE AGAINST MATHIEU NGUDJOLO CHUI. On July 6, 2007, Pre-Trial Chamber I issued a warrant of arrest for Mathieu Ngudjolo Chui, leader of the FNI. The warrant focuses on actions committed during a joint FRPI-FNI attack on the village of Bogoro, which occurred February 2003. He was taken into custody by Congolese authorities February 2008 and transferred to the Hague. As the actions in question were engaged in conjointly with Katanga's FRPI, the cases are being brought forth in a single trial.

THE CASE AGAINST BOSCO NTAGANDA. On August 22, 2008, Pre-Trial Chamber I issued an arrest warrant for Bosco Ntaganda. Ntaganda, a Tutsi veteran of the Rwandan Patriotic Army and deputy chief of the general staff of the FPLC, which was active in the Ituri region. The FPLC was the military wing of the Union of Congolese Patriots (UPC). He was third in command of the militia, subordinate only to Thomas Lubanga Dyilo and Floribert Kisembo.

He refused to join the coalition-established military in 2005. Ntaganda traveled to North Kivu province and joined the Congres National pour la Defense du People (CNDP), being appointed chief of staff. As leader of the FPLC, he was allegedly responsible for overseeing the recruitment and training of child soldiers.

Pre-Trial Chamber I found reasonable grounds to issue a warrant on three counts of war crimes involving child soldiers: the enlistment of children under fifteen in armed forces, the conscription of children under fifteen in the armed forces, and the use of children under fifteen to participate actively in hostilities (Art. 8(2)(b)(xxvi) or Art. 8 (2)(e)(vii) (ICC-01/04–02/06–2-Anx-tEng). As of early 2009, Ntaganda was at large. The court's prosecutor has sought assistance from all concerned parties to capture Ntaganda and surrender him to the court. He remains at large.

Sudan-Darfur

On March 31, 2005, the United Nations Security council adopted Resolution 1593 referring the situation in Darfur since July 2002 to the prosecutor of the ICC (UN Press Release SG/SM/9797/AFR/1132). This represented the first referral of a case to the ICC by the UNSC. Sudan is not a party to the Rome Statute, yet under Article 13(b) the Rome Statute provides the court jurisdiction with a UNSC referral. In response to the prosecutor's ongoing investigation, the court has issued three arrest warrants in the Darfur region of Sudan.

THE CASE AGAINST AHMAD MUHAMMAD HARUN. On May 2, 2007, Pre-Trial Chamber I issued an arrest warrant for Ahmad Harun. Harun served as minister of the state for the interior of the government of Sudan, specifically as head of the Darfur Security desk, from April 2003 until around September 2005. Under the auspices of his office, he was responsible for all military activities in the area. His actions were instrumental in bringing the Janjaweed militias under the command of the Sudanese army. He incited governmental and militia forces to engage in violations of international criminal law on numerous instances, primarily directing them against the Fur, Zaghawa, and Lasalit peoples. Due to the nature of the actions being charged, Harun is being tried jointly with Ali Kushayb.

The arrest warrant lists fifty-one counts against Harun and Ali Kushayb, focusing on actions alleged to have occurred in attacks in and around Kodoom, Bindisi, Mukjar, Arawala. The warrant lists four counts of persecution as a crime against humanity (Art. 7(1)(h) and Art. 25 (3)(d)); seven counts of murder as a crime against humanity (Art. 7(1)(a) and 25 (3)(d)); seven counts of murder as a war crime (Art. 8(2)(c)(i) and 25 (3)(d)); four counts of attacks against civilians as a war crime (Art. 8(2)(e)(i) and 25 (3)(d)); four counts of destruction of property as a war crime (Art. 8(2)(e)(xii) and 25 (3)(d)); three counts of forcible transfer of a population as a crime against humanity (Art. 7(1)(d) and Art. 25 (3)(d)); two counts of rape as a crime against humanity (Art. 7(1)(g) and 25 (3)(d)); two counts of rape as a war crime (Art. 8(2)(e)(vi) and 25 (3)(d)); two counts of inhumane acts as a crime against humanity (Art. 7(1)(1)(k) and 25 (3)(d)); four counts of pillage as a war crime (Art. 8(2)(e)(v) and 25 (3)(d)); one count of imprisonment or severe deprivation of liberty as a crime against humanity (Art. 7(1)(e) and 25 (3)(d)); one count of torture as a crime against humanity (Art. 7(1)(f) and 25 (3)(d)); and one count of outrages against personal dignity as a war crime (Art. 8(8(2)(c)(ii) and 25 (3)(d)) (ICC-02/05–01/07–2). As of now he is at large.

THE CASE AGAINST ALI MUHAMMAD ALI ABD-AL-RAHMAN. In May 2007, Pre-Trial Chamber I issued an arrest warrant for Ali Muhammad Ali Abd-al-Rahman, known as "Ali Kushayb." Ali Kushayb acted as a key leader of the Janjaweed militia between August 2003 and March 2004, which has been alleged to have committed numerous atrocities in Darfur. The prosecutor alleges he was the key mediator between the Janjaweed and the GoS and thus had considerable command and control of Janjaweed forces, especially in relaying and carrying out orders coming from the GoS (Hurna specifically). The warrant for his arrest identifies the same counts as Harun (ICC-02/05–01/07–3). Due to the coordination of the command chains, his trial has been conjoined with Ahmad Harun's. For a time, Ali Kushayb was in the custody of the Sudanese government. As of now, he is at large.

THE CASE AGAINST OMAR HASSAN AHMAD AL BASHIR. On March 4, 2009, the ICC made history by issuing an arrest warrant for the president of Sudan for crimes committed as head of state between March 2003 and July 2008. While former heads of state have had arrest warrants issued, indicted, and prosecuted, for violations of IHL, none were currently sitting as heads of state. Citing Article 27, Sections 1 and 2 of the Rome Statute, Pre-Trial Chamber I established the validity of the court to apply the statute "equally to all persons without any distinction based on official capacity . . . as Head of State or Government." The warrant states that the chamber found reasonable suspicion existed to believe that during Sudan's war of a noninternational character against rebel forces in the west (Darfur), al Bashir was involved with the planning and ordering of activities that violated the Rome Statute.

The warrant lists seven counts of violations committed against the Sudanese people in Darfur, especially those of the Fur, Masalit, and Zaghawa tribal groups. Two are for war crimes, specifically the direction of attacks against civilians (Art. 8 (2)(e)(i)) and for the encouragement of pillage (Art. 8(2)(e)(v)). Five are for crimes against humanity, specifically murder (Art. 7

(1)(a)), extermination (Art. 7(1)(b)), rape (Art. 7(1)(g)), torture (Art. 7(1)(f)), and forcible transfer of a population (Art. 7 (1)(d)) (ICC-02/05–01/09–1).

Pre-Trial Chamber I split on the issue of whether or not the activities of Sudan's military and militia forces, as orchestrated and ordered by al Bashir, constituted genocide. Two of the judges, Kuenyehia and Steiner, ruled that the prosecutor did not establish strong enough evidence to include genocide as a count in the warrant. Usacka dissented on this issue (ICC-02/05–01/09–3). Central to the arguments within the chamber was the evidentiary standard used to determine whether or not a crime should be listed on the arrest warrant. The court majority ruled that, based on the evidence presented to them, there were other reasonable interpretations of the government's activities other than genocide. Relying upon the ICJ's judgment on genocide, the majority found that the prosecution did not establish specific intent to commit genocide. While the chamber did see the actions committed as crimes against humanity, especially as a form of ethnic cleansing, they stated the acts were not tantamount to genocide, as the actions do not attempt to destroy a population in whole or in part. Thus, the evidence presented did not "show that the only reasonable conclusion to be drawn" was a genocidal intent (ICC-02/05–01/09–3). However, in accordance with the Rome Statute, the majority pointed out that if the prosecutor can marshal additional evidence before the case comes to trial, he is not precluded from filing charges of genocide at a later date.

This ruling does not reduce the culpability the chamber found in al Bashir's actions, nor does it reduce the historical nature of the ruling. It mirrors a similar argument made by the UNSC special investigation into the situation in Darfur. It establishes a very high legal bar for charging the crime of genocide at the ICC: a bar too high in the opinion of Judge Anita Usacka, who wrote her own partial dissent on this issue. Judge Usacka suggests that for the issuing of an arrest warrant the standard of evidence is inherently lower. At this stage of proceedings, she suggests, as the majority opinion noted, the standard should be "reasonable suspicion," not "reasonable doubt," which is the suggested conviction standard. Reasonable suspicion would suggest that the interpretation presented by the prosecutor be one, but potentially not the only, reasonable inference from evidence.

It is there that the majority and Usacka differ. While all judges accepted that other inferences were possible from the evidence presented, the majority ruled that genocide, especially within specific intent, must be the *only* reasonable conclusion; the dissent suggests that as long as the specific intent is *one* reasonable conclusion, it is a valid conclusion in the warrant. For Judge Usacka, whether or not there is reasonable doubt is to be decided at the trial when considering conviction. This logic mirrors the general western norms of criminal evidence, with the requirements to arrest being much lower than those required to convict.

Uganda

In December of 2003, the president of Uganda, Yoweri Museveni, requested that the ICC open an investigation into activities by the Lord's Resistance Army (LRA) during the protracted internal conflict with the Ugandan state (ICC-20040129–44). The prosecutor did so; to date, this investigation has produced a warrant calling for the arrest of four LRA leaders.

THE CASE AGAINST JOSEPH KONY, VINCENT OTTI, OKOT ODIAMBO, RASKA LUKIYA, AND DOMINI ONGWEN. In July 2005, Pre–Trial Chamber II issued a warrant of arrest for many of the acting commanders of the LRA. Initially, five individuals were named: Joseph Kony, the LRA's commander in chief; Vincent Otti, vice chairman of second in command of the LRA; Okot Odhiambo, deputy commander and brigade commander of Trinkle and Stockree Brigades of the LRA; Dominic Ongwen, brigade commander of the LRA's Sinia Brigade; and Raska Lukiya, deputy army commander.[5] The warrant contains thirty-three counts related to the LRA's ongoing activities in its insurgency against the seated government of Uganda.[6]

The prosecutor alleges LRA responsibility for six counts of attacks versus civilians as a war crime (Art. 8(2)(e)(i)) and 25(3)(b)); five counts of pillage as a war crime (Art. 8(2)(e)(v)) and 25(3)(b)); four counts of enslavement of civilians as a crime against humanity (Art. (1)(c) and 25 (3)(b)); four counts of murder as a crime against humanity (Art. 7(1)(a) and 25 (3)(b)); four counts of murder as a war crime (Art. 8(2)(c)(i) and 25(3)(b)); two counts of inhumane acts as a crime against humanity (Art. 7(1)(k) and 25(3)(b)); three counts of cruel treatment as a war crime (Art. 8(2)(c)(i) and 25(3)(b)); two counts of enlistment of children as a war crime (Art. 8(2)(e)(vii) and 25(3)(b)); one count of sexual enslavement as a crime against humanity (Art. 7(1)(g) and 25(3)(b)); one count of rape as a crime against humanity (Art. 7(1)(g)); and one count of inducing rape as a war crime (Art. 8(2)(e)(vi) and Art. 25(3)(b)) (ICC-02/04–01/05–53; ICC-02/04–01/05–54; ICC-02/04–01/05–55; ICC-02/04–01/05–56; ICC-02/04–01/05–57).

Currently, all five individuals are at large. The LRA has attempted to use the ICC warrants as a bargaining tool, suggesting that they will surrender themselves to Ugandan justice if the ICC terminates its proceedings against them. To date, the prosecutor has refused to do so. As of March 2003, the LRA leaders were thought to be in the northeastern provinces of the Democratic Republic of the Congo.

Rejected Cases: Iraq and Venezuela

Due to the ability of individuals and NGOs to submit referrals to the prosecutor, a number of parties submitted the behavior of the U.S.-led coalition in its invasion of Iraq in 2002 to the prosecutor's office. The prosecutor declined to launch an investigation for several reasons. First, he noted the lack of jurisdiction of the court, as neither Iraq nor the United States were state parties to the Rome Statue. Second, he questioned whether or not the incidents referred to him met the criterion of being grave, widespread, and/or systematic abuses. Third, he noted that where serious incidents had occurred, the controlling states in question (i.e., especially the United States and the United Kingdom) had initiated domestic prosecutions of alleged war criminals. Thus, due to the court's complementary principle, it had no cause to act (Moreno-Ocampo 2006a).

The Office of the Prosecutor also conducted preliminary investigations into the events in Venezuela surrounding the coup of April 2002. While the state in question is a state party, the prosecutor only has authority to investigate aspects of the situation that occurred after July 1, 2002, or the date of a state's ratification if later. The prosecutor declined to open a full investigation, as the evidence submitted to the court was of poor quality with numerous errors and omissions. The office also decided that the gravity threshold was not reached by the information provided (Moreno-Ocampo 2006b). During remarks given to League of Arab States, Prosecutor Moreno-Ocampo mentioned that his office also opened preliminary investigations of situations in Colombia, Afghanistan, and Georgia. He also unequivocally stated that he has no jurisdiction in the Gaza conflict (Moreno-Ocampo 2009).

PROBLEMS AND POSSIBILITIES

Critics of the court, as well as those under warrant of the court, have tried to paint the court as a political body. Sudanese President Bashir has called the court another aspect of European Colonial domination. Members of the George W. Bush administration went to great lengths to undermine the legal and political legitimacy of the court, in part, by suggesting it would be the tool of those with political interests counter to the United States (see Rothe and Mullins 2006a). Such discourses focused on the functional independence of the Office of the Prosecutor as a disadvantage, rather than the advantage it was perceived to be during the process of negotiating the Rome Statute.

Yet, an examination of the court's extant, if scant, procedural record, shows the opposite. There are several high-profile politically charged events the ICC could step into but has expressly refused to (i.e., Iraq, Gaza). The Office of the Prosecutor has carefully selected cases to pursue and has not shown itself to be overly (or even overtly) political. Indeed, certain public relations missteps have been made (i.e., announcing the opening of the investigation into the Uganda situation in a joint press conference with President Museveni, whose Ugandan Defense Forces have engaged in systematic violations of IHL in their pursuit of the LRA (see Mullins and Rothe 2008a). No serious critic, however, can deny that the cases currently under investigation and trial exhibit widespread criminal actions that deserve criminal justice attention.

One could critique the Office of the Prosecutor for the charges filed as focusing on less serious aspects of these conflicts. For example, the DRC cases focus on the recruitment of child soldiers—a serious problem both legally and socially—but only one of a host of problematic behaviors seen in the ongoing conflict within the DRC, which has seen widespread murder of civilians, systematic rape of women, and almost daily pillage. Contextually, though, this case is a perfect example of how evidence must (and does) drive prosecution. Clearly, the violation of the laws regarding the use of child soldiers was not the only illegal action committed in the Ituri region of the DRC since the Rome Statute came into force, but it is the violation on which the Office of the Prosecutor has amassed evidence. If the Office of the Prosecutor were more politically driven, one would suspect that Thomas Dyilo, Germain Katanga, Mathieu Ngudjolo, and Bosco Ntaganda would be facing far more criminal counts based on the actions of their militia in the Ituri region.

The judiciary of the court has also showed itself more interested in the adjudication of law than in political processes. For example, the pretrial chamber has not uncritically accepted and approved the requests for arrest warrants made by the Office of the Prosecutor. As discussed above, in the Bashir case, they expressly refused to affirm charges of genocide, and in the Jean-Pierre Bemba Gombo case the judges made express suggestions concerning the nature of charges filed. Further, even when a pretrial chamber has issued a warrant, it has not automatically confirmed those charges at that stage of proceedings. Similarly, the Trial Chamber I judges have been critical and controlling of the Office of the Prosecutor. Recall they ordered the release of Dyilo when the UN refused to provide certain information about the collectors and witnesses in some of the evidence filed in the case. Such decisions establish that not only is the court serious about trying those suspected of engaging in crimes prohibited by the Rome Statute, they are also serious about establishing fairness and transparency within their proceedings. Such acts strongly show that the court is not merely a politically driven process.

One of the major shortcomings of the court is its limited jurisdiction. The requisite ratification to the Rome Statute or acquiescence to the court's authority allows those who would seek to violate the crimes covered by the ICC to avoid accountability for their actions through this venue. States, like the United States for example, seek to maintain future impunity through avoiding subjection to the court's authority. While a truly universal jurisdiction could increase any deterrent value that ICC prosecutions might hold, as seen in the Sudanese cases, the UNSC can in essence give the court jurisdictional authority over a state through a resolution referring the case to the Office of the Prosecutor. Pre-Trial Chamber I has ruled that the court is jurisdictionally able to act upon a Security Council recommendation even if the state in question in not a party to the Rome treaty. This, of course, precludes such a move against one of the permanent members of the Security Council or an ally due to the innate veto power those states have. Yet, the overall precedent is clear: even if major world powers refuse to intervene militarily in a conflict with widespread human rights violations, the ICC will not stand by unacting. In and of itself, this sends a strong message about the ending of impunity.

Some have suggested that the ICC's issuing of arrest warrants for individuals in active conflicts has prolonged those conflicts instead of bringing them to a quicker resolution. The situations in Uganda and Sudan-Darfur are prime examples. The general suggestion is that the court should wait until conflicts are over to engage in investigations and issue warrants, as once the court issues an arrest warrant, any combatant is then further motivated to continue their fighting. Specifically, controversy has emerged over the LRA leadership claiming that it would seek peace if the ICC warrants were removed. One, however, should not take such statements at face value. Joseph Kony has publicly stated that he would be willing to face trial at the hands of a Uganda court, but one must be skeptical of how genuine he is. He has had numerous opportunities to turn himself into Ugandan authorities, which he has not done. Further, as the court's jurisdiction activates when a state is unwilling or unable to apply the principles of law, if Uganda were to begin trial proceedings, the court might be convinced to withdraw its extant warrant. While chief prosecutor Ocampo has said that he would not do this, his statements are in the context of a suspect at large and are by their nature contingent.

If the court waited until conflicts were fully resolved to begin investigatory work, its ability to accumulate the evidence necessary to conduct trials would be severely hampered. While it is difficult and dangerous to collect evidence in the midst of an ongoing conflict, if one waits until the conflicts are over, that evidence may not be collectable. Witnesses need to be interviewed soon after the events in question, and other material evidences can easily be destroyed by perpetrators or simply lost to time. Especially in light of the length of the conflicts the ICC is currently investigating (i.e., DRC, Darfur, and Uganda), waiting until such conflicts are over is simply not a practical measure. Further, it reinforces impunity in the minds of perpetrators who see other groups go uninvestigated.

Ultimately, the major goal of the ICC is to eliminate impunity and provide a mechanism of accountability that has long been absent for those most responsible for crimes covered by the statute. This involves bringing justice for victims and punishing offenders. It also involves deterring future offense from occurring by establishing that there will be a price to pay for resorting to such tactics. While agents of the ICC would suggest that issuance of warrants has in and of itself generated deterrence, there is no existing evidence to evaluate their claims. Further, drawing from extant criminological theories on deterrence, deterrence itself cannot come into existence until punishment has been administered. As of this writing, no individual has been found guilty of any charge by the ICC. Thus, discussions of a potentially deterrent value of the ICC are empirically premature. Due to the innate rationality within organizations and the leadership positions held by those under warrant and trial at the ICC (and others similarly situated but not under warrant or in custody), this population should be subject to the generally deterrent effects of law. I still agree with this assessment, yet, it will be years before any true deterrent effect can manifest, much less be empirically measured.

As such, any sweeping assessment of the ICC's functions or performances is premature to say the least. The court has only held temporal jurisdiction, as of this writing, for almost six years. It has yet to take a single case from start to finish, much less deal with an entire set of cases from a single conflict. It faces a situation where it has more fugitives than people in custody. However, it has begun case processing in a number of conflicts and has two trials under way. While the Office of the Prosecutor has made some initial missteps, it has also been judicious and active in pursuit of its mandate. The judges active in the various chambers have shown discipline and acuity in their application of both the Rome Statute and international law more generally. Judges are actively dissenting from decisions, suggesting a serious examination of legal issues and processes instead of a political exercise. These early actions will not only set the stage for conducting future business but also build and ensure legitimacy. To succeed in its overall mission, the Office of the Prosecutor must be seen as a valid and valuable organ of international criminal justice. Its actions now will strongly determine future perceptions. It appears to be building that future reputation on a solid foundation.

NOTES

1. See Rothe and Mullins (2006a, esp. chap. 3), for a full history of the development of an International Criminal Court.
2. Unless otherwise noted, all references cited as "Art." refer to the Rome Statute of the International Criminal Court.
3. See also Rothe and Mullins (2006a) and Sadat and Carden (2000) for a more extensive discussion of the structure of the ICC.
4. Further, considering that many of those are active arrest warrants for military personnel currently in the field or hiding in active war zones, it will take more than an international police force to secure them for the purposes of trial.
5. Originally, Raska Lukwiya was also named in the warrant. His name was removed upon the confirmation of his death (SEE ICC-02/04/01/05).
6. Unlike other warrants, the specific campaigns and action locales have been redacted in the public release of the warrant.

References

Achenbach, J. 2004. *The Grand Idea: George Washington's Potomac and the Race to the West*. New York: Simon and Schuster.

Agee, P. 1988. "The Role of the CIA, Anticommunism and the U.S.: History and Consequences, Institute for Media Analysis." Paper presented at Harvard University, November 11–13.

Akcam, T. 2006. *A Shameful Act: The Armenian Genocide and the Question of Turkish Responsibility*. New York: Metropolitan Books.

Almond, G. 1956. "Comparative Political Systems." *Journal of Politics* 18 (3): 391–409.

Alperovitz, G. 1965. *Atomic Diplomacy: Hiroshima and Potsdam: The Use of the Atomic Bomb and the American Confrontation with Soviet Power*. New York: Simon and Schuster.

———. 1995. *The Decision to Use the Atomic Bomb and the Architecture of an American Myth*. New York: Alfred A. Knopf.

Alterman, E. 2003. *What Liberal Media? The Truth about Bias and the News*. New York: Basic Books.

Ambos, K., and I. Stegmiller. 2008. "German Research on International Criminal Law: With a Special Focus on the Implementation of the ICC Statute in National Jurisdiction." *Criminal Law Forum* 19 (1): 181–198.

Amnesty International. 1999. "Chile: Torture: An International Crime: Even One Torture Victim Is One Too Many." http://www.amnesty.org/en/library/asset/AMR22/010/1999/en/dom-AMR220101999en.html.

———. 2002a. *Africa Report*. AFR 47/007/2002.

———. 2005. *Press Release*. AFR 54/059/2005. News Service No. 150.

———. 2007. *Africa Report*. AFR 47/007:1.

Amnesty International News Service. 1998. "UK/Chile: Pinochet—The Absence of Immunity for Crimes against Humanity: Amnesty International Submits Case to the House of Lords News Service." EUR 45/022/1998. November 3, 1998. http://www.amnesty.org/en/library/asset/EUR45/022/1998/en/dom-EUR450221998en.html.

Anderson, F., and A. Cayton. 2005. *The Dominion of War: Empire and Liberty in North America, 1500–2000*. New York: Penguin Books.

Arendt, H. 1963. *Eichmann in Jerusalem—A Report on the Banality of Evil*. New York: Viking Press.

Armstrong, D. 2002. "Dick Cheney's Song of America: Drafting a Plan for Global Dominance." *Harper's Magazine* (October): 76–83.

Aronowitz, S. and H. Gautney, eds. 2003. *Implicating Empire*. New York: Basic Books.

Associated Press. 2000. "September 9 (S. A. Record, Producer) October 12, 2007, from Indian Affairs Head Apologies for 'Legacy of Racism.'" *St. Augustine Archive*. http://staugustine.com/stories/090900/nat_20000909.032.shtml.

Aulette J., and R. Michalowski. 1993. "Fire in Hamlet: A Case Study of State-Corporate Crime." In *Political Crime in Contemporary America*, ed. Kenneth Tunnel, 171–206. New York: Garland.

Ayala, B. 1912. *Three Books on the Law of War and on the Duties Connected with War and on Military Discipline*. Trans. John P. Bate. New York: Carnegie Institution.

Bacevich, A. 2002. *American Empire: The Realities and Consequences of U.S. Diplomacy*. Cambridge, MA: Harvard University Press.

———. 2005. *The New American Militarism: How Americans Are Seduced by War*. New York: Oxford University Press.

———. 2008. *The Limits of Power: The End of American Exceptionalism*. New York: Metropolitan Books.

Bachrach, P., and M. S. Baratz. 1962. "Two Faces of Power." *American Political Science Review* 56:947–952.

Badiou, A. 2007. *The Century*. Malden, MA: Polity Press.

Balint, J. 2008. "Dealing with International Crimes: Towards a Conceptual Model of Accountability and Justice." In *Supranational Criminology: Towards a Criminology of International Crimes*, ed. A. Smeulers and R. Haveman, 311–334. Antwerp: Intersentia.

Balkin, J. M. 2009. "A Body of Inquiries." *New York Times*, January 11.

Bamford, J. 2005. *A Pretext for War: 9/11, Iraq, and the Abuse of America's Intelligence Agencies*. New York: Anchor Books.

Barak, Greg. 1991a. *Crimes by the Capitalist State: An Introduction to State Criminality*. Albany: State University of New York Press.

———. 1991b. "Toward a Criminology of State Crime." In *Crimes by the Capitalist State: An Introduction to State Criminality*, ed. G. Barak, 3–16. Albany: State University of New York Press.

———. 1998. *Integrating Criminologies*. Boston: Allyn & Bacon.

———. 2000. *Crime and Crime Control: A Global View*. Westport, CT: Greenwood Press.

———. 2009. *Criminology: An Integrated Approach*. Lanham, MD: Rowman and Littlefield.

Barak, G., and R. Bohm. 1989. "The Crimes of the Homeless or the Crime of Homelessness? On the Dialectics of Criminalization, Decriminalization, and Victimization." *Contemporary Crises: Law, Crime, and Social Policy* 13 (4): 275–288.

Bassiouni, M. C., ed. 1975. *International Terrorism and Political Crimes*. Springfield, IL: Charles C. Thomas.

———. 1979. "International Law and the Holocaust." *California Western International Law Journal* 9:202–298.

———. 1996. "Searching for Peace and Achieving Justice: The Need for Accountability." *Law and Contemporary Problems* 59 (4): 9–28.

———. 1998. *The Statute of the International Criminal Court: A Documentary History*. Ardsley, NY: Transnational Publishers.

———. 1999a. *Crimes against Humanity in International Criminal Law*. Norwell, MA: Kluwer Academic Publishing.

———. 1999b. *International Criminal Law: Crimes*. Ardsley, NY: Transnational Publishers.

———. 1999c. *International Criminal Law: Procedural and Enforcement Mechanisms*. 2d rev. ed. Ardsley, NY: Transnational Publishers.

———. 2000a. *A Casebook on International Criminal Law*. Durham, North Carolina: Carolina Academic Press.

———. 2000b. *International Humanitarian Law and Arms Control Agreements*. Ardsley, NY: Transnational Publishers.

———. 2000c. *A Manual on International Humanitarian Law and Arms Control Agreements.* Ardsley, NY: Transnational Publishers.

———. 2002a. *Post-Conflict Justice.* Ardsley, NY: Transnational Publishers.

———. 2002b. *International Terrorism: 2000. A Compilation of U.N. Documents 1972–2001.* 2 vols. Ardsley, NY: Transnational Publishers.

———. 2003. *Introduction to International Criminal Law.* Ardsley, NY: Transnational Publishers.

———. 2008a. *International Criminal Law.* Vols. 1–3. Leiden, The Netherlands: Martinus Nijhoff Publishers/Brill Academic.

———. 2008b. "The Perennial Conflict between Realpolitik and the Pursuit of International Criminal Justice." Public lecture presented at University of Northern Iowa, April 2008.

BBC News. 1998. Special Report. "South Africans Reconciled?" January 9. http://news.bbc.co. uk/1/hi/world/africa/142673.

———.1999. "Pinochet Must Go to Spain, Says Amnesty." April 10. http://news. bbc.co.uk/1/hi/world/260124.stm.

Beard, C., and M. Beard. 1930. *The Rise of American Civilization.* New York: Macmillan.

Becker, H. 1963. *Outsiders: Studies in the Sociology of Deviance.* New York: Free Press.

Beirne, P., and J. Messerschmidt. 1991. *Criminology.* Toronto: Harcourt, Brace, Jovanovich.

Bekker, P.H.F. 1997. "Legality of the Threat or Use of Nuclear Weapons." *American Journal of International Law* 91 (1): 126–138.

Bello, W. 2005. *Dilemmas of Domination: The Unmaking of the American Empire.* New York: Metropolitan Books.

Bennis, P. 2006. *Challenging Empire: How People, Governments, and the UN Defy US Power.* Northampton, MA: Olive Branch Press.

Berkman, A. 1971. *ABC of Anarchism.* London: Freedom Press.

Bess, M. 2006. *Choices Under Fire: Moral Dimensions of World War II.* New York: Alfred A. Knopf.

Bird, K., and L. Lifschultz, eds. 1998. *Hiroshima's Shadow.* Stony Creek, CT: Pamphleteer's Press.

Bledsoe, R., and B. Boczek. 1987. *The International Law Dictionary.* Santa Barbara: ABC-CLIO.

Blix, H. 2004. *Disarming Iraq.* New York: Pantheon Books.

———. 2008. *Why Nuclear Disarmament Matters.* Cambridge, MA: MIT Press.

Blum, W. 2000. *Rogue State.* Monroe: Common Courage Press.

———. 2005. *Killing Hope.* Monroe: Common Courage Press.

Boed, R. 1999. "An Evaluation of the Legality and Efficacy of Lustration as a Tool of Transitional Justice." *Columbia Journal of Transitional Law* 37:357–402.

Bohlander, M. 2009. "Killing Many to Save a Few? Preliminary Thoughts about Avoiding Collateral Civilian Damage by Assassination of Regime Elites." In *International Law and Power: Perspectives on Legal Order and Justice—Essays in Honour of Colin Warbrick*, ed. K. Kaikobad and M. Bohlander, pp. 207–34. Martinus Nijhoff Publishers.

Bonifaz, J. 2003. *Warrior-King: The Case for Impeaching George W. Bush.* New York: Nation Books.

Boston Globe. 1991. "Report on Torture in Chile Undermines Military's Denials." 10, 3(91), 4.

Boyle, F. 1989a. *The Future of International Law and American Foreign Policy.* Ardsley-on-Hudson, NY: Transnational Publishers.

———. 1989b. The Hypocrisy and Racism behind the Formulation of U.S. Human Rights Foreign Policy. *Social Justice: A Journal of Crime, Conflict, and World Order* 16 (1): 71–93.

———. 2002. *The Criminality of Nuclear Deterrence: Could the U.S. War on Terrorism Go Nuclear?* Atlanta: Clarity Press.

———. 2004. *Destroying World Order: U.S. Imperialism in the Middle East before and after September 11.* Atlanta: Clarity Press.

Brachet, J., and H. Wolpe. 2005. "Conflict-Sensitive Development Assistance: The Case of Burundi." November 11. http://www.worldbank.org/conflict.

Brahm, E. 2004. "Lustration." June 15. http://www.beyondintractability.org/essay/Lustration/.

———. 2005. "The Chilean Truth and Reconciliation Commission." July 6. http://www.beyondintractability.org/case_studies/Chilean_Truth_Commission.jsp?nid=5221).

Braithwaite, J. 1989. "Criminological Theory and Organizational Crime." *Justice Quarterly* 6:333–358.

Braithwaite, J., and T. Makkai. 1991. "Testing an Expected Utility Model of Corporate Deterrence." *Law and Society Review* 25:7–40. Reprinted in *Regulation and Regulatory Process*, ed. C. Coglianese and R. Kagan, Aldershot: Ashgate Publishing, 2007.

Brecher, J., J. Cutler, and B. Smith. 2005. *In the Name of Democracy: American War Crimes in Iraq and Beyond.* New York: Metropolitan.

Breitman, R. 1992. *Architect of Genocide: Himmler and the Final Solution.* Hannover, NH: University Press of New England.

Brittain, V. 1944. *Seed of Chaos.* London: New Vision Press.

Brody, R., and M. Ratner. 2000. *The Pinochet Papers: The Case of Augusto Pinochet in Spain and Britain.* Leiden, The Netherlands: Martinus Nijhoff Publishers.

Broomhall, B. 2003. *International Justice and the International Criminal Court: Between Sovereignty and the Rule of Law.* Oxford: Oxford University Press.

Brown, D. 1970. *Bury My Heart at Wounded Knee.* New York: Henry Holt & Co.

Browning, C. R. 1992. *The Path to Genocide: Essays on Launching the Final Solution.* Cambridge, UK: Cambridge University Press.

Brustein, W. 1996. *The Logic of Evil: The Social Origins of the Nazi Party, 1925–1933.* New Haven, CT: Yale University Press.

Bugliosi, V. 2008. *The Prosecution of George W. Bush for Murder.* Cambridge, MA: Vanguard Press.

Burnham, G., R. Lafta, S. Doocy, and L. Roberts. 2006. "Mortality after the 2003 Invasion of Iraq: A Cross-Sectional Cluster Sample Survey." *Lancet* (October 21). 1421-1428.

Bush, G. W. 2002. "Remarks by the President at 2002 Graduation Exercise of the United States Military Academy, West Point, New York." June 1. http://www.whitehouse.gov.

Byers, M. 2005. *War Law: Understanding International Law and Armed Conflict.* Vancouver, BC: Douglas & McIntyre.

Cabrera, N. 1995. "Control and Prevention of Crimes Committed by State-Supported Educational Institutions." In *Controlling State Crime*, ed. J. I. Ross, 163–206. New York: Garland.

Calhoun, C., P. Price, and A. Timmer, eds. 2002. *Understanding September 11.* New York: New Press.

Callinicos, A. 2003. *The New Mandarins of American Power.* Cambridge, UK: Polity Press.

Card, C. 1996. "Rape as a Weapon of War." *Hypatia* 11 (4): 5–17.

Carroll, J. 2004. *Crusade: Chronicles of an Unjust War.* New York: Metropolitan Books.

Caulfield, S. 1991. "Subcultures as Crime: The Theft of Legitimacy of Dissent in the United States." In *Crimes by the Capitalist State: An Introduction to State Criminality*, ed. G. Barak, 49–64. Albany, NY: State University of New York Press.

Chakravarty, A. 2006. "Gacaca Courts in Rwanda: Explaining Divisions within the Human Rights Community." *Yale Journal of International Affairs* (Winter/Spring): 132.

Chambliss, William J. 1989. "State-Organized Crime." *Criminology* 27 (2): 183–208.

———. 1995. "Commentary." *Society of Social Problems Newsletter* 26 (1): 9.

Chamorro, E. 1988. Remarks presented at "The Role of the CIA, Anticommunism and the U.S.: History and Consequences," Institute for Media Analysis, Harvard University, November 11–13.

Chernus, I. 2006. *Monsters to Destroy: The Neoconservative War on Terror and Sin.* Boulder, CO: Paradigm Publishers.

Chicago Commission of Inquiry. 1973. *Chile: Under Military Rule.* New York: International Documentation (IDOC).

Chilean National Commission on Truth and Reconciliation. 1991. *Report of the Chilean National Commission on Truth and Reconciliation.* Trans. Phillips E. Berryman. Notre Dame: University of Notre Dame Press.

Chomsky, N. 1994. *World Orders Old and New.* New York. Columbia University Press.

———. 1999. *The Umbrella of U.S. Power: The Universal Declaration of Human Rights and the Contradictions of U.S. Policy.* New York: Seven Stories Press.

———. 2003. *Hegemony or Survival: America's Quest for Global Dominance.* New York: Metropolitan Books.

———. 2006. *Failed States: The Abuse of Power and the Assault on Democracy.* New York: Metropolitan Books.

Christie, N. 2001. "Answers to Atrocities: Restorative Justice in Extreme Situations." In *Victim Policies and Criminal Justice on the Road to Restorative Justice: Essays in Honour of Tony Peters*, ed. E. Fattah and S. Parmentier, 379–392. Leuven, The Netherlands: Leuven University Press.

Churchill, W. 1997. *A Little Matter of Genocide: Holocaust and Denial in the Americas, 1492 to the Present.* San Francisco: City Lights.

Churchill, W., and J. Vander Wall. 1990. *Agents of Repression: The FBI's Secret War against the Black Panther Party and the American Indian Movement.* Boston: South End Press.

Cirincione, J. 2007. *Bomb Scare: The History and Future of Nuclear Weapons.* New York: Columbia University Press.

Clark, P. 2009. "The Rules (and Politics) of Engagement." In *After Genocide: Transitional Justice, Post-Conflict Reconstruction and Reconciliation in Rwandan and Beyond*, ed. P. Clark and Z. D. Kaufman, 297–320. London: Hurst & Co.

Clark, R. 2004. *Against All Enemies: Inside America's War on Terror.* New York: Free Press.

Clendinnen, I. 1999. *Reading the Holocaust.* Cambridge, UK: Cambridge University Press.

Coady, C.A.J. 2002. "The Ethics of Armed Humanitarian Intervention." *Peace Works* 45:2–47.

Cohen, S. 1993. "Human Rights and Crimes of the State: The Culture of Denial." *Australian and New Zealand Journal of Criminology* 26:97–115.

Collins, O., ed. 1999. *Speeches that Changed the World.* Westminster: John Knox Press.

Comfort, A. 1950. *Authority and Delinquency in the Modern State.* London: Routledge and Kegan Paul Ltd.

Commission on the Truth for El Salvador. 1992. http://www.mississippitruth.org/documents/EL-SALVADOR.pdf.

Conot, R. E. 1983. *Justice at Nuremberg*. New York: Harper & Row.

Conway-Lanz, S. 2006. *Collateral Damage: Americans, Noncombatant Immunity, and Atrocity after World War II*. New York: Routledge.

Conyers, J. 2003. Foreword to *Warrior-King: The Case for Impeaching George W. Bush*, ed. J. Bonifaz, ix–xii. New York: Nation Books.

Corn, D. 2003. *The Lies of George W. Bush: Mastering the Politics of Deception*. New York: Crown Publishers.

Corrado, R., and G. Davies. 2000. "Controlling State Crime in Canada." In *Varieties of State Crime and Its Control*, ed. J. I. Ross, 59–88. Monsey, NJ: Criminal Justice Press.

Cryer, R. 2005. *Prosecuting International Crimes: Selectivity and the International Criminal Law Regime*. Cambridge: Cambridge University Press.

Daly, E. 2002. "Between Punitive and Reconstructive Justice: The Gacaca Courts in Rwanda." *International Law and Politics* 34:355.

Danner, M. 2006. *The Secret Way to War: The Downing Street Memo and the Iraq War's Buried History*. New York: New York Review Books.

De Bonno, E. 1979. *Future Positive*. New York: Penguin.

de la Vega, E. 2006. *United States v. George W. Bush et al.* New York: Seven Stories Press.

Denzin, N. K., and Y. S. Lincoln, eds. 2003. *9/11 in American Culture*. Walnut Creek, CA: Altamira Press.

Derber, C. 2002. *People before Profit: The New Globalization in an Age of Terror, Big Money, and Economic Crisis*. New York: St. Martin's Press.

Derechos Chile. 2008. "History of Human Rights Abuses in Chile." http://www.beyondintractability.org/case_studies/Chilean_Truth_Commission.jsp?nid=5221.

de Vattel, E. 1916. *The Law of Nations or the Principles of Natural Law*. Trans. Charles Fenwick. New York: Carnegie Institution.

Diamond, L. 1995. *Promoting Democracy in the 1990s*. Report to the Carnegie Commission on Preventing Deadly Conflict, New York.

Dickinson, T., and J. Stein. 2006. "Chronicle of a War Foretold: Truth Was a Casualty Long Before We Invaded Iraq." *Mother Jones* 31 (September/October): 61–69.

Dinges, J. 2004. *The Condor Years: How Pinochet and His Allies Brought Terrorism to Three Continents*. New York and London: New Press.

Domke, D. 2004. *God Willing? Political Fundamentalism in the White House, The "War On Terror," and the Echoing Press*. London: Pluto Press.

Dorrien, G. 2004. *Imperial Designs: Neo-conservatism and the New Pax Americana*. New York: Routledge.

Doyle, M. W. 1986. *Empires*. Ithaca: Cornell.

Drost, P. 1959. *The Crime of State: Penal Protection for Fundamental Freedoms of Persons and Peoples*. Bk. 2, *Genocide*. Leyden, The Netherlands: Sythoff.

Drumbl, M. 2007. *Atrocity, Punishment, and International Law*. New York: Cambridge University Press.

Dyer, G. 2004. *Future Tense: The Coming World Order*. Toronto: McClelland and Stewart.

Edelman, M. 1971. *Politics as Symbolic Action: Mass Arousal and Quiescence*. Chicago: Markham Publishing Co.

Elliot, W., ed. 1955. *The Political Economy of American Foreign Policy: Its Concepts, Strategy and Limits*. New York: Henry Holt & Co.

Englehardt, T. 2006. *Mission Unaccomplished: Tom Dispatch Interviews with American Iconoclasts and Dissenters*. New York: Nation Books.

————. 2008. *The World According to Tom Dispatch: America in the New Age of Empire.* London: Verso.

Ensalaco, M. 1994. "Truth Commissions for Chile and El Salvador: A Report and Assessment." *Human Rights Quarterly* 16 (4): 656–675.

————. 2000. *Chile under Pinochet: Recovering the Truth.* Philadelphia: University of Pennsylvania Press.

Everrest, L. 2004. *Oil, Power, and Empire: Iraq and the U.S. Global Agenda.* Monroe, ME: Common Courage Press.

Ewald, U. 2008. "Reason and Truth in International Criminal Justice." In *Supranational Criminology: Towards a Criminology of International Crimes*, ed. A. Smeulers and R. Haveman, 399–432. Antwerp: Intersentia.

Falk, R. 1965. "The Shimoda Case: A Legal Appraisal of the Atomic Attacks upon Hiroshima and Nagasaki." *American Journal of International Law* 59:759–793.

————. 1983a. "Towards a Legal Regime for Nuclear Weapons." *McGill Law Journal* 28 (3): 519–541.

————. 1983b. "Is Nuclear Policy a War Crime?" *Human Rights* 11:18–55.

————. 1989. *Revitalizing International Law.* Ames: Iowa State University Press.

————. 1997. "Nuclear Weapons, International Law and the World Court: A Historic Encounter." *American Journal of International Law* 91 (1): 64–75.

————. 2004a. "State Terror versus Humanitarian Law." In *War and State Terrorism: The United States, Japan, and the Asia-Pacific in the Long Twentieth Century*, ed. M. Selden and A. So, 41–61. Lanham: Rowman & Littlefield.

————. 2004b. *The Declining World Order: America's Imperial Geopolitics.* New York: Routledge.

————. 2008a. "Non-Proliferation Treaty Illusions and International Lawlessness." In *At the Nuclear Precipice: Catastrophe or Transformation?* ed. R. Falk and D. Krieger, 9–47. New York: Palgrave Macmillan.

————. 2008b. "Nuclear Weapons, War, and the Discipline of International Law." In *At the Nuclear Precipice: Catastrophe or Transformation?* ed. R. Falk and D. Krieger, 225–233. New York: Palgrave Macmillan.

Falk, R., I. Gendzier, and R. J. Lifton, eds. 2006. *Crimes of War: Iraq.* New York: Nation Books.

Fallows, J. 2004. "Bush's Lost Year." *Atlantic Monthly*, October, 68–84.

Farebrother, G., and N. Kollerstrom, eds. 2004. *The Case against War.* Rev. ed. Nottingham, UK: Spokesman.

Farson, S. 1991. "Old Wine, New Bottles, and Fancy Labels: The Rediscovery of Organizational Culture in the Control of Intelligence." In *Crimes by the Capitalist State*, ed. G. Barak, 185–218. Albany: State University of New York Press.

Faust, K. L., and D. Kauzlarich. 2008. "Hurricane Katrina Victimization as a State Crime of Omission." *Critical Criminology* 16 (1): 85–103.

Felice, B. 1989. "Rights in Theory and Practice: An Historical Perspective." *Social Justice: A Journal of Crime, Conflict, and World Order* 16 (1): 34–56.

Feller, M. 2001. Implementation of the Convention on the Elimination of All Forms of Discrimination against Women by Burundi. Committee on the Elimination of Discrimination against Women 24th Session, January 15–February 2.

Ferguson, N. 2004. *Colossus: The Price of America's Empire.* New York: Penguin Press.

Fest, Joachim C. 1970. *The Faces of the Third Reich.* New York: Ace.

Fiala, A. 2008. *The Just War Myth: The Moral Illusions of War.* Lanham, MD: Rowman & Littlefield.

Finkielkraut, A. 1992. *Remembering in Vain: The Klaus Barbie Trial and Crimes against Humanity.* New York: Columbia University Press.

Fischer, C. 1995. *The Rise of the Nazis.* Manchester, UK: Manchester University Press.

Frank, A. G. 1969. *Capitalism and the Underdevelopment of Latin America.* New York: Monthly Review Press.

Fraser, D. 1996. "Law before Auschwitz: Aryan and Jew in the Nazi Rechtsstaat." In *Thinking through the Body of Law*, ed. P. Cheah, D. Fraser, and J. Grbich, 63–79. New York: New York University Press.

Freire, P. 1985. *The Politics of Education.* South Hadley, MA: Bergin and Garvey.

Friday, K. 2006. "Might Makes Right—Just War and Just Warfare in Early Medieval Japan." In *The Ethics of War in Asian Civilizations: A Comparative Perspective*, ed. T. Brekke, 159. New York: Routledge.

Friday, P., J. Hartman, V. Lord, and M. Exum. 2007. *Batterers and the Battered: Role Reversals in Domestic Violence.* Paper presented at the annual meeting of the American Society of Criminology, Atlanta, 14 November.

Friedlander, H. 1995. *The Origins of Nazi Genocide—From Euthanasia to the Final Solution.* Chapel Hill: University of North Carolina Press.

Friedrichs, D. O. 1985. "The Nuclear Arms Issue and the Field of Criminal Justice." *Justice Professional* 1:5–9.

———. 1995. "State Crime or Governmental Crime: Making Sense of the Conceptual Confusion." In *Controlling State Crime*, ed. Jeffrey Ian Ross, 53–80. New York: Garland.

———. 1996. "Governmental Crime, Hitler and White Collar Crime: A Problematic Relationship." *Caribbean Journal of Criminology and Social Psychology* 2:44–63.

———. 1998. *State Crime.* Vols.1–2. Aldershot, UK: Ashgate Publishing.

———. 2000. "The Crime of the Century? The Case for the Holocaust." *Crime, Law and Social Change* 34 (1): 21–41.

———. 2004. *Trusted Criminals: White Collar Crime in Contemporary Society.* Belmont, CA: Wadsworth.

———. 2007a. "Transnational Crime and Global Criminology: Definitional, Typological and Contextual Conundrums." *Social Justice* 34: 4–18.

———. 2007b. *Trusted Criminals: White Collar Crime in Contemporary Society.* Belmont, CA: ITP/Wadsworth Publishing Co.

———. 2008. "Towards a Criminology of International Crimes: Producing a Conceptual and Contextual Framework." In *Supranational Criminology: Towards a Criminology of International Crimes*, ed. A. Smeulers and R. Haveman, 29–50. Antwerp: Intersentia.

Friedrichs, D., and J. Friedrichs. 2002. "The World Bank and Crimes of Globalization: A Case Study." *Social Justice* 29 (1–2): 1–12.

Friel, H., and R. Falk. 2004. *The Record of the Paper: How the New York Times Misreports US Foreign Policy.* London: Verso.

Fruhling, H. 1983. "Stages of Repression and Legal Strategy for the Defense of Human Rights in Chile: 1973–1980." *Human Rights Quarterly* 5 (4): 510–533.

Galliher, J. F. 1989. *Criminology: Human Rights, Criminal Law and Crime.* Englewood Cliffs, NJ: Prentice Hall.

Garcas, J. 1999. *Pinochet, before the High Court of Spain and International Criminal Law.* http://www.memoriayjusticia.cl/english/en_issues-garcas.html.

Gardner, L. C., W. F. LaFeber, and T. J. McCormick. 1973. *Creation of the American Empire: U.S. Diplomatic History.* Chicago: Rand McNally & Co.

Geis, G., and L. B. Bienen. 1998. *Crimes of the Century: From Leopold and Loeb to O. J. Simpson.* Boston: Northeastern University Press.

Gentili, A., 1933. *De iure belli libri tres: The Classics of International Law*, No. 16. Trans. John C Rolfe. Oxford: Oxford University Press.

Georges-Abeyie, D. 1991. "Piracy, Air Piracy, and Recurrent U.S. and Israeli Civilian Aircraft Interceptions." In *Crimes by the Capitalist State*, G. Barak, 129–144. Albany: State University of New York Press.

Georgetown Law Library. 2008. International Criminal Court, Article 98, Agreements Research Guide. http://www.11.georgetown.edu/guides/article_98.cfm.

Gerson, J. 2007. *Empire and the Bomb: How the U.S. Uses Nuclear Weapons to Dominate the World*. Ann Arbor, MI: Pluto Press.

Gill, P. 1995. "Controlling State Crimes by National Security Agencies." In *Controlling State Crime*, ed. J. I. Ross, 81–114. New York: Garland.

Ginger, A. F., ed. 1998. *Nuclear Weapons Are Illegal: The Historic Opinion of the World Court and How It Will Be Enforced*. New York: Apex Press.

———. *Dominate the World*. London: Pluto Press.

Giroux, H. 1983. *Theory and Resistance in Education: A Pedagogy for the Opposition*. South Hadley, MA: Bergin and Garvey.

Glauner, L. 2001. "The Need for Accountability and Reparation: 1830–1976. The United States Government's Role in the Promotion, Implementation, and Execution of the Crime of Genocide against Native Americans." *DePaul Law Review* 51:911–962.

Glueck, S. 1943a. "Punishing the War Criminals." *New Republic* 109:706–709.

———. 1943b. "By What Courts Shall War Offenders Be Tried?" *Harvard Law Review* 66:1059.

———. 1944. *War Criminals: Their Prosecution and Punishment*. New York: Alfred A. Knopf.

———. 1946. *The Nuremberg Trial and Aggressive War*. New York: Alfred A. Knopf.

Gonzales, G. 2004. "Secret Report on Testimony from Torture Victims Triggers Debate." *Global Policy Forum*. November 10. http://www.globalpolicy.org/intljustice/wanted/2004/1110torturereport.htm.

Gottlieb, R. S., ed. *Radical Social and Political Theory*. New York: State University of New York Press.

Gottschall, J. 2004. "Explaining Wartime Rape." *Journal of Sex Research* 41(2): 129–136.

Gourevitch, P. 1998. *We Wish to Inform You That Tomorrow We Will Be Killed with Our Families: Stories from Rwanda*. New York: Picador.

Gray, J. 2007. *Black Mass: Apocalyptic Religion and the Death of Utopia*. New York: Farrar, Straus and Giroux.

Graybill, L. S. 2001. "Gender and Post-Conflict Resolution in South Africa and Rwanda." *Mind and Human Interaction* 12:261–277.

Grayling, A. C. 2006. *Among the Dead Cities: The History and Moral Legacy of the WW II Bombing of Civilians in Germany and Japan*. New York: Walker & Co.

Green, P. 2005. "Disaster by Design: Corruption, Construction and Catastrophe." *British Journal of Criminology* 45 (4): 528–546.

Green, P., and T. Ward. 2000. "State Crime, Human Rights, and the Limits of Criminology." *Social Justice* 27 (1): 101.

———. 2004. *State Crime*. London: Pluto Press.

Greene, F. 1970. *The Enemy: What Every American Should Know about Imperialism*. New York: Vintage Books.

Gurr, T. R. 1988. "War, Revolution and the Growth of the Coercive State." *Comparative Political Studies* 21 (1): 45–65.

Gutman, R., D. Rieff, and A. Dworkin, eds. 2007. *Crimes of War*. Rev. ed. New York: W. W. Norton & Co.

Haas, R. N. 2000. *What to Do with American Primacy*. http://www.brookings.edu/articles/1999/09diplomacy_haass.aspx.

Hackett, D. A. 1998. *Elusive Justice: War Crimes and the Buchenwald Trials*. Boulder, CO: Westview Press.

Hagan, F. E. 1997. *Political Crime: Ideology and Criminality*. Boston: Allyn and Bacon.

Hagan, J., and S. Greer. 2002. "Making War Criminal." *Criminology* 40:231–264.

Hagan, J., W. Rymond-Richmond, and P. Parker. 2006. "The Criminology of Genocide: The Death and Rape of Darfur." *Criminology* 43(3): 525–562.

Halper, S., and J. Clarke. 2004. *America Alone: The Neoconservatives and the Global Order*. Cambridge, UK: Cambridge University Press.

Halpern, J., and H. M. Weinstein. 2004. "Empathy and Rehumanization after Mass Violence." In *My Neighbor, My Enemy*, ed. Eric Stover and Harvey M. Weinstein, 303–304. Cambridge, UK: Cambridge University Press.

Hamber, B. 1998. Remembering to Forget: Issues to Consider When Establishing Structures for Dealing with the Past. In *Past Imperfect: Dealing with the Past in Northern Ireland and Societies in Transition*, ed. B. Hamber. Londonderry, Ireland: Initiative on Conflict Resolution and Ethnicity.

Hamilton, R. F. 1982. *Who Voted for Hitler?* Princeton, NJ: Princeton University Press.

Hamm, M. 1991. "The Abandoned Ones: A History of the Oakdale and Atlanta Prison Riots." In *Crimes by the Capitalist State*, ed. G. Barak, 145–182. Albany: State University of New York Press.

Harding, R. 1983. "Nuclear Energy and the Destiny of Mankind—Some Criminological Perspectives." *Australian and New Zealand Journal of Criminology* 16:81–92.

Hardt, M., and A. Negri. 2004. *Multitude: War and Democracy in the Age of Empire*. New York: Penguin Putnam.

Hartman, G. H. 1996. *The Longest Shadow: In the Aftermath of the Holocaust*. Bloomington: Indiana University Press.

Hartnett, S. J., and L. A. Stengrim. 2006. *Globalization and Empire: The U.S. Invasion of Iraq, Free Markets, and the Twilight of Democracy*. Tuscaloosa: University of Alabama Press.

Hartung, W. 2004. *How Much Are You Making on the War Daddy? A Quick and Dirty Guide to War Profiteering in the Bush Administration*. New York: Nation Books.

Hartung, W. D., and B. Moix. 2000. "Deadly Legacy: U.S. Arms to Africa and the Congo War." *Arms Trade Resource Center*. http://www.worldpolicy.org/projects/arms/reports/congo.htm.

Harvey, D. 2003. *The New Imperialism*. Oxford, UK: Oxford University Press.

Hasegawa, T. 2005. *Racing the Enemy: Stalin, Truman, and the Surrender of Japan*. Cambridge, MA: Belknap Press of Harvard University Press.

Haveman, R. 2008. "Doing Justice to Gacaca." In *Supranational Criminology: Towards a Criminology of International Crimes*, ed. A. Smeulers and R. Haveman, 357–398. Antwerp: Intersentia.

Hayes, P. 1991. *Lessons and Legacies: The Meaning of the Holocaust in a Changing World*. Evanston, IL: Northwestern University Press.

Hazlehurst, K. 1991. "Passion and Policy: Aboriginal Deaths in Custody in Australia, 1980–1989." In *Crimes by the Capitalist State*, ed. G. Barak, 21–48. Albany: State University of New York Press.

Henckaerts, J. M., and L. Doswald-Beck. 2005. *Customary International Humanitarian Law*. Vol. 1, *Rules*. Cambridge, UK: Cambridge University Press.

Henkin, L. 1995. *International Law: Politics and Values*. Dordrecht, The Netherlands: Martinus Nijhoff.

Henry, S. 1991. "The Informal Economy: A Crime of Omission by the State." In *Crimes by the Capitalist State*, ed. G. Barak, 253–272. Albany: State University of New York Press.

Higgens, D. R. 2006. "After Pinochet: Developments on Head of State and Ministerial Immunities." Incorporated Council of LAW Reporting for England and Wales Annual Lecture Series. http://www.lawreports.co.uk/AboutICLR/Lecture% 20PDF/ A4%20Transcript%20ICLR%20Pinochet.pdf.

Hillyard, P., C. Pantazis, S. Tombs, and D. Gordon. 2004. *Beyond Criminology: Taking Harm Seriously*. London: Pluto Press.

Hinch, R. 1991. "Contradictions, Conflicts, and Dilemmas in Canada's Sexual Assault Law." In *Crimes by the Capitalist State*, ed. G. Barak, 233–252. Albany: State University of New York Press.

Hirsch, A. 2009. "Lawyers See Threat to Open Justice in Growing Number of Secret Trials." http://www.guardian.co.uk/uk/2009/feb/09/law-sectret-trials-torture-allegations.

Hitchins, C. 2001. *The Trial of Henry Kissinger*. London: Verso Press.

Hodgson, G. 2009. *The Myth of American Exceptionalism*. New Haven: Yale University Press.

Hofmeister, H. 2005. "Neither the 'Caroline Formula' nor the 'Bush Doctrine'—An Alternative Framework to Assess the Legality of Pre-Emptive Strikes." *University of New England Law Journal* 2:31.

Human Rights Watch. 1996. "Human Rights Watch World Report 1996—Burundi." January 1. *UNHCR Refworld*. http://www.unhcr.org/refworld/docid/3ae6a8a30 .html.

———. 1998a. "The Pinochet Case—A Wake-up Call to Tyrants." http:// www.hrw.org/campaigns/ chile98/precedent.htm.

———. 1998b. "The Pinochet Prosecution." http://www.hrw.org/campaigns/ chile98/index.html.

———. 2000. "Brutal Burundi War Draws in Rwandan Combatants." http://www.hrw.org/en/news/2000/03/23/brutal-burundi-war-draws-rwandan-combatants.

———. 2006a. "Chile: Pinochet's Legacy May End Up Aiding Victims: London Arrest Gave Hope of Justice for Dictators." http://www.hrw.org/english/docs/ 2006/12/10/chile14805.htm.

———. 2006b. "Summary and Recommendations: When Tyrants Tremble." http:// www.hrw.org/reports/1999/chile/Patrick.htm.

———. 2006c. "Importance of War Crimes Prosecutions in Republika Srpska." http://www.hrw.org/reports/2006/bosnia0306/3.htm.

———. 2008a. "Burundi: Release Civilians Detained without Charge." http:// hrw.org/english/docs/2008/05/29/burund18974.htm.

———. 2008b. "Letter to the United Nations Human Rights Council from Human Rights Organizations in Burundi." http://hrw.org/english/docs/208/9/12/ burund19797.htm.

Iadicola, P. 2008a. "Centrality of the Empire Concept in Study of State Violence." Paper presented at the Workshop on State Crime in the Global Age, held at the International Institute for the Sociology of Law, Onati, Spain, May 29–30.

———. 2008b. "Globalization and Empire." *International Journal of Social Inquiry* 1 (2): 3–37.

References

Iadicola, P., and A. Shupe. 2003. *Violence, Inequality, and Human Freedom*. Boulder: Rowman and Littlefield.

Ingraham, B. L. 1979. *Political Crime in Europe*. Berkeley: University of California Press.

International Centre for Transitional Justice (ICTJ). 2004. *Iraqi Voices: Attitudes towards Transitional Justice and Social Reconstruction*. New York: Human Rights Centre, University of Berkeley California/ International Centre for Transitional Justice.

———. 2006. *Colombian Perceptions and Opinions on Justice, Truth, Reparations, and Reconciliation*. New York: International Centre for Transitional Justice.

———. 2007. *When the War Ends: A Population Based Survey of Attitudes about Peace, Justice, and Social Reconstruction in Northern Uganda*. New York: Human Rights Centre, University of Berkeley California/ International Centre for Transitional Justice.

International Court of Justice (ICJ). 1986. *Military and Paramilitary Activities in and against Nicaragua (Nicaragua v. United States of America)*. Archives of International Court of Justice, Peace Palace, The Hague. http://www.icj-cij.org/docket/files/70/9973.pdf?PHPSESSID=dc54883eaf.

———. 1996. *The Legality of the Threat or Use of Nuclear Weapons (Request for Advisory Opinion Submitted by the General Assembly of the United Nations)*. General List, No. 95, Advisory Opinion of July 8, 1996.

International Crisis Group. 2008. http://www.crisisgroup.org/home/index.cfm?action=conflict_search&1=1&t=1&c_country20.

Integrated Regional Information Networks. 2007. "Burundi: UN Office of Coordination of Humanitarian Affairs." http://www.irinnews.org/report.aspx?ReportID=74983.

Isikoff, M., and D. Corn. 2006. *Hubris: The Inside Story of Spin, Scandal, and the Selling of the Iraq War*. New York: Crown Publishers.

Jackall, R. 1980. "Crime in the Suites." *Contemporary Sociology* 9:354–358.

Jackson, Andrew. (1830) "Andrew Jackson—President's Message to Twenty-First Congress, Second Session, 1830." http://www.tngenweb.org/cessions/jackson.html.

Jackson, R. H. 1946. Foreword to *The Nuremberg Trial and Aggressive War*, S. Glueck, vii–xii. New York: Alfred A. Knopf.

Janis, I. 1982. *Groupthink*. Boston: Houghton Mifflin.

Jensen, R. 2004. *Citizens of the Empire: The Struggle to Claim Our Humanity*. San Francisco: City Lights Books.

Jochnick, C., and R. Normand. 1994. "The Legitimation of Violence: A Critical History of the Laws of War." *Harvard International Law Journal* 35 (1): 49–95.

Johns, C., and J. Borrero N. 1991. "The War on Drugs: Nothing Succeeds Like Failure." In *Crimes by the Capitalist State: An Introduction to State Criminality*, ed. G. Barak, 67–100. Albany: State University of New York Press.

Johnson, C. 2004. *The Sorrows of Empire*. New York: Metropolitan Books.

Jonas, S. 2004. "The Ripple Effect of the Pinochet Case." *Human Rights Brief* 11 (3): 36–38.

Bartle, Ronald David. "Judgment of the English Court Allowing the Extradition of Pinochet." 1999. *Equipo Nizkor and Derechos Human Rights*, October 8. http://www.derechos.org/nizkor/chile/juicio/extra2.html.

Juhasz, A. 2006. *The Bush Agenda: Invading the World, One Economy at a Time*. New York: Regan Books.

Just, R. 2008. "The Truth Will Not Set You Free." *New Republic*, August 27, 36–47.

Kauzlarich, D. 1995. "A Criminology of the Nuclear State." *Humanity and Society* 19 (3): 37–57.

———. 1997. "Nuclear Weapons on Trial: The Battle at the International Court of Justice." *Social Pathology* 3 (Fall): 157–164.

———. 2007. "Seeing War as Criminal: Peace Activist Views and Critical Criminology." *Contemporary Justice Review* 10 (1): 67–85.

———. 2008. "Victimisation and Supranational Criminology." In *Supranational Criminology: Towards a Criminology of International Crimes*, ed. A. Smeulers and R. Haveman, 435–453. Antwerp: Intersentia.

Kauzlarich, D., and R. Kramer. 1995. "The Nuclear Terrorist State." *Peace Review* 7 (3/4): 333–337.

———. 1998. *Crimes of the American Nuclear State: At Home and Abroad.* Boston: Northeastern University Press.

Kauzlarich, D., R. Kramer, and B. Smith. 1992. "Toward the Study of Governmental Crime: Nuclear Weapons, Foreign Intervention, and International Law." *Humanity and Society* 16 (4): 543–563.

Kauzlarich, D., R. A. Matthews, and W. J. Miller. 2001. "Toward a Victimology of State Crime." *Critical Criminology: An International Journal* 10 (3): 173–194.

Kauzlarich, D., C. Mullins, and R. Matthews. 2003. "A Complicity Continuum of State Crime." *Contemporary Justice Review* 6:241–254

Kellner, D. 2005. *Media Spectacle and the Crisis of Democracy: Terrorism, War, and Election Battles.* Boulder, CO: Paradigm Publishers.

Kennedy, P. 2006. *The Parliament of Man: The Past, Present, and Future of the United Nations.* New York: Random House.

Kern, K. 2007. "The Human Cost of Cheap Cell Phones." In *A Game as Old as Empire*, ed. S. Hiatt, 93–112. San Francisco: Berrett-Koehler Publishing.

Kiernan, B. 2007. *Blood and Soil.* New Haven: Yale University.

Kinzer, S. 2004. *All the Shah's Men: An American Coup and the Roots of Middle East Terror.* New York: John Wiley & Sons.

———. 2007. *Overthrow: America's Century of Regime Change from Hawaii to Iraq.* New York: New York Times Books.

Kirkby, C. 2006. "Rwanda's Gacaca Courts: A Preliminary Critique." *Journal of African Law* 50 (2): 94–117.

Kittrie, N. 2000. *Rebels with a Cause.* Boulder, CO: Westview Press.

Klare, M. 2004. *Blood and Oil: The Dangers and Consequences of America's Growing Petroleum Dependency.* New York: Metropolitan Books.

Klein, N. 2007. *The Shock Doctrine: The Rise of Disaster Capitalism.* New York, NY: Metropolitan Books.

Koh, H. H. 2003. "Foreword: On American Exceptionalism." *Stanford Law Review* 55:1479–1527.

Kolko, G. 1984. *Main Currents in Modern American History.* New York: Pantheon Books.

Kopel, D., and M. Krause. 2002. "Losing the War on Terrorism in Peru: The U.S. Government Has Undermined the War on Terrorism in Peru." http://www.nationalreview.com/kopel/kopelprint0322202.html.

Kornbluh, P. 2004. *The Pinochet File: A Declassified Dossier on Atrocity and Accountability— A National Security Archive Book.* New York: New Press.

Kramer, R. C. 1992. "The Space Shuttle *Challenger* Explosion: A Case Study of State Corporate Crime." In *White Collar Crime Reconsidered*, ed. K. Schlegel and D. Weisburd, 214–243. Boston: Northeastern University Press.

———. 1995. "Exploring State Criminality: The Invasion of Panama." *Journal of Criminal Justice and Popular Culture* 3 (2): 43–52.

————. 2008. "From Guernica to Hiroshima to Baghdad: The Normalization of the Terror Bombing of Civilian Populations." Paper presented at the Workshop on State Crime in the Global Age, held at the International Institute for the Sociology of Law, Onati, Spain, May 30.

————. 2010. "From Guernica to Hiroshima to Baghdad: The Normalization of the Terror Bombing of Civilian Populations." In *State Crime in the Global Age*, ed. W. Chambliss, R. Michalowski, and R. Kramer. Devon, UK: Willan Publishing.

Kramer, R., and D. Kauzlarich. 1999. "The International Court of Justice Opinion on the Illegality of the Threat and Use of Nuclear Weapons: Implication for Criminology." *Contemporary Justice Review* 4 (2): 395–413.

Kramer, R., and R. Michalowski. 1990. "Toward an Integrated Theory of State-Corporate Crime." Paper presented at the American Society of Criminology, Baltimore, November.

————. 2005. "War, Aggression, and State Crime: A Criminological Analysis of the Invasion and Occupation of Iraq." *British Journal of Criminology* 45 (4): 446–469.

————. 2006a. "The Invasion of Iraq as State-Corporate Crime." In *State-Corporate Crime: Wrongdoing at the Intersection of Business and Government*, ed. R. Michalowski and R. Kramer. Piscataway, NJ: Rutgers University Press.

————. 2006b. "The Original Formulation." In *State-Corporate Crime: Wrongdoing at the Intersection of Business and Government*, ed. R. Michalowski and R. Kramer, 18–26. New Brunswick, NJ: Rutgers University Press.

Kramer, R., R. Michalowski, and D. L. Rothe. 2005. "The Supreme International Crime: How the US War in Iraq Threatens the Rule of Law." *Social Justice* 32 (2): 52–81.

Krauthammer, C. 1989. "Universal Domination: Toward a Unipolar World." *National Interest* 18 (Winter): 48–49.

————. 1991. "The Unipolar Moment." *Foreign Affairs* 70:23–33.

————. 2007. "On Genocide, Fools Rush In." *New York Post*, October 19.

Kurtz, L. 1988. *The Nuclear Cage: A Sociology of the Arms Race*. Englewood Cliffs, NJ: Prentice Hall.

Lange, P., and H. Meadwell. 1985. "Typologies of Democratic Systems: From Political Inputs to Political Economy." In *New Directions in Comparative Politics*, ed. H. J. Wiarda, 82–117. Boulder, CO: Westview Press.

Langer, L. 1995. *Admitting the Holocaust: Collected Essays*. New York: Oxford University Press.

Lawyers' Committee on Nuclear Policy. 1990. *Statement on the Illegality of Nuclear Warfare*. Rev. ed. New York: Lawyers' Committee on Nuclear Policy.

Lemarchand, R. 1998. "Genocide in the Great Lakes: Which Genocide? Whose Genocide?" *African Studies Review* 41 (1): 3–16.

Lemkin, R. 1944. *Axis Rule in Occupied Europe*. New York: Columbia University Press.

Lenning, E., and S. Brightman. 2009. "Oil, Rape and State Crime." *Critical Criminology* 17 (1): 34–38.

Lens, S. 2003. *The Forging of the American Empire: From the Revolution to Vietnam: A History of U.S. Imperialism*. London: Pluto Press.

Lieven, A., and J. Hulsman. 2006. *Ethical Realism: A Vision for America's Role in the World*. New York: Vintage Books.

Lifton, R. J., and R. Falk. 1982. *Indefensible Weapons: The Political and Psychological Case against Nuclearism*. New York: Basic Books.

Lifton, R. J., and G. Mitchell. 1995. *Hiroshima in America: Fifty Years of Denial*. New York: Grosset/Putnam.

Lijphart, A. 1984. *Democracies.* New Haven, CT: Yale University Press.

Lippman, M. 1993. "They Shoot Lawyers Don't They? Law in the Third Reich and the Global Threat to the Independence of the Judiciary." *California Western International Law Journal* 23:257–318.

Loft, F. 1998. "Background to the Massacres in Burundi." *Review of African Political Economy* 43:88–93.

Lukacs, J. 1997. *The Hitler of History.* New York: Knopf.

Maalouf, M. 2006. *The Crusades through Arab Eyes.* London: Saqi Books.

Mahajan, R. 2003. *Full Spectrum Dominance: U.S. Power in Iraq and Beyond.* New York: Seven Stories Press.

Maier, C. S. 2005. "An American Empire? The Problems of Frontiers and Peace in Twenty-First Century Politics." In *The New American Empire,* L. C. Young, xi–ix. New York: New Press.

Makkai, T., and J. Braithwaite. 1991. "Criminological Theories and Regulatory Compliance." *Criminology* 29:191–220.

———. 1994a. "The Dialectics of Corporate Deterrence." *Journal of Research in Crime and Delinquence* 31:347–373.

———. 1994b. "Reintegrative Shaming and Regulatory Compliance." *Criminology* 32:361–385.

———. 2007. "Reintegrative Shaming and Regulatory Compliance." In *Corporate Crime,* ed. S. Simpson and C. Gibbs, 217–240. Aldershot: Ashgate Publishing.

Mamdani, M. 1996. *Citizen and Subject: Contemporary Africa and the Legacy of Late Colonialism.* New York: Princeton.

———. 2008. "The New Humanitarian Order." *The Nation,* September 28, 17–22.

Mandel, M. 2004. *How America Gets Away with Murder: Illegal Wars, Collateral Damage and Crimes against Humanity.* London: Pluto Press.

Mann, J. 2004. *Rise of the Vulcans: The History of Bush's War Cabinet.* New York: Viking Publishers.

Marcuse, H. 2008. "Martin Niemöller's famous quotation: 'First they came for the Communists.'" http://www.history.ucsb.edu/faculty/marcuse/niem.htm.

Marshall, T. 1996. "The Evolution of Restorative Justice in Britain." *European Journal on Criminal Policy and Research* (Special Issue on Restorative Justice and Mediation) 4 (4): 21–43.

Marx, G. T. 1981. "Ironies of Social Control: Authorities as Contributors to Deviance through Escalation, Nonenforcement and Covert Facilitation." *Social Problems* 28:221–246.

———. 1988. *Undercover: Police Surveillance in America.* Berkeley: University of California Press.

Massing, M. 2004. *Now They Tell Us: The American Press and Iraq.* New York: New York Review of Books.

McCormack, T. L. H., and H. Durham. 2009. "Aerial Bombardment of Civilians: The Current International Legal Framework." In *Bombing Civilians: A Twentieth Century History,* ed. Y. Tanaka and M. B. Young, 215–238. New York: New Press.

McCulloch, J., and S. Pickering. 2005. "Suppressing the Financing of Terrorism: Proliferating State Crime, Eroding Censure and Extending Neo-colonialism." *British Journal of Criminology* 45 (4): 470–486.

McGoldrick, D. 2004. *From "9–11" to the "Iraq War 2003": International Law in an Age of Complexity.* Oxford: Hart Publishing.

Melzer, N. 2008. *Targeted Killings in International Law.* Oxford: Oxford University Press.

Menzies, K. 1995. "State Crime by the Police and Its Control." In *Controlling State Crime*, ed. J. I. Ross, 141–162. New York: Garland.

Meyer, J. 2009. "Waterboarding Is Torture: Attorney General Nominee Vows Review of Bush Administration's Practices." *Chicago Tribune*, January 16.

Meyrowitz, E. 1990. *Prohibition of Nuclear Weapons: The Relevance of International Law.* Dobbs Ferry, NY: Transnational Publishers.

Michaels, H. 2003. "Washington's Use and Abuse of the Geneva Conventions." *World Socialist Website.* http://www.wsws.org/articles/2003/mar2003/pows-m29.shtml.

Michalowski, R. 1985. *Order, Law and Crime.* New York: Random House.

———. 2008. In Search of the State and Crime in State Crime Studies. Workshop on State Crime in the Global Age, held at the International Institute for the Sociology of Law Onati, Spain.

Michalowski, R., and R. Kramer. 2006. *State-Corporate Crime: Wrongdoing at the Intersection of Business and Government.* New Brunswick, NJ: Rutgers University Press.

Migdal, J. 1988. *Strong Societies and Weak States.* Princeton, NJ: Princeton University Press.

Migdal, J., A. Kohli, and V. Shue. 1994. *State Power and Social Forces.* Cambridge, UK: Cambridge University Press.

Miller, D., ed. 2004. *Tell Me Lies: Propaganda and Media Distortion in the Attack on Iraq.* London: Pluto Press.

Miller, R. L. 1995. *Nazi Justiz: Law of the Holocaust.* Westport, CT: Praeger Publishers.

———. 2000. "Controlling State Crime in Israel: The Dichotomy between National Security and Coercive Powers." In *Varieties of State Crime and Its Control*, ed. J. I. Ross, 89–118. Monsey, NY: Criminal Justice Press.

Moeller, S. 2004. *Media Coverage of Weapons of Mass Destruction.* College Park: Center for International Studies at Maryland, University of Maryland.

Moreno-Ocampo, L. 2006a. "OTP Response to Communications Received Concerning Iraq." http://www2.icc-cpi.int/NR/rdonlyres/04D143C8–19FB–466C-AB77–4CDB2FDEBEF7/143682/OTP_letter_to_senders_re_Iraq_9_February_2006.pdf.

———. 2006b. OTP Response to Communications Received Concerning Venezuela." http://www2.icc-cpi.int/NR/rdonlyres/4E2BC725–6A63–40B8–8CDC-ADBA7BCAA91F/143684/OTP_letter_to_senders_re_Venezuela_9_February_2006.pdf.

———. 2009. Conference on Justice in Post Armed Conflicts and the ICC: Reduction of Impunity and a Support to International Justice. Cairo, January 15.

Morris, B. 2008. "Why Israel Feels Threatened." *New York Times*, December 30.

Morrison, W. 2006. *Criminology, Civilisation and the New World Order.* New York: Routledge-Cavendish.

Muhlberger, D. 1990. *Hitler's Followers: Studies on the Sociology of the Nazi Movement.* London: Routledge.

Mukagasana, Yolande. 2007. Letter to Amnesty International. Copy available upon request to author.

Muller, Ingo. 1991. *Hitler's Justice: The Courts of the Third Reich.* Cambridge, MA: Harvard University Press.

Mullins, C. W. 2009. "He Would Kill Me with His Penis: Genocidal Rape as a State Crime." *Critical Criminology: An International Journal* 17:1.

Mullins, C. W., and D. L. Rothe. 2007. "The Forgotten Ones: The Darfur Genocide." *Critical Criminology: An International Journal* 15 (2): 135–158.

———. 2008a. *Blood, Power, and Bedlam: Violations of International Criminal Law in Post-Colonial Africa.* Oxford, UK: Peter Lang Press.

———. 2008b. "Gold, Diamonds and Blood: International State-Corporate Crime in the Democratic Republic of the Congo." *Contemporary Justice Review* 11 (2): 81–99.

Mullins, C. W., and D. Kauzlarich. 2000. "The Ghost Dance: A Criminological Examination." *Social Pathology* 6 (4): 264–283.

Mullins, C., D. Kauzlarich, and D. Rothe. 2004. "The International Criminal Court and the Control of State Crime: Problems and Prospects." *Critical Criminology: An International Journal* 12 (3): 285–308.

Munkler, H. 2007. *Empires.* Malden, MA: Polity.

Naqvi, Y. 2003. "Amnesty for War Crimes: Defining the Limits of International Recognition." *International Committee Red Cross and Red Crescent* 85:851.

National Law Journal. 2004. "Justices Weigh Alien Tort Act." http://www.store.law.com/nlj_results.asp?lqry=Alien+tort+Act&x=15y=7.

New Internationalist. 1987. "Visions of Freedom: A Journey through Pinochet's Chile." *New Internationalist* 174:6.

Nichols, J., and R. McChesney. 2005. *Tragedy and Farce: How the American Media Sell Wars, Spin Elections, and Destroy Democracy.* New York: New Press.

Normand, R. 2003. *Tearing Up the Rules: The Illegality of Invading Iraq.* Brooklyn: Center for Economic and Social Rights.

Nugent, W. 2008. *Habits of Empire: A History of American Expansion.* New York: Alfred A. Knopf.

Obama, B. 2009. "Executive Order—Review and Disposition of Individuals Detained at the Guantánamo Bay Naval Base and Closure of Detention Facilities." http://www.whitehouse.gov/the_press_office/ClosureOfGuantanamoDetentionFacilities.

O'Conner, J. 1973. *The Fiscal Crisis of the State.* New York: St. Martins Press.

O'Malley, P. 1987. "Marxist Theory and Marxist Criminology." *Crime and Social Justice* 29:70–87.

O'Shaughnessy, N. J. 2004. *Politics and Propaganda: Weapons of Mass Seduction.* Ann Arbor: University of Michigan Press.

Ott, W., and R. Buob. 1993. "Did Legal Positivism Render German Jurists Defenseless during the Third Reich?" *Social and Legal Studies* 2:91–104.

Panitch, L., and S. Gindin. 2006. "Theorizing American Empire." In *Empire's Law*, ed. A. Bartholomew, 21–43. London: Pluto Press.

Parmentier, S. 2001. "The South African Truth and Reconciliation Commission: Towards Restorative Justice in the Field of Human Rights." In *Victim Policies and Criminal Justice on the Road to Restorative Justice: Essays in Honour of Tony Peters*, ed. E. Fattah and S. Parmentier, 401–428. Leuven, The Netherlands: Leuven University Press.

———. 2003. "Global Justice in the Aftermath of Mass Violence. The Role of the International Criminal Court in Dealing with Political Crimes." *International Annals of Criminology* 41:203–224.

Parmentier, S., K. Vanspauwen, and E. Weitekamp. 2008. "Dealing with the Legacy of Mass Violence: Changing Lenses to Restorative Justice." In *Supranational Criminology: Towards a Criminology of International Crimes*, ed. A. Smeulers and R. Haveman, 335–356. Antwerp, Belgium: Intersentia.

Parmentier, S., and E. Weitekamp. 2005. "The Truth and Reconciliation Commission in South Africa." In *Introduction to International Criminal Justice*, ed. M. Natarajan, 151–158. New York: McGraw-Hill.

———. 2007. "Political Crimes and Serious Violations of Human Rights: Towards a Criminology of International Crimes." In *Crime and Human Rights*, Series in Sociology of Crime, Law and Deviance, ed. S. Parmentier and E. Weitekamp, 9:109–144. Oxford: Elsevier/JAI Press.

Paternoster, R., and A. Piquero. 1995. "Reconceptualizing Deterrence: An Empirical Test of Personal and Vicarious Experiences." *Journal of Research in Crime* 32 (3): 251–286.

Paternoster, R., and S. Simpson. 1992. "A Rational Choice Theory of Corporate Crime." In *Crimes of Privilege: Readings in White-Collar Crime*, ed. N. Shover and J. P. Wright, 194–210. New York: Oxford University Press.

Patterson, I. 2007. *Guernica and Total War*. Cambridge, MA: Harvard University Press.

Pepinsky, H. E. 1980. *Crime Control Strategies*. New York: Oxford University Press.

Peters, B. G. 1989. *The Politics of Bureaucracy*. 3d. ed. New York: Longman.

Pillar, P. 2006. "Intelligence, Policy, and the War in Iraq." *Foreign Affairs* 85 (March/April): 15–27.

Piquero, A., and R. Paternoster. 1998. "An Application of Stafford and Warr's Reconceptualization of Deterrence to Drinking and Driving." *Journal of Research in Crime and Delinquency* 35 (1): 5–41.

Pitt, W. R. 2002. *War on Iraq*. New York: Context Books.

Politi, M., and G. Nesi, eds. 2001. *The Rome Statute of the International Criminal Court: A Challenge to Impunity*. Burlington, VT: Ashgate.

Potter, D. 2000. "Controlling State Crime in Japan: A Case Study of Political Corruption." In *Varieties of State Crime and Its Control*, ed. J. I. Ross, 31–57. Monsey, NY: Criminal Justice Press.

Power, S. 2003. *A Problem from Hell: America and the Age of Genocide*. 3d ed. New York: Harper Perennial.

———. 2007. "Honesty Is the Best Policy." *Time*, October 29, 26.

Prados, J. 2004. *Hoodwinked: The Documents That Reveal How Bush Sold Us a War*. New York: New Press.

Privacy International. 2004. "Terrorism Profile—Peru." http://www.privacyinternational.org/article.shtml?cmd%5B347%5D=x-347-359623.

Proal, L. 1973. *Political Crime*. Montclair, NJ: Patterson Smith.

Proctor, R. N. 1999. *The Nazi War on Cancer*. Princeton, NJ: Princeton University Press.

Progressive Magazine. 2003. "Comment: Bush's Messiah Complex." *Progressive Magazine* (February): 8–10.

Project for the New American Century (PNAC). 2000. *Rebuilding America's Defenses: Strategy, Forces and Resources for a New Century*. Washington, DC: Project for the New American Century.

Prunier, G. 1995. *The Rwandan Crisis: A History of Genocide*. New York: Columbia University Press.

Quinn, J. R. 2001. "Dealing with a Legacy of Mass Atrocity: Truth Commissions in Uganda and Chile." *Netherlands Quarterly on Human Rights* 19 (4): 20.

———. 2006. *The Best War Ever: Lies, Damned Lies, and the Mess in Iraq*. New York: Jeremy P. Tarcher/Penguin.

Ratner, R. 1991. "Multi-Tiered Terrorism in Peru." In *Crimes by the Capitalist State: An Introduction to State Criminality*, ed. G. Barak, 101–128. Albany: State University of New York Press.

Redress Trust (REDRESS) and the International Federation of Human Rights (FIDH). 2007. *European Union Update on International Crimes*. July 3. http://www.redress.org/publications/EU%20Report%20Vol%203%20July%202007.pdf.

Reed, T. C., and D. B. Stillman. 2009. *The Nuclear Express: A Political History of the Bomb and Its Proliferation.* Minneapolis: Zenith Press.

Reichberg, G. M., H. Syse, and E. Begby, eds. 2006. *The Ethics of War.* Oxford, UK: Blackwell Publishing.

Reiman, J. 2006. Reviews. *British Journal of Criminology* 46 (2): 362–64 .

Reynolds, J. 2005. "Collateral Damage on the 21st Century Battlefield: Enemy Exploitation of the Law of Armed Conflict, and the Struggle for a Moral High Ground." *Air Force Law Review* 56:1.

Reuters News Service. 2007. "House Panel OKs Armenian Genocide Resolution." http://www.reuters.com/article/politicsNews/idUSWAT00825320071010?pageNumber=2.

Reyntjens, F. 1993. "The Proof of the Pudding Is in the Eating: The June 1993 Elections in Burundi." *Journal of Modern African Studies* 31 (4): 563–583.

Rich, F. 2006. *The Greatest Story Ever Sold: The Decline and Fall in Truth from 9/11 to Katrina.* New York: Penguin Press.

Ricks, T. 2006. *Fiasco: The American Military Adventure in Iraq.* New York: Penguin Press.

Risen, J. 2006. *State of War: The Secret History of the CIA and the Bush Administration.* New York: Free Press.

Ritter, S. 2003. *Frontier Justice: Weapons of Mass Destruction and the Bushwhacking of America.* New York: Context Books.

———. 2006. *Target Iran: The Truth about the White House's Plans for Regime Change.* New York: Nation Books.

Roberts, L., R. Lafta, R. Garfield, J. Khudairi, and G. Burnham. 2004. "Mortality before and after the 2003 Invasion of Iraq: Cluster Sample Survey." *Lancet* 364:1857–1864.

Rodrigues, A. 2006. "The War Crimes Chamber of Bosnia and Herzegovina: A New Solution for the Impunity Gap." Paper presented at The Hague Guest Lecture Series of the Office of the Prosecutor, June 23, The Hague.

Roebuck, J., and S. C. Weeber. 1978. *Political Crime in the United States.* New York: Praeger.

Roht-Arriaza, N. 2005. *The Pinochet Effect: Transnational Justice in the Age of Human Rights.* Philadelphia: University of Pennsylvania Press.

Rosenberg, A., and G. E. Myers. 1988. *Echoes from the Holocaust: Philosophical Reflections from a Dark Time.* Philadelphia: Temple University Press.

Rosenfeld, A. 1995. "The Americanization of the Holocaust." *Commentary* (June): 35–40.

———. 1997. *Thinking About the Holocaust: After Half a Century.* Bloomington: Indiana University Press.

Ross, J. I. 1988. "Attributes of Domestic Political Terrorism in Canada, 1960–1985." *Terrorism: An International Journal* 11 (3): 214–233.

———. 1992. Review of *Crimes by the Capitalist State*, ed. Gregg Barak. *Justice Quarterly* 9 (June 2): 347–354.

———. 1995a. *Controlling State Crime: An Introduction.* New York: Garland

———. 1995b. *Varieties of State Crime and Its Control.* Monsey, NY: Criminal Justice Press.

———. 1998. "Situating the Academic Study of Controlling State Crime." *Crime, Law and Social Change* 29: 331–340.

———. 2000a. *Controlling State Crime: An Introduction.* 2d ed. New York: Garland.

———. 2000b. *Varieties of State Crime and Its Control.* 2d ed. Monsey, NY: Criminal Justice Press.

———. 2000c. "Introduction: Protecting Democracy by Controlling State Crime in Advanced Industrialized Countries." In *Varieties of State Crime and Its Control*, ed. J. I. Ross, 1–10. Monsey, NY: Criminal Justice Press, 2000.

———. 2002. *The Dynamics of Political Crime*. Thousand Oaks, CA: Sage Publications.

Ross, J., G. Barak, J. Ferrell, D. Kauzlarich, M. Hamm, D. Friedrichs, R. Matthews, S. Pickering, M. Presdee, P. Kraska, and V. Kappeler. 1999. "The State of State Crime Research: A Commentary." *Humanity and Society* 23 (3): 273–281.

Ross, J. I., and D. L. Rothe. 2008. "The Ironies of Controlling State Crime." *International Journal of Law, Crime and Justice* 36 (3): 196–210.

Roth, K. 2004. *War in Iraq: Not a Humanitarian Intervention*. New York: Human Rights Watch.

Rothe, D. L. 2006. "The Masquerade of Abu Ghraib: State Crime, Torture, and International Law." Ph.D. diss., Western Michigan University, Kalamazoo.

———. 2009a. "Beyond the Law: The Reagan Administration's Dirty War on Nicaragua." *Critical Criminology: An International Journal* 17:1.

———. 2009b. *State Criminality: The Crime of All Crimes*. Lanham, MD: Roman and Littlefield.

Rothe, D. L., and D. O. Friedrichs. 2006. "The State of the Criminology of Crimes of the State." *Social Justice* 33 (1): 147–161.

Rothe, D., and D. Kauzlarich. 2010. "State-Level Crime: Theory and Policy." In *Crime and Public Policy: Putting Theory to Work*, 2d ed., ed. H. Barlow and S. Decker, 166–187. Philadelphia: Temple University Press.

Rothe, D. L., and C. W. Mullins. 2006a. *Symbolic Gestures and the Generation of Global Social Controls: The International Criminal Court*. Lanham, MD: Lexington Books.

———. 2006b. "The International Criminal Court and United States Opposition: A Structural Contradictions Model." *Crime, Law and Social Change* 45:201–226.

———. 2007. "Darfur and the Politicalization of International Law: Genocide or Crimes against Humanity." *Humanity and Society* 31 (1): 83–107.

———. 2008a. "Genocide, War Crimes and Crimes against Humanity in Central Africa: A Criminological Exploration." In *Supranational Criminology: Towards a Criminology of International Crimes*, ed. A. Smeulers and R. Haveman, 135–158. Antwerp: Intersentia.

———. 2008b. "State Crime." *Encyclopedia of Social Problems*. Ed. Vince Parillo. Thousand Oaks, CA: Sage.

———. 2009. "Toward a Criminology for International Criminal Law: An Integrated Theory of International Criminal Violations." *International Journal of Comparative and Applied Criminal Justice* 33(1): 97–118.

Rothe, D., C. W. Mullins, and K. Sandstrom. 2009. "The Rwandan Genocide: International Finance Policies and Human Rights." *Social Justice* 35 (3): 66–86.

Rothe, D., and S. Muzzatti. 2004. "Enemies Everywhere: Terrorism, Moral Panic, and U.S. Civil Society." *Critical Criminology: An International Journal* 12 (3): 159–180.

Rousseau, J.-J. 1990. "Reading Rousseau in the Nuclear Age." In *The State of War*, trans. G. Roosevelt, 185. Philadelphia: Temple University Press.

Roy, A. 2004. *An Ordinary Person's Guide to Empire*. Cambridge, MA: South End Press.

Rutherford, P. 2004. *Weapons of Mass Persuasion: Marketing the War against Iraq*. Toronto: University of Toronto Press.

Ryan, D. 2007. *Frustrated Empire: U.S. Foreign Policy, 9/11 to Iraq*. London: Pluto Press.

Sadat, L., and R. Carden. 2000. "The New International Criminal Court: An Uneasy Revolution." *Georgetown Law Journal* 88:381–415.

Salzman, T. A. 1998. "Rape Camps as a Means of Ethnic Cleansing: Religious, Cultural and Ethical Responses to Rape Victims in the Former Yugoslavia." *Human Rights Quarterly* 20 (2): 348–378.

Sands, P. 2005. *Lawless World: The Whistle-Blowing Account of How Bush and Blair Are Taking the Law into Their Own Hands.* New York: Penguin Books.

Sarkin, J. 2001. "The Tension Between Justice and Reconciliation in Rwanda: Politics, Human Rights, Due Process, and the Role of the Gacaca Courts in Dealing with the Genocide." *Journal of African Law* 45 (2): 143–172.

Schabas, W. A. 2002. "Geonocide Trials and Gacaca Courts." *Journal of International Criminal Justice* 3:879–895.

Schaffer, R. 1985. *Wings of Judgment: American Bombing in World War II.* New York: Oxford University Press.

———. 2009. "The Bombing Campaigns in World War II: The European Theater." In *Bombing Civilians: A Twentieth-Century History*, ed. Y. Tanaka and M. Young, 30–45. New York: New Press.

Schafer, Stephen. 1974. *The Political Criminal.* New York: Free Press.

Schechter, D. 2006. *When News Lies: Media Complicity and the Iraq War.* New York: Select Books.

Scheer, C., R. Scheer, and L. Chaudry. 2003. *The Five Biggest Lies Bush Told Us about Iraq.* New York: Seven Stories Press and Akashic Books.

Scheffer, C. 2006. "Genocide and Atrocity Crimes." *Genocide Studies and Prevention* 1:229–250.

Schell, J. 1982. *The Fate of the Earth.* New York: Avon.

———. 2007. *The Seventh Decade: The New Shape of Nuclear Danger.* New York: Metropolitan Books.

Schell, O. 2004. Preface to *Now They Tell Us: The American Pressa Iraq*, ed. M. Massing, ii–xviii. New York: New York Review of Books.

Scheper-Hughes, N., and P. Bourgois. 2004. *Violence in War and Peace: An Anthology.* Oxford, UK: Blackwell.

Schmitt, M. 1992. "State-Sponsored Assassination in International and Domestic Law." *Yale Journal of International Law* 17:609–685.

Schoenfeld, G. 1998. "Auschwitz and the Professors." *Commentary* (June): 42–46.

Schmitt, M. 1992. "State-Sponsored Assassination in International and Domestic Law." *Yale Journal of International Law* 17:609.

Schomburg, J. 2004. "Separate Opinion of Judge Schomburg in Appeals Chamber Judgement XIV p 260." In *Judgment, Prosecutor v. Tihomir Blaskic*, July 2004, Case No. IT-95-14-A.

Schwartz, M. 2008. *War without End: The Iraq War in Context.* Chicago: Haymarket Books.

Schwendinger, H., and J. Schwendinger. 1970. "Defenders of Order or Guardians of Human Rights." *Issues in Criminology* 5 (2): 123–157.

Selden, M. 2004. "The United States and Japan in Twentieth-Century Asian Wars." In *War and State Terrorism: The United States, Japan, and the Asia-Pacific in the Long Twentieth Century*, ed. M. Selden and A. So, 19–40. Lanham, MD: Rowman and Littlefield.

———. 2009. "A Forgotten Holocaust: U.S. Bombing Strategy, the Destruction of Japanese Cities and the American Way of War from the Pacific War to Iraq." In *Bombing Civilians: A Twentieth-Century History*, ed. Y. Tanaka and M. Young, 77–96. New York: New Press.

Selden, M., and A. So. 2004. "Introduction: War and State Terrorism." In *War and State Terrorism: The United States, Japan, and the Asia-Pacific in the Long Twentieth Century*, ed. M. Selden and A. So, 1–18. Lanham, MD: Rowman and Littlefield.

Sellin, T. 1938. *Culture, Conflict and Crime.* New York: Social Science Research Council.

Shaddad, I. 2000. *Tale of Salah Al-din, Al Kadi (Sirat Salah Al-din, Maktabat Al-Thakafat Al Diniat).* Port Saïd.

———. 2002. *The Rare and Excellent History of Saladin.* Trans. D. S. Richards. Aldershot, UK: Ashgate Publishing.

Shalabi, A. 1983. "Crusade Wars." *Encyclopedia of Islamic History.* Vol. 6. 6th ed. N.p., n.p.

Sharkansky, I. 1995. "A State Action May Be Nasty but Is Not Likely to Be a Crime." In *Controlling State Crime,* ed. J. I. Ross, 35–52. New York: Garland.

Shelton, D. 2005. "The United Nations Principles and Guidelines on Reparations: Context and Contents." In *Out of the Ashes: Reparation for Victims of Gross and Systematic Human Rights Violations,* ed. K. De Feyter, S. Parmentier, M. Bossuyt, and P. Lemmens, 11–33. Oxford: Intersentia.

Sherry, M. 1987. *The Rise of American Air Power: The Creation of Armageddon.* New Haven: Yale University.

———. 1995. *In the Shadow of War: The United States since the 1930s.* New Haven: Yale University Press.

———. 2009. "The United States and Strategic Bombing: From Prophecy to Memory." In *Bombing Civilians: A Twentieth-Century History,* ed. Y. Tanaka and M. Young, 175–190. New York: New Press.

Sierra Leone Truth Commission Charter. 2000. *The Final Report of the Truth and Reconciliation Commission of Sierra Leone.* http://trcsierraleone.org/drwebsite/publish/v1c1.shtml.

Sierra Leone Truth and Reconciliation Commission. 2004. *Witness to Truth: Report of the Sierra Leone Truth and Reconciliation Commission.* Accra, Ghana: Graphic Packaging Ltd.

Sink, J. M. 1974. *Political Trials: How to Defend Them.* New York: Clark, Boardman Co.

Sklar, M. J. 1988. *The Corporate Reconstruction of American Capitalism, 1890–1916.* New York: Cambridge University Press.

Slomanson, W. 2003. *Fundamental Perspectives on International Law.* 4th ed. Belmont, CA: Thomson/West.

Smeulers, A., and R. Haveman. 2008. *Supranational Criminology: Towards a Criminology of International Crimes.* Portland, OR: Intersentia.

Snow, K. H. 2008. *Over Five Million Dead in Congo? Fifteen Hundred People Daily? OpEdNews.com.* http://www.opednews.com/articles/1/genera_keith_ha_080130_over_five_million_de.htm

Sofsky, W. 1996. *The Order of Terror: The Concentration Camp.* Princeton, NJ: Princeton University Press.

Solomon, J. 2009. "U.S. Drops 'War on Terror' Phrase, Clinton Says." *Wall Street Journal,* March 31, 2009.

Solomon, N., and R. Erlich. 2003. *Target Iraq: What the News Media Didn't Tell You.* New York: Context Books.

Stafford, M., and M. Warr. 1993. "A Reconceptualization of General and Specific Deterrence." *Journal of Research in Crime and Delinquency* 30:123–135.

Stannard, D. E. 1996. "Uniqueness as Denial: The Politics of Genocide Scholarship." In *Is the Holocaust Unique? Perspectives on Comparative Genocides,* ed. A. S. Rosenbaum, 163–208. Boulder, CO: Westview Press.

Steinmetz, G. 2005. "Return to Empire: The New U.S. Imperialism in Comparative Historical Perspective." *Sociological Theory* 23 (4): 339–367.

Stiglitz, J. E., and L. J. Bilmes. 2008. *The Three Trillion Dollar War: The True Cost of the Iraq Conflict.* New York: W. W. Norton & Co.

Stohl, Michael, and George Lopez, eds. 1984. *The State as Terrorist: The Dynamics of Governmental Violence and Repression.* Westport, CT: Greenwood Press.

Stolleis, M. 1998. *The Law under the Swastika.* Chicago: University of Chicago Press.

Styron, R. 1974. *New York Review of Books* 21 (May 30): 9.

Sugerman, D. 2008. "The Pinochet Case and Its Consequences Ten Years On." Paper presented at the Institute of Advanced Legal Studies, London, November 11.

Suskind, R. 2004. *The Price of Loyalty: George W. Bush, the White House, and the Education of Paul O'Neil.* New York: Simon & Schuster.

———. 2006. *The One Percent Doctrine: Deep Inside America's Pursuit of Its Enemies since 9/11.* New York: Simon & Schuster.

Sutherland, E. 1939. "White Collar Criminality. Presidential Address to the American Society of Sociology." *American Sociological Review* 5:1–12.

———. 1949. *White Collar Crime.* New York: Holt, Rinehart & Winston.

Tabb, B. 2004. "The Two Wings of the Eagle." In *Pox Americana: Exposing the American Empire*, ed. B. J. Foster, J. B. McChesney, and R. W. McChesney, 95–103. New York: Monthly Review Press.

Taft, W. H., and T. Buchwald. 2003. "Preemption, Iraq, and International Law." *American Journal of International Law* 97 (3): 557–563.

Tanaka, Y., and M. Young, eds. 2009. *Bombing Civilians: A Twentieth Century History.* New York: New Press.

Taylor, Telford. 1992. *The Anatomy of the Nuremberg Trials.* New York: Knopf.

Terkel, S. 1984. *The "Good War": An Oral History of World War Two.* New York: Pantheon.

Thomas, H. 1971. *Cuba: The Pursuit of Freedom.* New York: Harper and Row.

Tiemessen, A. E. 2004. "After Arusha: Gacaca Justice in Post-Genocide Rwanda." *African Studies Quarterly* 8 (1): 69. http://web.africa.ufl.edu/asq/v8/v8i1a4.htm.

Traub, J. 2008. *The Freedom Agenda: Why America Must Spread Democracy (Just Not the Way George Bush Did).* New York: Farrar, Strauss and Giroux.

Truth and Reconciliation Commission. 2003. *Final Report.* Sect. 5. http://www.info.gov.za/otherdocs/2003/trc/.

Tunnell, K. D. 1993a. "Political Crime and Pedagogy: A Content Analysis of Criminology and Criminal Justice Texts." *Journal of Criminal Justice Education* 4 (1): 101–114.

———. ed. 1993b. *Political Crime in Contemporary America.* New York: Garland.

———. 1995. "State Crime against the Labor Movement." In *Controlling State Crime*, ed. J. I. Ross, 207–232. New York: Garland.

Turk, Austin. 1982. *Political Criminality.* Beverly Hills: Sage Publications.

United Nations (UN). 1948a. *UN Convention on the Prevention and Punishment of the Crime of Genocide, Article II.* UN Documents Cooperation Circles. http://un-documents.net/cppcg.htm.

———. 1948b. Universal Declaration of Human Rights, GA. Res. 217A (III0, UN Doc A/810).

———. 2000. Resolution S/RES/1315. Adopted by the Security Council at its 4,186th meeting, August 14.

———. 2006. "Basic Principles and Guidelines on the Right to a Remedy and Reparation for Victims of Violations of International Human Rights and Humanitarian Law." General Assembly, A/RES/60/147

———. 2008. Office for the Coordination of Humanitarian Affairs, IRIN 2008.

U.S. Department of State. 1995. "Burundi Human Rights Practices." http://dosfan.lib.uic.edu/ERC.democracy/1994_hrp_report/94hrp_report_africa/Burundi.htm.

U.S. Institute of Peace. 2008. Truth Commissions Digital Collection. http://www .usip.org/library/truth.htm.

Uvin, P. 1999. "Ethnicity and Power in Burundi and Rwanda: Different Paths to Mass Violence." *Comparative Politics* 31 (3): 253–271.

Valiñas, M., and K. Vanspauwen. 2009 "The Promise of Restorative Justice in the Search for Truth after a Violent Conflict. Experiences from South Africa and Bosnia-Herzegovina." *Contemporary Justice Review.* 12 (3): 269–287.

Van Alstyne, R. W. 1960. *The Rising American Empire.* New York: W. W. Norton & Co.

Vann, B. 2002. "The Unquiet Death of Patrice Lumumba." *World Socialist Website.* http://www.wsws.org/articles/2002/jan2002/lumu-j16_prn.shtml.

Vanspauwen, K., S. Parmentier, and E. Weitekamp. 2007. "Restorative Justice for Victims of Mass Violence: Reconsidering the Building Blocks of Post-Conflict Justice." Presentation at Expert Meetings, Maastricht University, April 13–14.

———. 2008. "Restorative Justice for Victims of Mass Violence: Reconsidering the Building Blocks of Post-Conflict Justice." In *Supranational Criminology: Towards a Criminology of International Crimes,* ed. R. Haveman and A. Smeulers Antwerp: Intersentia.

Vaughan, D. 1996. *The Challenger Launch Decision: Risky Technology, Culture, and Deviance at NASA.* Chicago: University of Chicago Press.

———. 1999. "Boundary Work: Levels of Analysis, the Macro-Micro Link, and the Social Control of Organizations." In *Situated Action, Theory Elaboration, and Boundary Work: An Agenda Social Science, Social Policy, and the Law,* ed. P. Ewick, R. Kagan, and A. Sarat, 291–321. New York: Russell Sage Foundation.

———. 2007. "Beyond Macro- and Micro-Levels of Analysis, Organizations, and the Cultural Fix." In *International Handbook of White-Collar and Corporate Crime,* ed. H. Pontell and G. Geis, 3–24. New York: Springer.

Vasquez, C. M. 1995. "The Four Doctrines of Self-Executing Treaties." *American Journal of International Law* 89 (October 4): 695–723.

Villa-Vicencio, C. 2000. "Why Perpetrators Should Not Always Be Prosecuted: Where the International Criminal Court and Truth Commissions Meet." *Emory Law Journal* 49:101–118.

Walgrave, L. 1994. "Beyond Rehabilitation: In Search of a Constructive Alternative in the Judicial Response to Juvenile Crime." *European Journal on Criminal Policy and Research* (Special Issue on the Juvenile Justice System) 2 (2): 57–75, 62–67.

Walker, R. 2004. "Rwanda Still Searching for Justice." BBC, March30. http://www .news.bbc.co.uk/2/hi/africa/3557753.stm.

Walker, Samuel. 1985. *Sense and Nonsense about Crime: A Policy Guide.* Monterey, CA: Brooks/Cole.

———. 2004. *Prompt and Utter Destruction: Truman and the Use of Atomic Bombs against Japan.* Rev. ed. Chapel Hill: University of North Carolina Press.

Wallerstein, I. 1989. *The Modern World System.* New York: Academic Press.

Walzer, M. 2006. *Just and Unjust Wars.* 4th ed. New York: Basic Books.

Ward, T. 2005. "State Crime in the Heart of Darkness." *British Journal of Criminology* 45 (4): 434–445.

Waxman, H. A. 2004. *Secrecy in the Bush Administration.* http://oversight.house.gov/ documents/20050317180908–35215.pdf.

Weeramantry, C. G. 2003. *Armageddon or Brave New World? Reflections on the Hostilities in Iraq.* Ratmalana, Sri Lanka: Sarvodaya Vishva Lekha.

Weitekamp, E., S. Parmentier, K. Vanspauwen, M. Valiñas, and R. Gerits. 2006. "How to Deal with Mass Victimization and Gross Human Rights Violations: A Restorative

Justice Approach." In *Large Scale Victimisation as a Potential Source of Terrorist Activities: Importance of Regaining Security in Post-Conflict Societies*, ed. U. Ewald and K. Turkovic, 217–241. Amsterdam: IOS Press.

Weston, B. 1983. "Nuclear Weapons and International Law: Prolegomenon to General Illegality." *New York Law School Journal of International and Comparative Law* 4:227–256.

White, R. 2008. "Depleted Uranium, State Crime and the Politics of Knowing." *Theoretical Criminology* 12 (1): 31–54.

White House. 2002. *National Security Doctrine of the United States of America.* http://www.whitehouse.gov/nsc/nss.pdf.

Wiesel, E. 1970. *One Generation After.* New York: Avon.

Wildeman, J. 1991. "When the State Fails: A Critical Assessment of Contract Policing in the United States." In *Crimes by the Capitalist State: An Introduction to State Criminality*, ed. G. Barak, 219–232. Albany: State University of New York Press.

Williams, W. A. 1969. *The Roots of the Modern American Empire: A Study of the Growth and Shaping of Social Consciousness in a Marketplace Society.* New York: Random House.

———. 1988. *The Tragedy of American Diplomacy.* New York: Norton Paperback Edition.

Williams, W. A. 2007. *Empire as a Way of Life.* Brooklyn: Ig Publishing.

Wilson, J. Q., and P. Rachel. 1977. "Can the Government Regulate Itself?" *Public Interest* 46 (1): 3–14.

Wingfield, T., 1998. "Taking Aim at Regime Elites: Assassination, Tyrannicide, and the Clancy Doctrine." *Maryland Journal of International Law of Trade* 22:287.

Wolfe, R. 1998. "Flaws in the Nuremberg Legacy: An Impediment to International War Crimes Tribunals' Prosecution of Crimes against Humanity." *Holocaust and Genocide Studies* 12:434–453.

Wood, E. M. 2003. *Empire of Capital.* London: Verso.

Wood, E., Jr. 2006. *Worshipping the Myths of World War II: Reflections on America's Dedication to War.* Washington, DC: Potomac Books.

Woodward, B. 2004. *Plan of Attack.* New York: Simon and Schuster.

World Bank. 1999. *World Development Report: Poverty.* New York: Oxford Press.

Wright, R. 2008. *What Is America? A Short History of the New World Order.* Philadelphia: Da Capo Press.

Yarnold, B. 1995. "A New Role for the International Court of Justice: Adjudicator of International and State Transnational Crimes." In *Controlling State Crime* , ed. J. I. Ross, 317–345. New York: Garland.

Young, M. 2009. "Bombing Civilians from the Twentieth to the Twenty-first Centuries." In *Bombing Civilians: A Twentieth-Century History*, ed. Y. Tanaka and M. Young, 154–174. New York: New Press.

Zinn, H. 1980. *A People's History of the United States: 1492–Present.* New York: Harper-Collins.

Contributors

Gregg Barak is a professor of criminology and criminal justice at Eastern Michigan University; former visiting distinguished professor in the College of Justice and Safety at Eastern Kentucky University; and fellow of the Academy of Criminal Justice Sciences.

M. Cherif Bassiouni is a distinguished research professor of law emeritus; president emeritus, International Human Rights Law Institute, DePaul University, Chicago; and president, International Institute of Higher Studies in Criminal Sciences, Siracusa, Italy.

Michael Bohlander is a professor in the Durham Law School at Durham University; chair of LLB Board of Examiners, Durham Law School; director of the Centre for Criminal Law and Criminal Justice; and associate director of the International State Crime Research Consortium, Old Dominion University, College of Arts and Letters.

William J. Chambliss is a professor at George Washington University; recipient of an honorary doctorate of law from the University of Guelph; and former president of the American Society of Criminology and the Society for the Study of Social Problems.

David O. Friedrichs is a professor at the University of Scranton, Department of Sociology and Criminal Justice; former president of the White Collar Crime Research Consortium; member of the Working Groups on Crime as Business; and recipient of the Rufus Putnam Visiting Professor at Ohio University.

Roelof H. Haveman is vice rector of the ILPD/Institute of Legal Practice and Development, the postgraduate training institute for the justice sector in Rwanda.

Kara Hoofnagle is a Ph.D. student at Old Dominion University, Department of Sociology and Criminal Justice.

Peter Iadicola is a professor at Indiana University–Purdue University in the Department of Sociology and Anthropology. He is the recipient of the

Fulbright Senior Specialist Award, Department of Criminology, National Taipei University, Taipei, Republic of China.

DAVID KAUZLARICH is a professor at Southern Illinois University, Edwardsville; chair of the Department of Sociology and Criminal Justice Studies; and recipient of the William and Margaret Going Endowed Professor Award.

RONALD C. KRAMER is a professor at Western Michigan University, Department of Sociology, and director of the Criminal Justice Program at Western Michigan University, Department of Sociology.

RAYMOND J. MICHALOWSKI is a professor at Northern Arizona University, Department of Criminology and Criminal Justice; graduate program director at Northern Arizona University, Department of Criminology and Criminal Justice; and Arizona Regents' Professor of Criminal Justice.

ALPHONSE MULEEFU is lawyer at the NSGJ/National Service of Gacaca Jurisdictions in Rwanda and founder and president of the nongovernmental organization Together against Impunity/Great Lakes Region.

CHRISTOPHER W. MULLINS is a professor in the Department of Criminology and Criminal Justice at Southern Illinois University, Carbondale.

STEPHAN PARMENTIER is a professor at Katholieke Universiteit Leuven, Faculty of Law, Research Unit Penal Law and Criminology, and coordinator of the Research Unit Penal Law and Criminology.

JEFFREY IAN ROSS is a professor in the Division of Criminology, Criminal Justice, and Forensics and a fellow at the Center for International and Comparative Law at the University of Baltimore.

DAWN L. ROTHE is a professor at Old Dominion University, Department of Sociology and Criminal Justice; director of the International State Crime Research Consortium, Old Dominion University, College of Arts and Letters; and chair of the American Society of Criminology Division of Critical Criminology.

MARTA VALIÑAS is an affiliated researcher for the Department of Criminal Law and Criminology, Faculty of Law, Katholieke Universiteit Leuven.

ELMAR WEITEKAMP is a professor in the Department of Criminal Law and Criminology, Faculty of Law, Katholieke Universiteit Leuven, and co-responsible of the International Network for Research on Restorative Justice for Juveniles.

Index

9/11. *See* September 11 attacks
"The Abandoned Ones" (Hamm), 40
Abd-al-Rahman, Ali Muhammad Ali, 286–287
Abu Ghraib (prison), 172, 201
Afghanistan, 84, 114, 140
AFRC (Armed Forces revolutionary Council), 207
African Charter on Human and People's Rights, 159
Agee, Phillip, 45
Alaska (state), 126
Albania, 217
Al-Bashir, Omar, 13, 172, 206, 278, 287, 289–290
Albigensian Crusades, 57
Alexander (Yugoslavian king), 129
Alien Tort Claims Act (ATCA), 201
Ali Kushayb, 286–287
Allende, Salvador, 45, 162
Alperovitz, Gar, 86
Al Queda (terror group), 102, 105, 107, 114, 117
Althusius, Johannes, 253
Alvarez, Alexander, 59
American Empire, 77–78, 85–89, 104–111, 122–140. *See also* United States
American Indian Movement, 195
American Society of Criminology, 23, 51, 54, 123
American Sociological Association, 124
Amin, Idi, 162
Amnesty International, 170, 187, 237
apartheid (state crime), 11–12, 16

Apra Party, 215
Arciniegra, Alberto, 42
Arendt, Hannah, 8
Argentina, 56, 165, 202, 204, 212–213
Armed Forces of Rwanda (FAR), 151, 154
Armed Forces Revolutionary Council (AFRC), 207
Armenians (people), 53, 135, 140
Armistice Agreement, 19
Arusha Peace Accords, 151, 158–59, 200, 219
assassination (as legal issue), 244–260
Assembly of State Parties, 276
Association of Progressive Prosecutors, 170, 204
ATCA (Alien Tort Claims Act), 201
Atlantic Charter, 99–100
atrocities. *See* state crime; *specific events, nations, regions, wars*
Aulette, Judy, 27
Auschwitz, 61
Australia, 36, 38
Austria, 18, 203
Austro-Hungarian empire, 109
Avocates sans Frontières (group), 235
Ayala, Balthazar, 253
Aylwin, Patricio, 168–169, 212

Baath Party, 105, 216–217
Baez, Joan, 21
Bagaza, Jean-Baptists, 148
Baghdad (city), 93
Baldwin IV (King), 250

Available titles in the Critical Issues in Crime and Society series:

www.ingramcontent.com/pod-product-compliance
Lightning Source LLC
Chambersburg PA
CBHW021808270326
41932CB00007B/101